LAST CHANCE FOR LIFE

CLARENDON STUDIES IN CRIMINOLOGY

Published under the auspices of the Institute of Criminology, University of Cambridge; the Mannheim Centre, London School of Economics; and the Centre for Criminology, University of Oxford.

RECENT TITLES IN THIS SERIES:

Police Unlimited: Policing, Migrants, and the Values of Bureaucracy
Mutsaers

Personalizing the State: An Anthropology of Law, Politics, and Welfare in Austerity Britain
Koch

Common Enemies: Crime, Policy, and Politics in Australia-Indonesia Relations
McKenzie

Embodying Punishment: Emotions, Identities, and Lived Experiences in Women's Prisons
Chamberlen

Professionalizing the Police: The Unfulfilled Promise of Police Training
Fielding

Getting Out: Early Release in England and Wales, 1960–1995
Guiney

Sentencing Policy and Social Justice
Henham

Last Chance for Life

Clemency in Southeast Asian Death Penalty Cases

DANIEL PASCOE

OXFORD
UNIVERSITY PRESS

OXFORD
UNIVERSITY PRESS

Great Clarendon Street, Oxford, OX2 6DP,
United Kingdom

Oxford University Press is a department of the University of Oxford.
It furthers the University's objective of excellence in research, scholarship,
and education by publishing worldwide. Oxford is a registered trade mark of
Oxford University Press in the UK and in certain other countries

First Edition published in 2019

Published in the United States of America by Oxford University Press
198 Madison Avenue, New York, NY 10016, United States of America

British Library Cataloguing in Publication Data
Data available

Library of Congress Control Number: 2018961479

ISBN 978–0–19–880971–5

General Editors' Introduction

The *Clarendon Studies in Criminology* series aims to provide a forum for outstanding theoretical and empirical work in all aspects of criminology and criminal justice, broadly understood. The Editors welcome submissions from established scholars, as well as excellent PhD work. The Series was inaugurated in 1994, with Roger Hood as its first General Editor, following discussions between Oxford University Press and Oxford's Centre for Criminological Research. It is edited under the auspices of three centres: the Institute of Criminology at the University of Cambridge, the Mannheim Centre for Criminology at the London School of Economics, and the Centre for Criminological Research at the University of Oxford. Each supplies members of the Editorial Board and, in turn, the Series Editor or Editors.

Last Chance for Life: Clemency in Southeast Asian Death Penalty Cases has involved deep research in four countries – Thailand, Singapore, Malaysia, and Indonesia – within broader contextual discussion of the use of the death penalty and the role and place of clemency within Southeast Asia. The book is an attempt to explain how we can best understand the push and pull factors towards commutation of the death penalty or pardon from the decision-makers, including sultans, kings, presidents, cabinets and boards. These four countries (alongside Vietnam) have been described by Amnesty International as death penalty 'retentionists' because they have carried out executions during the past ten years. At the same time, there is evidence of grants of clemency via the executive branch of government, replacing the death penalty with imprisonment, or in some cases, the removal of punishment altogether. Yet clemency practices across the four countries which form the basis of this book vary enormously.

This is an innovative study involving the systematic collection and analysis of clemency data in the different jurisdictions using both archival and 'elite' interview sources in a difficult research terrain. Indeed, this is a sophisticated study despite methodological complications and the challenges associated with comparative analysis in contexts not known for openness and invitation to research. Daniel Pascoe poses a puzzle about differences in clemency rates and practices. What becomes clear through his research is that the volume of death sentences and the exercise of clemency are shaped by the interplay between law and politics, the different components of the criminal justice 'system'. Pascoe subtly and deftly teases out the importance of these kinds of relations, pointing to the extent to which the granting of clemency enhances or detracts from the political power of the different decision-makers. Other factors contribute to the variance across the four countries too – the length of time prisoners spend on death row, for example – but the key insight is that clemency in such 'retentionist' countries means so much more than mere ambivalence over the death penalty. This is a fascinating and significant contribution.

As Editors, we commend the author for making such important contribution to the field of criminology and to our understanding of the complexities of decision-making about clemency in the modern Southeast Asian political context. This is a scholarly, theoretically grounded and insightful book and we are very pleased to welcome *Last Chance for Life: Clemency in Southeast Asian Death Penalty Cases* to the *Clarendon Studies in Criminology* series.

Loraine Gelsthorpe and Kyle Treiber
Institute of Criminology, University of Cambridge
January 2019

Acknowledgements

This book evolved from a doctoral dissertation completed at the University of Oxford in October 2013. As a final product it is part statistical compilation, part comparative legal analysis, part journalism, and part instruction manual. Finishing the final manuscript, with all the data collection and overseas fieldwork it entailed, would not have been possible without the assistance of many different people and organizations. Having promised confidentiality, I cannot do this by name, but I would like to thank all of my interview and personal communication sources for their input. My hope is that this book, including all of your contributions, goes some small way towards providing a more informed understanding of state killing, and its decline, in Southeast Asia and the Asian continent more generally. Clemency grants, both for individual prisoners on death row and when issued collectively, form a key part of that story. As the book demonstrates, even in the most punitive regimes, political leaders are still capable of showing mercy, compassion, and forgiveness.

By name, I can thank Lucy Alexander, Amy Baker, and Peter Daniell from the editorial team at OUP, as well as Damien Chng, Ngeow Chow Ying, Andrew Khoo, Sutawan Chanprasert, Todung Mulya Lubis, Ricky Gunawan, Bhatara Ibnu Reza, Michael Hor, and Andrew Novak for their comments on various chapter drafts and the direction of the book as a whole. Several research assistants have helped in the project's latter stages, including Mark Law Hiu Fung, Toni Tong Yihan, Herbert Cheng Hoi Fai, Kenny Siu, Muhammad Arif Hidayah, Hugo Ho, Hung Ching Ada, and Tsang Wing Kwan Karen. Over the past few years, I have also received tremendous career advice and encouragement from Roger Hood, Danthong Breen, Pip Nicholson, Tim Lindsey, Antonios Kouroutakis, Maria Cristina Dorado, Simon Butt, Dave McRae, Julian McMahon, Geraint Howells, Melissa Crouch, John Beaton, David Johnson, Timothy Webster, Julian Roberts, and Mary Bosworth, just to name a few. To my former DPhil colleagues from the Centre for Criminology, in particular Marie Manikis,

Dan Alati, Fernanda Fonseca Rosenblatt, Harry Annison, Marie Tidball, George Mawhinney, Chris Giacomantonio, Rudina Jasini, Michelle Miao, Marion Vannier, and Julia Viebach—I am fortunate to have you as my friends.

I would also like to thank a number of people who provided me accommodation and companionship during the course of the fieldwork investigations: Pete in Singapore, Paul and Sharon in Kuala Lumpur, Sam and Charlotte in Hong Kong, Richard and Steve in Bangkok, and John in Jakarta. Frank Morgan at the University of Western Australia generously provided facilities in Perth for the part of the DPhil writing-up phase. My family were, as always, an invaluable and ongoing source of support during good times and bad: Sue, Bruce, Malcolm, Jan, Alex, and Meredith, I could not have produced the book without your love and support (and proofreading). My academic supervisor, Professor Carolyn Hoyle, provided frequent and timely advice over the course of my doctoral degree, often after being asked at short notice. Thank you, Carolyn.

Moreover, I would not have been able to complete two research degrees as an overseas student at Oxford without a number of funding organizations placing their faith in my potential as a researcher: these were the Trustees of the Keith Murray Award Fund at Lincoln College, the Oxford Law Faculty, the Wingate Foundation, the Menzies Centre for Australian Studies at King's College London, and the Gowrie Scholarship Trust Fund. City University of Hong Kong helped to get me to the finish line with a generous start-up grant soon after the commencement of my employment at the School of Law there in 2014. To all these funders, I will continue to repay your trust in me throughout my career.

Finally, Bruce Hunt (1951–2018) was an enormous influence on my life and academic career, and I am deeply saddened that he was not able to see this book in print. Bruce, I dedicate this book to you.

Daniel Pascoe
Hong Kong, September 2018

Table of Contents

List of Illustrations, Tables, and Figures

List of Cases, Statutes, and International Instruments

People's Republic of China

Republic of Indonesia

Republic of Iraq

Federation of Malaysia

Republic of Singapore

Kingdom of Thailand

United States

International Instruments

Introduction: Six Paradigmatic Cases

If the crossroads of legal traditions are nodal points where comparatists are to be found, then one ought to be tripping over them in South East Asia

Andrew Harding, focusing comparative scholarly attention on an 'ideal laboratory'[1]

This is a book about hope in the tropics. Far more so than is commonly believed, death row prisoners in Southeast Asia who have exhausted all their judicial appeals still cling to a hope of avoiding execution from the most unlikely of sources: the political executive. This book attempts to explain the factors underlying death row prisoners' hopes of commutation or pardon from clemency arbiters as varied as kings, sultans, presidents, cabinets, and boards. Although some decision makers have ultimately proven more generous than others, modern Southeast Asia provides a cogent demonstration of the fact that the executive clemency power, and therefore hope for death row prisoners, will continue to exist as long as the death penalty remains as a judicial punishment in some countries of the world.[2] In other words, commutation goes hand in hand with condemnation.

I begin with the regional context. Five countries within the Association of Southeast Asian Nations (ASEAN)—Indonesia, Malaysia, Thailand, Singapore, and Vietnam—have performed executions on a regular basis over the past few decades. At the beginning of 2017, Amnesty International classified each of these five nations as death penalty 'retentionists' because they had conducted executions over the previous ten-year period.[3] However,

[1] Harding (2001) 199.

[2] Kobil (1992–3) 214–15; Sebba (1977a) 234–6.

[3] Amnesty International AI Index ACT 50/5740/2017, 43. Of the remaining five members of ASEAN, Brunei, Laos, and Myanmar are classified as abolitionist de facto, not having conducted an execution for more than ten years and

notwithstanding this common willingness to execute, the number of death sentences passed by courts that are reduced to a term of imprisonment, or where the prisoner is released from custody altogether, through grants of clemency by the executive branch of government[4] varies remarkably among these neighbouring jurisdictions. In Thailand, during the twenty-six-year period under analysis from 1991 to 2016,[5] more than 95 per cent of death row prisoners who exhausted judicial remedies received clemency

having a settled policy not to execute, whereas the Philippines and Cambodia abolished capital punishment for all crimes in 2006 (for a second time) and in 1989, respectively (Amnesty International AI Index ACT 50/5740/2017, 42–3; Johnson and Zimring (2009) 16, 103–4). ASEAN presently denotes as 'observers' two states: Papua New Guinea and Timor-Leste. Papua New Guinea is classified as abolitionist de facto, albeit with twelve persons on death row in July 2017 (Cornell Center on the Death Penalty Worldwide, 'Papua New Guinea'), whereas Timor-Leste has been abolitionist for all crimes since its independence in 2002 (Hood and Hoyle (2015) 100).

[4] For the purposes of this book, I use the term 'clemency' to refer to the executive branch of government replacing a sentence of death with a lesser punishment, usually a term of imprisonment. This type of clemency is sometimes termed a 'commutation' of sentence. I also define clemency as where the executive branch abrogates punishment altogether through 'pardon' (Novak (2016) 819). For more detailed discussion on terminology, see Chapter 2.

[5] The book's temporal scope is limited to the period 1991–2016 inclusive. The doctoral dissertation on which this study is based covered the period 1975–2009 for Thai, Singaporean, Malaysian, and Indonesian death penalty practice. A new end date of 2016 takes account of more recent cases and data, particularly the changing political context with the election of Indonesian President Joko Widodo (a strong supporter of the death penalty) in October 2014 and Thailand's military coup of the same year (thereby reducing the possibility of death penalty abolition in the short term). The extended temporal scope also serves to include Singapore's unprecedented 2012 curtailment of the mandatory death penalty for certain categories of drug trafficking and murder cases, via the Penal Code (Amendment) Act 2012 (Singapore) and the Misuse of Drugs (Amendment) Act 2012 (Singapore).

The study's start date is set at the beginning of 1991 due to the higher relevance of more recent cases and to even out data access across time. More specifically, across Southeast Asia, by the late 1980s the mentality of 'emergency' borne of real or perceived Communist Party threats from the 1960s onwards began to wane or disappear altogether. Instead, during the 1990s a majority of death sentences were passed in the region for drug trafficking and murder, rather than for subversion or security/firearms offences, much like the situation today ('121 Convicts in "Death Row" (2003); Amnesty International AI Index ASA 36/001/2004, 6; International Federation for Human Rights (2005) 9, 18; Amnesty International AI Index ASA 39/02/99; McRae (2012) 6).

via royal pardon from King Bhumibol Adulyadej or his successor Maha Vajiralongkorn, whereas over the same period, fewer than 1 per cent of capital prisoners with finalized cases received clemency from the various presidents of Singapore. In Malaysia and Indonesia, the clemency 'rates' in capital cases from 1991 to 2016 stand in between these two extremes. In these two nations, approximately 55–63 per cent and (at a minimum) 26–33 per cent of death row prisoners' sentences were mitigated by the executive, respectively (depending on which sources are to be believed and the precise methodology used to count).[6] Vietnam's clemency rate, with fewer data points available than the other four jurisdictions, is likely to have fallen somewhere between 5 per cent and 50 per cent of finalized death penalty cases since data first became available in the mid-1990s.[7]

The discrepancy in capital clemency incidences among Southeast Asian jurisdictions is both extraordinary and puzzling. Accordingly, within this book, I analyse the differences in clemency practice among the Southeast Asian jurisdictions that continue to employ the death penalty as a form of criminal punishment (Thailand, Singapore, Malaysia, and Indonesia, minus

Moreover, attempting to cover the entire period 1975–2016 would also lead to a shortage and consequent imbalance of information on clemency cases from the 1970s and 1980s, as compared with the much greater detail available from the 1990s and 2000s. While one reason for this disparity in coverage is the lack of widespread interest in the death penalty as an international human rights issue until the early 1990s (Hood and Hoyle (2008) 18–20; Banchoff (2011) 304), the contrast becomes even more pronounced once the influence of the internet and the digitization of media reporting is taken into account, together with the more recent recollections of potential interview subjects (see Chapter 1).

[6] See Chapter 1.

[7] See Pascoe (2016a) 174–5. I have previously estimated, based on severely limited data from 1997 to 2008, that 6–23 per cent of finalized capital cases received clemency in Vietnam (Pascoe (2014) 5, 16). A recently released but unverified government report suggests that, beginning with Vietnam's change to lethal injection as a method of execution in July 2011, 179 commutations were passed in death penalty cases and 429 prisoners were executed through to July 2016 (The (2017); Vietnam Ministry of Public Security (2017) 10). This represents a clemency rate of approximately 29 per cent, comparable with Indonesia's minimum clemency rate from 1991 to 2016.

Vietnam),[8] in a search for patterns which explain why some countries in the region make use of capital clemency far more often than do others.

Southeast Asia is an excellent place to begin the long overdue conversation on comparative capital clemency practices in empirical perspective. Southeast Asia contains just under 10 per cent of the world's population, is one of the few world regions (alongside East Asia, the Middle East, and the Caribbean) where it is still possible to engage in a comparison of neighbouring countries' death penalty regimes, and, perhaps most significantly, functions as a regional barometer of death penalty trends worldwide. Although, over the past few years, comparative death penalty scholars have begun to give Southeast Asia a greater share of attention,[9] their focus generally remains either on a comparison between retentionist and abolitionist states or on substantive criminal laws and sentencing practice, rather than the quasi-legal, quasi-political decision to grant or refuse executive clemency.

Moving well beyond Amnesty International's simplistic observation in 1979 that 'although, in many countries, there is provision for act of presidential clemency, nowhere in Asia has the ready availability of such clemency been marked',[10] in this book I employ empirical analysis to examine the intricacies of clemency practice in Indonesia, Malaysia, Singapore, and Thailand, informed by relevant theory and previous comparative studies on

[8] Vietnam is excluded as a comparative case study because: (a) its socialist political system makes it more amenable to comparison with similarly situated states (particularly China) rather than states to the right of the political spectrum (Harding (2002) 49; Johnson and Zimring (2009) 132, 382–6; Buhmann (2001) 60, 410–11); and (b) unlike the other four nations under study, Vietnam's death penalty data is an official state secret, and has been since 2004 (Johnson and Zimring (2009) 388 n9, 389). For reasons of fieldwork safety and access to data, I was not able to conduct interview-based fieldwork in Vietnam, unlike in Singapore, Kuala Lumpur, Bangkok, and Jakarta from 2011 to 2013 (see Chapter 1). For recent academic research on the death penalty in Vietnam in English, see Lindsey and Nicholson (2016), Pascoe (2016a), Thayer (2015), Luong (2014), Nguyen (2014), Giao (2013), Johnson and Zimring (2009), Nicholson and Truong (2008), Nicholson (2008), and Sidel (1998).

[9] See Nicholson (2017); McRae (2017); Lindsey and Nicholson (2016); Leechaianan and Longmire (2013); Johnson and Zimring (2009).

[10] Amnesty International (1979) 67. See also Anti-Death Penalty Asia Network (2011) 32, for a more recent statement asserting the rarity of capital clemency in the Asia-Pacific region.

clemency—particularly the work undertaken by Douglas Hay,[11] Leslie Sebba,[12] Kathleen Dean Moore,[13] Elizabeth Rapaport,[14] Daniel Kobil,[15] Michael Heise,[16] Austin Sarat,[17] and Andrew Novak.[18] From 1991 to 2016, the situation on the ground in actively retentionist Southeast Asia was not nearly as dire as had been suggested by Amnesty International back in 1979, with capital clemency having been granted at different rates and for a variety of justifications. Condemned prisoners' hopes of winning a permanent reprieve from the executive rested not only on their individual case characteristics, but also on the jurisdiction in which they found themselves and the political administration then in power.

The findings presented here complement the scarce bodies of literature on comparative clemency in capital cases (globally), and the death penalty in Southeast Asia (locally). While extrapolating the findings of a study of only four retentionist jurisdictions to other parts of the world must be undertaken with caution, in the future, the hypothesis developed here may be tested elsewhere. No scholar has yet formulated a coherent, overarching theory as to why clemency is granted at vastly different rates and in different circumstances across the retentionist world, despite these differences being plain to see.[19] In fact, this is the first research study anywhere in the world to compare clemency across national borders using empirical methodology.

Why might the comparative and empirical literature on clemency remain so scarce? The answer is in the data. Clemency deliberations by executive decision makers, in whichever jurisdiction they occur, are usually performed in secret, with public justification for the exercise of clemency rarely given.[20] Accordingly, possible reasons behind death sentence commutations are rarely analysed in any systematic way.[21] However, this does not make

[11] Hay et al (2006).
[12] Sebba (1977a; 1977b).
[13] Moore (1989).
[14] Rapaport (1998–2000; 2001).
[15] Kobil (1991; 2003; 2007).
[16] Heise (2003; 2013; 2015).
[17] Sarat (2005; 2008).
[18] Novak (2015; 2016).
[19] Strange (1996) 9.
[20] Sebba (1977a) 229; Kobil (1991) 608–9.
[21] Landes and Posner (2009) 62; Kobil (1991) 608–9; Heise (2013) 7–8.

such research any less urgent. As Kobil observes, clemency and pardons now demand academic explanation to an even greater degree:

> like the monarchical power from which it derives, clemency is shrouded in mystery and often fraught with arbitrariness at a time when other aspects of [criminal justice systems] are becoming more open and fair.[22]

Despite limited information on how clemency decisions are made and the factors that contribute to their frequency or scarcity, clemency deliberations usually determine whether or not a prisoner sentenced to death ultimately lives or dies, and hence are of vital importance in a criminal justice system that retains capital punishment.[23] Although the frequency of clemency grants appears to have declined in a range of jurisdictions throughout the course of the twentieth century,[24] clemency is typically still the final avenue of appeal for a condemned prisoner, recourse to which is mandated by the International Covenant on Civil and Political Rights in Article 6(4),[25] by the UN Safeguards Guaranteeing Protection of the Rights of Those Facing the Death Penalty,[26] and perhaps even by customary international law, given its widespread availability in retentionist states.[27] Clemency is a condemned prisoner's indispensable last chance for life.

The Six Cases

As noted above, Southeast Asia's retentionist jurisdictions are striking in the diversity of their clemency practice. Thailand grants clemency extremely liberally in death penalty cases, Singapore extremely frugally; Indonesia and Malaysia fall somewhere in between, when considering data from the period 1991 to 2016. While those who make decisions on executive clemency are not

22 Kobil (1992–3) 202.

23 Burnett (2002) 16; Scott (1952) 95; Kobil (1992–3) 214–15.

24 Strange (1996) 14–15; Novak (2015) 2, 5, 166; Sebba (1977a) 234.

25 Of the four jurisdictions under study, Indonesia (as of 23 February 2006) and Thailand (as of 29 October 1996) are state parties to the International Covenant on Civil and Political Rights, whereas Singapore and Malaysia are neither parties nor signatories.

26 UN Economic and Social Council Resolution 1984/50, art 7.

27 *Fermin Ramirez v Guatemala* (Inter-American Court of Human Rights, 20 June 2005), [109]; Amnesty International AI Index 01/023/2011, 31.

obliged to follow precedent when making political decisions on petitions, over many hundreds of cases and years of practice, discernible patterns begin to emerge in most jurisdictions. The following are six paradigmatic cases whose features echo each of the four Southeast Asian nations' clemency practices as a whole. I introduce the volume with these six short vignettes to provide a human face to Southeast Asia's recent capital clemency story, given that the focus in Chapters 3–7 tends to be on clemency in an aggregate form.

The following examples juxtapose a serious Thai drug-trafficking case, in which the three defendants nonetheless escaped capital punishment via royal pardon, with a Singaporean case where the defendant, also a convicted drug trafficker, exhibited compelling mitigating features and yet clemency was denied. For Malaysia and Indonesia, the contrasting tales of clemency rejection and success described in what follows begin to show why those two jurisdictions fall somewhere in between Singapore's extremely low rate of clemency and Thailand's extremely high rate.[28] For certain categories of prisoners in Malaysia and Indonesia, clemency has been an expected remedy in more cases than not, whereas for other convicts, clemency is a forlorn hope that exists as a right only on paper. Singapore and Thailand's clemency practice encapsulates these two extremes, demonstrating significant regional disagreement over the political and legal functions that executive discretion should serve in capital cases.

1. Leung Chi Fai, Ng Shun Wa, and Leung Kam Chuen—Thailand

Leung Chi Fai, Ng Shun Wa, and Leung Kam Chuen (Image 1) were three fishermen from Hong Kong who were arrested in 2005 and sentenced to death for drug possession and trafficking in Thailand, but were eventually granted clemency by King Bhumibol Adulyadej via collective royal pardon in August 2012.[29] At the time, the suspects'

[28] On this classification see Chapter 1.

[29] Reprieve (2012a) 6; Reprieve (2012b); Bellivier and Lahidji (2013). Kong Chun Wah (the ship's captain) and Lee Foon were the other accomplices arrested who were not sentenced to death and later pardoned, possibly because they pleaded guilty at first instance ('Captain the Only One to Admit to Drug Trafficking' (2005)).

Image 1 Leung Chi Fai (second from left), Ng Shun Wa (far right), and Leung Kan Chuen (middle) following their arrest

Source: *Sing Pao Daily News*, 22 March 2005 (reprinted with permission)

arrests resulted in the Thai police's largest capture of illicit heroin in 10–15 years—a total of 546 kilograms with a street value of USD 7.1 million[30]—and the largest ever drugs seizure involving foreign suspects.[31] Moreover, there was some evidence that the three men were repeat offenders, having smuggled drugs between Hong Kong and Thailand on previous occasions.[32] At the time of their arrest, the suspects were alleged to be planning to traffic the drugs through Thailand and on to Hong Kong, the United States, and Russia.[33]

The three fishermen's case provides a salient example of the role played by collective royal pardons in removing prisoners from Thailand's death row, even for cases that are among the most serious. Leung, Ng, and Leung, who held overseas British nationality as pre-1997 Hong Kong residents, had concurrently submitted petitions to the Thai King for individual royal pardon, assisted

[30] Tang (2005); 'Captain the Only One to Admit to Drug Trafficking' (2005).
[31] 'HK Men on Drug Charges in Bangkok' (2006).
[32] 'HK Men on Drug Charges in Bangkok' (2006).
[33] 'Captain the Only One to Admit to Drug Trafficking' (2005).

by pro bono lawyers from Hong Kong and by London-based non-governmental organization (NGO) Reprieve.[34] The death sentences imposed on foreigners in Thailand are usually commuted to lesser punishments through individual royal pardons, if backed by senior figures from within their own governments.[35] However, it was through a periodic collective royal pardon celebrating Queen Sirikit's eightieth birthday and Crown Prince Maha Vajiralongkorn's sixtieth birthday that the petitioners in this case were spared execution. All fifty-seven prisoners on Thailand's death row had their sentences commuted to lesser punishments following the decree,[36] despite drug trafficking being a category of crimes for which collective royal pardons are sometimes prohibited.[37] Collective royal pardons, as a periodic method of reducing or clearing death row to celebrate important national events, constitute the most common form of leniency in Thai death penalty cases,[38] reflecting a long tradition of personal benevolence and Buddhist piety among Thai monarchs.[39] Leung, Ng, and Leung can now hope that, pursuant to a prisoner transfer agreement between Hong Kong and Thailand, they will be moved to a prison in Hong Kong to be closer to their families.[40]

2. Tong Chieng Mun—Singapore

Tong Chieng Mun was a young woman from Hong Kong who was executed for drug trafficking in 1995 in Singapore. At the time of her arrest at Singapore's Changi Airport in 1988, she was only several months past her eighteenth birthday.[41] Other than her youth, further potentially attenuating circumstances in Tong's case included the sentence of imprisonment imposed on her seventeen-year-old accomplice; Tong's status as a Hong Kong resident rather

[34] Reprieve (2012a) 6; Reprieve (2012b).

[35] Hands Off Cain, 'Thailand' (2001); interview with Thai criminal defence lawyer #2. See also Friedman (2012).

[36] Bellivier and Lahidji (2013); '10,000 Inmates Released under Royal Pardon' (2012); 'Current Statistics of Prisoners Condemned to Death' (2012).

[37] Union for Civil Liberty (2011) 36; Amnesty International AI Index ACT 50/001/2002, 11.

[38] See Appendix (Thailand).

[39] Chotibal (1990).

[40] Reprieve (2012b).

[41] 'Keep Death Penalty but Allow Leeway' (2009).

than being Singaporean; her sole intention to transit heroin from Thailand to Brussels, via Singapore's Changi Airport; and her difficult upbringing. Nevertheless, the case's determinative factor was the high street value (more than SD 2 million) of the heroin Tong was caught carrying at Changi.[42]

Tong's case therefore provides an example of several mitigating circumstances that Singapore's High Court, obliged since 1975 to apply the mandatory death penalty upon conviction for serious drug-trafficking offences, could not take into account in sentencing.[43] Moreover, despite the High Court's hands being tied at the sentencing phase, the Singaporean president (on the advice of the Cabinet) later rejected clemency and Tong was hanged. If clemency was rejected in a case such as Tong's, it is easy to see why one prominent Singaporean criminal lawyer described applying for clemency as invariably 'a waste of time'.[44] Only six petitions have been granted, from approximately five hundred capital cases, since the mandatory death penalty for drug trafficking was introduced by the Misuse of Drugs (Amendment) Act 1975.[45]

3. Kenneth Lee Fook Mun—Malaysia

Malaysia's king, the *Yang di-Pertuan Agong*, granted clemency to fifty-nine-year-old Kenneth Lee Fook Mun in 2008 (Image 2). Lee shot dead a female accountant through her car window in a road rage incident[46] and was sentenced to death by the Malaysian Court of Appeal in 2005, after prosecutors successfully appealed the initial eight-year prison sentence imposed at trial.[47] As the grandson of Malaysia's first Finance Minister, Tun Henry S Lee, and the nephew of a former deputy minister,[48] the defendant is strongly suspected to have benefited from his family ties to the then ruling political party, the United Malays National Organisation (UMNO).[49]

[42] 'Keep Death Penalty but Allow Leeway' (2009).
[43] Misuse of Drugs Act 2001 (Singapore), s 5 and sch 2.
[44] Anandan (2009) 90.
[45] Chan (2016) 200. Execution data sourced from Chan (2016) 183; Amnesty International (1979) 98; Amnesty International Annual Report (1978) 187; Cornell Center on the Death Penalty Worldwide, 'Singapore' (2017).
[46] Cheah (2008).
[47] Aaron (2007).
[48] Aaron (2007).
[49] Ting (2008).

Image 2 Kenneth Lee Fook Mun (left)

Source: *The Star Malaysia*, 1 July 2003 (reprinted with permission)

However, Lee may also have received clemency after settling a civil suit brought by the family of his victim, Lee Good Yew, for RM 550,000,[50] and because there was some evidence of hypoglycaemia or intoxication at the time of the killing, albeit not enough to establish a full defence.[51] Lee's case is indicative of clemency being granted to Malaysian defendants with political connections or previous service to the country,[52] as well as where compelling mitigating circumstances first appear at trial[53]—factors discussed in further detail in Chapter 5. Clemency as political reward, together with clemency for foreign nationals and for retributive and rehabilitative purposes, ensures that Malaysia's clemency totals far

[50] Aaron (2007).

[51] 'Kenneth Lee Sentenced to Death' (2005); interview with Malaysian prosecutor; interview with Malaysian criminal defence lawyer.

[52] Liu (2003); 'Will King Go against UMNO? Agong Has Last Word in Anwar's Pardon—Lawyers' (2015).

[53] Donoghue (2013) 191.

outstrip those of neighbouring Singapore, despite the close similarities in the two neighbours' historical and legal circumstances.

4. Michael McAuliffe—Malaysia

Michael McAuliffe was a thirty-nine-year-old Australian citizen who was denied clemency by the Penang Pardons Board and was executed in Selangor's Kajang Prison in June 1993. McAuliffe (Image 3) was sentenced to the mandatory death penalty for attempting to traffic 141 grams of pure heroin through Penang International Airport.[54] His case demonstrates that during the 1980s and early 1990s, under the stewardship of Prime Minister Mohamad Mahathir, Malaysia's 'one law for all' drugs policy spared no prisoner on the grounds of nationality.[55] If McAuliffe had been arrested for trafficking drugs in neighbouring Thailand, he would likely have not been executed,

Image 3 Michael McAuliffe (left)

Source: News Ltd, 23 January 2015 (reprinted with permission)

[54] Murdoch (1993); Donoghue (2013) 196.
[55] Donoghue (2013) 199.

given that his clemency appeal was supported by Australian Prime Minister Paul Keating and Foreign Minister Gareth Evans.[56] However, before the notable rise in executions in the mid-1990s in neighbouring Singapore and a softening of its own position,[57] Malaysia could lay claim to the ASEAN region's most punitive drug laws, which included the mandatory death penalty for trafficking, coercive drug rehabilitation schemes for addicts, administrative detention without trial,[58] and—of most relevance here—a near blanket prohibition on clemency in drug-trafficking cases,[59] irrespective of any impact on international relations or considerations of a prisoner's rehabilitation or mitigating characteristics.

5. Asep Suryaman—Indonesia

Professor Dr Asep Suryaman was a PKI (*Partai Komunis Indonesia*—Indonesian Communist Party) official who, while still under a death sentence, was granted a presidential pardon and released from Jakarta's Cipinang Prison in March 1999 (Image 4).[60] He was first arrested in 1971 and then sentenced to death for subversion in the Central Jakarta District Court in August 1975,[61] accused of 'building contacts for the PKI within the military'.[62] Suryaman was part of the PKI's intelligence agency and, between 1965 and his arrest in 1971, was a member of the party's Central Java provincial committee.[63] During Suryaman's long period of detention, he was told at least twice that he would be executed, only for those plans to be cancelled. His case became a prominent cause for international human rights NGOs as part of their broader effort to pressure the Suharto government over its treatment of political prisoners.[64]

Suryaman was one of several surviving PKI conspirators under sentence of death who were released from prison as part of

[56] 'Drugs Hanging' (1993); Donoghue (2013) 198.

[57] See Appendix (Malaysia, Singapore); Donoghue (2013) 236, 239.

[58] See Leechaianan and Longmire (2013) 132.

[59] 'Rocky Man to Hang' (1992); Baker (1992); Donoghue (1990) 119–20.

[60] 'President Grants Clemency to 10 More Political Prisoners' (1999); TAPOL (1999) 17; 'Eks Tapol PKI Minta Nyoblos' (1999).

[61] Amnesty International AI Index ASA 21/27/87, 11.

[62] Human Rights Watch and Amnesty International (1998).

[63] Murray (1991).

[64] Lev (2011) 348.

Image 4 Asep Suryaman (far left, white shirt) being released from Cipinang Prison in March 1999, alongside fellow political prisoners. Standing three to Suryaman's left is Colonel Abdul Latief (white shirt), a major figure in the coup attempt of 1965

Source: Tempo.co (reprinted with permission)

Indonesia's democratization after the fall of President Suharto in May 1998. In addition to the need to distance his government from that of the military autocrat Suharto through granting the pardons, Indonesia's new President BJ Habibie also took into account the men's old age, their failing health, their rehabilitation within prison, and finally their waning political threat to the Indonesian state.[65] Notably, one year before Suryaman was released, he was suffering from severe health problems, with fellow prisoners requesting that prison authorities transfer him to a prison hospital.[66]

Importantly, the prisoners who were released alongside Suryaman (up to ten altogether, although not all may have still been under sentence of death)[67] contribute significantly to the list of Indonesian capital clemency recipients since 1991. Not only do

[65] 'Coup Plotter to Be Freed After Years of Failed Efforts' (1999); England (1999).

[66] Amnesty International AI Index ASA 21/01/98.

[67] See Appendix (Indonesia).

the repercussions of the alleged PKI coup on the night of 30 August to 1 September 1965 continue to shape modern Indonesian politics and society,[68] but when associated capital subversion cases are considered in their aggregate, the events of 1965 also loom large over Indonesian clemency practice in the period under study. Asep Suryaman's case, where the accused was retrospectively sentenced to death under the 1969 Subversion Law and made to wait more than two decades for his death sentence to be lifted,[69] is symptomatic of the political function played by the post-coup trials and the tardiness of the Indonesian criminal justice system under Suharto. However, much has changed since Indonesia's democratization from 1998 onwards, as the sixth and final case indicates.

6. Rodrigo Gularte—Indonesia

Rodrigo Gularte was a Brazilian citizen arrested for trafficking in six kilograms of cocaine through Jakarta's Soekarno-Hatta

Image 5 The funeral of Rodrigo Gularte, Jakarta, 29 April 2015

Source: Anadolu Agency/Getty Images (reprinted with permission)

[68] Metcalf (2001) 20.
[69] Lev (2011) 348–9; Murray (1991).

airport in 2004. In the nearby Tangerang District Court, Gularte was sentenced to death, with the judicial panel holding that he was part of an international drug-trafficking syndicate aiming to distribute drugs within Indonesia. After Gularte's appeals to the Banten High Court and the Indonesian Supreme Court failed, he applied for presidential clemency in July 2012.[70] Gularte's clemency appeal was rejected by Indonesian President Joko Widodo in February 2015,[71] despite the fact that he had expressed significant remorse in his petition[72] and was suffering from cerebral dysrhythmia, paranoid schizophrenia, and bipolar disorder; his legal team had obtained ample evidence to prove his medical condition.[73] Gularte was subsequently executed in April 2015 (Image 5).[74] His case provides a stark example of the policies of Indonesia's democratically elected presidents relating to capital drug-trafficking crimes since 1999—in particular President Widodo, who has promised never to grant clemency in a drug-trafficking case, irrespective of the attenuating circumstances.[75]

Although, according to available figures, clemency in capital murder and PKI subversion cases has proven reasonably common in post-1991 Indonesia,[76] Indonesia's post-1991 clemency rate remains at a 'medium' level largely due to the consistent execution of drug traffickers in the post-1998 democratic era. This represents a substantial change in policy, as only one drug trafficker was executed during President Suharto's reign,[77] despite capital drug offences first being introduced in 1976.[78] Gularte's case, as a foreigner from an openly abolitionist nation,[79] suffering from severe mental health problems which would normally require admission to a psychiatric treatment facility,[80]

[70] Gunawan (2016) 37–40.

[71] Presidential Decree 5/G 2015 (Indonesia).

[72] Gunawan (2016) 39–40.

[73] Choudhury (2015–16) 31; Gunawan (2016) 41–3. The Indonesian Attorney General sought a second opinion supporting his own view of Gularte's mental condition, which was not divulged to Gularte's lawyers (Choudhury (2015–16) 32).

[74] Safi (2015).

[75] 'Bali Nine: Indonesian President Rules Out Clemency for Inmates on Death Row' (2014); Parlina et al (2015).

[76] See Chapter 6; Appendix (Indonesia).

[77] KontraS (2010).

[78] See Law 9/1976 on Narcotics (Indonesia), art 23(4)–(5).

[79] See Watts (2015).

[80] Topsfield (2015).

demonstrates the inflexibility of presidential clemency policy in drug-trafficking cases in post-Suharto Indonesia. As Gunawan has argued, Gularte's case is probably the clearest Indonesian example where not only was the defendant sentenced to death, but so was 'common sense' itself.[81]

Chapter Structure of the Book

This book is divided into nine chapters, four of which directly relate to the Southeast Asian jurisdictions under analysis: Thailand, Singapore, Malaysia, and Indonesia. However, before elaborating on the respective nations' death penalty and clemency policies, I first summarize the relevant academic literature that informs the study, and outline the precise methodology employed in collecting data on an often secretive and politically sensitive topic in retentionist states.

The book's later findings (contained in the national case studies in Chapters 3–6, as well as the broader discussion in Chapter 7 and the Conclusion) are guided and informed by an amalgam of previous research on: (a) comparative criminal justice methodology; (b) the role of data triangulation; (c) clemency in death penalty cases, both from a justificatory and an empirical perspective; and (d) specific regional material on the death penalty itself. Accordingly, Chapters 1 and 2 set the context within which I later present data on capital clemency in Southeast Asia obtained through archival and interview-based research.

Each of the four national case studies proceeds as an examination of the clemency laws and procedures, and the death penalty and capital clemency practice, within the relevant jurisdiction over the period 1991–2016, concluding with a list of potentially influential factors shaping clemency incidence in that jurisdiction. I begin with Thailand, with its extremely high clemency rate in capital cases, and move to diametrically opposed Singapore: by far the most frugal capital clemency jurisdiction in Southeast Asia. For these two nations, with their respective clemency rates falling at either end of the 0–100 per cent spectrum, deriving potential

[81] Gunawan (2016) 60. Gunawan also notes several fair trial concerns at the outset of the case. Gularte was denied access to an interpreter and a lawyer in the period immediately after his arrest (at 46–7).

explanatory factors is far simpler than is the case for Malaysia and Indonesia, where clemency practice is more nuanced. For Malaysia and Indonesia, I describe contradictory factors either enhancing or suppressing capital clemency, given the evident longitudinal variation in clemency practice and the differing interests of contemporary criminal justice actors in those jurisdictions. The Appendix at the end of the book provides the numerical data upon which analysis of each country's practice is based.

Chapter 7 and the Conclusion to this volume draw together comparative trends across the four case studies to develop an overarching hypothesis explaining clemency incidence in retentionist Southeast Asia. These chapters also comment on the implications of this hypothesis for practitioners, policymakers, and future scholarship. In brief, I suggest that in the four nations under study, capital clemency incidence from 1991 to 2016 has been largely determined by three structural and political factors:

1. The extent to which clemency operates as a form of lenient discretion, given the relative 'attrition rate' of capital cases at earlier stages of the criminal justice system;
2. The extent to which granting clemency enhances or detracts from political power for the final decision maker;
3. The length of time prisoners spend on death row, whether due to negligence by state officials or procedural obstacles to execution.

In other words, clemency in retentionist Southeast Asia symbolizes far more than official ambivalence over capital punishment as a criminal sentence, as its presence (or absence) can coincide with both high *and* low rates of execution. Instead, certain structural and political factors largely explain its prominence within one of the world's few remaining retentionist blocs.

1

Sources and Methods

> *According to competent authorities, stemming from our humanitarian policy, President Tran Duc Luong has signed decisions to commute [the] death penalty to life imprisonment for some people, including Mai Cong Thanh.*
>
> Vietnam Foreign Ministry spokesman Le Dung, after a convicted drug trafficker's sentence was commuted in 2006. No further explanation was forthcoming.[1]

In the preceding Introduction, I identified the traditional shortage of research on the death penalty in Southeast Asia, in addition to the reasons why clemency decisions in death penalty cases make for a compelling comparative and empirical analysis. The present chapter discusses important issues relating to the study's methodology, given clemency's generally opaque decision-making processes and outcomes and the semi-secretive nature of the four criminal justice systems under study. The discussion begins with the comparative criminal justice case study framework employed, and then moves to the availability of sources, including a need to 'triangulate' death penalty and clemency data from primary sources, secondary sources, and interviewees. This chapter's final section concerns the study's defining quantitative feature—each jurisdiction's clemency rate in capital cases from 1991 to 2016. I discuss how this figure is calculated, and relay potential problems of accuracy and comparability.

Overall, although this study relies heavily on unofficial data sources together with the recollections of 'elite' interviewees from both within and outside of Southeast Asia, the analysis in Chapters 3–7 is based on the most complete information presently available. As the four jurisdictions under study gradually come to

[1] 'Vietnam Commutes Aussie's Death Sentence' (2006).

Last Chance for Life: Clemency in Southeast Asian Death Penalty Cases. First Edition. Daniel Pascoe. © Daniel Pascoe 2019. Published 2019 by Oxford University Press.

open their criminal justice institutions to public and international scrutiny in the future, death penalty researchers will take these findings even further, gaining a more complete understanding of the extent to which the death penalty is practised in Southeast Asia, and the precise role of executive clemency in that practice.

Comparative Criminal Justice Case Studies

This four-country study employs a comparative criminal justice methodology, through the presentation of four national case studies preceding a comparative discussion section. A subset of the academic discipline of comparative criminology,[2] comparative criminal justice research analyses the similarities and differences of particular criminal justice phenomena across two or more national or provincial systems.[3] As a predominantly qualitative approach,[4] the comparative criminal justice methodology is a particularly useful framework for a hypothesis-generating study involving only a few jurisdictions, where the explanatory candidates for similarity and difference are not known ahead of time,[5] and where there are too few data points upon which to base a purely quantitative analysis.[6] Nevertheless, Boulanger and Sarat have advised against any methodological straitjacket in conducting comparative death penalty research.[7] As such, from time to time throughout the book, I make reference to the numerical data collected in the Appendices. Moreover, in the Conclusion, I also describe the untapped potential of this data to inform future multivariate regression studies of death penalty clemency.

What value does comparison itself bring to a study like this one? There are three main benefits: first, without referring to the state of affairs in otherwise similar jurisdictions, researchers have

[2] Newman and Howard (2001) 8.

[3] Hardie-Bick et al (2006) 1; Bennett (2004) 4; Nelken (2011) 396.

[4] Bennett (2004) 6, 15; Miethe et al (2005) 124, 128.

[5] Merriam (1995) 52; Tavallaei and Abu Talib (2010) 571.

[6] Previous transnational quantitative regression analyses of capital punishment such as those undertaken by Suh (2015), Kim (2015), Anckar (2014; 2004), McGann and Sandholtz (2012), Kent (2010), Neumayer (2008a; 2008b), Greenberg and West (2008), and Miethe et al (2005) have pursued a global focus, sampling a much larger number of retentionist jurisdictions, sometimes extending to *all* retentionist countries.

[7] Boulanger and Sarat (2005) 4.

no way of knowing what is 'normal' or what is 'exceptional'[8] within clemency practice. For example, the frequent use of the death penalty, when justified by nation-states, can appear ordinary, utilitarian, and benign (and indeed this is what a number of authoritarian governments would like their constituents and foreign critics to think about the ultimate punishment). It is only when it is compared with the penal policies of more liberal societies that state killing takes on a more repressive character. In the present context, how are academic researchers and criminal justice policymakers to know whether clemency is 'normally' granted in a majority or a small minority of finalized capital cases, absent statistical data or qualitative narrative from more than one jurisdiction? Without international comparison, observers cannot know whether clemency has largely vanished along with the absolute monarchies that gave birth to the concept,[9] or whether it remains very much an essential cog in the functioning of modern retentionist justice systems.

Second, the field of social science, for many researchers, revolves around 'the search for systematic regularities and generalizable laws'.[10] A number of comparable events or cases are required to provide a broader explanation, and perhaps even a cautious prediction of social and historical phenomena.[11] The approach chosen here is similar to inductive 'quasi-experimentation': a matching of broadly similar cases which nonetheless result in different outcomes, in order to isolate plausible explanatory factors in the formation of that outcome.[12] Admittedly, Thailand, Singapore, Malaysia, and Indonesia possess distinct legal systems, historical backgrounds, predominant religious creeds, and systems of government. However, each of these four nations has justified retaining and enforcing capital punishment for very similar reasons since the end of the Vietnam War in 1975: to provide retribution and public condemnation for murder,[13] to deter and

[8] Nelken (2011) 395–6; Johnson and Zimring (2009) 38.

[9] Sebba (1977a) 221–8; Sebba (1977b) 83; Kobil (1991) 571.

[10] Steinmo (2008) 133; Øyen (1990) 8; Nelken (2011) 398.

[11] Steinmo (2008) 133; Kohli et al (1995) 3; Nelken (2011) 398.

[12] Kohli et al (1995) 17; Lijphart (1971) 687.

[13] Interview with Singaporean law professor and Singaporean NGO staff #5 (with reference to Singapore); Handley (2006) 374 (Thailand); interview with Australian academic expert on Indonesia #4 (Indonesia); Human Rights Commission of Malaysia (2004) 7 (Malaysia).

eliminate those individuals and groups who pose a fundamental threat to the survival of the state in its present political form,[14] and to deter drug trafficking in a world region where narcotic drugs are regarded as a serious threat to the youth population, as well as to national stability more generally.[15]

Although the importance of the second stated function has declined in recent decades, alongside the Cold War mentality of 'emergency',[16] the first and third stated justifications for capital punishment in Southeast Asia remain very much operative at the time of writing in 2018. The list of crimes for which the death penalty is predominantly enforced in modern Southeast Asia is remarkably similar across the region's retentionist states: premeditated murder and serious drug crimes such as trafficking and manufacturing.[17] Not only are Thailand's, Singapore's, Malaysia's, and Indonesia's death penalty offences reasonably similar, but each of these four nations also make prominent constitutional provision for executive clemency from the head of state.[18] What differs so remarkably is the extent to which these clemency provisions are used in capital cases.

The third and final justification for comparison is to enable researchers to learn from the experience of otherwise similarly situated jurisdictions which have developed markedly different criminal justice policies: in other words, relying on the study's results to effect policy transfer.[19] For death penalty abolitionists, the key policy lesson from this book will be an awareness of the

[14] For communist insurgents: interview with Singaporean law professor and Singaporean NGO staff #5 (with reference to Singapore); interview with Malaysian human rights lawyer; interview with Malaysian Member of Parliament (both Malaysia); interview with Australian academic expert on Indonesia; KontraS (2010); interview with London-based Indonesian human rights activist (all Indonesia); Funston (2001b) 332; interview with Thai human rights commissioner; 'Death Penalty Should Be Abolished' (1996) (all Thailand). For Islamic extremists: Murray (1991); Kaye (1985); Glasius (1999) 98–9 (Indonesia). For military coup plotters: Amnesty International (1977); Amnesty International (1979) 66 (both Thailand).

[15] Johnson and Zimring (2009) 308–9; Hor (2004) 108 n30; Lindsey (2008).

[16] See Introduction.

[17] See Chapters 3–6; Johnson and Zimring (2009) 311; Lindsey and Nicholson (2016) 276.

[18] Constitution of Singapore 1965, art 22P(2); Constitution of Malaysia 1957, art 42(1); Constitution of Indonesia 1945, art 14; Muntarbhorn (2009); Constitution of Thailand 2014, s 22; Constitution of Thailand 2017, art 179.

[19] Pakes (2015) 5.

potential conditions that support executive clemency in Southeast Asian death penalty cases, and of how activists, lawyers, and policymakers might bring those conditions about in the future, assuming the death penalty is retained in each jurisdiction for the medium term. The exact opposite applies for readers who are supporters of the death penalty.

Structurally, the crux of the method used in this book involves presenting death penalty and clemency data in a narrative format, before proposing several nationally specific factors contributing to each country's clemency rate. Each of the legal and political factors proposed are supported by the local and theoretical literature on clemency and the death penalty, together with the views of in-country and foreign interview subjects. In Chapter 7, I compare and contrast these factors and draw regional conclusions as to the reasons for Southeast Asia's stark national differences on capital clemency. Within a monograph format, a similar comparative case study approach has recently been employed by scholars such as Tim Lindsey and Pip Nicholson (comparing the narcotics laws of Indonesia, Singapore, and Vietnam),[20] Andrew Novak (documenting the decline in the mandatory death penalty worldwide),[21] David Johnson and Franklin Zimring (comparing the death penalty laws and practices of East Asian nations),[22] and Sangmin Bae (evaluating international norm compliance among retentionist and abolitionist states).[23] This book adds to the transnational comparative literature on the death penalty, albeit with a different focus to that of previous authors: clemency in empirical perspective. In the following two sections, I elaborate on the difficulties encountered in adopting such an empirical approach within Southeast Asia.

Triangulating Sources in Four Semi-Secretive Jurisdictions

In an ideal world, the primary data relied upon in completing this study would come from official (government) sources only, in

[20] Lindsey and Nicholson (2016).

[21] Novak (2014).

[22] Johnson and Zimring (2009).

[23] Bae (2007). For more on the present state of global comparative death penalty scholarship, see Pascoe (2016b) 199–200, 199 n4.

order to maximize its reliability and authenticity. Unfortunately, researchers working on capital punishment—a highly politicized and sensitive criminal justice issue in Southeast Asia, as in other retentionist regions—are often left to rely on incomplete statistics, speculative recounting and interpretations of factual events, opaque reasoning behind official decisions, and even apathy or downright hostility from potential interview subjects. With complete death penalty clemency statistics over time largely inaccessible to researchers within Indonesia, Malaysia, and Thailand, and moreover the official reasoning behind each grant or rejection only sporadically placed on the public record within all four jurisdictions under analysis,[24] in conducting this study I faced a potential crisis of source material.

The accepted academic means of overcoming defects and omissions within official sources is an epistemological technique known

[24] Singapore's data includes only six grants of clemency since independence in 1965, all recorded prominently in local newspaper reports. However, the President of Singapore does not provide any official reasons when granting or refusing clemency (interview with Singaporean criminal defence lawyer #2; 'Keep Death Penalty but Allow Leeway' (2009); Amnesty International AI Index ASA 36/001/2004, 16).

In Malaysia, detailed statistical information on the use of capital punishment generally only appears in the public domain after a question by an opposition member of parliament (interview with international human rights NGO staff #2; interview with Malaysian human rights lawyer). The justifications for granting or rejecting capital clemency are rarely made public (interview with international human rights NGO staff #3; interview with Malaysian criminal defence lawyer; Roy (1986)).

In Indonesia, presidential clemency decrees have traditionally not been available to the public ('Joint Stakeholders' Report on the UPR of Indonesia (Third Cycle)—On Issues Relating to the Death Penalty' (2016) [20]; Amnesty International AI Index ASA/21/2434/2015, 67). For example, they are not listed on the website of the State Secretariat (https://www.setneg.go.id/) and local NGOs have been unsuccessful in trying to gain access to the data (Scholastica Gerintya (2018)). After succeeding with a legal challenge in 2016, an NGO called Institute for Criminal Justice Reform (ICJR) established a right to view a list of *rejected* clemency applications from death penalty prisoners, although not the president's reasoning on these petitions (Eddyono et al (2016) 20–1; Mulyana (2016)).

In Thailand, clemency statistics are occasionally available from unofficial sources, but are not currently listed on the website of the Department of Corrections (http://www.correct.go.th/eng/index.html). The king's reasons for granting individual royal pardons are not directly provided to prisoners (interview with Thai human rights activist (2012); interview with Thai prison caseworker), but will often be announced for collective royal pardons, which celebrate as 'triangulation of proof', which involves cross-referencing various official and non-official, quantitative and qualitative sources of data, in the hope that the aggregate of a number of flawed sources will reveal the 'true' picture on sensitive topics.[25]

Within the present study, I therefore rely upon both official (government press releases and archival data, speeches, autobiographies) and non-official sources (such as independent media reports, journal articles, and NGO publications), together with 'elite' interviews.[26] Given that Southeast Asian governments have often been reluctant to publicize clemency grants to prisoners on death row, due to the political capital gained by regular executions and an outwardly impartial enforcement of the law, the leading public sources of information on capital clemency grants are independent media articles and NGO reports—hence the heavy reliance on those materials in Chapters 3–6.

'Elite' interviews in Southeast Asia, the United Kingdom, Australia, and elsewhere

Beyond the written sources employed, 'elite' interviews perform a particularly important role within the present study, given that the executive rarely reveals the decision-making processes and operative reasons for clemency decisions to the public. According to Lilleker, interviews have the potential to provide

> insights into events about which we know little: the activities that take place out of the public or media gaze, behind closed doors ... interviews can provide immense amounts of information that could not be gleaned from official published documents or contemporary media accounts.[27]

important national events and reward good behaviour in prison (interview with Thai law professor; interview with former employee of the Thailand Department of Corrections).

[25] Johnson and Zimring (2009) 234; Davies (2001) 75, 78; Miller (2003) 327; Merriam (1995) 54.

[26] I refer to interviews with political and legal decision makers and relevant experts as 'elite' interviews to distinguish these from interviews with potentially vulnerable parties such as defendants, prisoners, voters, and children. With 'elite' interviews, the power imbalance generally favours the interviewee over the interviewer, whereas when interviewing 'down', the opposite is true (Bailer (2004) 171).

[27] Lilleker (2003) 208.

To complete the triangulation process, the categories of persons approached for interview included:

- academic staff;
- journalists;
- criminal defence lawyers;
- non-governmental organization (NGO) staff and volunteers;
- government personnel (including judges, prosecutors, and other members of the criminal justice bureaucracy);
- politicians (from both government and opposition parties).

In accordance with the 'elite' interviewing literature, the interview subjects were chosen on the basis of their proximity to decision-making power in the criminal justice and political hierarchy of the jurisdiction concerned, or else their own expertise on the issues of relevance.[28] All identities have since been anonymized within this book, in accordance with ethical requirements.[29]

Overall, during fieldwork trips to Kuala Lumpur and Singapore (from September 2011 to January 2012) and Bangkok and Jakarta (September to October 2012; April 2013), together with further interviews carried out at other times in the United Kingdom, in Australia, and by email and telephone, 64 individuals and organisations consented to participate (some more than once), whereas 105 declined. Although fewer government contacts agreed to speak on the record, the interviews managed to capture a plurality of views on capital clemency and its potential socio-political explanations, from both pro- and anti-'establishment' sources.[30]

Data availability challenges—death penalty statistics

The annual clemency totals for each of the four jurisdictions under study are listed in the four Appendices, together with the annual

[28] Leech (2002) 663; Lilleker (2003) 207.

[29] Further information regarding the University of Oxford's CUREC policy, which shaped the fieldwork for this study, is available at http://www.admin.ox.ac.uk/curec/policystatement/.

[30] See Seldon (1996) 353–5; Lilleker (2003) 208; Richards (1996) 204; Davies (2001) 75.

Table 1 Appendix data

Year	First instance death sentences passed[a]	Death row prisoners (exhausted appeals)[b]	Clemency (pardons)[c]	Executions
1991				
1992				
etc.				
2016				

[a]This figure includes death sentences imposed at first instance, together with prison sentences that are increased to death sentences on appeal.

[b]Numbers in brackets indicate prisoners who have *exhausted all judicial appeals*, in other words, clemency by commutation or pardon is their final procedural hope of avoiding execution. Where there are several sources covering the same year, I indicate a range from lowest to highest.

[c]Numbers in brackets here indicate the number of clemency grants *from the total* which are pardons. For the Thai data, I split this column into clemency granted pursuant to *individual* royal pardon and clemency granted as part of a *collective* royal pardon. For capital prisoners in Thailand, collective royal pardons are invariably granted as commutations rather than pardons.

number of death sentences passed by the courts, the death row population, and yearly totals for executions (see Table 1).

These figures allow the calculation of each country's clemency rate (I elaborate on this later in this chapter), and also help to illustrate Chapters 3–7 with numerical detail. Nevertheless, one of the first things the reader will notice about each of the tables in the Appendices is the amount of blank space within certain columns. Additionally, a number of sampling biases leave the data that have been collected open to criticism.

The tables in the Appendices contain empty cells for a variety of reasons. Sometimes the data that do exist have proved inaccessible, whereas on other occasions the data may not exist at all.[31] The general problem with the official data obtained is not that Southeast Asian governments have systematically lied or deliberately downplayed the number of death sentences issued, clemency grants made and executions carried out, but rather that they adopt deliberate policies of non-disclosure regarding any

[31] For example, given that I do not speak Thai, 'elite' interviews play a larger role within Chapter 3 on Thailand than is the case in the other chapters. My language proficiency extends to Indonesian and Malay.

information concerning capital punishment,[32] even if (unlike in Vietnam) the information is not technically 'classified' as a state secret.[33] On the whole, between 1991 and 2016 the governments of Singapore, Malaysia, and Indonesia published very little official statistical information on the administration of the death penalty, whereas Thailand adopted a more open approach, at least until the current military government took power in May 2014.[34]

Even where death penalty statistics are available in some form, there are still a number of potential shortcomings with this data. First, the tables in the Appendices provide contrasting figures for the same year from different sources, as is obvious from multiple entries in many fields. The triangulation technique demands that multiple sources (from official and unofficial data) be considered, in order to arrive at a consensus or median position. Moreover, as NGO-sourced statistics are often themselves based upon media reports, these best serve as reliable *minimum* estimates for executions in a particular year in systems that are otherwise 'closed' to the outside world.[35] Where applicable, the '+' symbol is used to denote a 'minimum' figure in each case, following the practice adopted by Amnesty International.[36]

There may also be multiple-year ranges provided by a source rather than single-year figures;[37] 'yearly' figures may have been

[32] Interview with international human rights NGO staff (Asia-wide relevance); Interview with Singaporean Human Rights Activist; Interview with Singaporean NGO Staff #3 (both Singapore); interview with international human rights NGO staff #2 (Malaysia); Amnesty International AI Index ASA 36/004/2009; 'Death Sentence for Canadian Father, Son' (1993) (Thailand); Amnesty International AI Index ASA 21/003/2008, 29; Amnesty International AI Index ASA 21/017/1994, 104 (Indonesia).

[33] The Official Secrets Act 2012 (Singapore) may be an exception here (Singapore Anti Death Penalty Campaign (2011) 2).

[34] Interview with Thai human rights activist (2012); Malakunas (2004). Official death penalty statistics were previously available on the Thailand Department of Corrections website (Thailand Department of Corrections (2006)), and still appear occasionally on the Death Penalty Thailand blog: http://deathpenaltythailand.blogspot.com.

[35] Interview with international human rights NGO staff; Johnson and Zimring (2009) 235. The latter authors note that 'Amnesty [International] bends over backward not to overestimate execution numbers'.

[36] See, for example, Amnesty International AI Index ACT 50/001/2012, 2.

[37] I do not consider multiple-year figures if they relate to years outside the 1991–2016 timeframe. Nor do I record clemency grants or executions in the Appendix if it is unclear which year/s they occurred in.

collected before the end of a calendar year,[38] and there may be confusion in media sources between death sentences, executions, and statistics which only relate to particular crimes or punishments (e.g. drug offences, or the mandatory death penalty). For clemency in particular, media reports describing 'commutations' or 'clemency grants' may in fact refer to death sentences that have been reduced to a term of imprisonment following a judicial appeal, rather than by executive action. Indeed, this is the terminology that Amnesty International employs in its annual death penalty reports.[39]

Given these problems, the numbers relayed in the Appendices to this volume provide a good indication of death penalty and clemency trends over time, but should not be taken as representing an official record of each jurisdiction's practice. Further democratization is likely to increase data transparency in Southeast Asia, but until then researchers must make do with whatever limited information is available, all the while specifically acknowledging the caveats of such an approach.

Data availability challenges—clemency reasoning

Annual or periodic clemency figures may be necessary to establish each jurisdiction's clemency rate, but by themselves these are not sufficient to answer this study's primary research question: why do different retentionist nations grant clemency at vastly different rates? Within each jurisdiction under study, the questions of who receives clemency in death penalty cases, for which reasons, and from which precise decision maker/s help greatly to explain 'how many' prisoners receive clemency overall. For a truly exhaustive analysis, the executive decision makers' reasons for all documented clemency grants and refusals would need to be publicly available. However, in retentionist jurisdictions these reasons often remain secret,[40] and where public justifications are offered

[38] I prioritize 'yearly' (calendar year) figures only for executions and death sentences, but record figures for death row prisoners collected at any time of year: the latter figure may be constantly changing as prisoners are sentenced to death throughout the year and move off death row for various reasons.

[39] See, for example, Amnesty International AI Index ACT 50/001/2015, 6; Amnesty International AI Index ACT 50/003/2009, 9–10.

[40] Kobil (1991) 608–9; Acker et al (2010) 188.

the explanation given will often be framed in an extremely general or politically convenient manner, encapsulated by expressions such as 'because of the peculiar circumstances of the crime' or 'because it is considered that justice will be satisfied without the taking of this [petitioner's] life'.[41]

Absent full and honest disclosure from the executive decision maker/s in each case, outside observers may only speculate on the political or legal reasons for each grant of clemency. Without the input of key decision maker/s, researchers are often limited to making assumptions based on a pattern of previous decisions (such as clemency granted in cases of youth or old age, to women, for a particular crime, and so forth),[42] or relying on the opinions of analysts and 'experts' on the law and politics of each national jurisdiction. In most Southeast Asian cases, even the lawyers of the prisoners granted clemency have no right to receive information on the reasons for the grant or its refusal (although they may make written or oral representations to the decision-making body, depending on the jurisdiction).[43] Case reports and transcripts, together with media articles, can provide background to the factual circumstances of the case and the offender, but the official reasons for the clemency grant will usually remain a mystery.

Even the direct input of an insider close to the decision-making process will not always constitute an authoritative and reliable source on the reasons for clemency grants. 'Elite' interviews, which form such an integral part of the research design for this study, pose particular problems of reliability here. Smith admits to being fundamentally 'uncertain how easy it is to identify the people who influence "important decisions"'.[44] In the clemency context, with many layers of bureaucracy potentially contributing to the final recommendation and decision, who is the right 'decision maker' to contact for interview? Furthermore, for 'elite' interviewees on the government side, there will usually be an

[41] Scott (1952) 98; Acker et al (2010) 188. See also note 1 and associated text.

[42] Pridemore (2000) 163, 165.

[43] Interview with Malaysian criminal defence lawyer (Malaysia); interview with Singaporean criminal defence lawyer #2 (Singapore); International Federation for Human Rights (2005) 27; interview with Thai human rights activist (2012); interview with former employee of the Thailand Department of Corrections (all Thailand); interview with Indonesian human rights lawyer (Indonesia).

[44] Smith (2006) 645.

'official' line to be promulgated.[45] Will the answer provided to the question 'why was clemency granted in that particular case?' be based upon only one person's input into or opinion about a collective decision,[46] or alternatively be the kind of generic response designed to disguise more calculated political considerations?[47] For these reasons, even interview responses from prominent civil servants or serving politicians have been treated with caution, and triangulated with other data sources wherever possible.

During the fieldwork for this study, although I interviewed several current or former direct advisers on clemency petitions,[48] in no case was it possible to interview a member of the highest prima facie decision-making body for clemency (i.e. the Singapore Cabinet, the King of Thailand, members of the Malaysian State and Federal Pardons Boards, Malaysia's state rulers or governors, or the Indonesian president). Moreover, the identities of these decision makers have not, of course, remained consistent throughout the period 1991–2016. Over two and a half decades, official policies and subjective inclinations to grant or refuse clemency will change with the personnel involved. This also assumes that clemency decisions are actually made at the highest political level, rather than the constitutionally empowered decision maker simply rubber-stamping recommendations made by the judiciary, prosecutors, prison authorities, or other civil servants.[49] As described previously, at best, interviews form part of a strategy of triangulation, whereby the responses of purported decision makers are reconciled with information on clemency reasoning contained within primary and secondary documentary sources.

Calculating and Comparing Clemency Rates

The figures provided in the Appendices have been collated not only as a source of quantitative illustration for each country chapter, but also, crucially, in order to ascertain the country's 'clemency

45 Nelken (2010) 92.

46 Lilleker (2003) 208.

47 See Davies (2001) 75.

48 Interview with Indonesian deputy minister; interview with Indonesian Supreme Court judge; interview with Singaporean prosecutor.

49 Interview with London-based death penalty lawyer; Abramowitz and Paget (1964) 184–5; Sebba (1977b) 115; Lardner and Colgate Love (2004) 213.

rate', defined here as the percentage of *finalized* death penalty cases in which the prisoner receives clemency. This figure is calculated not by comparing death sentences or numbers of death row prisoners with clemency grants, but rather by comparing total clemency grants with total executions over the temporal limits of the study.[50] For example, a clemency rate of 20 per cent means that of the total sum of prisoners executed and granted clemency over a defined yearly range, one in five 'finalized' death sentences are spared by the executive, either through a commutation to life imprisonment or a term of years, or through outright release by pardon. While a prisoner executed in a particular year may have been sentenced to death at a completely different time to another prisoner granted clemency in that same year (given appeal processes of differing lengths and evolving political priorities), the ratio of clemency grants to executions in a particular year, or over the entire period 1991–2016, is broadly indicative of the importance each nation accords to executive clemency as a form of discretionary relief from the death penalty.

In addition to the impact of missing data just described, there are several further caveats relating to the way that national clemency rates are calculated. These are shortcomings which may affect the accuracy and legitimacy of the clemency rate percentage as a measure of how frequently clemency is employed as a discretionary means of avoiding capital punishment. First, there are more than two binary outcomes (beyond simply execution or commutation/pardon) once a condemned prisoner exhausts judicial appeals: some prisoners die in prison before execution; some escape;[51] a few might be moved to mental health facilities if they are unfit for execution;[52] some are cruelly held indefinitely on death row (until their later death from natural causes), without an order for clemency or a warrant for execution ever being signed.[53]

Second, research from the United States suggests that a significant minority of prisoners eventually executed are death row 'volunteers', meaning they have voluntarily renounced their right to

[50] This is similar to the definition adopted by Argys and Naci Mocan (at 265) and Heise (2013 at 12). Contrast Bedau (1990–1) 263–6.

[51] Scott (1952) 99.

[52] Argys and Naci Mocan (2004) 265, 271.

[53] Interview with London-based death penalty lawyer #2; interview with British academic expert on the death penalty; Bedau (1990–1) 266.

appeal against the sentence of death, either at the judicial or clemency stages.[54] However, in Southeast Asia this problem is not as significant as it is in the United States. Within three of the jurisdictions under analysis, all prisoners sentenced to death are automatically considered for clemency on an individual basis (Singapore and Malaysia) or collectively (Thailand).[55] In Indonesia, a 2010 amendment to the nation's Clemency Law allows for the Minister of Law and Human Rights to petition the president for clemency on a capital prisoner's behalf if the prisoner or the prisoner's family will not do so personally.[56] Before the 2010 amendment, a condemned prisoner's family member was entitled to appeal for clemency on his or her behalf.[57]

Third, because the clemency rate is a measure of clemency success in *finalized* cases, if clemency is granted at an earlier stage of the proceedings (i.e. before all judicial appeals have failed), this will distort the figures. Executive leniency before all judicial appeals are exhausted are possible in both Thailand and Indonesia (via collective amnesty grants)[58] and in Thailand, Indonesia, and Malaysia (where the prisoner fails to pursue all available judicial appeals).[59]

Fourth, where necessary the clemency rates calculated in this study are expressed as low-to-high ranges rather than as precise percentages, due to contradictory yearly figures for clemency and for executions, as noted previously. I combine four figures to produce a clemency 'range' for both Malaysia and Indonesia over the entire period 1991–2016:[60]

[54] Cooper (2009) 107; Heise (2013) 12, 12 n34.

[55] Criminal Procedure Code 2006 (Malaysia), s 281(c); Talib (1989) 62–3 (both Malaysia); Constitution of Singapore 1965, art 22P(2) (Singapore); interview with Thai Prison caseworker (Thailand).

[56] Law 5/2010 on Clemency (Indonesia), art 6A; Law 22/2002 on Clemency (Indonesia), art 8(1).

[57] Law 3/1950 on Clemency (Indonesia), art 1; Law 22/2002 on Clemency (Indonesia), art 6(1), 8(1).

[58] Constitution of Indonesia 1945, art 14(2); interview with Thai criminal defence lawyer #2. See also Criminal Procedure Code 1934 (Thailand) s 262.

[59] Law 22/2002 on Clemency (Indonesia), elucidation; Cornell Center on the Death Penalty Worldwide, 'Thailand' (2017); Criminal Procedure Code 2006 (Malaysia) s 281(b)(i).

[60] I do not consider years in the cumulative total unless *both* execution and clemency figures are available for the year in question. This means that I only include years where clemency or execution totals are reported as zero, rather than years where such totals are not reported at all. For Thailand, however,

1. the lowest minimum number of clemency grants indicated by available sources;
2. the highest minimum number of clemency grants indicated by available sources;
3. the lowest minimum execution total over the same period;
4. the highest minimum execution total over the same period.

Use of the lowest and highest 'minimum' totals for clemency grants and executions is the inevitable result of a reliance on unofficial data, in particular NGO-sourced statistics.[61]

Despite such difficulties, incomplete statistics do still enable rough calculations to be made. For the nations with more imprecise data (Malaysia and Indonesia), what I term the jurisdiction's 'low-end' clemency percentage is calculated by comparing the lowest minimum clemency total with the highest minimum execution total, and likewise the 'high-end' clemency percentage is calculated by comparing the highest minimum clemency total with the lowest minimum execution total over common temporal limits. A narrower final clemency range here implies that there are fewer discrepancies in the triangulated data for clemency and executions, but whether this comes as a result of increased *accuracy* is not necessarily certain. Moreover, for Indonesia, the overt lack of yearly totals for clemency, combined with the precise yearly figures available for executions, suggests that whatever numerical result range is reached will itself be a 'minimum' estimate for clemency frequency anyway.

After determining each country's clemency rate using available data, it is then possible to compare that country alongside others within and outside the study in three groups of magnitude: those jurisdictions with 'low' clemency rates (below 5 per cent), those with 'medium' clemency rates (between 5 and 50 per cent), and those with 'high' clemency rates (above 50 percent). Countries with low rates only use clemency very sparingly,

I include years in the sample where there are known totals for *either* individual royal pardons or collective royal pardons, but not necessarily both (see Appendix (Thailand) and Chapter 3: Kingdom of Thailand). When calculated in this way, Thailand's final clemency 'range' comes to 94.8–95.3 per cent, which I round to 95 per cent, although in reality this figure may be even higher given the unavailability of clemency data in certain years. Singapore's unambiguous data means a range is unnecessary for that jurisdiction.

[61] See notes 35–36 and associated text.

in what the executive deems truly exceptional cases. Countries with high rates of clemency actually spare more prisoners than they execute. Execution is the unusual measure here, rather than clemency. Between these two extremes lie the countries espousing what I term medium rates. Here, the death sentence is upheld and later carried out by the executive in the majority of cases, yet clemency still appears to play a significant role in the criminal justice system as an extra layer of appeal against the harshness of a death sentence, as a means to reward prisoner rehabilitation, or perhaps as a demonstration of political benevolence. By way of comparison, the collective post-1976 death penalty clemency practice of the United States places that nation firmly within the 'medium' category,[62] alongside pre-abolition twentieth-century Britain.[63] In Vietnam, the remaining actively retentionist Southeast Asian nation not covered in this book, the clemency rate from the limited period July 2011–July 2016 also falls into the 'medium' designation, at 29 per cent.[64] In both Japan and China, the recent clemency rate is zero. Executive clemency, either as a collective amnesty or as an individual commutation, has not been granted in a death penalty case in either jurisdiction since 1975.[65]

[62] Following the death penalty's reinstatement by the US Supreme Court in *Gregg v Georgia* 428 US 153 (1976), between 1977 and 2016 (inclusive) 1,442 executions were carried out in the United States (Death Penalty Information Center (2017b)) and 280 prisoners were granted clemency for *humanitarian* reasons, that is, excluding clemency granted only in order to avoid a retrial or for other procedural reasons (Death Penalty Information Center (2017a)), resulting in a clemency rate of approximately 16 per cent. However, if the 167 death sentences commuted by Illinois governor George Ryan in a single 2003 decree are removed from these statistics (Death Penalty Information Center (2003)), the national humanitarian clemency percentage drops to approximately 6.5 per cent. Before the death penalty was initially declared unconstitutional by the US Supreme Court in *Furman v Georgia* 408 US 238 (1972), Coyne and Entzeroth (2001, at 840) calculated the country-wide clemency rate between 1960 and 1970 as approximately 44 percent.

[63] Chan (2016) 182 n15 (46 percent). Novak (2015) relays a 50 per cent pardon rate in British colonies in Africa during the first half of the twentieth century (at 35).

[64] The (2017); Vietnam Ministry of Public Security (2017) 10.

[65] Johnson and Zimring (2009) 64 n30; Dui Hua Foundation (2016); Andrew and Rapp (2000) 75.

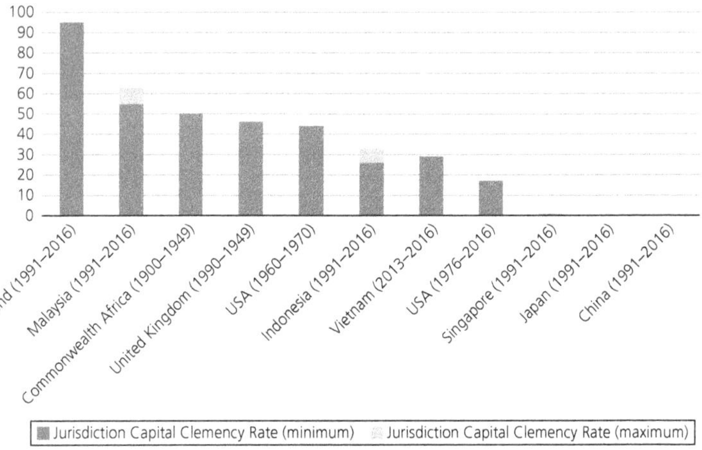

Figure 1 Death penalty clemency rate in selected jurisdictions

For the four jurisdictions comprising the current study, on the basis of the 1991–2016 data provided in the Appendices, the relevant clemency rates, in ascending order, are the following:

- Singapore: a 'low' rate of clemency, at 0.6 per cent;
- Indonesia: a 'medium' rate of clemency, from 26 per cent to 33 per cent, at a minimum;
- Malaysia: a 'high' rate of clemency, from 55 per cent to 63 per cent;[66]
- Thailand: a 'high' rate of clemency, at 95 per cent,[67] or above.

Alongside the other jurisdictions referred to in Figure 1, actively retentionist Southeast Asia therefore provides examples of each of the three identified categories of clemency use—clemency granted at low, medium, and high rates. As legal historian Carolyn Strange has observed, 'The most striking aspect of pardoning is that rates of commutation differed between jurisdictions and

[66] I use a slightly different calculation method to arrive at Malaysia's total, due to missing yearly clemency data from 1991 to 1997. See further Chapter 5.

[67] Excluding the years 2006, 2008, 2013, 2014, and 2015 (no clemency data). See further note 60.

varied over time within jurisdictions'.[68] Such vast differences in clemency incidence are the puzzle that this book ultimately seeks to resolve.

Rigour or 'Guesswork'?

Death penalty research within semi-secretive criminal justice jurisdictions must overcome many different methodological challenges. In particular, within the present study, the scarcity of death penalty statistics and clemency case reports from official sources creates special difficulties in arriving at academically rigorous findings. Again, it should be stressed that the present study is by no means exhaustive, but provides an exploratory analysis of the reasons behind clemency grants and their relative incidence across four neighbouring retentionist jurisdictions. The sources and methods employed here echo Johnson and Zimring's observations on carrying out death penalty scholarship on China, for which their research was necessarily 'constructed around limits that sound scholarship would ordinarily find unacceptable'.[69] As the same two authors have noted in the comparative Asian context:

> Research on the death penalty ... [is] so thick in some parts of the subject that no one can master it, yet so thin in others that storytellers are 'reduced to guesswork, weaving great swatches of narrative from little rags of data' ... research on capital punishment outside the USA is so thin that [even] guesswork must sometimes be considered progress.[70]

While engaging in frivolous 'guesswork' would not produce academically rigorous hypotheses, some liberties must nevertheless be taken. Tellingly, even in the United States, the retentionist nation that has attracted the vast majority of English-language academic scholarship on the death penalty, debates on capital clemency justifications are rarely informed by systematically collected data.[71] In this context, the book's heavy reliance on independent media, NGO

[68] Strange (1996) 9.

[69] Johnson and Zimring (2009) 225.

[70] Johnson and Zimring (2006) 94, quoting Friedman (1993) ix. See also Boulanger and Sarat (2005) 18.

[71] Heise (2003) 262; Hoffman (1998).

reports, and ‘elite’ interviews as sources of empirical data on the clemency practice of each national jurisdiction, while falling short of comprehensive government data in terms of coverage and reliability, nonetheless represents a significant improvement on the status quo.

2

Four Models of Clemency

On the one hand, pardons were frequently granted for no discernible reason, as if some were spared through the luck of the draw; on the other, certain types of crimes and offenders have consistently inspired either sympathy or intolerance.

Carolyn Strange, *Qualities of Mercy: Justice, Punishment, and Discretion*[1]

This chapter provides a theoretical framework for the study of clemency in death penalty cases. It begins with a primer on terminology, both within the western and the Southeast Asian contexts, before moving to the reasons why clemency is granted, and the categories of prisoners who tend to benefit. Here, I suggest four justificatory models for clemency in death penalty cases, based upon a survey of the previous academic literature: (1) 'mercy from the sovereign' granted solely for the ruler's benefit; (2) retributivist clemency; (3) redemptive clemency; and (4) clemency for political advantage or utilitarian reasons. Finally, although transnational clemency research is still very much in its infancy, I conclude by relaying the results of the few multi-jurisdictional studies on capital clemency conducted in the past, supplemented by factors that the theoretical literature suggests as potentially contributory to clemency frequency or scarcity.

Terminology

Defining 'clemency' grants

Once a defendant is sentenced to death by a court of law and has exhausted all available judicial appeals,[2] his or her last remaining

[1] Strange (1996) 9.

[2] Unless domestic law prohibits it, there is no reason why commutation or pardon cannot be granted *before* the prisoner has exhausted all judicial options, or

Last Chance for Life: Clemency in Southeast Asian Death Penalty Cases. First Edition. Daniel Pascoe. Published 2019 by Oxford University Press.

procedural hope is usually a grant of clemency from the political executive.[3] In the Introduction, clemency was briefly defined as the executive branch of government replacing a death sentence with a lesser punishment, or alternatively the executive branch abrogating judicially imposed punishment altogether. Throughout this book, I label executive clemency that permanently mitigates but does not completely alleviate punishment as 'commutation', whereas executive clemency that releases a death row prisoner from incarceration altogether I label a 'pardon'.[4] Sometimes a grant of pardon also erases criminal responsibility in its entirety.[5] Within this book's definition, commutations and pardons may be granted individually, or to an entire group of prisoners at once.[6]

While the outright release from prison of a convict previously condemned to death was once the most common form of executive leniency in capital cases,[7] the advent of long-term imprisonment and rehabilitative punishments in the nineteenth century,[8] together with the development of additional layers of judicial review following conviction, means that when an executive order for leniency is now made, it normally comes as a commutation.[9] Here, the death sentence is replaced by a sentence of imprisonment, such as a life sentence with or without the possibility of parole or a (lengthy) fixed term of imprisonment. In the modern

even before criminal charges are laid (Acker and Lanier (2000) 204). Nonetheless, this course of action is rare across the retentionist world. See Chapter 1 on clemency in this context in Southeast Asian nations.

3 Sebba (1977a) 230; Sarat (2005) 19. Throughout the world, grants of clemency are made by a range of executive decision makers, from a monarch or head of state to a senior government minister, a provincial governor, a parliamentary committee, or a specially constituted clemency or pardons board (Sebba (1977b) 111–15; Robertson (2006) 147).

4 Under the common law model, clemency also extends to lesser forms of leniency such as reprieves (delays in sentence execution, particularly in death penalty cases), respites (temporary breaks in the middle of a sentence), and remissions of fines and forfeitures (Novak (2016) 819; Novak (2015) 4; Sebba (1977b) 116). Clemency's permanent impact on a death sentence is limited to commutations, pardons, and amnesties, hence the book's focus on these powers.

5 Acker et al (2010) 184; Acker and Lanier (2000) 204–5; Abramowitz and Paget (1964) 138.

6 Novak (2015) 7, 9, 20.

7 Abramowitz and Paget (1964) 138.

8 Kaminer (1995) 171; Fairchild and Dammer (2006) 251.

9 Acker et al (2010) 184; Lardner and Colgate Love (2004) 212–13.

context, a pardon (whether conditional or unconditional) is extremely rare for a prisoner sentenced to death,[10] irrespective of the jurisdiction, unless there are significant doubts over the propriety of the prisoner's conviction, or where a state transitions suddenly from autocracy to democracy, delegitimizing the prior regime's punishments. For this reason, the focus of the book is primarily on executive leniency by commutation. Nevertheless, although they are far outnumbered by commutations, pardons are occasionally passed in Southeast Asian death penalty cases. Given the limited data available, I estimate that approximately 3 per cent of Southeast Asian death sentence clemency grants from 1991 to 2016 were pardons rather than commutations.[11]

More controversially, I also include executive 'amnesties' within this broad definition of capital clemency, even if collective amnesties have the potential to dominate data on executive discretion to the detriment of commutations and pardons.[12] Compared with common law jurisdictions, which are usually reliant upon commutations and pardons as lenient discretion in death penalty cases, civil law jurisdictions most commonly make constitutional and legislative provision for amnesty.[13] The effect of an amnesty proclamation on capital crimes is that a group of suspects may be immune from prosecution in the future,[14] many existing prisoners' death sentences may be commuted to lesser punishments at the same time, many existing prisoners may be released from prison altogether, or any of these acts may occur in combination.[15] Amnesties normally differ from commutation and pardon grants in that the prisoners who stand to benefit from the former do not need to petition the head of state or other executive decision maker directly, and are instead assessed on the basis of generic categories.[16] Therefore, amnesties usually reflect broader political goals,[17] rather than case-based humanitarian considerations.

[10] Novak (2015) 111; Smith (1983) 417, 422; Bedau (1990–1) 256.

[11] See Appendix.

[12] Heise (2015) 985. Note Mallinder (2008, at 6), who states that 'some academics have begun to use the term "amnesty" in an all-encompassing manner to describe both [amnesty and commutation/pardon]'.

[13] Novak (2016) 819, 820 n14; Close (2015); Novak (2015) 1, 7.

[14] Close (2015); Novak (2015) 45.

[15] Mallinder (2008) 6.

[16] Novak (2015) 7, 9, 45; Close (2015); Mallinder (2008) 6.

[17] Tait (2000–1) 134; Novak (2015) 45, 163; Mallinder (2008) 13.

A second difference is that pardons and commutations are usually granted *after* trial and conviction, whereas amnesty may relieve the consequences of a crime at any stage.[18] A third difference is that amnesties encompass acts by both the executive and the legislature branches of government,[19] whereas typically commutations and pardons may only be issued by the executive.

For present purposes, the key is to capture the extent to which national or provincial governments utilize discretionary powers rooted in constitutions, legislation, or the sovereign prerogative to negate capital punishment for a broad range of legal and political reasons. This makes it irrelevant whether the power is used on an individual or a group basis,[20] although I do exclude *legislative* amnesty from the overall definition of 'clemency' adopted in the book. Legislative amnesty is not as readily comparable with commutations and pardons as executive remedies, due to the additional checks and balances inherent in the former power. An executive amnesty, much like an individual commutation or pardon, can (depending on the jurisdiction's precise procedural framework) be granted speedily by a single decision maker for a variety of compassionate, legal, political, or self-serving justifications. Legislative amnesties, although they are common in some civil law jurisdictions, require slower deliberation. They have a closer analogy in domestic legislation, rather than in the executive's extraordinary, discretionary powers.[21]

Clemency and the Southeast Asian context

Having defined death penalty clemency as including executive commutations, pardons, and amnesties, when reading Chapters 3–7 it is also important to bear in mind the local terms used to describe various types of executive leniency in Thailand, Singapore,

[18] Novak (2015) 46; Mallinder (2008) 6. However, see note 2.

[19] Mallinder (2008) 30.

[20] See Sitze (2007) 201: 'Clemency's qualitative difference from amnesty is … reducible to a difference of degree. Whereas amnesties punish the fewest number possible, clemency remits punishment from the fewest number possible.'

[21] For example, in the Thai context, see Haberkorn (2015). Thailand is the only one of the four countries under study where the legislature has granted amnesty to persons who might otherwise be tried for capital crimes.

Malaysia, and Indonesia. Wherever possible I have attempted to employ the local terms most commonly in use.

In Thailand, despite its name, a 'royal pardon' in capital cases usually only reduces a death sentence to life imprisonment.[22] A prisoner will often receive a series of royal pardons, over a number of years or decades, to reduce a death sentence to life imprisonment, then to a term of years, and eventually to outright release from prison.[23] However, in exceptional cases a royal pardon may release a prisoner immediately and unconditionally from death row.[24] As reflected in the relevant Appendix,[25] royal pardons may be issued collectively, or individually following a petition.[26] With its mass application and predominant political function,[27] a collective royal pardon is a type of executive 'amnesty', as described earlier, whereas an individual royal pardon in capital cases fits within a more conventional definition of clemency, as a 'commutation' (or, in very rare cases, a 'pardon').

In both the Singaporean and Indonesian contexts, the English-language term 'clemency' is the word commonly used by lawyers, politicians, and academic commentators to refer to the commutation of a death sentence to life or termed imprisonment. Nevertheless, the expression 'pardon' is used in the Singaporean Constitution of 1965 to mean either commutation or pardon, with or without conditions attached.[28] The bahasa Indonesia word *grasi*, listed as a presidential prerogative in Indonesia's 1945 Constitution,[29] derives from the Dutch *gratie*, meaning pardon, or grace.[30] Article 14(1) of the 1945 Constitution allows

[22] Thailand Department of Corrections (12/2/2008); Criminal Procedure Code 1934 (Thailand), ss 259–67.

[23] 'Death Penalty Should Be Abolished' (1996); 'Capital Punishment Called into Question' (1998); 'Amnesty for Drug Offenders Reflects King's Generosity' (1996).

[24] Criminal Procedure Code 1934 (Thailand), s 265; Thailand Department of Corrections (12/2/2008).

[25] See Appendix (Thailand).

[26] See Chapter 3.

[27] See Chapter 3.

[28] Constitution of Singapore 1965, art 22P(1)(a)–(c). This provision applies to any criminal punishment, including the death sentence. The Singaporean president also has the power to 'remit', 'reprieve', or grant 'respite' from any lawfully imposed sentence.

[29] Constitution of Indonesia 1945, art 14(1).

[30] Sahid (2014) 56–7.

the Indonesian president, through *grasi*, to grant death sentence commutations, prison sentence commutations, as well as pardons for any crime.[31] Although Indonesia is one of the few jurisdictions worldwide to make written constitutional provision for both clemency *and* amnesty, and to vest both of these powers in the president as head of state rather than in the legislature,[32] according to official records no Indonesian president since 1945 has ever extended *amnesti* (amnesty) to a group of prisoners on death row.[33] Accordingly, all references in this book to 'clemency' in the Indonesian context are limited to commutations or pardons, or in other words, *grasi*.

Singapore's 1965 Constitution contains no provision empowering the president to grant amnesty. Furthermore, all six clemency grants in Singapore since independence in 1965 have been issued as commutations to a twenty-year term of imprisonment,[34] although the precise legal consequences of a death sentence commutation in Singapore changed in 1997.[35] Several of the six prisoners granted commutations were subsequently released from prison on parole, or via a further presidential clemency grant.[36]

Finally, the State and Federal Pardons Boards are the constitutional decision-making bodies for executive discretion in Malaysia. The Boards advise the Malaysian king (*Yang di-Pertuan Agong*) in federal and security cases, and the state governors and Malay hereditary rulers in state cases.[37] The mandate of the *Agong*, rulers, and governors extends to commuting death sentences to natural life imprisonment or to a set term of imprisonment (known locally as a 'pardon', or *pengampunan* in Malay), the reduction of prison sentences to a lesser term, and, occasionally, the unconditional

[31] Rachman (2010); Judicial System Monitoring Programme (2010) 4. See further Pascoe (2017a) on the debate over the impact of *grasi* on a prisoner's guilt in Indonesia.

[32] Close (2015); Constitution of Indonesia 1945, art 14(1)–14(2).

[33] Indonesian Ministry of Law and Human Rights (2016).

[34] Peters (1995); Chan (2016) 200; Appendix (Singapore).

[35] *Hamsah v Public Prosecutor* [1997] 2 SLR(R) 842. In 1997, this case changed the meaning of 'life imprisonment' in Singapore, increasing it from a twenty-year sentence to a natural life sentence.

[36] See Chapter 4.

[37] See Chapter 5.

release of prisoners from jail.[38] Although, by legislation, each death row prisoner must be individually considered for clemency by the relevant State or Federal Pardons Board,[39] in several instances commutations have been announced by the Malay hereditary rulers benefiting multiple prisoners at once,[40] thus resembling an executive amnesty in practice.

Reasons and Recipients: The Four Models of Clemency

Given that death penalty clemency in Southeast Asia is under-researched and under-theorized, the present section returns to focus on the global academic literature. To map out a theoretical framework for the country case studies in Chapters 3–6, here I delineate four existing models of clemency, based upon previous cases, commentary, and scholarship.

The previous academic literature, particularly the work of Douglas Hay et al (1975), Leslie Sebba (1977a; 1977b); Kathleen Dean Moore (1989), Daniel Kobil (1991; 2003; 2007), Elizabeth Rapaport (1998–2000; 2001), and Austin Sarat (2005; 2008), reveals four justificatory models of capital clemency practice:

1. Mercy from the sovereign.
2. Retributivist clemency.
3. Redemptive clemency.
4. Clemency for political advantage or utilitarian reasons.

Mercy from the sovereign

Here, clemency is granted as a merciful 'gift' from the political executive to the prisoner, with its bestowal a reflection of the ruler's benevolence[41] and his or her desire for social control and to

[38] Criminal Procedure Code 2006 (Malaysia), s 281(c); Talib (1989) 67–72; Damis (11/04).

[39] Criminal Procedure Code 2006 (Malaysia), s 281(c); Talib (1989) 62–3.

[40] Hood and Hoyle (2015) 318.

[41] Kobil (1991) 571. Acker and Lanier (2000, at 201) describe the appropriateness of a festive metaphor where an absolute monarch grants pardons—prisoners in such societies have sometimes 'cheated the executioner through the fortuitous timing of royal births, coronations, and other official celebrations'.

exercise power over life and death,[42] rather than a response to any particularly deserving features of the case. Clemency granted by an absolute monarch or dictatorial ruler, often to an entire class of condemned persons as an amnesty,[43] usually accords with this classification. Whether prisoners benefit collectively or individually, granting frequent clemency is an ancient strategy to enhance sovereign power. As Pufendorf observes, 'by the granting of pardon [or commutation] in the proper place and time, the safety of a state is not undermined but is in fact sometimes strengthened'.[44]

However, in modern democracies, where national leaders' decisions are scrutinized through electoral choice rather than being justified as benevolence, clemency as 'mercy from the sovereign' is not as widespread.[45] Unlike the case of absolute monarchs or autocrats who rule through charisma, grace, or coercive terror,[46] the democratically elected leaders of modern states must instead govern and gain legitimacy through legally prescribed and predictable rules.[47]

Retributivist clemency

Where 'mercy from the sovereign' is dispensed on a purely discretionary and perhaps even arbitrary basis,[48] a retributivist model of clemency mandates commuting or pardoning a death sentence in circumstances where strict conformity with the original sentence would result in undeserved or disproportionate punishment.[49] Hence, clemency is granted to enhance retributive justice, rather than to detract from it.[50] Although in each individual case the executive

[42] Sarat (2005) 16; Hay et al (1975) 42, 48; Coyne and Entzeroth (2001) 839; Kobil (1991) 582. Strange (1996, at 4) and Tuckness and Parrish (2014, at 32) observe that the power to grant pardons may have been appropriated by pre-modern autocratic rulers as a means of demonstrating semi-divinity, given the public's belief that only God could forgive.

[43] Botsman (2007) 45; Sebba (1977a) 232; Novak (2015) 163.

[44] Pufendorf, *De jure naturae et gentium*, quoted in Sitze (2007) 186, emphasis added. See also Garland (2010) 78.

[45] Kobil (2007) 47; Sarat (2005) 108.

[46] Of course, there is nothing stopping an autocratic sovereign, accustomed to reprieving condemned prisoners as a show of benevolence, from also granting clemency for *retributive* or *redemptive* or *utilitarian* reasons.

[47] See Weber (2004) 33–6; Strange (1996) 3.

[48] Sarat (2005) 20–1; Kobil (1991) 574; Strange (1996) 9.

[49] DeCoste (2003) 9; Moore (1989) 129.

[50] Meyer (2007) 86; Acker et al (2010) 185.

decision maker must weigh the retributive costs and benefits of enforcing or lessening punishment, actual and hypothetical examples of retributivist clemency include pardons or commutations made in response to:

- wrongful conviction, deriving from procedural improprieties in the original trial, error or procedural bars at the appeal stage, or the discovery of new evidence exonerating the prisoner;[51]
- one or more dissenting judgments contained in the original conviction, casting doubt on the accused's guilt;[52]
- the death sentence being a far more severe punishment than is usually imposed in cases of comparable severity,[53] or likewise where the death sentence is disproportionate compared with the prison sentences imposed on co-offenders;[54]
- the crime being committed 'out of necessity, coercion or adherence to moral principles';[55]
- the facts of the case, while insufficient to found a full defence in law, suggesting a degree of mental incapacity, intoxication, provocation, duress, self-defence, or 'battered woman syndrome';[56]
- a prisoner's youth diminishing culpability, a prisoner's old age increasing the severity of punishment over time,[57] or other mitigating factors in the offender's background that ordinarily might have been considered during sentencing;[58]
- the 'death row effect', adding to a death sentence's severity long before it is ever implemented;[59]

[51] Sebba (1977a) 229; Kobil (2000) 572; Ledewitz and Staples (1993) 234; Sarat (2008) 220.

[52] Robertson (2006) 147; Burnett (2002) 158; Abramowitz and Paget (1964) 170.

[53] Coyne and Entzeroth (2001) 843; Rapaport (1998–2000) 1521; Sarat (2005) 155.

[54] Burnett (2002) 158; Berlow (2003) 91.

[55] Coyne and Entzeroth (2001) 843; Moore (1989) 97, 156–65; Meyer (2007) 67.

[56] Meyer (2007) 67; Abramowitz and Paget (1964) 165, 168; Burnett (2002) 158.

[57] Blumenthal (2007); Heise (2003) 284; Crouch (2009) 25; Pridemore (2000) 164.

[58] Sarat (2008) 205–6; Berlow (2003) 91; Burnett (2003) 192.

[59] Hood and Hoyle (2015) 202–18.

- the gender of the prisoner. In some societies, political leaders and the public may believe that the execution of a woman is never justifiable.[60] Moreover, international law clearly provides that a pregnant woman should never be executed;[61]
- compassionate family grounds, for example where the prisoner has infant children, or a dying spouse or parent;[62]
- compassionate medical grounds, such as a prisoner being diagnosed with a terminal illness while in prison, or developing a serious mental illness rendering the prisoner unfit for execution.[63]

Redemptive clemency

Within the redemptive model, clemency is granted not as a criticism of the original conviction and sentence, or the way that languishing on death row affects the prisoner over time, but in reference to the prisoner's character, behaviour, or meritorious activities before arrest and before conviction, or in prison after conviction.[64] For example, the executive decision maker may grant commutation or pardon pursuant to:

- demonstrated rehabilitation, remorse, and repentance by the prisoner during the time spent in detention;[65]
- the prisoner embracing religion in prison;[66]
- compensation paid to or forgiveness granted by the victim or victim's family;[67]

[60] Rapaport (2001) 968, 982; Heise (2003) 275, 277; Moore (1989) 208–9; Robertson (2006) 150.

[61] International Covenant on Civil and Political Rights, art 6(5). Strange (1996, at 15) notes that pregnant women 'pled the belly' for centuries in England in order to avoid hanging. However, in other societies, pregnancy may only have resulted in a temporary reprieve from execution, in order to deliver the child (Kobil (1991) 578).

[62] Rapaport (2001) 987; Heise (2003) 287–8; Kobil (2007) 44–5; Rapaport (1998–2000) 1522.

[63] Blumenthal (2007); Ministry of Justice (UK) (2009) 17; Death Penalty Information Center (2017a).

[64] Harris and Redmond (2007) 7; Moore (1989) 204–5; Rapaport (1998–2000) 1523.

[65] Sebba (1977a) 230–1; Rapaport (2001) 987, 998; Blumenthal (2007).

[66] Moucarry (2004) 271; Abramowitz and Paget (1964) 168.

[67] Acker and Lanier (2000) 209; Death Penalty Worldwide (2013) 77; Moore (1989) 146.

- compensation paid or restitution made to the state for economic crimes such as fraud, embezzlement, or corruption;[68]
- a prisoner's significant previous national service—for example, as a politician, soldier, judge, or other state employee.[69]

Clemency for political advantage or utilitarian reasons

Within this fourth and final model, capital clemency is the secular form of 'mercy from the [semi-divine] sovereign',[70] albeit in this case typically exercised by democratically elected leaders rather than by absolute monarchs or autocrats.[71] Here, the executive grants commutation, pardon, or amnesty for self-serving political benefit,[72] or to provide a broader public benefit,[73] rather than acting on the basis of any redeeming qualities of the prisoner or the prisoner's case. For example:

- an amnesty granted to combatants on both sides of a civil war, in order to facilitate societal 'healing';[74]
- an amnesty or pardon releasing political prisoners following a transition from autocracy to democracy;[75]
- a conditional pardon in exchange for a promise to serve in the military, to be deported to a penal colony, or to undertake some other conduct in the national interest;[76]
- clemency granted to the citizen of an abolitionist nation (or in response to a request made by a powerful international ally), to maintain good diplomatic and trade relations with that nation;[77]
- clemency for a prisoner who acts as an informant or as a witness in a case against his or her accomplices or ringleader;[78]

[68] Salinger (2005) 48; Pascoe (2016a) 183.
[69] Moore (1989) 204; Kobil (2003) 222.
[70] See note 42.
[71] Sarat and Hussain (2004) 1319.
[72] Crouch (2009) 3; Sebba (1977a) 231; Heise (2003) 289; Coyne and Entzeroth (2001) 842.
[73] Crouch (2009) 28–9; Moore (1989) 199–200.
[74] Kobil (2003) 222; Crouch (2009) 20; Sarat (2005) 20.
[75] Mallinder (2008) 4.
[76] Meyer (2007) 74; Moore (1989) 90, 199.
[77] Johnson and Zimring (2009) 318, 334; Neumayer (2008a) 242.
[78] Sebba (1977a) 227, 229; Blumenthal (2007); Robertson (2006) 297; Kobil (1991) 589.

- clemency granted as a reward after the prisoner assists 'prison authorities in preventing [another prisoner's] escape, injury or death';[79]
- clemency granted in response to changing public, political, judicial, or international law views on the 'morality, justice and effectiveness' of the death penalty after the sentence has been imposed;[80] and, most obviously,
- clemency to gain direct political or financial favour from the recipient, or from the wider community.[81]

Explaining Variation: A Summary of the Theoretical and Empirical Literature

As first noted in the Introduction, some jurisdictions grant clemency extremely rarely in death penalty cases, whereas in other jurisdictions execution is the exceptional outcome, with most prisoners expecting commutation, pardon, or amnesty instead. Remaining jurisdictions fall in between, with clemency not the expected outcome in a death penalty case, but not altogether uncommon.

How have previous academic commentators attempted to explain such wide variation in clemency incidence, whether across provincial borders (such as between US states) or national ones (as with the present study)? Significantly, most of the previous scholarship on clemency incidence derives from a normative or theoretical standpoint, rather than from empirical data.[82] As Ruckman

[79] Ministry of Justice (UK) (2009) 17. Clearly this ground, together with acting as an informant or witness (as previously described), could also fall within the 'redemptive' category. In both scenarios, the state benefits from the prisoner's actions and issues clemency as a 'reward'. The subtle difference between the two categories is that 'redemptive' clemency is awarded to prisoners who have demonstrated virtue *for themselves*, whereas 'utilitarian' clemency rewards a specific and practical action that benefits the state or the general public.

[80] Sebba (1977a) 230, 232; Rapaport (2001) 1001; Alston (2007) 14; Sarat (2005) 67. Clemency may be awarded en masse if a death penalty law is found to be unconstitutional or otherwise legally invalid (Burnett (2003) 192; Acker and Lanier (2000) 208), or if other sentencing options such as life without parole had been available at the time the death sentence was originally passed (Sarat (2008) 220).

[81] Sebba (1977a) 231; Rapaport (2001) 982; Heise (2003) 289, 298; Tait (2000–1) 136.

[82] Heise (2003) 262.

observed in 1997, in reference to the United States—a nation with an entirely transparent criminal justice system—let alone for those jurisdictions evincing significant state secrecy:

For all of the mania surrounding 'empirical tests' and 'multivariate modeling' in political science seventy years after [the first US data became available], political scientists have made little or no effort to apply the rigor of modern methodology to many of the relationships [which purportedly influence clemency].[83]

The same applies to clemency practice in other retentionist countries. The theoretical determinants of clemency incidence have not been tested across national borders using quantitative methodology, unlike the determinants of death penalty retention and abolition, for which there already exists a large and growing literature.[84] Most previous international comparative studies of clemency have utilized qualitative approaches, such as comparative case studies (Turrell 2000; Pascoe 2017b), comparative legal or constitutional analyses (Sebba 1977b; Baumgartner and Morris 2001; The Parliamentary Monitoring Group 2004; Dascalu 2012; Novak 2015), or comparative historical analyses (Strange 1996; Tait 2000–1), to discern the reasons for similarities and differences in national clemency laws and practice and to build and test hypotheses on capital clemency incidence. Since Ruckman's plea for more quantitative analysis, only Heise (2003; 2013; 2015), Kraemer (2008), and Pridemore (2000) have attempted to systematically test various hypotheses explaining death penalty clemency, although their comparative work has focused exclusively on US states, and largely on *who* is granted clemency in each jurisdiction, rather than *how many* prisoners benefit.

In the following subsections I draw upon the above-mentioned studies' findings, in combination with further untested hypotheses which academic theorists have proposed to explain capital clemency incidence. In summary, previous scholarship has pointed to the nature of the political regime, the separation of powers, the precise clemency decision-making structure, justifications for punishment, structural opportunities for leniency elsewhere in the

[83] Ruckman (2011) 23.

[84] See, for example, Suh (2015); Kim (2015); Anckar (2014; 2004); McGann and Sandholtz (2012); Kent (2010); Neumayer (2008a, 2008b); Greenberg and West (2008); Miethe et al (2005).

criminal justice system, procedural idiosyncrasies, average time spent on death row, and predominant religious practice as factors which all potentially contribute towards the proportion of finalized death penalty cases which result in clemency.

Political regime

Some scholars have focused on the nature of the political regime in which clemency is granted. According to this hypothesis, capital clemency will be granted more often by autocratic or unelected leaders seeking to boost their own legitimacy[85] by what Botsman labels 'strategies of benevolence'.[86] When combined with Johnson and Zimring's plausible suggestion of a positive relationship between autocracy and execution rates,[87] the resulting hypothesis is that autocratic states tend to execute more prisoners, but also grant clemency to a higher proportion of those originally sentenced to death.

The corollary of this theory is that directly elected clemency decision makers within a democratic state governed strictly by the 'rule of law' are unlikely to grant clemency as often.[88] Democratic retentionist nations will execute fewer prisoners, but will also keep finalized death sentences intact through the clemency stage. Streib's comments, although made in reference to the United States, have resonance in any retentionist democracy or semi-democracy: 'clemency decisions are intensely political decisions, being made by political leaders beholden to the voting public for their present jobs and ... re-election.'[89] Likewise, according to Toney Anaya, former governor of New Mexico, 'politics is the most important consideration in a governor's mind [in deciding on clemency] and often may be the *only* consideration'.[90] If, as is usually the case, public opinion strongly supports the death penalty in a particular democratic jurisdiction, most attempts

[85] Novak (2015) 12. Thurschwell (2009, at 278) describes 'the Foucauldian distinction between the ancient state that exercises the right to kill or let live and the modern state that exercises the right to foster life or allow to die'.

[86] Botsman (2007) 45–9.

[87] Johnson (2010) 338 (Asia-wide reference); Johnson and Zimring (2009) 289–90 (worldwide reference).

[88] Novak (2015) 195.

[89] Streib (2005) 209; see also Strange (1996) 14, and Acker et al (2010) 183.

[90] Sullivan (1993) emphasis added.

by a member of the executive branch to ameliorate punishment through the use of clemency will prove unpopular.[91] This does not mean that the executive need always act in accordance with popular demand, but nonetheless adverse public opinion generally forms an obstacle to independent decision-making on clemency petitions in democracies.[92]

Separation of powers

Another group of scholars has highlighted the relationship between clemency and the separation of powers between the executive, the legislature, and the judiciary. One noticeable problem here is that a clemency frequency hypothesis can be constructed both ways. While it is commonly stated that a separation of powers or functions forms a key component of democratic governance,[93] in practice a 'strict' separation may see the executive paying extreme deference to the death penalty policies and practices of the other two branches, or alternatively may see the executive acting as a check on the power of the judiciary.[94] The political executive repeatedly 'overruling' the judiciary in single cases[95] (and not merely a single court, but usually multiple courts which have confirmed the death sentence) or disregarding the legislature's established retentionist policy when granting a 'mass' commutation[96] may be a symptom of either (a) no separation of powers at all, as judicial, legislative, and executive functions blur, or (b) a properly exercised safeguard within the separation of powers.[97] Resolving this problem may depend on a distinction in the political science and constitutional law literature between the executive 'checking' legislative and judicial powers and the executive 'usurping' these powers.[98] Only

[91] Sarat (2005) 22, 24, 36; Kobil (1998) 680; VanBrocklin (2003).

[92] Kobil (2007) 49; Breslin and Howley (2002) 253; Kobil (1991) 610.

[93] Bellamy (1996) 34–5; Turpin and Tomkins (2007) 103, 107; Crouch (2009) 14; Sebba (1977a) 226.

[94] Shane (1993) 363.

[95] Sebba (1977b) 83.

[96] Novak (2015) 163.

[97] Turpin and Tomkins (2007) 106–7; Shane (1993) 384–5; Novak (2015) 164.

[98] Shane (1993) 373–4, 405; Burns and Markham (1987) 582; Mojapelo (2013) 39. Note Marshall's ambivalence (1971, at 102):

> neither [Montesquieu] nor many others down to the present day seem clear as to whether [the] 'checking' of one branch by another is a participation

the former is a healthy part of the separation of powers in democracies, whereas the latter is rather associated with autocratic governance or 'illiberal democracies'.[99] The concluding assumption is that a properly functioning separation of powers tolerates clemency only as an uncommon or exceptional measure in capital cases rather than as a regular, institutionalized criminal justice remedy, or in its most extreme form a 'functional nullification' of the death penalty through blanket commutations.[100]

Clemency decision-making structure

American scholars, in particular, have also focused on the way in which each jurisdiction's precise decision-making structure affects clemency outcomes. In some US states the state governor makes clemency decisions alone; in some states a pardons board makes the decision alone; in other states there must be agreement between the board and the governor; and in a fourth group of states the board makes a non-binding recommendation to the governor.[101] Studies have found that capital clemency is most likely to be granted by a politically insulated board acting alone, whereas a sole decision maker is the decision-making structure next most likely to afford leniency to death row prisoners.[102] Clemency appears less likely where there exists a 'diffusion of responsibility' between an advisory body recommending a particular course of action to the final decision maker.[103] Importantly, this analysis appears consistent with the idea of clemency frequency in authoritarian states, as described previously. If clemency is capricious and personality-driven, it tends to be granted more generously,

in the other's function and a partial *violation* of the separation of powers doctrine, or whether it is actually an *exemplification* of the doctrine, which carries out the very purpose of the separating and balancing off against each other of the three branches of government. (emphasis added)

[99] See Zakaria (1997); Cameron (2002) 134, 154.

[100] Bedau (2004) 193; Bedau (1990–1) 272.

[101] Death Penalty Information Center (2017a).

[102] Novak (2016) 828; Novak (2015) 135–6; Gill (2010) 23.

[103] Mandery (2005) 614–15; Novak (2016) 828; Novak (2015) 135–6. Contrast Novak (2015, at 80), who argues that American clemency boards are more reluctant to use *mass* grants of clemency as a policy tool. Similarly, after excluding mass clemency decrees to focus on individualized grants, in two separate studies Heise (2013, at 21; 2015, at 978–9) found no differences in outcome between single decision makers and boards.

whereas if the power has been bureaucratized and diffused among different criminal justice actors, its use becomes scarcer.

Nevertheless, the problem with decision-making structure as an explanatory hypothesis is that the sheer volume of clemency petitions and other pressing government tasks means that the chief executive, or the collective decision-making body, will usually have to rely upon a recommendation arising from elsewhere, for example from a trusted adviser, a government department, a prosecutor, or a judge.[104] And given that this is a non-binding recommendation, the same literature tells us that neither party will take the initiative to commute the death sentence, preferring to pass political risk on to the 'other' party. Where the volume of clemency petitions is small, thereby allowing the final decision maker to personally review each document,[105] an overall hypothesis linking unassisted decision makers with clemency generosity seems plausible. Yet in high-volume jurisdictions, most purported decision-making by a single actor or a single board is, in reality, a collective effort involving various government agencies.

Other than following a bureaucratic recommendation, the political executive's alternative is to rely on guidelines and informal 'rules of thumb' developed as pragmatic measures to deal with large clemency caseloads.[106] Cases for decision might be categorized by class (on the basis of crime committed, behaviour in prison, or some other measure), or could be subject to a prevailing presumption that all petitions will be rejected, or accepted, unless extraordinary circumstances exist. Accordingly, precedent, even if it does not play a formal legal role in clemency decisions,[107] nonetheless becomes more important from year to year in the same jurisdiction, or cumulatively before the same decision maker. Over time, decisions that were once made on an individualized basis 'can acquire the same binding force as legal rules', at least within the same political administration.[108] Of course, this hypothesis does not, by itself, clarify whether a particular jurisdiction will

[104] Novak (2016) 828, 839; Abramowitz and Paget (1964) 184–5; Novak (2015) 120, 149–52; Sebba (1977b) 120.

[105] Hawkins (1992) 39–40.

[106] Hawkins (1992) 39.

[107] Abramowitz and Paget (1964) 176; Lavinsky (1965) 38; Meyer (2007) 64.

[108] Abramowitz and Paget (1964) 177, 182; Hawkins (1992) 43; Morison (2006) 153.

grant clemency frequently or infrequently. However, its implication is that, absent any radical change in leadership or caseload volume, clemency practice is likely to remain consistent over time, both in terms of *who* receives clemency and also *how often* death sentences are set aside.

Structural opportunities for leniency

For another group of scholars, capital clemency is more likely to be granted in less advanced criminal justice systems which do not contain as many in-built due process safeguards and opportunities for leniency.[109] According to this hypothesis, clemency must not be seen in isolation from earlier criminal justice processes.[110] Examples of prior opportunities to filter out cases undeserving of death include where independent prosecutors exercise their charging discretion,[111] where defendants possess the opportunity to strike plea bargains, where there are multiple levels of credible judicial appeal available, where there is an array of partial and complete legal defences upon which the defendant may rely,[112] where there is discretionary capital sentencing (as opposed to the mandatory death penalty),[113] and where there are automatic judicial appeals (thereby lessening the problem of death row 'volunteers').[114] As Colgate Love summarizes:

> History teaches that the demand for clemency increases when the legal system lacks other mechanisms for delivering individualized justice, recognizing changed circumstances, and correcting errors and inequities. Clemency is less necessary, and is therefore less justifiable, when mercy 'shines in the code'.[115]

The most famous scholarly example is John Beattie, Douglas Hay, and Peter King's historical work on the English legal system.[116]

[109] Novak (2015) 36; Sebba (1977a) 230–1; Colgate Love (2010) 39.

[110] Ammons (1994) 40; Tait (2000–1) 134; Scott (1952) 95.

[111] Hawkins (1992) 36; Acker et al (2010) 193.

[112] Acker and Lanier (2000) 206; Colgate Love (2010) 17–18; Burnett (2002) 14.

[113] Novak (2015) 140; Ruckman (2011) 42–3; Bedau (1990–1) 268.

[114] Heise (2013) 12, 12 n34; Hood and Hoyle (2015) 321.

[115] Colgate Love (2010) 39, quoting Cesare Beccaria.

[116] See Hay et al (1975); Hay (2006); Beattie (1986); King (1984). Hay (2006, at 40 n9) provides a comprehensive summary of prior research on royal pardons in England from the seventeenth to the nineteenth centuries.

Up to 300 crimes attracted the mandatory death penalty during the eighteenth century as part of England's 'Bloody Code' and defendants had no opportunity to appeal conviction and sentence until the creation of the Court of Appeal in 1907;[117] more than 50 per cent of condemned prisoners were eventually pardoned by the king,[118] following recommendations by trial judges or petitions from influential community members.[119] The high proportion of pardons here did not necessarily indicate official ambivalence over capital punishment: execution rates in eighteenth-century England were also high.[120] Instead, the situating of lenient discretion at the 'back end' of the criminal justice system, together with clemency's role in endearing the king to his subjects (following the 'mercy from the sovereign' paradigm described previously), combine to explain how prolific pardons became at the time.[121] As Novak observes:

> the prerogative of mercy allowed the class that passed one of the bloodiest penal codes in European history to congratulate itself on its humanity … The mandatory nature of the death penalty was by far the most important contributor to the high rate of clemency and pardon in early modern England.[122]

Although in general this theory appears useful in explaining clemency incidence across the globe, scholars must be careful not to assume that where discretion is restricted at one stage of the criminal justice system it will automatically reappear as executive clemency.[123] Clemency is but one form of discretion available to mitigate the harshness of a mandatory death sentence, albeit a highly visible political power, as opposed to the lower-profile legal decisions made by actors at earlier stages of the criminal justice system. The largest measure of discretion in most jurisdictions (whether utilizing mandatory sentencing or not) is exercised

[117] Novak (2015) 21–3.

[118] Beattie (1986) 404; King and Ward (2015) 185; Acker and Lanier (2000) 211–12.

[119] Hay (2006) 42, 45–6.

[120] See generally King and Ward (2015).

[121] Hay (2006) 40.

[122] Novak (2015) 20–1.

[123] Hawkins (1992) 32, 36; interview with Canadian academic expert on the death penalty.

at the front end of the process, by the police and prosecuting authorities.[124]

Procedural idiosyncrasies

Some scholars have seen capital clemency as less likely to be granted in systems with procedural idiosyncrasies that operate to obstruct petitioners. These are not deep underlying causes of clemency incidence based on history, political structure, or legal culture, but are instead symptoms of increasing bureaucratization within modern criminal justice systems.[125] Essentially, this hypothesis posits that the more regulated the clemency power becomes, the less likely it is to be used.[126] Previous scholarship has identified the potentially restrictive impact of:

- bureaucratic obstacles to clemency petitions, such as waiting periods[127] or time limits within which the prisoner must apply;[128]
- a requirement for victim notification or consent before a petition is considered;[129]
- a requirement for the decision maker to provide reasons for clemency grants;[130]
- the practice, followed in some jurisdictions, of the executive decision maker consulting the case prosecutor as to whether the death sentence should be commuted. The prosecutor is unlikely to recommend clemency after spending the state's time and money prosecuting the case and seeking the death sentence in the first place;[131]
- although it is prohibited by the International Covenant on Civil and Political Rights' Article 6(4), an outright prohibition on clemency applications and grants for particular crimes,

[124] Sarat (2005) 133; Barkow (2007–8) 1351.

[125] See Novak (2015) 145; Barkow (2007–8) 1334–5.

[126] One exception is automatic clemency appeals, which of course make clemency grants more likely (Pridemore (2000) 180; Sebba (1977b) 116).

[127] Novak (2015) 149. However, see also notes 133–134 and associated text.

[128] Interview with London-based NGO staff.

[129] Barkow (2007–8) 1349.

[130] Novak (2015) 196.

[131] Colgate Love (2002) 192–3; Novak (2015) 15, 139.

which does occasionally appear in retentionist jurisdictions.[132] Although this restriction may not extend to all capital crimes, any prohibition on crimes that are regularly prosecuted will affect the overall volume of clemency grants.

Each of these factors are logical correlates. Yet the direction of causation is uncertain. Does a regulated, bureaucratized clemency power result in fewer grants of clemency as a side effect of such regulation, or does the state (via the executive and legislative branches) impose regulation on clemency because national leaders prefer to execute in most cases? Or is there an interaction effect between the two? No scholar has yet provided a satisfactory explanation.

Time on death row

Relatedly, capital clemency appears more likely to be granted where, due to a system's in-built waiting periods, general inefficiencies, or the negligence of criminal justice actors (rather than any official ambivalence over capital punishment itself), the prisoner spends a very long time (such as ten years or more)[133] waiting for arraignment, first instance adjudication, legal appeals, and a final clemency determination.[134] Over a decade or more spent incarcerated, many different justifications for capital clemency may emerge: rehabilitation in prison, old age, reconciliation with victims, terminal or psychiatric illness, shifting public opinion, new evidence to prove innocence, testifying against co-offenders, the opportunity to bribe officials, and so forth.[135] Whether death penalty 'efficiency' is linked to a criminal justice system's procedural and substantive level of 'advancement' is open to debate, however. The more procedural safeguards available, and the more regulated the clemency process, the longer prisoners' cases take to resolve.[136] Ironically, the more closely a criminal justice system

[132] For example, the Constitution of Iraq 2005, art 73(1) (prohibiting special pardon for international crimes and terrorism) and within the six nations that have most strictly incorporated Sharia (where clemency is not available for *hudud* offences and for *qisas* offences) into their positive criminal law: Saudi Arabia, Libya, Yemen, Iran, United Arab Emirates, and Sudan (Pascoe and Miao (2017) 974).

[133] Hood and Hoyle (2015) 203–5.

[134] Acker et al (2010) 195; Abramowitz and Paget (1964) 168.

[135] Pascoe (2014) 15; Abramowitz and Paget (1964) 153; Acker et al (2010) 195.

[136] Hood and Hoyle (2015) 213, 216–17.

follows the United States' 'super due process' model for capital cases,[137] the more cruel it becomes to execute once a prisoner's judicial appeals are exhausted.

Religion—Buddhism, Islam, Confucianism

Religion is the final theoretically supported factor that may have some impact on clemency incidence. Given that this study's geographical scope extends to Southeast Asia's actively retentionist jurisdictions (minus Vietnam), the most appropriate religions to consider here are Buddhism (the predominant religion in Thailand), Islam (the predominant religion in Indonesia and the state religion of Malaysia), and Confucianism (the dominant governance philosophy of Singapore).

With the irony that some political science research has identified Islamic-majority and Buddhist-majority societies as more likely to retain capital punishment in the first place,[138] the first religion-based clemency hypothesis holds that a devout Muslim or Buddhist leader is more likely to commute death sentences that come before him or her when compared with leaders of other religious faiths, or atheists. The strong strand of mercy and compassion within both Islamic and Buddhist philosophy[139] may operate to increase capital clemency rates, although a confounding explanation is that a greater proportion of Muslim-majority and Buddhist-majority jurisdictions possess autocratic rather than democratic leaders.[140]

More specifically, which factors influence Islam's relationship with executive clemency? While a strict incorporation of Sharia into positive criminal law is only found in a small minority of countries with an Islamic majority (and only within Brunei in Southeast Asia),[141] in Muslim-majority jurisdictions criminal

[137] Hood and Hoyle (2015) 267.

[138] Kim (2015) 6; Anckar (2014) 15–16; Anckar (2004) 91, 100; Miethe et al (2005) 122; Boulanger and Sarat (2005) 5.

[139] Horigan (1996) 288; Tuckness and Parrish (2014) 29–30, 36, 41; Abu-Nimer (2001) 248.

[140] Boulanger and Sarat (2005) 5. Of the five remaining retentionist or abolitionist de facto nations with Buddhist majority, three (Thailand, Myanmar, and Laos) possessed governments classified by NGO Freedom House as 'not free' in 2016. Sri Lanka's government was classified as 'partly free' in 2016 (Freedom House (2016)).

[141] Moucarry (2004) 282; Al Saqqaf (2010); Anckar (2014) 13.

justice actors such as prosecutors, judges, and ultimately the chief executive may nonetheless draw on Islamic precepts to inform decision-making on death penalty cases.[142] As such, even in secular or religiously pluralist societies, Sharia's disposition toward mercy and forgiveness remains relevant.

Here—contrary to occasional western perceptions[143]—Islamic law and jurisprudential traditions, while mandating death sentences for particular crimes,[144] are nonetheless dedicated to upholding the sanctity of human life,[145] and are 'characterized by a strong undercurrent of clemency and sympathy for the oppressed'.[146] In those Middle Eastern, North African, and South Asian nations which have most strictly incorporated Sharia into their positive criminal law, enforcement is characterized by the imposition of harsh punishments, tempered by mercy.[147] However, other than for *tazir* crimes (with discretionary punishments which the ruler may remit),[148] such leniency derives not from the commutation of death sentences by political figures, but from the precept of legality, the burden of proof imposed on an accuser, strict evidential requirements,[149] the availability of complete defences,[150] or, if a death sentence for murder survives these procedural hurdles, the forgiveness of the victim's heirs.[151] Therefore, while relief from the death sentence through executive clemency may fall within the *spirit* of Islamic law in some instances, it does not always reflect the letter of the doctrine. Although interpretations of the classical doctrine differ, for both *qisas* (offences against the person) and *hudud* (offences against religion) crimes, the political ruler has no discretionary power at all to remit punishment.[152]

Buddhism, on the other hand, is often described by academic commentators as a religion that is entirely incompatible with

[142] Neumayer (2008a) 254; Anckar (2014) 13.
[143] Hooker (2002) 225.
[144] El-Awa (1982) 1–2; Peters (2006) 7, 53–4.
[145] Abou El Fadl (2004) 79–80, 87.
[146] Schabas (2000) 230.
[147] Abou El Fadl (2004) 91.
[148] Tuckness and Parrish (2014) 43.
[149] Abou El Fadl (2004) 101–2; Postawko (2002) 285, 287; Mulia (2010).
[150] Postawko (2002) 285–6.
[151] Abou El Fadl (2004) 97. See generally Pascoe (2016c).
[152] See Tuckness and Parrish (2004) 42–3; Peters (2006) 39, 54; Baderin (2003) 73; El-Awa (1982) 1–2.

death penalty retention, due to its compassionate requirement to refrain from intentional killing.[153] Nevertheless, in most countries where Buddhism is or was the official religion, government authorities have carried out judicial executions at some point during the state's history.[154] While Buddhists in secular nations might adopt an anti-death penalty stance on the basis of the First Precept's injunction against taking life, in Buddhist-majority countries such as Sri Lanka, Bhutan, and Thailand the Buddhist religion is seen as separate from politics and its moral teachings as separate from state laws.[155] Greenberg and West suggest that, in such jurisdictions, 'Buddhist precepts may not carry weight when it comes to the formulation of criminal justice policy'.[156]

Nevertheless, despite death sentences continuing to be passed in more than half of the Buddhist-majority countries in Asia (Thailand, Myanmar, Sri Lanka, Japan, and Laos),[157] one plausible hypothesis suggests that Buddhist political executives may still display a more forgiving attitude towards many of those condemned to die.[158] Buddhist teaching recognizes the capacity of all human beings to change and reform, a notion which even extends to the most hardened convicted criminals.[159] Miethe et al state the point succinctly:

Punishment in Buddhism is restricted to the purpose of protecting society from further criminal activity and should be administered in the spirit of

[153] Greenberg and West (2008) 309; Boulanger and Sarat (2005) 5; Cho (2008) 173; Alarid and Wang (2001).

[154] Alarid and Wang (2001); Keyes (2011) 158; Breen (2010). Alarid and Wang suggest that capital punishment as a cultural institution long pre-dated the arrival of Buddhist influence in India in 400–500 BC, hence its continued use by Buddhist rulers there and elsewhere.

[155] Breen (2010); interview with Thai law professor. Bhutan abolished the death penalty in 2004, in part due to the influence of a devoutly Buddhist king (Johnson and Zimring (2009) 406). Moreover, Theravada Buddhism's influence may explain the failure of the previous military regime in Myanmar to carry out any judicial executions from 1989 onwards (Johnson and Zimring (2009) 320 n25).

[156] Greenberg and West (2008) 309; see also Alarid and Wang (2001).

[157] See Amnesty International AI Index ACT 50/001/2015, 64. Mongolia was recently part of this list, until it abolished the death penalty for all crimes in July 2017 (Anti-Death Penalty Asia Network (2017)).

[158] Greenberg and West (2008) 309; Miethe et al (2005) 119; Amnesty International (1990) 8; Horigan (1996) 278. See Cho (2004, at 270–1) for historical examples.

[159] International Federation for Human Rights (2005) 14; Hubert (2008); Alarid and Wang (2001); Amnesty International (1990) 8–9.

compassion. The goal of punishment from this religious perspective is to help offenders correct their path of life.[160]

Interpretations of classical Buddhist scripture (*Dhamma*—the Divine Law of Kings) suggest that a devout ruler should pardon a majority of convicted criminals, whose behaviour will instead be cosmically judged through karma. To rule through piety (and moreover to guarantee the ruler's good karma and reincarnation), violence should be countered by non-violence.[161] As such, of the three religions mentioned in this section, Buddhism appears to be the faith most likely to embrace a generous use of the clemency power, particularly as its limited influence on the positive criminal law has not brought about formal abolition of the death penalty in most Buddhist-majority societies.

Confucianism is the dominant governance philosophy in Singapore. Here, the public and political establishment appear to be heavily influenced 'by the traditional Chinese view which held that harsh punishment deterred crime, restored normalcy and maintained "Confucian peace and harmony"'.[162] However, it is debatable whether this view constitutes an accurate interpretation of Confucian doctrine. In South Korea, the Asian country where Confucian precepts have most influenced governance over the centuries,[163] Cho asserts that 'the religious influences of Buddhism and Confucianism and the social norms of Confucian morality have collectively acted to *constrain* the practice of capital punishment throughout history'.[164] Likewise, throughout the history of imperial China the death penalty was frequently administered as a criminal punishment, *despite* perceived moral limitations imposed by 'the widespread and persistent influence of Confucius' principles of benevolence and humaneness'.[165]

While the Confucian notion of rigid social order and authoritarian governance has sometimes been interpreted as requiring the 'situational administration of "retributive justice"' and strong

[160] Miethe et al (2005) 119; Amnesty International (1990) 8. See also 'Seminar on Religious Aspects of Death Penalty' (2008).

[161] van Oosten (2008) 258; Tuckness and Parrish (2014) 34, 36; Amnesty International (1990) 8.

[162] Kuppusamy (2007).

[163] Hahm (2003) 257; Weightman (2011) 10.

[164] Cho (2008) 173, emphasis added.

[165] Liang et al (2006) 120; Boxer (1998–9) 598.

general deterrence, the competing notion of 'humanitarian punishment' in light of the individual offender's circumstances gives rise to more compassionate implications for criminal justice policy.[166] Moreover, with relevance for clemency practice, Confucian governance is not averse to benevolent discretion by elites in preference to the rigid application of rules,[167] suggesting that condemned prisoners need not invariably be executed. Arguably, the supposed influence of Confucian morality on modern criminal justice policy (leading to the rigid and merciless application of death penalty laws in countries such as Singapore and the People's Republic of China) derives from a doctrinal misinterpretation, or even deliberate manipulation.[168] Bae, as well as Johnson and Zimring, have argued that no aspect of traditional Confucian or 'Asian' values implores a state to ruthlessly enforce the death penalty. It is authoritarian government, rather than cultural values, that determines the frequency with which capital punishment is used in the countries of East Asia heavily influenced by Confucianism.[169] The same principle applies to leniency through clemency—it is clearly not the spread of Confucian philosophy that separates East and Southeast Asian nations with 'low' or absent capital clemency (e.g. China, Japan, Singapore, Taiwan) from those with 'medium' rates (South Korea, Vietnam),[170] but some other factor or factors. This chapter provides many different alternative explanations.

Becoming Ever Rarer

The existing empirical and theoretical literature provides a sense of why capital clemency has declined across the world over time, both from an absolute point of view and in proportion to executions.[171] Although the trends documented in this chapter have led some progressive nations to abolish the death penalty altogether, where states choose to remain retentionist, features of modern

[166] Cho (2008) 174; Liang et al (2006) 120.

[167] Cho (2008) 174, 190; Boxer (1988–9) 596. Contrast Davis (1987, at 307) who argues that the infusion of Confucian principles into imperial criminal codes in China brought 'fairness and predictability' to punishment.

[168] Cho (2004) 271–2.

[169] Bae (2008) 55; Johnson and Zimring (2009) 297–9.

[170] See Chapter 1; Cho (2008) 183; Novak (2015) 12.

[171] Strange (1996) 14–15, Novak (2015) 2, 5, 166; Sebba (1977a) 234; Kobil (2007) 37.

governance operate to severely constrain clemency practice. As nations become more secular and democratic, as their legal systems are better able to individualize punishments and provide safeguards against wrongful conviction, and as the clemency power becomes less personality-driven and more transparent and bureaucratized, capital clemency will inevitably decline. Whether it declines to an absolute total of zero or merely to infrequency will vary by country.[172] In some jurisdictions, the very fact that a clemency power still exists at all is largely due to colonial legal inheritance,[173] as well as international law standards.[174] However, as long as the formal clemency power survives on paper, in most jurisdictions capital clemency practice will survive as well, albeit in a diminished form.[175] Throughout Chapters 3–6 of this book, Thailand, Singapore, Malaysia, and Indonesia prove cogent examples of this. During the 1990s, 2000s, and 2010s, capital clemency was granted in all four of these retentionist Southeast Asian nations, for retributivist, redemptive, political, and utilitarian reasons, in addition to 'mercy from the sovereign'. The unresolved question is why these nations' respective clemency rates varied so remarkably over this timeframe.

[172] Some scholars have unsuccessfully grappled with an 'ideal' rate of clemency in democratic societies (Heise (2015) 987; Perry (2017) 65).

[173] Novak (2015) 5.

[174] International Covenant on Civil and Political Rights, art 6(4); American Convention on Human Rights, art 4(6); *Fermin Ramirez v Guatemala* (Inter-American Court of Human Rights, 20 June 2005) [109]; UN Economic and Social Council Resolution 1984/50, art 7.

[175] Scott (1952) 95; Novak (2015) 196–7.

3

Kingdom of Thailand

[H]e must be forthright, gentle, merciful, generous, and pious; he must never be violent, angry, or vindictive; and he must give alms and care for the welfare of his citizens before considering his own needs.

The *Thammasat*'s 'ten kingly virtues'[1]

Of the four countries under examination, Thailand is Southeast Asia's notable outlier in terms of clemency rates. In finalized death penalty cases, clemency by individual or collective royal pardon appears to be the rule rather than the exception in Thailand, despite the state carrying out regular executions between 1996 and 2009.[2] The most compelling reason to investigate clemency patterns in Thailand is the influence of the reigning monarch, although Thailand's lengthy clemency procedures, history of arbitrary and extrajudicial killings, and reluctance to execute foreigners each help, in their own way, to explain the prominence of royal pardons in capital cases. All twenty permanent and interim Thai constitutions since the abolition of absolute monarchy in 1932 have conferred on the monarch the prerogative to grant royal pardons in death penalty cases[3]—a power which the late king Bhumibol Adulyadej, who died in October 2016, frequently exercised over the course of his seventy-year reign.[4] While members of the Thai political establishment and civil service demonstrated increasing

[1] Goodman (2004) 20.

[2] See Appendix (Thailand).

[3] Muntarbhorn (2009); Constitution of Thailand 2014, s 22; Constitution of Thailand 2017, s 179.

[4] See Appendix (Thailand). Maha Vajiralongkorn, King Bhumibol's heir, has so far continued his father's regular use of royal pardons (see Constant (2016); King Maha Vajiralongkorn Brunthirin, 'First Pardon Decree Since the Royal Succession' (Thailand Government Gazette, 11 December 2016)).

Last Chance for Life: Clemency in Southeast Asian Death Penalty Cases. First Edition. Daniel Pascoe. © Daniel Pascoe 2019. Published 2019 by Oxford University Press.

influence over the royal pardons process in the last years of King Bhumibol's reign, Thailand constitutes an important case study of the effect of a traditionally powerful monarchy on executive discretion in death penalty cases.[5] Although the heads of state in the three other countries under study each have a formal or substantive role to play in granting clemency, none match the Thai monarchy's long unbroken tradition of granting individual and collective royal pardons.

Death Penalty and Clemency Practice 1991–2016

Death sentences and executions

In Thailand, executions are now carried out by lethal injection (which replaced shooting in 2001).[6] A total of thirty-eight different civilian offences carry the death penalty: they are contained within the Penal Code 1956; the Prevention and Suppression of Prostitution Act 1996; the Firearms, Ammunition, Explosives, Fireworks and Imitation Firearms Act 1947; and the Narcotics Act 1979.[7] In addition, seventeen different offences under the Military Penal Code 1911 also carry the death sentence as a maximum punishment.[8] However, among all these crimes, of greatest importance are the smaller number of offences for which executions have been carried out over the course of Thailand's history as a constitutional monarchy from 1932:

- murder;
- robbery causing death;
- murder of a government official;
- rape causing death;
- manufacturing/importing/exporting 'type 1' drugs for commercial purposes, or possession of trafficable quantities of 'type 1' drugs;[9]

[5] Johnson and Zimring (2009) 406.
[6] Thailand Department of Corrections (12/2/2008).
[7] Thailand Rights and Liberties Protection Department.
[8] Thailand Rights and Liberties Protection Department.
[9] In practice, the narcotic drugs that now lead to death sentences for trafficking or manufacturing in Thailand are heroin and methamphetamine (Gallahue and Lines (2010) 33). While heroin trafficking and possession attract the death penalty as part of the Narcotics Act 1979 (Thailand) (ss 7, 65), methamphetamine was only added to the list of 'type 1' drugs in 1996 (Amnesty International AI Index ASA 39/002/1997; Pouaree (1999a)).

- offences against the monarchy;
- offences against the Royal Family.[10]

In practice, death is only a discretionary sentence. While the statutory provisions regulating capital punishment in Thailand appear to impose the mandatory death penalty for offences deemed the most serious (regicide, abetting regicide, murder, rape causing death, kidnapping causing death, robbery causing death, gang robbery causing death, drug trafficking, and murder of a government official),[11] the Thai Penal Code also allows certain extenuating circumstances to mitigate punishment in all cases.[12] As the Thai Union for Civil Liberty observes:

> Judges in Thailand heavily rely on evidence of aggravating or mitigating circumstances from the offender's background and take into account the offender's behaviour, even during the trial. A well respected man will be condemned to a lighter sentence than another one for exactly the same offense.[13]

With particular importance in capital cases, under Thai law a guilty plea at the earliest possible stage will, in a majority of cases, reduce a death-eligible crime to one attracting a term of imprisonment.[14] Moreover, the execution of pregnant women,[15]

[10] Thailand Department of Corrections (2006). These figures reflect 280 executions where the offence type was known from 1935 to 2001. From 1935 to 2018, 326 convicts were executed in total (Mala (2018); Agerholm (2018)).

[11] Penal Code 1956 (Thailand), ss 107, 108, 109, 111, 277 ter, 289, 313, 339, 339 bis, 340, 340 bis; Narcotics Act 1979 (Thailand), ss 65, 93. In January 2017, legislative amendments to the Narcotics Act 1979 (Thailand) passed in November 2015 took effect, replacing the nominally mandatory death penalty in s 65 with the discretion to choose between life imprisonment plus a fine, or death (Akbar and Lai (2017)).

[12] See Penal Code 1956 (Thailand), s 78. The enumerated extenuating circumstances include low intelligence, a minimal criminal record, distress, voluntary surrender, repentance, and cooperation with the authorities.

[13] Union for Civil Liberty (2011) 9.

[14] Pouaree (1999a); Union for Civil Liberty (2011) 9; interview with Thai criminal defence lawyer #2; interview with Thai human rights lawyer.

[15] Criminal Procedure Code 1934 (Thailand), ss 246–7. Execution is delayed for three years in this case. Before amendment in 2007, execution was only delayed by one year (Hands Off Cain, 'Thailand' (2007); Charoonbara (1981) 52 n47); however, in practice, the vast majority of new mothers are granted individual royal pardon anyway ('Death Penalty Should Be Abolished' (1996)).

juveniles,[16] and the mentally disabled[17] is also prohibited by law.

Statistically, Thailand's capital appeal process reveals a high attrition rate, followed by relatively few executions. The general pattern over the period from 1991 to 2016 involves the Courts of First Instance passing very large numbers of death sentences (109 is the highest figure for a single year in the 1990s, 447 in the 2000s, and 392 in the 2010s),[18] fewer death sentences remaining after judicial appeals are exhausted (70 being the highest finalized death row population in the 1990s, 127 in the 2000s, and 253 in the 2010s),[19] but only a comparatively small number of executions at the end of the process (an average of 1.9 per year from 1991 to 2016, with a yearly minimum of zero and yearly maximum of 16).[20] With a condemned prisoner afforded two stages of judicial appeal (in the Court of Appeal and in the Supreme Court) against both conviction and the severity of sentence,[21] the overwhelming discrepancy between sentence and execution numbers suggests that not only are many death sentences reduced to lesser punishments on judicial appeal (or that the defendant is acquitted), but also that executive clemency is widely utilized for cases which remain.[22] Figure 2 summarizes Thailand's capital case attrition rate over several years for which complete data are available:

16 Penal Code 1956 (Thailand), s 18. The execution of 14–18-year-olds was only officially prohibited in 2003 (Hands Off Cain, 'Thailand' (2003); Hands Off Cain, 'Thailand' (2009)). In prior cases involving younger prisoners (variously listed as under eighteen or under twenty years), death sentences were always commuted to a term of imprisonment by individual royal pardon (Hands Off Cain, 'Thailand' (2001); International Federation for Human Rights (2005) 20, 33).

17 Criminal Procedure Code 1934 (Thailand), ss 246–8.

18 See Appendix (Thailand).

19 See Appendix (Thailand). One interviewee labelled Thailand the 'world capital of overcharging' (interview with American academic expert on the death penalty).

20 See Appendix (Thailand).

21 Finch and Tangprasit (2012); Union for Civil Liberty (2011); interview with Thailand Department of Corrections staff. Sentences cannot be increased on appeal (interview with Thai criminal defence lawyer #2).

22 Note however that in Thailand, 'historically a large percentage of those on death row are not executed but die of natural causes' (Union for Civil Liberty (2011) 42).

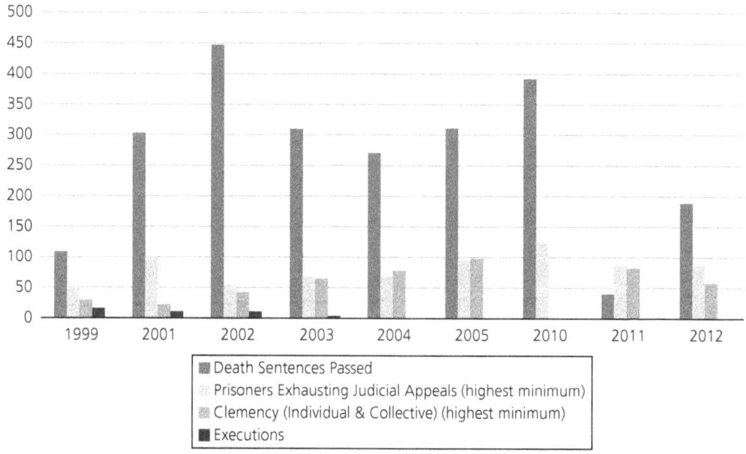

Figure 2 Thailand's death penalty attrition rate (selected years)

Source: Appendix (Thailand)

Clemency procedures in death penalty cases

In contrast to the three other national jurisdictions considered in this study, clemency is a regular, institutionalized form of leniency within the Thai criminal justice system,[23] rather than a hopeful chance to make new retributive and redemptive arguments in mitigation that have not already been considered in judicial appeals. The King of Thailand is empowered by the Thai Criminal Procedure Code to grant two kinds of clemency: an individual royal pardon and a collective royal pardon.[24] The former, as its name suggests, involves an individual petition submitted through prison authorities by the prisoner, by a relative, or by a diplomatic representative (for foreign prisoners).[25] In capital cases, a prisoner has sixty days to submit a petition after the final appeal judgement is delivered.[26] Once completed, the

[23] Junlakan et al (2013) 317.

[24] Thailand Department of Corrections (2009). See Criminal Procedure Code 1934 (Thailand), ss 259, 261 bis (on Individual and Collective Royal Pardons, respectively).

[25] Thailand Department of Corrections (2009); Junlakan et al (2013) 20.

[26] Criminal Procedure Code 1934 (Thailand), s 262; Thailand Department of Corrections (2009). This deadline is not always strictly enforced, as it will take

petition for individual royal pardon will contain the following information:

- A letter from the prisoner to the king, written in formal language, containing information such as the petitioner's personal background, previous employment details, family ties, details of the vocational and religious courses undertaken in prison, what the prisoner would do if the death sentence were to be commuted (or if released), why the prisoner committed the crime, any mitigating circumstances arising within the facts of the case, and finally, if the pardon were to be granted, how it might affect public respect for the Royal Family;
- extrinsic documents such as children's birth certificates, marriage certificates, medical certificates;
- supporting letters from family, friends, employers, and NGOs.[27]

The Thailand Department of Corrections, charged with running the prison system, will then build on the petition by adding several other documents:

- the prisoner's criminal record;
- the prisoner's behavioural record in prison;[28]
- court documents from the prisoner's case.[29]

Once filed, individual petitions are considered by various bureaucratic and political entities—the Department of Corrections, the Ministry of Justice, the prime minister and Cabinet, the king's Principal Private Secretary, and the king's Privy Council—before a recommendation on whether to commute or affirm the death

some time for court documentation to arrive at the prison (interview with Thai human rights activist (2012)).

27 Interview with Thailand Department of Corrections staff; 'King's Pardon Application' (2016); Union for Civil Liberty (2011) 9; interview with Thai criminal defence lawyer #2; interview with Thai prison caseworker; interview with Thai criminal defence lawyer; interview with Thai criminal defence lawyer and Thai NGO staff; Thailand Department of Corrections (2008). Thailand Department of Corrections (2008) provides a sample individual royal pardon petition (at 17–18).

28 Interview with Thailand Department of Corrections staff.

29 Interview with former employee of the Thailand Department of Corrections; interview with Thai criminal defence lawyer and Thai NGO staff.

sentence finally makes its way to the monarch.[30] In practice, the chief decision makers on individual royal pardon petitions appear to be civil servants within the Ministry of Justice and the Ministry of Interior,[31] although Cabinet ministers retain the power to veto recommendations for pardon in particularly serious cases.[32] Moreover, the monarch himself retains absolute discretion to act against any recommendation from civil servants or politicians.[33]

Upon disposal, a petition may be rejected, may result in a death sentence being commuted to life imprisonment (in which case the prisoner may submit another pardon request immediately to reduce the life sentence to a forty to fifty-year term), or may, in rare cases, allow unconditional release.[34] A rejected petitioner must wait at least two years before making another application.[35] Nevertheless, the tedious bureaucratic decision-making process for individual royal pardons, allied to the innate respect accorded to the monarch's formal role within the petition process, combine to indirectly increase a condemned prisoner's chances of eventually receiving royal pardon and avoiding execution.

Collective royal pardons are granted by royal decree, and take place to celebrate an important national event such as the king or queen's birthday or a significant event in the reign of the monarch.[36] Unlike the procedure for individual royal pardon,

[30] Thailand Department of Corrections (12/2/2008); Thailand Department of Corrections (2009); International Federation for Human Rights (2005) 28; Boriboonthana (1999) 354; interview with Thai human rights lawyer. An interviewee from the Department of Corrections added that a recommendation from the Office of the Narcotics Control Board (ONCB) will also be sought in drug-trafficking cases (interview with Thailand Department of Corrections staff).

[31] Thailand Department of Corrections (2009); Finch and Tangprasit (2012); interview with Thai law professor; interview with Thai criminal defence lawyer. An interviewee from the Department of Corrections viewed officers of his department as making the decision, whereas the Ministry of Justice merely *confirmed* it (interview with Thailand Department of Corrections staff).

[32] Interview with Thailand Department of Corrections staff.

[33] 'Chavalit Honours Anti-Drug Efforts' (2001); interview with Thai law professor; interview with Thailand Department of Corrections staff.

[34] Criminal Procedure Code 1934 (Thailand), ss 259–67; Thailand Department of Corrections (12/2/2008).

[35] Criminal Procedure Code 1934 (Thailand), s 264.

[36] Thailand Department of Corrections (2009); interview with Thai Prison caseworker. For a full list of collective royal pardons from 1977 to 1996, see Boriboonthana (1999) 358. For a full list from 1999 to 2007, see Barrow (2017). King Bhumibol granted thirty collective royal pardons during his reign from 1946

no separate petition is necessary.[37] The process is as follows: the Ministry of Justice and the elected government form a committee to formulate a pardon decree in honour of the royal occasion, with the draft decree being forwarded for discussion and approval to the Cabinet, the Council of State (legal advisers to the government), the king's Principal Private Secretary, and the king's Privy Council, before the decree is passed to the king himself for final approval and signature.[38]

While many thousands of inmates sentenced to terms of imprisonment will receive sentence reductions or releases pursuant to the pardon decree,[39] death sentences have also been commuted as a part of most recent collective royal pardons, and in some cases *all* finalized death sentences passed before a particular date have been commuted to lesser punishments.[40] When state authorities plan to commute only a portion of existing death sentences by collective royal pardon, cases are assessed ahead of the pardon decree, according to clear criteria based on the type and severity of crime committed and the prisoner's assigned category of behaviour in prison.[41] Often, prisoners who have committed an offence which poses a 'serious danger to society' are excluded from collective royal pardons.[42] Nonetheless, the chronological regularity of important national events such as royal birthdays and anniversaries and the long tradition of pardons being granted to celebrate these occasions give most death row prisoners hope that their sentence will eventually be reduced to a lesser punishment, even if their application for individual royal pardon has already failed,

to 2016 ('Prison Inmates Pay Last Respects' (2017)). Collective royal pardons do not always take place on the same day year after year, such as the king or queen's birthday: prisoner releases in 'celebration' generally only occur every few years (interview with Thai criminal defence lawyer #2).

[37] Thailand Department of Corrections (2009); Thailand Department of Corrections (12/2/2008).

[38] Criminal Procedure Code 1934 (Thailand), s 261 bis; Thailand Department of Corrections (2009); Thailand Department of Corrections (12/2/2008). The Privy Councillors' general function is to 'debate with the king on actions he could take' (Stevenson (2001) 251).

[39] See Boriboonthana (1999) 358; Barrow (2017); Thailand Department of Corrections (2009).

[40] See International Federation for Human Rights (2005) 27.

[41] Union for Civil Liberty (2011) 16; Jaruboon (2006) 87; Pouaree (1999a).

[42] Thailand Department of Corrections (2008).

or has been pending for a long period of time.[43] In practice, it is via collective royal pardon that most capital prisoners who have exhausted judicial appeals manage to leave death row.[44]

Features of cases where royal pardon was refused (and the prisoner was executed)

According to the limited data available from 1991 to 2016, the annual average total for royal pardon grants of both types ranges from 43+ to 48+, compared with a much smaller annual average total for executions (1.9).[45] The clear pattern is that a royal pardon is the *expected*, rather than a remote, outcome in each capital case, with the overall clemency rate reaching a staggering 95 per cent, at the very minimum.[46] This is not a recent trend. Royal pardons were granted to the majority of prisoners sentenced to death during King Bhumibol's seventy-year reign (from 1946 to 2016).[47] In most retentionist jurisdictions, scholars tend to analyse clemency grants on a case-by-case basis.[48] In Thailand, clemency is so frequent that patterns are instead best revealed by studying the cases of prisoners who do *not* receive commutation or pardon: hence the focus of this section.

Executions over the past two and a half decades (exactly fifty from 1991 to 2016)[49] have generally served to highlight the Thai state's lack of tolerance for particular crimes. Only in cases deemed especially shocking, or where the government has sought

[43] International Federation for Human Rights (2005) 27; Pouaree (1999a); 'Pardoned Inmates "Must Serve at Least 25 Years"' (1995). Prisoners must have exhausted or waived judicial appeals to be eligible for either type of royal pardon (Union for Civil Liberty (2011) 16).

[44] See Appendix (Thailand).

[45] See Appendix (Thailand).

[46] If anything, complete clemency statistics over the period 1991–2016 would reveal Thailand's actual clemency rate to be higher than 95 percent. Although complete execution figures by year are available, no precise individual *and* collective royal pardon figures (whether zero or higher) are available for the years 1993, 1997–2000, 2003–10, and 2013–16. See Appendix (Thailand).

[47] Interview with Australian academic expert on Thailand; interview with Thai human rights lawyer; Johnson and Zimring (2009) 405. Bhumibol ascended to the throne after his brother's death in 1946, but was not officially crowned until 1950.

[48] Pridemore (2000) 181.

[49] See Appendix (Thailand).

to 'make an example' of the offender, has an execution proceeded after a prisoner was sentenced to death.[50] The period under study began with an undeclared moratorium from 1988 to 1995, as Thailand looked to be headed towards death penalty abolition. However, from the beginning of the 1990s, concern grew within the Thai political establishment over the country's serious violent crime problem (particularly with regard to murders involving police officers, both as perpetrators and victims)[51] and society's permissive attitude to drug abuse.[52] Executions in murder cases resumed from January 1996,[53] and from 1999 onwards, executions of large-scale narcotics traffickers recommenced for the first time since the 1970s.[54] Since the resumption of executions in 1996, it is these same two crimes (murder and drug trafficking) that have led to the majority of executions in Thailand.[55]

The crimes for which prisoners have been considered 'disqualified' from collective royal pardons in past grants, providing a key indicator of the government's punishment priorities, consisted of drug trafficking,[56] treason or offences against the state,[57] and rape causing death[58] during the 1980s and early 1990s, and drug

[50] Interview with Singaporean criminal defence lawyer #2; interview with Thai human rights activist (2012).

[51] Handley (2006) 374; 'Ex-Police Officer Executed' (1998); Alford (2000); Amnesty International AI Index ASA 39/002/1997; interview with Thai human rights activist (2012).

[52] Handley (2006) 374–5, 425; interview with Thai human rights activist (2010).

[53] See 'Murderer First Convict to Be Executed in Eight Years' (1996).

[54] Thailand's Narcotics Act, explicitly authorizing the death sentence for drug trafficking, only came into effect in 1979, and was not invoked to execute a drug trafficker until 1999 (Pouaree (1999a); Amnesty International AI Index ASA 39/05/99). Since then, approximately fifteen heroin and methamphetamine traffickers have been executed pursuant to this law (Gallahue and Lines (2010) 33). Also, twelve suspected drug traffickers were extrajudicially executed pursuant to constitutional national security provisions in the 1960s and 1970s (Pouaree (1999a); Amnesty International (1979) 102).

[55] Johnson and Zimring (2009) 400–1; Gallahue and Lines (2010) 33.

[56] 'Pardon for Drug Convicts Possible' (1994); 'Amnesty for Drug Offenders Reflects King's Generosity' (1996); 'Persons Detained by Special Orders and Condemned to Death' (1983); 'Royal Pardon to Mark Bicentennial' (1981).

[57] 'Persons Detained by Special Orders and Condemned to Death' (1996); 'Human Rights Situation' (1988); 'Royal Pardon to Mark Bicentennial' (1981).

[58] 'Prisons to Free 15,000 under Amnesty' (1990); 'Royal Pardon to Mark Bicentennial' (1981).

trafficking alone since the resumption of executions from the mid-1990s and into the 2000s.[59] In 2001, former prime minister Thaksin Shinawatra even moved (unsuccessfully) to legally prohibit newly sentenced drug traffickers from submitting petitions for *individual* royal pardon, pursuant to his administration's 'war on drugs',[60] which resulted in the extrajudicial execution of 2,800 drug dealers and users during 2003.[61]

Nonetheless, in the recent past Thailand's position has softened once again. The four most recent collective royal pardon grants commuting death sentences to lesser punishments (2011, 2012, 2015, and 2016) each included prisoners sentenced to death for drug trafficking,[62] representing a significant change in policy. Since the two executions conducted in August 2009,[63] Thailand's Second and Third National Human Rights Action Plans (2009–13 and 2014–18) have even outlined concrete plans to abolish the death penalty,[64] as does Thailand's 2016 UN Universal Periodic Review statement.[65] However, with a coup in May 2014 returning the military to power once more, and an unexpected resumption of executions in June 2018,[66] it is far from certain when Thailand's government might take this significant step.

Aside from the nature and severity of the offence, which impacts both individual and collective royal pardons,[67] the various other criteria for individual royal pardons invoked in past cases

[59] Union for Civil Liberty (2011) 36; Amnesty International AI Index ACT 50/001/2002, 11.

[60] Amnesty International AI Index ASA 39/002/2002; Amnesty International AI Index ASA 39/005/2001; International Federation for Human Rights (2005) 27.

[61] Lefevre (2016); International Harm Reduction Association and Human Rights Watch (2008).

[62] Breen (2013); Breen (2012); 'Death Row for Women in Thailand Is Empty' (2012); Constant (2016); King Maha Vajiralongkorn Brunthirin, 'First Pardon Decree Since the Royal Succession' (Thailand Government Gazette, 11 December 2016); King Bhumibol Adulyadej, 'Pardon Decree' (Thailand Government Gazette, 30 March 2015).

[63] See Hands Off Cain, 'Thailand' (2009); Thamnukasetchai (2009). During the period under study, these were the final executions to take place in Thailand. However, see also note 66 on the recent resumption of executions in June 2018.

[64] Cornell Center on the Death Penalty Worldwide, 'Thailand' (2017).

[65] Anti-Death Penalty Asia Network (2016).

[66] Agerholm (2018).

[67] Interview with Thai law professor; Pouaree (1999a).

have included the following demographic, utilitarian, and rehabilitative/redemptive considerations:

- the prisoner's nationality, which is of critical importance;[68]
- rehabilitation as demonstrated within prison, which is also of significant importance;[69]
- admitting to the crime and showing remorse;[70]
- wrongful conviction, on the rare basis of new evidence becoming available;[71]
- gender (a female prisoner, especially one with young children, is more likely to receive commutation);[72]
- age (with both teenage and elderly prisoners being almost certain to be granted commutation);[73]
- employment in the civil service or the military;[74]
- terminal illness in prison (including 'untreatable cancers, organ failure, AIDS or mental diseases');[75]
- providing assistance to ongoing police investigations.[76]

Prisoners who satisfy none of these criteria undoubtedly face a higher risk of execution, although failing to meet any of the terms of this 'list' was a necessary but not sufficient criterion for execution over the period of study from 1991 to 2016. The condemned

[68] See the section entitled 'International relations and foreign prisoners'.

[69] 'Amnesty for Drug Offenders Reflects King's Generosity' (1996); interview with Thailand Department of Corrections staff; Pouaree (1999a). Nevertheless, Chanprasert's fieldwork at Bang Khwang Central Prison revealed that 'there are no official programs for prisoners on death row that especially focus on rehabilitation'. Death row prisoners are largely left to rehabilitate themselves (Chanprasert (2012) 129).

[70] 'Legality of Pardon Move Doubted' (2009); 'Of Amnesties and Royal Pardons' (2008); Hands Off Cain, 'Thailand' (1999); Crawford (2002).

[71] Interview with Thai criminal defence lawyer; interview with Thai human rights activist (2010).

[72] Cornell Center on the Death Penalty Worldwide, 'Thailand' (2017); 'Death Penalty Should Be Abolished' (1996). From 1935 to 2009, men executed in Thailand outnumbered women by 318 to 3 (Chitsawang (2015)).

[73] Hands Off Cain, 'Thailand' (2006); Hands Off Cain, 'Thailand' (2001); International Federation for Human Rights (2005) 33; interview with Thai prison caseworker.

[74] Cornell Center on the Death Penalty Worldwide, 'Thailand' (2017); interview with Thai human rights lawyer.

[75] Thamnukasetchai (2007); Hands Off Cain, 'Thailand' (2006); 'When Couriers Fail to Deliver' (1996).

[76] Burrell (1999); 'Activities of CGRS' (1983).

prisoner's case would need to have been finalized in the courts around the time of a Thai government 'crackdown' on particular crimes such as large-scale drug trafficking, rape with murder, or murder involving state officials, as described previously. And even then, given the large numbers of finalized death sentences for each of these crimes,[77] arbitrariness in selecting the prisoner or prisoners to execute as a deterrent example undoubtedly played an important role. During the period under study, most death row prisoners, irrespective of the crime they committed and when they committed it, eventually benefited from collective royal pardon grants, such as those which emptied death row entirely in 2012, 2015, and 2016.[78]

Explaining the High Clemency Rate in Thailand

There are four noteworthy factors that operate to explain the very high proportion of clemency grants in finalized capital cases in Thailand. First and probably most influential are Thailand's system of government and its national religion: a constitutionally constrained yet occasionally interventionist monarchy steeped in Buddhist tradition,[79] with the longest reigning monarch in the world until King Bhumibol's death in 2016.[80] Second is the process by which individual and collective royal pardons are granted, leading to protracted stays on death row for capital defendants before a decision on clemency is finalized. Third is the Thai political establishment's long-time use of arbitrary and extrajudicial executions to control petty crime and to eliminate political opponents. Finally, in light of the fact that foreigners make up a significant portion of those prisoners executed for drug offences in Singapore, Malaysia, and Indonesia over the period of study, some explanatory power is also found in the Thai authorities' reluctance to

[77] See note 19 and associated text.

[78] Breen (2012); Hands Off Cain, 'Thailand' (2016); Constant (2016); King Bhumibol Adulyadej, 'Pardon Decree' (Thailand Government Gazette, 30 March 2015).

[79] Johnson and Zimring (2009) 398.

[80] Ivarsson and Isager (2010) 2; 'A Royal Occasion' (1996).

carry out executions of foreigners, particularly prisoners from western nations.

King Bhumibol and the Buddhist monarchy

Thailand remains the only country in Southeast Asia never to have been colonized,[81] a fact reflected in the continuity of the Chakri dynasty from 1782 to the present.[82] In a fluid and unstable political system beset by nineteen military coups and twenty different constitutions since the end of absolute monarchy in 1932,[83] King Bhumibol Adulyadej (the ninth of the Chakri kings) proved a rare constant political influence from his official coronation in 1950 through to his death in October 2016.[84] Two particular aspects of the Thai monarchy as a cultural and historical institution—the 1,000-year history of granting pardons in order to demonstrate benevolence, and the monarchy's inalienable association with Theravada Buddhism—operate to substantially explain the continued award of individual and collective royal pardons in the vast majority of finalized capital cases.

First, the long tradition of granting royal pardons to a majority of prisoners sentenced to death and to lesser punishments continues to endear the Thai monarch to the public. Despite strong public support for the death penalty,[85] Thai politicians, sentencing judges, and the public rarely questioned King Bhumibol's generous granting of royal pardons over the seven decades of his rule.[86] Taking action to appear merciful and generous rather

[81] Choosup (1979) 81.

[82] 'A Royal Occasion' (1996); Ivarsson and Isager (2010) 6.

[83] Bremmer (2016). In 2011 Harding and Leyland noted that since 1932, no other country has enacted as many different written constitutions as Thailand (at 34, 34 n62).

[84] Johnson and Zimring (2009) 398; Funston (2001b) 342; Harding and Leyland (2011) 34. Handley (2006, at 433) quotes Bhumibol himself: 'when a constitution is abrogated or a parliament abolished ... the people's mandate reverts to me.'

[85] International Federation for Human Rights (2005) 8; Mala (2018). 'Seminar on Religious Aspects of Death Penalty' (2011) quotes a 2008 survey finding that 84 per cent of Bangkok residents favour the continued use of the death penalty.

[86] International Federation for Human Rights (2005) 12; Sherwell (1996). The failure to hold royal actions to account is explicable not only as a result of public respect and adulation for the late King Bhumibol, but also due to Thailand's increasingly draconian *lèse-majesté* laws, prohibiting criticism of the Royal Family, which have been more commonly enforced since 1976. According to a leading

than vengeful and punitive is by no means unique to the Thai monarch. Royal generosity in pardoning is generally associated with absolute monarchies, whereby popular approval is gained not through election but through 'strategies of benevolence'[87] which have little to do with the merits of each case. As described in Chapter 2, 'mercy from the sovereign' is one of four possible clemency models. In Thailand this phenomenon is exemplified by collective royal pardons as a symbol of royal power.[88] However, individual royal pardons may also, in certain individual cases and when taken as a cumulative whole, help to endear the Thai monarch to his subjects. As Chotibal observed in a major piece of research on the history of the Thai royal pardon, for almost a thousand years the institution of clemency helped to bind Siamese absolute monarchs and their royal subjects together.[89] Pardons in capital and non-capital cases have thus been an important means of maintaining the monarchy's power, prestige, and popularity.

Nevertheless, one of the important practical features of Thailand's pardoning process (both for individual and collective royal pardons) is the primarily ceremonial or signatory function of the king. Each individual case or collective proposal only reaches the reigning monarch after extensive vetting by successive levels of government bureaucracy.[90] Arguably, the long tradition of the monarch granting clemency to condemned prisoners (over a thousand years for the monarchy as a whole, and since coronation in 1950 for King Bhumibol)[91] proves more significant in explaining Thailand's high clemency rate than any personal influence of King Bhumibol or his heir, especially during the last fifteen years of Bhumibol's life.

The exact point at which the process evolved from detailed personal consideration of individual petitions and collective

academic expert on *lèse-majesté*, 'It is a dubious distinction that Thailand has what may well be one of the most repressive laws restricting freedom of speech in the world' (Streckfuss (2010) 109, 138).

[87] Botsman (2007) 45–9.

[88] Jayaphorn (2011); interview with Thai criminal defence lawyer and Thai NGO staff; interview with Thai human rights commissioner.

[89] Chotibal (1990). See also Jayaphorn (2011).

[90] Thailand Department of Corrections (2009); interview with Australian academic expert on Thailand; interview with Thailand Department of Corrections staff.

[91] See Chotibal (1990), Jayaphorn (2011), and note 47.

proposals by the Chakri monarchs to become a rubber-stamping exercise is uncertain. The Thai political establishment and the civil service bureaucracy may have usurped the power to grant collective royal pardons on behalf of the king as far back as the establishment of constitutional monarchy in 1932,[92] and under King Bhumibol the rate of royal assent to proposed collective royal pardon decrees approached 100 per cent.[93] Individual royal pardons, on the other hand, were certainly considered in detail by monarchs prior to 1932.[94] Although reliable evidence is not available given a lack of access to palace officials, it is also likely that, at the very minimum, Bhumibol read all or at least a majority of individual petitions during the course of his reign.[95] However, when the king's health problems became more severe from 2003 onwards, the roles of the Ministry of Justice and the Ministry of Corrections became more influential, as unread petitions 'piled up' on the king's desk.[96] Although the official position remained that Bhumibol read every document put before him, in 2012 a leading Thai human rights activist asserted that such a workload would not have been possible for 'many years'.[97] Moreover, even taking the time to read all pending petitions for individual royal pardon does not equate to individual decision-making by the king. Bhumibol's signature may have followed prior recommendations on all or a majority of petitions, but there is not enough evidence to know this with certainty. Two interviewees asserted that the king 'rarely' changed the recommendation given, thereby leaving open the possibility that he had previously done so in exceptional cases.[98]

[92] Chotibal (1990).

[93] Interview with Thailand Department of Corrections staff; interview with Thai human rights lawyer.

[94] Bangkok Corrections Museum (2012); Tips (1998) 28; interview with Thai criminal defence lawyer and Thai NGO staff.

[95] Interview with Thai human rights activist (2012); interview with Thai law professor.

[96] Interview with Thai human rights activist (2012); interview with Thai human rights activist (2010); interview with Thailand Department of Corrections staff.

[97] Interview with Thai human rights activist (2012). This account is confirmed by an NGO memo on file with the author (Anti-Death Penalty NGO Memo (2012)).

[98] Interview with Thailand Department of Corrections staff; interview with former employee of the Thailand Department of Corrections.

A related explanation for Thailand's high clemency rate over the period under study is the historical influence of Buddhism on royal and bureaucratic decision-making on capital punishment. Around 95 per cent of Thailand's population follows Theravada Buddhism.[99] In Thailand, Buddhism has attained the status of 'a social institution which is important in giving meaning to and being a symbol of national unity. It is a source and medium of the culture and traditions of the Thai nation.'[100] As described in Chapter 2, the Buddhist religion is generally regarded as incompatible with the practice of capital punishment,[101] providing one possible explanation for the general reluctance of Thai authorities to carry out judicial executions.[102] Buddhist teaching eschews the deliberate taking of life, promotes pacifism and compassion,[103] and recognizes the capacity of all human beings to change and reform, a notion which extends to convicted criminals.[104]

It is ironic, then, that public opinion polls in Thailand have long demonstrated mass support for capital punishment,[105] and even the majority of Buddhist monks support executions.[106] The retention of capital punishment as a criminal sanction is thus justified by the Thai political establishment as being in accordance with the public will, and consistent with democratic government.[107] Yet, in the royal pardon context, it is the personal piety of the Thai king and higher-level bureaucratic decision makers, together with the monarchy's historical tradition of Buddhist kingship, that are most relevant. In his 2006 biography of Bhumibol, Paul Handley asserted that the king appeared to view many capital crimes 'in a Buddhist sense, [such] that criminal behavior was unmeritorious

[99] Johnson and Zimring (2009) 397; Hubert (2008); International Federation for Human Rights (2005) 14.

[100] Jackson (1989) 2.

[101] Amnesty International (1990) 9; Miethe et al (2005) 119; Anckar (2004) 100.

[102] Interview with Australian academic expert on Thailand; interview with Thai human rights lawyer; Thongpao (2007); Torode (1998). Executions are not carried out during Buddhist holidays or festivals in Thailand (Amnesty International AI Index ASA 39/005/2001).

[103] Johnson and Zimring (2009) 397; Alarid and Wang (2001).

[104] International Federation for Human Rights (2005) 14; Hubert (2008).

[105] See note 85.

[106] Johnson and Zimring (2009) 397; interview with international human rights NGO staff #5; interview with Thai human rights activist #2 (2012); interview with Thai human rights activist (2012).

[107] Johnson (2009).

conduct and up to the criminal to correct lest he suffer bad karma'.[108] The Chakri monarchs' tradition of commuting most death sentences finalized by the courts accords with the Buddhist law of kingship, *Dhamma*,[109] which has informed pardon practice in Thailand since the thirteenth-century Sukhothai period.[110] As Handley observed:

> In the Buddhist paradigm, the leader steers his people not by harsh laws and punishments but by the suasive power of example, the sheer force of his virtue. Karma governs the cosmos, not constitutional law and secular judges. If people do wrong, they will eventually suffer their deserved consequences naturally.[111]

Irrespective of the fact that the most important decision makers on collective royal pardon decrees and individual royal pardon petitions are government officials rather than the king himself, personally held religious opposition to state-sanctioned killing and the state's need to portray the Royal Family as devout Buddhists have combined to result in the vast majority of finalized death sentences throughout Thailand's modern history being commuted to lesser punishments.

Pardoning process and long stays on death row

The slow-moving judicial and clemency appeal system in Thailand also helps to explain the kingdom's clemency rate of 95 per cent or above. To reiterate, following arrest, trial, and sentencing in the Courts of First Instance and two levels of judicial appeal (which alone will often take between five and ten years),[112] a prisoner's petition for individual royal pardon, when made within the sixty-day deadline, passes through multiple government departments and political committees for recommendation, before making its

[108] Handley (2006) 375.

[109] van Oosten (2008) 258; Jayaphorn (2011).

[110] Chotibal (1990); Anand (1996) 2; Jayaphorn (2011).

[111] Handley (2006) 434. Haberkorn (2015, at 53) notes a similar dynamic with legislative amnesties precluding prosecutions in Thailand.

[112] Union for Civil Liberty (2011, at 9) and Chanprasert (2012, at 3) describe a range of 7–10 years. A Thai law professor (at interview) asserted the time period is 5.5–7.5 years. A Thai criminal defence lawyer and a Thai NGO staff member (in a joint interview) estimated 6–10 years.

way to the king for ratification.[113] Although Thailand's Criminal Procedure Code (enacted in 1934) has always permitted an execution to proceed if the king neither accepts nor rejects a prisoner's petition for individual royal pardon within a further sixty-day period after its receipt by the Royal Palace,[114] in practice the Department of Corrections acts extremely cautiously in capital cases. Officers within the Department will usually wait for royal approval before initiating execution procedures, however long this may take.[115] As a Department of Corrections officer stated to the *Bangkok Post*: 'What would happen if the pardon [decree] arrived after we had killed the convict? How could we bring back his life?'[116]

Past practice suggests that, for capital prisoners who do not receive collective royal pardon in the interim, the king's final decision on individual royal pardon will only come five to ten years after judicial appeals have been exhausted.[117] The Thai bureaucracy and the royal palace appear to take the view that, after all judicial appeals fail, a five- to ten-year period on death row awaiting the petition's outcome, followed by imprisonment of similar length, constitute adequate retributive and deterrent punishment for most serious crimes. A senior Thai judge interviewed in the *Bangkok Post* in 1999 stated that in a majority of cases 'those who receive the death sentence could leave prison—alive—after spending between 15 to 20 years behind bars' following successive royal pardons.[118] Moreover, in the view of two Bangkok-based interviewees, as King Bhumibol advanced in years, the frequency with which he adjudicated on or approved recommendations on individual royal pardon petitions declined, contributing to an increase in the numbers on Thailand's death row and much longer waits for condemned prisoners if they were not granted collective

[113] Thailand Department of Corrections (12/2/2008); Thailand Department of Corrections (2009).

[114] Criminal Procedure Code 1934 (Thailand), s 247(1); Pouaree (1999a).

[115] Pouaree (1999a); International Federation for Human Rights (2005) 28; Breen (2013); interview with international human rights NGO staff #5.

[116] Pouaree (1999a).

[117] Handley (2006) 375; interview with Thai prison caseworker; interview with former employee of the Thailand Department of Corrections. Union for Civil Liberty (2011, at 10) and Chanprasert (2012, at 3) report a range of anywhere from one to ten years for the consideration of an application for individual royal pardon.

[118] Pouaree (1999a). In contrast, Rojanaphruk (2012) estimated ten years.

royal pardons in the interim.[119] In 2013, for example, Breen reported that no individual royal pardon petition had been ruled upon for four years.[120]

How does the lengthy period a condemned prisoner generally spends incarcerated affect the proportion of cases granted clemency in Thailand? As I noted in Chapter 2, rehabilitative and utilitarian justifications for clemency become stronger the longer a prisoner spends on death row. In fact, good behaviour and demonstrated reform in prison have been acknowledged by the Thai authorities as two of the three most important criteria for the award of an individual royal pardon (along with the type of crime committed).[121] By interview, an officer from the Department of Corrections revealed that the petition review process was so slow that sometimes a prisoner's papers were returned to the Department for amendment, given a beneficial change in circumstances during processing.[122] Furthermore, although the process for granting collective royal pardons is more streamlined than that for individual royal pardon petitions, the long period of time already spent in custody during court appeals and while awaiting consideration for pardon is influential in determining a prisoner's assigned behavioural 'category'—a crucial precondition determining eligibility for collective royal pardons.[123]

Arbitrary and extrajudicial executions

One of the reasons why Thailand's many elected civilian and unelected military governments have been able to tolerate an apparent 'thwarting' of death penalty laws by royal prerogative is the concurrent availability of extrajudicial punishments to control crime. Through individual and collective royal pardons in capital cases, the king's enduring image as a benevolent, God-like figure,[124] together with the Chakri monarchs' longstanding pardoning

[119] Interview with Thai human rights activist (2012); interview with Thailand Department of Corrections staff.

[120] Breen (2013).

[121] 'Amnesty for Drug Offenders Reflects King's Generosity' (1996); interview with Thailand Department of Corrections staff; Pouaree (1999a).

[122] Interview with Thailand Department of Corrections Staff.

[123] Jaruboon (2006) 87; Pouaree (1999a); interview with Thai criminal defence lawyer and Thai NGO staff.

[124] Ivarsson and Isager (2010) 2–3; Streckfuss (2011) 309.

tradition, are respected and maintained. At the same time, extrajudicial and arbitrary executions carried out by the military and police often do the 'dirty work' of eliminating political opponents and criminal elements.[125] As Handley notes, especially under Thailand's frequent military caretaker governments, 'the law was seen as a barrier to public order', hence the government's resort to arbitrary and extrajudicial killings.[126] Particularly during periods of political turmoil, bypassing conventional judicial processes allowed for a rapid and deadly response to crimes that posed a perceived threat to national security.[127] At the same time, the conventional route to trial, adjudication, sentencing, and (in most cases) royal pardon was still used for crimes that were undoubtedly serious (such as domestic murders, robbery, and rape), yet which were not perceived as existential threats to the state.[128]

Extrajudicial punishments have taken place by two methods throughout Thailand's modern history: in an 'official' manner as arbitrary executions sanctioned by several twentieth-century constitutions,[129] and in an 'unofficial' manner as targeted or negligent extrajudicial killings by security forces. Arbitrary executions were frequently performed by Thailand's military governments in the 1960s, 1970s, and early 1980s,[130] with the most recent constitutional provision explicitly authorizing lethal force without trial

[125] Arbitrary executions may prima facie conform to the domestic law of the executing state, yet do not take place after fair judicial adjudication (Schabas (2002) 99–100). Extrajudicial executions constitute 'unlawful and deliberate killing carried out by order of a government or with its acquiescence' (Amnesty International AI Index MDE 15/005/2001).

[126] Handley (2006) 375; 'Death Penalty Should Be Abolished' (1996); interview with Thai Human Rights Commissioner.

[127] Hickling (1973) 218.

[128] Amnesty International (1979) 102; 'Death Sentences' (1983) 10–11; '31 Were Sentenced to Death' (1982) 27–8; '17 Persons Executed and Sentenced to Death During April and May' (1982) 10–11. Historical anomalies do exist here, such that persons accused of rape causing death, or arson, have also been arbitrarily executed pursuant to constitutional provisions (see note 130 and associated text).

[129] See Constitution of Thailand 1959, art 17; Constitution of Thailand 1972, art 17; Constitution of Thailand 1976, art 21; Constitution of Thailand 1977, art 27; Constitution of Thailand 1978, art 200; Interim Constitution of Thailand 1991, art 27; Pouaree (1999a); 'Death Penalty Should Be Abolished' (1996). The power to order arbitrary executions did not exist in the democratic constitutions of 1968 and 1974.

[130] See generally Haberkorn (2018) 55–74.

dating to 1991.[131] Post-1991 royal pardon practice has instead been influenced by 'unofficial' state killings, conducted by military and police personnel in the field: hence this section's focus on the latter category.

Thailand has a long history of extrajudicial killings by security forces. Most notably, during a period of civil and political unrest in the mid-1970s, security forces conducted targeted killings of leftist political leaders, protesters, and communist insurgents[132] (some but not all of whom could have been prosecuted in the courts). Likewise, for non-political crimes, a 2002 Freedom House report observed that, even before Prime Minister Thaksin Shinawatra's later 'war on drugs' crackdown:

> Thailand's poorly trained police frequently are implicated in wrongful killings and rights violations against criminal suspects and detainees. Officers at times kill armed drug traffickers and other criminal suspects while apprehending them. While police in some of these cases may be justified in using lethal force, at least some of the killings are unwarranted.[133]

Similar allegations of killings by police and the army in the 1980s and 1990s have been made by the Thai NGO called the Coordinating Group for Religion in Society, by King Bhumibol's biographer Paul Handley, by Amnesty International, by the *Bangkok Post*, and by the US Department of State.[134] Prime Minister Thaksin Shinawatra's infamous policy to order or permit the extrajudicial executions of up to 2,800 drug dealers and users during 2003[135] was interpreted by one interviewee as a means of bypassing the slow court system and royal pardon petition process, in order to shock the public and deter future criminal activity.[136] The magazine *The Economist* has even suggested that King Bhumibol privately approved of the killings,[137] while continuing to play the role of benevolent monarch in public.

[131] Interim Constitution of Thailand 1991, art 27.

[132] Funston (2001b) 331–2; Yimprasert (2009); Haberkorn (2015) 45.

[133] Freedom House (2002c).

[134] See 'To Our Readers' (1982); Handley (2006) 375; Amnesty International AI Index ASA 39/004/2002; Amnesty International AI Index ASA 39/002/1997, 3, 6–7; 'Human Rights—US Document Cites Abuses in Thailand' (1997); US Department of State (2000).

[135] See note 61.

[136] Interview with Thai human rights activist #2 (2012).

[137] 'Thailand's King and Its Crisis' (2008).

Thereafter, Thaksin's policies were continued, albeit to a far lesser extent, by his successors Samak Sundaravej and Abhisit Vejjajiva, at least until 2010.[138] Most recently, in 2013 the World Coalition Against the Death Penalty reported that 'there has been considerable extra-judicial killing—especially of alleged drug dealers—by the police in recent years'.[139]

International relations and foreign prisoners

Unlike in Singapore, Malaysia, and Indonesia, no citizen of a western nation was executed in Thailand from 1991 to 2016, or indeed during King Bhumibol's entire seventy-year reign.[140] The judicial execution of foreigners from non-western nations has also proven relatively rare, with media sources asserting that none took place from the early 1960s at least to the resumption of executions in the mid-1990s.[141] The first execution of a foreigner from any nation under the period of study may have been that of Myanmar national Htaho Pauy, who had been convicted of murder, in 1999.[142] With foreign nationals constituting only around 5 per cent of the 223 executions conducted since the early 1960s,[143] and no westerners included in Thailand's 323 executions from 1935 to 2006,[144] on its face it does appear that foreigners (and especially westerners) are treated more leniently compared with local prisoners convicted of capital offences.

Two commentators attribute the rarity in foreign executions, when compared with those of Thai citizens, to the importance of

[138] Interview with Thai human rights activist (2010); interview with Thai Human Rights Commissioner; Windle (2016) 6.

[139] World Coalition against the Death Penalty et al (2011).

[140] Interview with London-based NGO staff; Kelly (1991); Kelly (1988); Drummond (1996).

[141] 'Death Sentence for Canadian Father, Son' (1993); Crawford (2002); Bellett (2008); Hands Off Cain, 'Thailand' (2002). However, two Hong Kong nationals were executed for drug trafficking in 1978, pursuant to constitutional provisions allowing for execution without trial (Pouaree (1999b)).

[142] See Amnesty International AI Index ASA 39/05/99.

[143] See variously Johnson and Zimring (2009) 403; 'Death Sentence for Canadian Father, Son' (1993); Crawford (2002); Bellett (2008); Hands Off Cain, 'Thailand' (2002); Warren (2017); 'Nigeria: Five Foreigners Executed in Thailand' (2002); 'Thai Executions Condemned' (2001).

[144] See Johnson and Zimring (2009) 403; Kelly (1991); Kelly (1988); Drummond (1996).

trade and tourism to the Thai economy.[145] Even for large-scale narcotics trafficking, where proceeding to execution would be a political priority in the case of Thai nationals, westerners have traditionally had their sentences commuted to lesser punishments through individual royal pardon, and have sometimes been released from prison after as few as ten years.[146] It is not that westerners are completely removed from the scope of the criminal law; they are merely exempted from being executed. Notably, the first westerner to be sentenced to death at first instance for drug trafficking in Thailand was convicted in 1985.[147] By the end of 2016, there were twenty-four foreigners under sentence of death for all crimes (from both developed and developing nations).[148]

Given the Thai authorities' clear reluctance to compromise relations with other governments by executing foreign citizens, why are death sentences typically reduced to lesser punishments by royal pardon rather than earlier in the process, through available judicial means? The answer may be that foreigners are treated on a par with locals within the generally well-regarded judicial system,[149] with legislatively enumerated mitigating factors sufficient to reduce death sentences to terms of imprisonment in many, but not all, cases. Where a death sentence imposed on a foreigner reaches the individual royal pardon phase, it is only here that extralegal considerations such as international relations become relevant. As described in Chapter 2, clemency may be interpreted by an executive decision maker not only as an extra 'layer' of

[145] Interview with London-based NGO staff; Skehan (2000).

[146] Kelly (1991); 'American Given Life for Trafficking in Heroin' (1995). A 2012 article reported the release from prison of the westerner who had served the longest ever stint in Bang Khwang Central Prison, at eighteen years (after initially being sentenced to death) (Friedman (2012)).

[147] Kelly (1985).

[148] Amnesty International AI Index ACT 50/7611/2017, 3; Cornell Center on the Death Penalty Worldwide, 'Thailand' (2017).

[149] Interview with Thai human rights activist (2010); interview with Thai criminal defence lawyer #2; interview with international human rights NGO staff #6. Prisoners with money and connections (including some westerners) may benefit from corruption at the *earlier* stages of police investigations, before recommendations are made to prosecutors (interview with Thai human rights activist (2010); interview with Thai human rights activist #2 (2010); interview with Thai criminal defence lawyer #2; interview with former employee of the Thailand Department of Corrections).

judicial appeal or as an incentive or reward for good behaviour and rehabilitation in prison, but also as a forum in which non-legal (political or utilitarian) considerations may be given weight. While the other three countries represented in this study have, to varying degrees and at varying points in their recent history, emphasized publicly a policy of enforcing the criminal law in an impartial manner, including that no one should be exempted from execution on the basis of their citizenship,[150] the Thai political authorities openly adopt a contrasting position.

As suggested previously, it is within petitions for individual royal pardon that foreign nationality influences Thai commutations, rather than citizenship acting as a distinguishing criterion within the regular death row amnesties granted by collective royal pardon.[151] For individual royal pardons, the advocacy role played by foreign embassies, governments, and heads of state is crucial. While in 2001 western diplomats in Thailand claimed that it was only a matter of time before a citizen of a developed country was executed for a narcotics offence,[152] high-level representations by foreign governments have thus far invariably resulted in the commutation of death sentences to terms of imprisonment,[153] even where a prisoner has been passed over for collective royal pardon after poor behaviour in prison, or based on the offence committed.

How then are the executions of certain non-westerners, including Hong Kong, Taiwanese, Nigerian, and Myanmar nationals from 1999 onwards,[154] to be explained? European diplomats have suggested that, for crimes where execution is deemed a political priority in Thailand,[155] a self-initiated pardon petition by a foreigner would fail unless there was high-level backing for clemency from the relevant foreign government.[156] Death penalty abolitionist

[150] See Chapter 4; Chapter 5; Chapter 6.

[151] Interview with Thailand Department of Corrections staff; Union for Civil Liberty (2011) 16.

[152] 'Western Prisoners Face Thai Firing Squad' (2011).

[153] Hands Off Cain, 'Thailand' (2001); Bellett (2008); interview with Thai human rights activist (2012); interview with international human rights NGO staff #5; Willcox (2008).

[154] See Hands Off Cain, 'Thailand' (2002); Corben (2001); 'Thai Executions Condemned' (2011); 'Nigeria: Five Foreigners Executed in Thailand' (2002); Amnesty International AI Index ASA 39/05/99; Warren (2017).

[155] See notes 56–59 and associated text.

[156] Hands Off Cain, 'Thailand' (2001); interview with Thai criminal defence lawyer #2.

countries and governments that adopt a 'protectionist' attitude to their citizens living and travelling abroad usually provide such consular support, which will form part of the individual royal pardon petition. Indeed, several interview sources speculated that the foreign prisoners executed since 1996 hail from countries and territories that:

1. do not play a major role in the Thai economy through trade and tourism or do not otherwise have a special bilateral relationship with Thailand;[157] and/or
2. do not engage in the zealous protection of citizens arrested and sentenced to death abroad[158] (which is often correlated with the negotiating nation's own stance on retention and abolition).[159]

In summary, the Thai king's commutation of the vast majority of finalized death sentences imposed on foreign nationals, especially for offences (such as large-scale drug trafficking) which would lead to the execution of Thai citizens during periodic political campaigns against particular crimes, remains a highly visible and controversial factor contributing to Thailand's extremely high clemency rate from 1991 onwards. This continued deference to requests from foreign governments finds no parallel within the clemency practice of the comparator countries: Singapore, Malaysia, and Indonesia.

Explaining Executions, Not Clemency

Commutation was the overwhelmingly likely outcome in any finalized capital case in Thailand during the period 1991–2016, which is noticeably different from the position in Singapore, Malaysia, and Indonesia over the same period. Indeed, the numerical gap between first-instance death sentences and executions in Thailand is among the highest in the retentionist world.[160] As described in this

[157] Interview with Thai prison caseworker; interview with Australian academic expert on Thailand.

[158] Interview with international human rights NGO staff #5; interview with Thai criminal defence lawyer #2; interview with international human rights NGO staff #6.

[159] Interview with international human rights NGO staff #6; interview with Thai human rights lawyer.

[160] Johnson and Zimring (2009) 405.

chapter, Thailand's clemency practice largely reflects the 'mercy from the sovereign' model identified in Chapter 2, although some of the precise criteria for individual and collective royal pardons also mirror the 'retributive', 'redemptive', and 'utilitarian' paradigms, particularly the latter two.

Given the four stated explanations for Thailand's recent clemency practice, an obvious question to ask is why any judicial executions have taken place *at all* over the course of Thailand's modern political history? With such strong incentives against executions (particularly the Thai monarchy's Buddhist and benevolent traditions), why is Thailand comparable with its actively retentionist Southeast Asian neighbours, rather than with the abolitionist de jure or abolitionist de facto Asian monarchies ruling Bhutan and Brunei?[161] The main reason is that despite the Thai monarchs' traditional role (or the bureaucracy's perpetuation of it) in commuting finalized death sentences, Thailand's political establishment has remained in favour of death penalty retention, and occasional executions as a deterrent measure, at least since the enactment of the present Penal Code in 1956.[162] As one human rights activist sees it, Thailand's modern history has followed the path of 'continual conflict between the people who want to stop [executions], and the people who want to start'.[163] And unlike Bhutan and Brunei, Thailand's status as a constitutional rather than an absolute monarchy results in a necessary balancing of, and tension between, royal and political interests.

More specifically, during King Bhumibol's long reign, capital punishment by firing squad or by lethal injection was solely enforced for death row prisoners whose offence category was deemed particularly serious at the time, or who behaved badly in prison, thereby disqualifying the prisoner from the most reliable source of clemency—regular collective royal pardons to celebrate important royal events.[164] As for why those same prisoners' petitions

[161] See Johnson and Zimring (2009) 16, 406.

[162] Interview with Thai human rights activist (2012); International Federation for Human Rights (2005) 10; interview with Thai Human Rights Commissioner.

[163] Interview with Thai human rights activist (2012).

[164] See notes 40-42 and associated text.

for individual royal pardon were not granted, commentators have suggested three potential explanations. Although direct evidence is scarce, it is likely that executions during the last decades of King Bhumibol's reign fell into three categories:

1. There was a breach of royal protocol. Where government officials seek to execute a convict, they are legally empowered to do so if the king does not rule on the petition within sixty days.[165] In important cases, politicians may have pressured officials from the Ministry of Justice or Department of Corrections to carry out an execution in these circumstances, in breach of the conventional protocol to wait indefinitely on a response from the royal palace;[166]
2. King Bhumibol explicitly authorized certain executions. Handley has speculated that Bhumibol, towards the end of his long rule, grew impatient with the drug and violent crime problems afflicting Thai society, and therefore refused several individual petitions,[167] or at least confirmed his advisers' recommendations for refusal. Data provided by the Thai Union for Civil Liberty appears to confirm this hypothesis. At least twenty-six petitions were actively rejected by the king during the period 2001–5, rather than merely being allowed to lapse beyond sixty days.[168] Coincidentally or not, the same number of executions took place between 2001 and 2005.[169] Available evidence also suggests that the final executions during the period under analysis, in August 2009, took place after the king had rejected their petitions two weeks beforehand.[170]
3. Some cases may have resulted in execution through an amalgam of explanations 1 and 2. Thailand's political leaders, *with the Royal Palace's acquiescence*, may have rushed through executions, contrary to bureaucratic convention, after the sixty-day

[165] See Criminal Procedure Code 1934 (Thailand), s 247(1).

[166] Johnson and Zimring (2009) 406; interview with Thai human rights activist (2012).

[167] Handley (2006) 375.

[168] Union for Civil Liberty (2011) 17.

[169] See Appendix (Thailand); Union for Civil Liberty (2011) 17.

[170] US Embassy Thailand Bangkok (2009). See also Millar (2018), speculating upon the role of the Royal Palace in authorizing Thailand's first execution in nine years, in June 2018.

period for royal adjudication lapsed. However, the same political leaders also took ultimate public responsibility for the execution orders, so as to protect the king's benevolent reputation and to maintain royal patronage.[171]

[171] For example, Handley (2006, at 425) speculates that Prime Minister Thaksin Shinawatra's unsuccessful move to ban serious narcotics traffickers from submitting pardon applications in 2001 may have originated as a convenient way for the government to employ executions as a deterrent and to make a strong political statement condemning drug crimes, while also allowing the king to save face (as he privately approved of certain drug-related executions).

4

Republic of Singapore

[T]he integrity of our legal system and the standing of our Judiciary are among the hard-earned assets of the Singapore brand name. We do not jettison them for transient political convenience. The law must take its course and we just have to be prepared for any fallout.

Former Singapore Deputy Prime Minister Shunmugan Jayakumar, on clemency in death penalty cases[1]

During the 1990s and the early 2000s the small island state of Singapore achieved worldwide notoriety as likely the most prolific executioner in the world, per head of population.[2] Although execution rates have dropped precipitously since then,[3] the same level of severity is evident in the fact that the Singapore Cabinet has granted only six clemency applications among the more than five hundred petitions received since Singapore became an independent state in 1965.[4] From 1991 to 2016, only three death row prisoners received clemency whereas more than 450 executions were carried out,[5] making Singapore by far the most frugal jurisdiction for pardons and commutations among the four retentionist Southeast Asian countries under analysis. One of Singapore's

[1] Jayakumar (2011) 153.

[2] Amnesty International AI Index ASA 36/001/2004, 1; Thio (2004a) 215; Hood (2002) 51.

[3] See Appendix (Singapore).

[4] Chan (2016) 182, 200; Amnesty International (1979) 98; Singapore Prison Service (2017) 10. Singapore's *The Independent* newspaper reports seven grants, including a third grant during the presidency of Wee Kim Wee (1985–93), without providing further details ('Nathan Grants Zero Presidential Pardon during His 2 Terms' (2016)). Hor (2013, at 160) also suggests a figure of seven, again without providing further details. It is unclear whether a seventh grant, if it did take place, came during the period of study from 1991 onwards.

[5] See Appendix (Singapore).

most experienced criminal lawyers, the late Subhas Anandan, related in his autobiography that filing a petition for clemency with the president was usually 'a waste of time' as it was invariably rejected.[6] Singapore is Thailand's polar opposite—a jurisdiction where the explicit constitutional right to be considered for clemency when judicial appeals fail[7] carries almost no practical effect.

What is special about the political, legal, and historical characteristics of this highly commercialized and prosperous city-state that, generally speaking, precludes the use of executive clemency in death penalty cases? I address this question in the present chapter, alongside detailed descriptions of each of the six successful clemency petitions to date. Based on data from 1991 to 2016, excepting jurisdictions where 'clemency procedures are either absent or exist only on paper' (such as China and Japan),[8] Singapore may well possess one of the world's lowest clemency rates among retentionist nations, at less than 1 per cent of finalized cases.

Death Penalty and Clemency Practice 1991–2016

Death sentences and executions

Hanging was the method of execution favoured by the British administration in colonial Singapore, yet, as with neighbouring Malaysia (the country from which Singapore split to form an independent state in 1965), the death penalty has long outlasted both British colonial rule and its own eventual abolition in all Western European countries. Since independence, the death penalty has, despite significant post-2003 declines in execution rates,[9] been an integral and operational part of Singapore's criminal justice system. Executions in Singapore have historically performed a strong deterrence and incapacitation function,[10] unlike the 'symbolic' function of capital punishment in Asian nations with lower execution rates (such as Japan and Indonesia).[11] Singapore's mandatory death penalty gives effect to this policy: excepting

[6] Anandan (2009) 90.

[7] Constitution of Singapore 1965, art 22P(2).

[8] Anti-Death Penalty Asia Network (2011) 32. See Johnson and Zimring (2009) 64 n30; Dui Hua Foundation (2016); Andrew and Rapp (2000) 75.

[9] See Appendix (Singapore).

[10] Johnson and Zimring (2009) 8, 22, 410–11; Tey (2010) 356.

[11] Johnson and Zimring (2009) 23.

defendants benefiting from landmark legislative changes enacted in November 2012,[12] every defendant convicted of murder, various firearms offences, and specified drugs offences[13] (in addition to the rarely prosecuted crimes of piracy and mutiny and the recently enacted mandatory death penalty crimes of genocide, terrorism, and nuclear sabotage)[14] must be sentenced to death upon conviction. Together, three offence groups (murder, firearms offences, and drugs offences) have provided the vast majority of Singapore's death sentences and executions in recent decades, with

[12] New legislation that came into force in January 2013 enabled trial judges to exercise the discretion to sentence defendants to death or life imprisonment in selected homicide and drug-trafficking cases previously subject to the mandatory death penalty (Penal Code (Amendment) Act 2012 (Singapore); Misuse of Drugs (Amendment) Act 2012 (Singapore)). See further notes 108–111 and associated text.

[13] See Penal Code 2008 (Singapore), s 302 (murder); Misuse of Drugs Act 2001 (Singapore), ss 5–7 and sch 2 (trafficking, manufacturing, importing/exporting scheduled narcotics); Arms Offences Act 1973 (Singapore), ss 4, 4A, 5 (using or attempting to use arms, being an accomplice thereto), and Internal Security Act 1985 (Singapore), s 58(1) (carrying firearms, ammunitions, or explosives in a security area).

The mandatory death penalty for murder was first introduced under British rule in 1883 (see *Yong Vui Kong v Public Prosecutor* [2010] SGCA 20, [84]). The mandatory death penalty for firearms offences has existed since 1960 (pursuant to the Malayan Internal Security Act 1960, largely superseded by the Arms Offences Act 1973 (Singapore)), while the mandatory death penalty for drug offences was established by the Misuse of Drugs (Amendment) Act 1975 (Singapore), as a response to increased rates of heroin addiction and the 'perceived influence of a decadent western culture' in Singapore during the Vietnam War (Ganapathy (2006) 166).

The two original drugs invoking the mandatory death penalty trafficking thresholds pursuant to the Misuse of Drugs (Amendment) Act 1975 (Singapore) were heroin (15 grams) and morphine (30 grams). In 1989 cocaine (30 grams), cannabis (500 grams), hashish (200 grams) and opium (1,200 grams) were added to the list, followed by cannabis mixture (1,000 grams) in 1993 and methamphetamine (250 grams) in 1998 (Phang (1990) 233; Amnesty International (1979) 44, 97; Misuse of Drugs (Amendment) Act 1993 (Singapore)). The 1993 amendments also enabled mandatory death penalty convictions for the possession of specified drugs for the *purpose* of trafficking, rather than merely the action of trafficking in drugs by, for example, selling or distributing.

[14] Penal Code 2008 (Singapore), s 130B (piracy), s 130E (genocide); Singapore Armed Forces Act 2000 (Singapore), s 15 (mutiny); Terrorism (Suppression of Bombings) Act 2007 (Singapore), s 3(1) (terrorist bombing causing death); Radiation Protection (Amendment) Act 2014 (Singapore), s 26DB(2)(c) (nuclear sabotage intentionally causing death).

drug offences alone accounting for 71 per cent of executions from 1991 to 2016.[15] By contrast, the larger range of crimes subject to the judicially discretionary death penalty[16] have not led to any executions since 1991.[17]

Official data reveals that the Singaporean authorities carried out 466 executions between 1991 and 2016.[18] The average is approximately eighteen executions per year, although the data reveals two distinct 'halves' to Singapore's execution practice. From 1991 to 2003, the execution rate was approximately thirty-two per year, before falling precipitously to only four per year from 2004 to 2016. Given Singapore's worldwide reputation for strict law and order governance,[19] it is at first tempting to view this decline in execution rates as a historical anomaly. However, the opposite may in fact be true. The high execution rate during the 1990s and early 2000s (when, with its low population as a city-state, Singapore was perhaps the global leader on a per capita basis) contrasts with comparatively lower totals from 2004

[15] See Chan (2016) 183, and Singapore Prison Service (2017) 10, for data.

[16] Discretionary death sentence offences in Singapore consist of the Hostage-Taking Act 2010 (Singapore), s 3 (hostage taking); Kidnapping Act 1961 (Singapore), s 3 (kidnapping); Arms Offences Act 1973 (Singapore), s 6 (trafficking in arms); Penal Code 2008 (Singapore), s 121–121A (treason), s 132 (abetment of mutiny), s 194 (perjury intending to lead to a death sentence), s 305 (abetting suicide), s 307 (attempted murder), s 364 (kidnapping to commit murder), s 396 (gang robbery with murder); Internal Security Act 1985 (Singapore), s 59 (firearms and explosives offences); Singapore Armed Forces Act 1973 (Singapore), s 11 (misconduct in action), s 12 (assisting the enemy), s 39 (offences by officer serving on a vessel); Radiation Protection (Amendment) Act 2014 (Singapore), s 26DB(2)(b) (nuclear sabotage causing death). Sections 121 and 121A of the Penal Code 2008 (Singapore), criminalizing treason, were mandatory death penalty offences until amendment in 2007.

[17] A discretionary death sentence for kidnapping has not been handed down in Singapore since the early 1970s, while only a small number of discretionary death sentences for gang robbery with murder were passed at first instance in the 1990s (Hor (2013) 161 n77; Kow (2009) 1120–2). The majority of the Penal Code offences listed here 'have no record of ever being used' (Hor (2006) 503 n15). A partial exception here is the case of Kho Jabing, whose death sentence for murder was imposed in 2015 by the Singapore Court of Appeal pursuant to the 2012 amendments allowing for discretionary sentencing in certain murder cases (see note 109 and associated text). Jabing was executed in May 2016 (Zeng (2016)). In the future, Singapore may well see more executions pursuant to discretionary death sentences in this manner.

[18] Appendix (Singapore).

[19] Skapinker (2015); Hor (2013) 142.

onwards, as well as during the 1980s (with Amnesty International recording eighteen hangings for that entire decade).[20]

Hor has argued that the 1990s saw a temporary execution 'bulge' as a backlog of finalized cases from the 1980s were cleared. During the 1980s, the need for two judges to try capital cases in Singapore's High Court meant that, for several years, defendants were charged with capital offences more frequently than the Court could process their trials and appeals. A backlog of pending cases gradually built up. Legislative amendments in 1992 allowed only one judge to consider capital cases,[21] and time limits were tightened. Cases could be processed through the system at twice the rate, hence the much higher number of executions during the 1990s.[22] Nevertheless, the apparent eighteen-fold increase in executions from the 1980s to the 1990s[23] has led Johnson and Zimring to speculate as to whether or not 'the apparent rise in Singapore's execution rate after the 1980s could be an artefact of reporting changes by the government ... [perhaps] there was a "hidden toll of executions" before the 1990s that studies could not capture'.[24]

In response, even abolitionist 'elite' interviewees in Singapore were sceptical as to whether misleading statistics have ever been provided by the government. 'Stonewalling' requests for information has proven a more common government tactic.[25] Nevertheless, whenever yearly execution totals are compiled piece by piece from media reports (as Amnesty International's unofficial 1980s figures on Singapore were)[26] to the exclusion of official aggregates, there is potential for significant undercounting. Data inaccuracies are far less likely for recent years, after the Ministry of Home Affairs and the Singapore Prison Service belatedly released official statistics covering the years from 1991 onwards.[27] Yet there remains a distinct possibility of undercounting during the 1980s.

[20] Johnson (2013) 54.
[21] See Criminal Procedure Code (Amendment) Act 1992 (Singapore).
[22] Hor (2004) 115; Hor (2013) 159–60.
[23] See Appendix (Singapore); Chan (2016) 183.
[24] Johnson and Zimring (2009) 414. See also Johnson (2013) 53.
[25] Interview with Singaporean NGO staff #3; interview with Singaporean law professor and Singaporean NGO staff #5.
[26] Johnson (2013) 53; interview with Singaporean NGO staff.
[27] Toh (2011); Singapore Prison Service (2017) 10; Johnson (2013) 53.

Since 2004, well after the 'backlog' of 1990s cases was cleared, Singapore's execution rate has probably fallen by design. Around this time the Singapore government became sensitive about its international image as 'world execution capital'[28] and encouraged the public prosecutor (the Attorney-General of Singapore and his deputies) to downgrade charges to non-capital offences in a number of cases.[29] The other potential explanations for a substantial drop in the number of executions—higher numbers of acquittals, or a reduction in serious crimes and arrests—have not arisen with the frequency necessary to explain such significant declines.[30] It is no coincidence that Singapore's reduction in executions coincided with Amnesty International's critical 2004 report 'A Hidden Toll of Executions'[31] and the international opprobrium that ensued.[32]

Nevertheless, irrespective of fluctuating execution rates during Singapore's modern history, as depicted in Figure 3, clemency grants have remained stubbornly rare, with the large number of executions overall interspersed with only six confirmed cases of clemency since independence[33] and three since 1991, leaving Singapore's 1991–2016 clemency rate at an extremely frugal 0.6 percent.[34] Given the remarkable consistency of Singapore's apparent 'no clemency' policy over time, the most important question to answer in explaining Singapore's exceptionalism is not why executions have increased or declined during different decades but rather why clemency has remained anathema to the People's Action Party (PAP) government,[35] despite the 1965 Singaporean Constitution's clear mandate for its exercise by the president.[36]

[28] 'Singapore, World Execution Capital' (1999); Amnesty International AI Index ASA 36/001/2004, 1; interview with international human rights NGO staff #4; interview with Singaporean human rights lawyer.

[29] Hor (2013) 163; statement by Singaporean law professor; interview with Singaporean criminal defence lawyer #2.

[30] Hor (2013) 161–2.

[31] See Amnesty International AI Index ASA 36/001/2004.

[32] Au (5/2011); Hor (2013) 141–2.

[33] Chan (2016) 200.

[34] See Appendix (Singapore).

[35] The PAP has ruled Singapore continuously since 1959, and held all the seats in the Parliament from 1968 to 1981 (Silverstein (2008) 93).

[36] See Constitution of Singapore 1965, art 22P. Presumably in reference to drugs and firearms offences from the mid-1970s onwards, Chan (2016, at 182) states that 'the death penalty was made mandatory on the expectation that clemency would be granted in appropriate cases'. See further note 13.

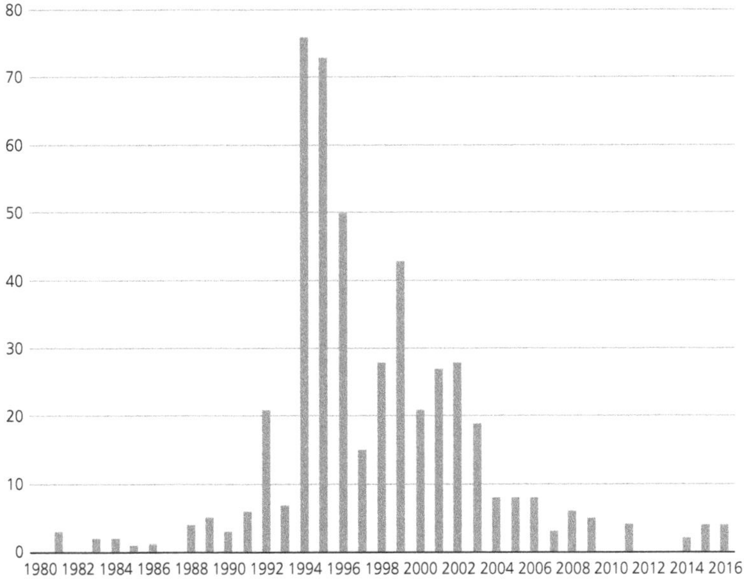

Figure 3 Executions in Singapore 1980–2016

Sources: Amnesty International Annual Report (1981); Johnson and Zimring (2009) (unofficial data 1980–90); Appendix (Singapore) (official data 1991–2016)

Clemency procedures in death penalty cases

Singapore's 1965 Constitution empowers the head of state, the president, to grant clemency in death penalty cases 'on the advice of the Cabinet'[37] (numbering twenty ministers in 2015).[38] In this context 'advice' means that, pursuant to the Westminster model of government which Singapore inherited from the United Kingdom, the Cabinet will collectively make the decision and the president must follow it, as has been confirmed by the Singapore Court of Appeal.[39] Irrespective of whether or not a prisoner asks

[37] Constitution of Singapore 1965, art 22P.

[38] Singapore Ministry of Communications and Information (2015).

[39] *Yong Vui Kong v Attorney-General* [2011] SGCA 9, [126], [150], [175], [180]; Lee (1994) 442–3.

for clemency, the Cabinet is mandated to consider the possibility of commuting every death sentence confirmed by the Court of Appeal.[40]

The Cabinet will rely on a number of documents during clemency deliberations. First, the Singaporean Constitution requires that the Attorney-General (the appointed government legal adviser, who is not a member of the Cabinet) considers reports written by the trial judge and lead appellate judge in the case, together with the evidence notes from the first instance trial, in making a written recommendation as to whether or not the death sentence should be commuted.[41] These four documents are put before the Cabinet for consideration as the constitutional 'clemency materials',[42] and are read in conjunction with the prisoner's clemency petition. Although it is not a formal legal right, allowing the prisoner to submit a written plea for clemency through the Singapore Prison Service within three months of the appeal judgement has become an established practice in capital cases.[43] Singaporean commentators and interviewees, and even former president SR Nathan (in office from 1999 to 2011), have all confirmed that, within Cabinet deliberations on clemency, the Attorney-General's constitutionally mandated advice is heavily influential, if not entirely determinative of each case.[44]

Before 1997, presidential clemency would reduce a death sentence to a twenty-year term of imprisonment, during which the petitioner could become eligible for full release after serving two-thirds of the term (at roughly thirteen years).[45] This occurred in all six of the cases described in this chapter, with several of the reprieved prisoners eventually released on parole. However, since

[40] *Yong Vui Kong v Attorney-General* [2011] SGCA 9, [82]–[83]. There is only one avenue of judicial appeal in capital cases in Singapore: from first-instance trial in the High Court, to the Court of Appeal (both part of the Supreme Court of Singapore). A second level of appeal, to the Privy Council in London, was abolished for death penalty appeals between 1989 and 1994 (Tan and Thio (2015) 99).

[41] Constitution of Singapore 1965, art 22P(2); Lee (2006) 472.

[42] Constitution of Singapore 1965, art 22P(2); *Yong Vui Kong v Attorney-General* [2011] SGCA 9, [82].

[43] *Yong Vui Kong v Attorney-General* [2011] SGCA 9, [114], [135]; Hor (2013) 152–3.

[44] 'Nathan Grants Zero Presidential Pardon during His 2 Terms' (2016); interview with Singaporean criminal defence lawyer #2; Lee (2006) 472, 477; Ghui (2011); interview with Singaporean NGO staff #3.

[45] Othman (2012); Siyuan (2012) 1–2.

a Court of Appeal ruling in 1997 which toughened the definition of 'life imprisonment', clemency in a death penalty case will now result in imprisonment for the term of the offender's natural life, with no prospect of parole.[46] No prisoner has yet been granted clemency under this new interpretation, with the most recent grant from President Ong Teng Cheong, in April 1998, operating under the 'old' rule.[47]

Features of cases where clemency was granted

As described earlier, the president of Singapore has granted clemency in only six death penalty cases during the post-independence era (1965 to the present). Despite this book's period of analysis commencing in 1991, it is worth relaying the facts of all historical cases to paint a complete picture of Singaporean clemency practice. The six cases, in the order that clemency was granted, are as follows:

1. 1978: Mohamad Kunjo Ramalan, 'a 56-year-old man convicted of murdering a friend during a drunken argument',[48] despite the defences of intoxication and 'sudden fight' being advanced by his lawyers during trial.[49] In rejecting Ramalan's appeal the Privy Council recommended clemency to the Singaporean authorities, based upon the mitigating factors of the case, and moreover the defendant's longer than usual wait on death row.[50]
2. 1980: Bobby Chung Hua Watt, who 'stabbed a man to death after his sister asked him to help her resolve her marital problems',[51] constituting an apparently 'spontaneous' murder, or a 'crime of passion'.[52] Watt was released from prison in 1993.[53]

46 *Hamsah v Public Prosecutor* [1997] 2 SLR(R) 842, [49]–[70].

47 *Kalimuthu v Attorney-General* [2012] SGHC 39, [24]–[27].

48 'A List of Death Row Inmates in Singapore Who Were Granted Clemency' (2005).

49 *Ramalan v Public Prosecutor* [1978] 2 WLR 130 (Privy Council), 132; 'Clemency Plea to Sheares by Man Sentenced to Die' (1978).

50 *Ramalan v Public Prosecutor* [1978] 2 WLR 130 (Privy Council), 136.

51 'A List of Death Row Inmates in Singapore Who Were Granted Clemency' (2005).

52 'President Grants Clemency to Mum on Death Row' (1992); statement by Singaporean law professor.

53 'Drug Trafficker Was Given Second Chance but She Blew It' (2001).

3. 1983:[54] Siti Aminah Jaafar,

> the first woman in Singapore to be sentenced to death for drug trafficking in 1978, was also the first drug trafficker to be given clemency in modern Singapore's history. Siti was 18 when convicted, and President Devan Nair's grant of clemency led to a term of life imprisonment.[55]

   Jaafar had been convicted 'for abetting her live-in lover in trafficking 43.5g of heroin … Her lover, who was 32, was hanged'.[56] Apart from her youth and gender, further mitigating circumstances may have included being the mother of a two-year-old son at the time of conviction,[57] and the impression that the accused had been 'used' by her lover to carry the drugs.[58] Jaafar was released in December 1991 after serving thirteen years and eight months,[59] but was later sentenced to a five-and-a-half year term of imprisonment for a new drugs offence.[60]
4. March 1992: Sim Ah Cheoh, 47, whose sentence for heroin trafficking was commuted by President Wee Kim Wee to life imprisonment. The Cabinet's reasons for recommending clemency are unknown, but Sim's expression of remorse for the crime, her clean criminal record, her being a mother of two, her poor and abusive upbringing,[61] and perhaps most importantly her manipulation by two men into being an accomplice in the crime[62] may each have proven influential. In 1995, while suffering from terminal cancer, Sim was released from prison by a second grant of clemency to allow her to

[54] 'Keep Death Penalty but Allow Leeway' (2009); Alfred (1983). Also reported as being granted in 1982 in 'A List of Death Row Inmates in Singapore Who Were Granted Clemency' (2005).

[55] 'A List of Death Row Inmates in Singapore Who Were Granted Clemency' (2005).

[56] 'Keep Death Penalty but Allow Leeway' (2009); Vijayan (2007).

[57] Alfred (1983).

[58] 'President Grants Clemency to Mum on Death Row' (1992).

[59] 'Drug Trafficker Was Given Second Chance but She Blew It' (2001).

[60] Chan (2016) 200.

[61] 'First Brush with Crime Nearly Sent Mum to Gallows' (1992).

[62] 'Murderer Escapes Gallows after President's Pardon' (1992); 'President Grants Clemency to Mum on Death Row' (1992).

spend the last few months of her life with her family. She died six weeks later.[63]

5. May 1992: Koh Swee Beng, 'convicted of killing a man who assaulted his foster father when he was 22', granted clemency by President Wee Kim Wee[64] possibly due to the fact that he had been diagnosed with the AIDS virus in prison.[65] The provocation defence had also been raised at trial,[66] although it is unknown whether this was a contributing factor toward the Cabinet's recommendation. Moreover, Koh's clemency petition stated that he 'came from a poor family, had a good and clean national service record and was not a secret society member'.[67]

(6) 1998: '19-year-old Mathavakannan Kalimuthu, who killed a 25-year-old gangster in a fight'[68] in the company of two other men.[69] Kalimuthu pleaded that 'it was the victim who had attacked and injured him first, and that he had not planned for [the victim] to die. He added that he was deeply remorseful ... His petition was supported by five letters, including one from his mother and another from her employer.'[70] Two Singaporean interviewees also speculated that Kalimuthu may have played a lesser role in the attack compared with his co-accused.[71] The two accomplices were hanged later the same year.[72] Kalimuthu was eventually released on parole in January 2012.[73]

Accordingly, although Cabinet deliberations and the official reasons for grants of clemency are kept secret (even from successful

[63] 'Prisoner Suffering from Cancer Granted Clemency' (1995); Chan (2016) 200; 'Thursday Special Report; Spared Death on Appeal' (2012).

[64] 'A List of Death Row Inmates in Singapore Who Were Granted Clemency' (2005).

[65] Statement by Singaporean law professor.

[66] *Public Prosecutor v Koh Swee Beng* [1990] SLR 405, 410; 'Labourer Gets Death for Killing Man Who Beat Up "Foster Father"' (1990).

[67] 'Presidential Pardon Saves Death Row Man from Gallows' (1992).

[68] 'A List of Death Row Inmates in Singapore Who Were Granted Clemency' (2005).

[69] 'Keep Death Penalty but Allow Leeway' (2009).

[70] Boon (1998).

[71] Statement by Singaporean law professor; interview with Singaporean criminal defence lawyer #2.

[72] See Amnesty International AI Index ASA 36/03/98.

[73] Othman (2012); 'Thursday Special Report; Spared Death on Appeal' (2012).

petitioners and their lawyers),[74] it is possible to deduce that commutations have historically been granted in select cases of:

- terminal illness;[75]
- youth or first offence;[76]
- a murder committed in spontaneous or provoked circumstances;
- the accused being an accomplice rather than the primary offender.

Expanding on the fourth factor, one further possibility is that defendants have been granted clemency after cooperating with police and prosecutors in securing the convictions of their accomplices in the crime. Three of those granted clemency since 1965 (Siti Aminah Jaafar, Sim Ah Cheoh, and Mathavakannan Kalimuthu) may have done so, based upon the known facts of their cases. Singapore's constitution explicitly provides for the possibility of sentence commutation or full pardon in these circumstances:

> The President, as occasion shall arise, may, on the advice of the Cabinet ... grant a pardon to any accomplice in any offence who gives information which leads to the conviction of the principal offender or any one of the principal offenders, if more than one.[77]

Notably, no other specific ground justifying clemency is listed in Article 22P. Nevertheless, this constitutionally sanctioned ground

[74] Interview with Singaporean criminal defence lawyer #2; 'Keep Death Penalty but Allow Leeway' (2009); Amnesty International AI Index ASA 36/001/2004, 16.

[75] One interviewee stated that 'my own view is that terminal illness is the safest bet for clemency ... I am almost [certain] that no one who was known to be terminally ill has been executed' (statement by Singaporean law professor).

[76] Statement by Singaporean law professor; interview with Singaporean criminal defence lawyer #2. In Singapore, no prisoner under eighteen years of age at the time of the offence may be executed (Criminal Procedure Code 2010 (Singapore), s 314). Juveniles who would be sentenced to death for the same crime are generally detained for 10–12 years, at the pleasure of the president (Anandan (2009) 205). In relation to the cases of Siti Aminah Jaafar and Mathavakannan Kalimuthu, 'it is not known if age was a factor in the deliberations' ('Keep Death Penalty but Allow Leeway' (2009)). The same article reports the 1995 execution of Tong Chieng Mun, a female drug trafficker who was only just past her eighteenth birthday at the time of the offence (see Introduction). The Singapore government once confirmed that around 5 per cent of prisoners executed between 1993 and 2003 were aged between eighteen and twenty years at the time of arrest (Singapore Government (2004)), which suggests that up to twenty very young prisoners were executed during that decade (see Appendix (Singapore)).

[77] Constitution of Singapore 1965, art 22P(1)(a).

for clemency may since have become redundant due to the short time span of recent cases from arrest to execution date. As I explain later in this chapter, agreeing to testify against co-defendants is now usually taken into account at the prosecutorial discretion stage, rather than at the clemency deliberation stage. Moreover, amendments passed to the Misuse of Drugs Act in 2012 now also allow for limited *judicial* discretion in similar circumstances, where the defendant (who must be a drug 'courier') provides information aiding drug enforcement efforts.[78] Yet within the three 1980s and 1990s cases just described, clemency as a reward for assisting the authorities remains a strong possibility.

Explaining the Low Clemency Rate in Singapore

Archival research and 'elite' interviews identify five factors that, together, explain why capital clemency has remained so rare throughout Singapore's independent history, irrespective of fluctuating execution rates. Of the explanations outlined in this chapter, three (rule of law ideology, the mandatory death penalty, and strong deterrence in drug-trafficking cases) reflect criminal justice philosophies long favoured by the PAP government. A fourth explanation concerns the resulting outlet for leniency in Singaporean death penalty cases—prosecutorial discretion—whereas the fifth factor relates to the Singapore Cabinet's decision-making processes.

The rule of law and the Singapore 'brand name'

The rule of law is a key component of Singaporean political ideology. A long-serving Chief Justice of Singapore, Yong Pung How (1990 to 2006), once stated: 'Singapore is a nation which is based wholly on the Rule of Law. It is clear and practical laws and the effective observance and enforcement of these laws which provide the foundation for our economic and social development.'[79]

In the present context, 'rule of law' embodies the notion that laws are applied equally to all subjects, all of the time,[80] and that executive discretion should not be allowed to subvert the outcome

[78] Lindsey and Nicholson (2016) 191.
[79] Silverstein (2008) 77.
[80] Nygh and Butt (1998) 387.

of judicial decisions.[81] During the PAP's long rule in Singapore, a purist philosophical position holding that defendants should be treated with absolute equality has been consistently applied within judicial and clemency decision-making.[82]

Throughout the period under study, and also long beforehand, Singaporean politicians believed that an award of clemency in less than compelling circumstances would create an unwelcome 'exception' to the equal application of the law to capital defendants. As Dr Teo Ho Pin, Chairman of the Government Parliamentary Committee for Home Affairs and Law, stated in 2007: 'I do not think that we should practise the King's pardon approach as in other countries which can be *quite ad hoc and arbitrary*.'[83] Over the years, the Singapore government has taken pride in portraying the image that every convicted capital prisoner is treated equally in the clemency process, whether foreign or Singaporean,[84] young or old,[85] male or female,[86] well-known or not.[87]

In this context, during Singapore's execution 'boom' of the 1990s and early 2000s, the execution of foreign nationals drew particular international attention. Amnesty International data suggest that of the executions carried out from 1993 to 2003, around 50 per cent were of foreign nationals,[88] while the

[81] Zee (2011) 38–9.

[82] Interview with London-based death penalty lawyer.

[83] Vijayan (2007), emphasis added.

[84] Shadrake (2011b) 78. For example, in 1994 Foreign Minister Shunmugan Jayakumar stated that any grant of clemency made to a foreigner:

> will be a serious breach in our battle to fight drug traffickers. All drug syndicates will start recruiting traffickers from countries opposed to [the] capital penalty once they know we will spare them. This is unacceptable. (Ngoo (1994))

[85] In 2011 the Minister for Law, K Shanmugam, stated that if clemency were extended to a young drug trafficker, 'drug lords would see it as a sign that young traffickers will be spared and would then use more of them as drug mules' (Shadrake (2011a) 7–8).

[86] Again, in a 2010 speech K Shanmugam emphasized the impartiality of Singapore's application of the death penalty. A grant of clemency would amount to:

> sending a signal to all the drug barons out there: Just make sure you choose a victim who is young, *or a mother of a young child*, and use them as the people to carry the drugs into Singapore. (Hands Off Cain, 'Singapore' (2010), emphasis added)

[87] See, for example, Anandan (2009) 166, and Johnson and Zimring (2009) 417 n13 and n15.

[88] Amnesty International AI Index ASA 36/001/2004, 7.

Singapore government admitted to a figure of 36 per cent over the same period.[89] Most of the foreigners executed came from neighbouring Southeast Asian nations;[90] however, a number of westerners were also hanged.[91] In 2011, Shadrake cited former foreign minister Shunmugan Jayakumar giving justification for the president's failure to award clemency to a single foreign national over the course of independent Singapore's history: '[Jayakumar] said that granting clemency on the grounds that capital punishment was [an] anathema to the country of origin of an offender would undermine Singapore's integrity and *reputation for impartial enforcement of the law*.'[92]

Neither widespread public support for death row prisoners,[93] nor diplomatic pressure from foreign governments,[94] nor vigorous campaigning from NGOs[95] has worked to produce executive clemency grants for foreigners or Singaporeans in the past. It appears that the Singapore Cabinet relies solely on its own evaluation of the case at hand when deciding clemency appeals,[96] apparently impervious to external political pressure at the clemency phase, which it considers an 'interference in the administration of justice'.[97] However, as I describe later in this section, the criminal justice system in Singapore is not entirely without mercy for defendants accused of mandatory death penalty offences. Selective leniency is instead present at the prosecutorial discretion stage, rather than at the executive clemency stage. All systems of justice, even those which proclaim the rule of law as sacred, contain some in-built avenues for lenient discretion[98]—Singapore

[89] Johnson and Zimring (2009) 416–17.

[90] 'Singapore, World Execution Capital' (1999); Oehlers and Tarulevicz (2005) 303.

[91] Markham and Phillips (2004); Fernandez (2005); 'Singapore Premier Says West Coddles Citizens' (1994).

[92] Shadrake (2011b) 78, emphasis added. See also Lee (2006) 477–9.

[93] See note 87.

[94] See for example, Hands Off Cain, 'Singapore' (2004); Hands Off Cain, 'Singapore' (2005); Amnesty International AI Index ASA 36/001/2004, 7, 11.

[95] Interview with international human rights NGO staff #4. Pressure from civil society groups may have contributed to the legislative reforms passed in 2012, but these allowed death row prisoners to be re-sentenced, rather than leading to executive clemency (Hor (2013) 164–5).

[96] Amnesty International AI Index ASA 36/001/2004, 16, quoting former prime minister Goh Chok Tong in 2003.

[97] Amnesty International AI Index ASA 36/001/2004, 7.

[98] Walker (1993) 4.

merely chooses to exercise this possibility at a less visible stage of proceedings.

Public justifications for the mandatory death penalty

The Singapore government's public justifications for retaining the mandatory death penalty for particular crimes provide a second explanation for clemency scarcity. As described above, the mandatory death penalty is imposed for selected murder, firearms, and drug-trafficking offences in Singapore. Together, these three offence groups have led to all of Singapore's executions from 1991 onwards.[99] The Singapore government has explicitly and implicitly invoked three main justifications for retaining mandatory capital punishment for these crimes, despite evolving international human rights standards which question the legality of mandatory death penalties under customary international law.[100] The government's three justifications are: to maximize marginal deterrence; to accord deserved retribution; and to maintain the consistency of political policies.

Regarding the latter, given PAP political leaders' long history of fervent statements in support of the mandatory death penalty in domestic politics and international forums such as the United Nations General Assembly,[101] arguably 'the Singapore government [has become] trapped by its own rhetoric',[102] and cannot completely abolish these laws without creating political liability. Indeed, the mandatory death penalty has been a deliberate 'flagship' policy for the PAP over the decades.[103] Instead of leading to the abolition of the mandatory death penalty altogether, the government's 2012 review only led to limited legislative exceptions,[104] which are discussed in further detail later in this chapter.

[99] Chan (2016) 183.

[100] See Hood and Hoyle (2015) 340, 348; *Yong Vui Kong v Public Prosecutor* [2010] SGCA 20, [43], [95]–[96]; McDermott (2010) 43–6.

[101] See, for example, Thio (2004b) 66–7; 'Singapore Defends Death Penalty in First Rights Report to UN' (2011); Kuppusamy (2007); Deen (1998); 'Row at UN over Call by EU for Moratorium on Death Penalty' (1999).

[102] Au (11/2011); interview with Singaporean NGO staff #4.

[103] Hor (2013) 148.

[104] Amnesty International AI Index ACT 50/7158/2017, 5–6.

On marginal deterrence (i.e. the purported increase in deterrent value between a discretionary death penalty and a stricter mandatory death penalty), Hor has observed that

> the attraction of a mandatory penalty to retentionist jurisdictions like Singapore is simple—if the purpose of the death penalty is maximum deterrence, then to make the penalty discretionary [at the judicial stage] would be likely to dilute the expected deterrence.[105]

Likewise, long-serving prime minister Lee Kuan Yew (in power from 1959 to 1990) articulated a fear that judges would not make use of discretionary death penalties if they were given the option to choose an appropriate sentence.[106] Lee's initial justification appears vindicated by the courts' treatment of kidnapping and gang robbery cases, which have not led to any executions in the period of study from 1991 to 2016, despite remaining capital offences.[107]

In this context, the 2012 legislative reforms in drug-trafficking and murder cases were, at least on their face, historically significant. The reforms constituted only the second occasion (following the new discretionary death sentence for treason in 2007) that capital punishment had been legislatively restricted since 1975.[108] Pursuant to the Penal Code (Amendment) Act 2012, only homicide committed with an intention to kill is now subject to the mandatory death penalty, with the other enumerated legal definitions of murder now attracting a discretionary death sentence.[109] For drug trafficking, following the Misuse of Drugs (Amendment) Act 2012, the mandatory death penalty no longer applies if the defendant can prove that he or she was simply a 'courier' in a trafficking operation, and if 'substantive assistance' is given to the authorities in an attempt to disrupt drug-trafficking activities, or

105 Hor (2004) 110.

106 Au (2010).

107 See note 16.

108 Hor (2013) 165.

109 Penal Code (Amendment) Act 2012 (Singapore), s 2. The other three *mens rea* for murder are an 'intention of causing such bodily injury as the offender knows to be likely to cause the death of the person to whom the harm is caused'; an 'intention of causing bodily injury to any person, and the bodily injury intended to be inflicted is sufficient in the ordinary course of nature to cause death', and 'if the person committing the act knows that it is so imminently dangerous that it must in all probability cause death, or such bodily injury as is likely to cause death, and commits such act' (Penal Code 2008 (Singapore), s 300(b)–(d)).

if he or she possessed impaired mental responsibility at the time of the offence.[110]

In these circumstances the court may sentence the person accused of murder or drug trafficking to death or to life imprisonment.[111] Yet defendants in firearms cases, non-couriers in drugs cases, and intentional killers remain unaffected by the reforms. Accordingly, activist Alex Au Waipang has argued that the 2012 legislation merely saw Singapore retreat from the mandatory death penalty 'by an inch'.[112] Publicly, the Singapore government still insists that the mandatory death penalty deters crime.[113]

Third, from a purely retributive point of view, the mandatory death penalty is also intended to signify publicly that, once committed with the requisite *mens rea*, a crime is considered so serious that forgiveness at any level is simply not an option, irrespective of any attenuating circumstances.[114] As Ledewitz and Staples observe, in a death penalty regime such as Singapore's, 'commutation is never deserved because the mandatory penalty dictates that death is deserved … The legal system has determined that such inmates deserve to die for what they did.'[115]

In light of these three factors underpinning Singapore's mandatory death penalty policy, the publicly reported use of lenient discretion to mitigate punishment here would, in the eyes of the PAP government, have the same compromising result irrespective of whether it were employed by the judiciary (i.e. in sentencing) or later by the executive (i.e. in sentence enforcement, via clemency). The purported criminological and political benefits of retaining the mandatory death penalty in Singapore strongly depend on there being very few public exceptions made to its enforcement.[116] Singapore's technocratic leaders perceive there is little to gain (and much to lose) from dispensing clemency freely in mandatory death penalty cases—a quite different position from

[110] Misuse of Drugs (Amendment) Act 2012 (Singapore), s 14.

[111] Misuse of Drugs Act 2001 (Singapore), s 33B(1); Penal Code 2008 (Singapore), s 302(2). Other than in cases of drug couriers suffering from impaired responsibility, the court must also pass a mandatory sentence of caning on the defendants covered by these reforms.

[112] Au (2012).

[113] Shanmugam (2017); Au (2012).

[114] See Singapore Government (2004).

[115] Ledewitz and Staples (1993) 230. See also Johnson and Zimring (2009) 309.

[116] Hor (2013) 142, 164; Chan (2016) 185–6.

that of the absolute monarchs and other unelected autocrats considered in Chapter 2.[117]

Drug-trafficking policy: Maximizing deterrence

The Singapore government's strong rhetoric against narcotics and the high proportion of executions for drug-trafficking crimes (71 per cent from 1991 to 2016)[118] justify consideration of the government's policy towards drug crime as a separate explanation for Singapore's historically low clemency rate. Singaporean politicians have historically seen drug trafficking as a kind of mass 'sabotage' of national economic productivity,[119] and an even more serious crime than murder,[120] or even serial killing,[121] due to its perceived implications for the long-term security of the state.[122] As Clammer notes, in Singapore:

> crime is not just an assault on private property or the person, but reflects something deeper—a pollution or cancer are terms often heard locally—which like a germ or virus must be stamped out before it begins to infect even wider ranges of the social order ... If crime in general is paradigmatic of social disorder in Singapore, drug offences are somehow the centre of that paradigm.[123]

In a manner similar to other Southeast Asian nations, Singapore likes to view itself as particularly vulnerable to drug-trafficking syndicates, owing to its 'small size and location near the Golden Triangle'[124] as well as its trade-based economy.[125] This is, of course, one reason for the high proportion of foreigners executed—many

[117] See Chapter 2.

[118] See note 15.

[119] Johnson and Zimring (2009) 415; Hor (2004) 109 n31; Lindsey and Nicholson (2016) 143.

[120] Jayakumar (1989); McDermott (2010) 51.

[121] Amnesty International AI Index ASA 36/001/2004, 12.

[122] Hor (2004) 108 n30; Phang (1990) 233–4; Lindsey and Nicholson (2016) 164.

[123] Clammer (1997) 142. See also Lindsey and Nicholson (2016) 137.

[124] Singapore Government (2004).

[125] McMahon (2017) 135.

are drug 'mules' caught attempting to smuggle narcotics into or out of Singapore from neighbouring Southeast Asian countries.[126]

Despite limited empirical evidence,[127] it has long been the Singaporean political establishment's view that a rational 'calculus' is being made by drug offenders. Syndicate masterminds and couriers are thought to weigh the risk of arrest, together with the severity of punishment, against the financial rewards for importing or exporting narcotics.[128] Accordingly, since 1975 one of the government's key criminal justice policies has been to maintain the 'purity' of deterrence against a crime regarded not only as the most serious criminal problem faced by Singapore's population, but also as an offence which may be prevented by the threat of severe punishment.[129] In contrast, the Singapore government does not regard deterrent punishment as equally effective in preventing 'spontaneous' or 'provoked' violent offences.[130]

To maintain the 'purity' of general deterrence for drug offences, the death penalty must be mandatory not only at the judicial level, but also at the level of executive clemency: there must be very few, if any, public exceptions made to its enforcement (although, as I will explain shortly, prosecutors frequently create exceptions behind closed doors). Among the hundreds of cases considered by the Cabinet since independence, only two drug traffickers have ever received clemency, and both were Singaporean-born mothers whose cases bore significant mitigating features. Only one of these cases (Sim Ah Cheoh) occurred after 1991. Numerically, the 1991–2016 clemency rate for drug cases stands at approximately 0.3 per cent—an extraordinarily low figure, even lower than the overall rate of 0.6 per cent.[131] As an experienced Singaporean criminal

[126] Johnson and Zimring (2009) 416; 'Singapore, World Execution Capital' (1999).

[127] Lindsey and Nicholson (2016) 164; Chan (2016) 186; Amnesty International AI Index 51/02/95, 67.

[128] Interview with London-based death penalty lawyer; Shanmugam (2012); Hor (2006) 522; McDermott (2010) 51.

[129] Hor (2006) 530; Chan (2016) 186; Lindsey and Nicholson (2016) 164.

[130] Shanmugam (2012); Kow (2009) 1116; McDermott (2010) 51; Hor (2006) 518 n64, 522.

[131] See Appendix (Singapore). Clemency has *never* been granted in a capital firearms or security case, although the total number of cases since 1991 (nine executions—around 2 per cent of the total) is much lower than for drugs offences (Chan (2016) 183; Singapore Prison Service (2017) 10).

defence lawyer noted when interviewed, other than when terminal illness triggers a compassionate response from the Cabinet, once a defendant's death sentence for drug trafficking is confirmed on appeal, 'the law will take its course'.[132]

Prosecutorial discretion supplanting executive discretion

Nevertheless, despite the government's longstanding mandatory death penalty policy for drug trafficking, murder and certain firearms offences, not all offenders who are arrested for capital crimes in Singapore end up being executed—far from it. The prominence of prosecutorial discretion as the government's preferred solution to the inherent inflexibility of the mandatory death penalty provides a fourth structural reason for Singapore's low clemency rate. In Singapore, as in other retentionist jurisdictions, quietly made discretionary decisions at the 'front end' of the criminal justice system (i.e. by prosecutors, and during police investigations) will have significant influence over the more public discretionary decisions at the 'back end' of the system (i.e. concerning commutations, pardons, and execution warrants).[133] In other words, the more often cases are filtered away from death eligibility before trial, the less use executive clemency has as a remedial mechanism.

The mandatory death penalty's inflexibility creates two main problems for the Singaporean executive and judiciary. The first is the inability to differentiate sentencing for offenders exhibiting strongly mitigating circumstances, such as youth or assistance to law enforcement authorities. In addition to case-specific inflexibility, the mandatory death penalty also prevents the Singapore government from reducing execution rates for policy reasons. Notably, after the adverse international attention focused on Singapore following its labelling as 'world execution capital' and 'a theme park with the death sentence' during the 1990s and 2000s,[134] national leaders sought to reduce annual execution totals to internationally acceptable rates. To do so publicly via mass clemency or through legislative reform would, however, have been seen as directly bowing to international pressure.[135]

[132] Interview with Singaporean criminal defence lawyer.
[133] Lim and Yong (2006); Johnson and Zimring (2009) 309; Han (2010).
[134] 'Singapore, World Execution Capital' (1999); Clammer (1997) 142; Au (11/2011); interview with international human rights NGO staff #4.
[135] Interview with Singaporean NGO staff; Hor (2006) 539.

For the Singapore government, the acceptable, face-saving solution has been to individualize punishment and avoid executions by bringing non-capital charges[136] (or, in a minority of cases, diversion to detention without trial).[137] Here, instead of consideration by the Cabinet during clemency deliberations, any evidentiary shortcomings,[138] together with mitigating circumstances that justify a lesser punishment such as the relative youth (18–21 years) or minimal criminal record of the offender,[139] mental impairment,[140] testifying against co-offenders,[141] or—most controversially—the

[136] Statement by Singaporean law professor; Lim and Yong (2006); Lee (2006) 480. In 2011, a senior criminal lawyer observed that the reduction of capital charges to non-capital charges had taken place far more often since the retirement of Attorney-General Tan Boon Teik (1969–92) (interview with Singaporean criminal defence lawyer #2).

[137] From the 1980s onwards, certain drug-trafficking suspects have been detained for renewable one-year periods pursuant to the Criminal Law (Temporary Provisions) Act 1955 (Singapore) (Freedom House (2002a); Tremewan (1996) 200; interview with Singaporean human rights lawyer; '366 Criminal Law Detentions in Five Years' (2009)). Terrorism suspects are also routinely detained under the Internal Security Act 1985 (Singapore) (Lee (2012) 6; US Department of State (2011) 4–5). Additionally, the Misuse of Drugs Act 2001 (Singapore), s 34(5) also allows the detention of drug addicts in rehabilitation centres for up to three years.

In some cases where the mandatory death penalty might otherwise apply but where a case exhibits mitigating circumstances, administrative detention enables the Singapore government to control the criminal threat without attracting even greater international scrutiny for adding to its total of judicial executions. However, it is unlikely that the diversion of cases away from prosecution to administrative detention is carried out in Singapore on such a scale as is conducted in Malaysia (see Chapter 5). The main cases dealt with by preventive detention in Singapore are those where there is insufficient evidence to conduct a prosecution (interview with Singaporean human rights lawyer; '366 Criminal Law Detentions in Five Years' (2009); Erlanger (1989)), hence administrative detention would have little practical impact on the clemency-to-execution ratio.

[138] 'Public Prosecutorial Discretion Exercised Carefully' (2012); *Ravinthran v Attorney-General* [2012] SGCA 2, [24], [52]. Evidentiary shortcomings and possible defences are generally taken into account at the prosecutor's discretion stage, rather than at the adjudication stage, where there are very few acquittals. As Hor notes, in Singapore 'an acquittal is analogous to judicial disagreement with an executive decision as to guilt. Thus, judicial disagreement with the executive is rare' (Hor (2002) 507).

[139] Statement by Singaporean law professor; interview with Singaporean criminal defence lawyer; 'Yong Vui Kong Gets to See His Next Birthday' (2010).

[140] Statement by Singaporean law professor; Vijayan (2012).

[141] Lum (2012); *Ravinthran v Attorney-General* [2012] SGCA 2, [52], [78].

offender's nationality (if he or she is from an abolitionist country or a powerful trading partner),[142] are taken into account during the prosecutor's consideration of the case, behind closed doors.[143] Following the conclusion of this process, the vast majority of defendants whose cases have been assessed by public prosecutors as still deserving of capital prosecution will not be able to find any novel extenuating circumstances to present before the Cabinet for clemency.

On the mechanics of charge reduction, the Attorney-General of Singapore and his deputy prosecutors have, in select cases, replaced mandatory death penalty murder charges with charges for non-capital 'culpable homicide' (equivalent to manslaughter under Singaporean law). Despite the defendant killing with the requisite *mens rea*, prosecutors classify the case as falling within one of seven partial statutory defences to capital murder, even if the *real* reasons for reducing the charge fall outside the legislation (as suggested previously).[144] Accordingly, Hor observes that the 'death penalty for murder is only mandatory in so far as the *courts* are concerned',[145] with the common practice being that defence lawyers write to the prosecutor after the preliminary hearing in order to make representations to amend the charge.[146]

For narcotics cases, the impact of prosecutorial discretion in potential mandatory death penalty cases is strikingly indicated by the so-called 14.99 charge, whereby the prosecutor artificially reduces the net weight of illegal drugs that an accused trafficker is found to be carrying to an amount fractionally below the capital threshold. Trafficking 15 grams or more of heroin is charged as trafficking in 'not less than' 14.99 grams; 30 grams of cocaine

142 MARUAH (2011) [6]; Shadrake (2011a) 67. Former foreign minister Shunmugam Jayakumar once denied that Singapore uses prosecutorial discretion in this manner (Jayakumar (2011) 152–3).

143 The official reasons for downgrading potential capital charges are not normally revealed to the public (*Ravinthran v Attorney-General* [2012] SGCA 2, [74]–[78]).

144 Hor (2006) 513–14, 533. The seven partial statutory defences are: provocation; defence of property; exceeding powers of law enforcement; sudden fight; assisting suicide; infanticide; and abnormality of mind (Penal Code 2008 (Singapore), s 300). The maximum punishment for culpable homicide is life imprisonment (s 304).

145 Hor (2006) 514, emphasis added.

146 Interview with Singaporean criminal defence lawyer; Hor (2006) 513.

is charged as 29.99 grams; 500 grams of cannabis is charged as 499.9 grams, and so forth.[147] Unlike when downgrading murder charges, Singapore's public prosecutors appear to make these reductions unilaterally,[148] on the basis of the policy factors and mitigating circumstances described previously. Indeed, in a 2013 speech, former Attorney-General Steven Chong stated that, based on the policy of the Attorney-General's Chambers, '[c]apital charges will generally not be preferred for trafficking between say 15 and 25 grammes of diamorphine [heroin]'.[149]

By reducing charges from capital to non-capital through these methods, the Singaporean executive (in the Attorney-General's guise as public prosecutor)[150] has been able to achieve a number of political and criminological aims. Compelling mitigating circumstances can be considered on a case-by-case basis, without outwardly compromising the marginal deterrence value of the mandatory death penalty.[151] Moreover, at least since 2004, the annual number of judicial executions could be stabilized at a level attracting far less international criticism, without abolishing the mandatory death penalty as a PAP flagship policy.[152] Indeed, Hor estimated in 2013 that Singapore's death row population was potentially as much as 70 per cent lower as a result of increased prosecutorial discretion from 2004 onwards.[153] With prosecutorial discretion being used so frequently in this manner, the executive

[147] Tey (2010) 317, 317 n15; Lum (2012); Hor (2013) 163, 164 n90; Shadrake (2011b) 143; Au (11/2011). See Hor (2006) 534 n114 for individual case examples. The Singapore Court of Appeal has stated that in circumstances such as these:

> the Prosecution is not denying any scientific fact, but is instead simply reducing the quantity of drugs specified in the charge against one offender in order to give effect to its decision to charge that offender differently from his co-offender. (*Ravinthran v Attorney-General* [2012] SGCA 2, [65])

[148] Interview with Singaporean criminal defence lawyer; Chong (2013) 7.

[149] Chong (2013) 7.

[150] Although the Singapore Attorney-General is nominally independent from the elected government (Constitution of Singapore 1965, art 35(8)), some commentators and interviewees have questioned the extent to which prosecutorial decisions are free from government interference (Tan (2016); interview with Singaporean human rights activist; interview with Singaporean NGO staff #4). Hor observes that public prosecutors in Singapore 'work together with the Executive in the pursuit of legitimate governmental aims' (Hor (2006) 510).

[151] See Shanmugam (2012).

[152] Hor (2013) 148.

[153] Hor (2013) 167.

clemency process is sidelined entirely as a means of preventing executions for humanitarian or policy reasons.

Finally, since the 2012 legislative amendments, slightly more discretion has been returned to the judiciary, who may now, in limited circumstances, sentence murderers and drug couriers to life imprisonment instead of death.[154] Yet it is difficult to know whether many more potential death sentences are now reduced to lesser punishments via the new laws, as opposed to the more traditional downgrading of charges by prosecutors alone. It may be that the legislative reforms simply codified prosecutors' existing practices.[155] The broad array of mitigating and policy factors identified earlier in the chapter suggests that prosecutorial discretion still continues to play a key role in downgrading capital charges.[156] If anything, these new outlets for discretion at the sentencing stage have only made it more difficult for condemned prisoners to plead for and receive clemency from the president of Singapore. As with prosecutorial discretion, any method which removes less deserving cases from the threat of execution at an earlier stage in the judicial process greatly reduces clemency's utility as a retributive safeguard against excessive or undeserved punishment, and as a means of effecting broader policy goals.

Aspects of the clemency decision-making process: Cabinet dynamics and bureaucratic efficiency

Finally, the Singapore Cabinet's decision-making processes, placed in the wider context of the culture of efficiency promoted within government and the civil service, also have a likely impact on the frequency of clemency grants. There are four possible factors at

[154] See notes 109–111 and associated text.

[155] Hor (2013) 165–6; Amnesty International AI Index ACT 50/7158/2017, 26. By November 2015, available data suggested that at least thirteen death row convicts had been 're-sentenced' pursuant to this provision (Amnesty International (2015)). From 1 January 2013 to 30 September 2017, of the combined total of prisoners resentenced, plus prisoners tried under the new provisions, thirty-eight defendants (41 per cent) were spared the death sentence (Amnesty International AI Index ACT 50/7158/2017, 6).

[156] Hor (2013) 167. Moreover, the recent amendments also empower the Attorney-General's Chambers to determine whether or not a drug courier has provided 'substantive assistance' (Misuse of Drugs Act 2001 (Singapore), s 33B(2)(b)).

play here. First, the fact that the president must accept the recommendation of the Cabinet, in accordance with the head of state's 'ceremonial' role within the Westminster tradition,[157] negates the president's chances of granting clemency 'on a whim', with compassionate mercy the sole guiding motive.[158] Over the years, only the most compelling retributivist or utilitarian justifications have prompted the Singapore Cabinet to approve clemency, as described earlier in the chapter. A group of between sixteen and twenty ministers during the period of study,[159] the Cabinet remains a forum where a communal, consensus-based decision-making structure may encourage what one interviewee labelled a 'lowest common denominator' approach to decision-making.[160] Within the Cabinet, a risk-averse presumption against granting clemency likely exists,[161] even if there is a legal duty to consider each and every death sentence for clemency. Two interviewees speculated that, given the large number of capital cases that pass before the Cabinet for consideration, unless specifically concerned ministers (such as those responsible for the home affairs or law portfolios) were to raise an issue regarding one of the petitions, a motion would be passed to reject all of them.[162]

It is also likely that Cabinet consideration of clemency applications was influenced by the views of the late Lee Kuan Yew, Singapore's first prime minister. During his forty-six-year period as a Cabinet minister (from Singapore's independence in 1965, through to retirement as prime minister in 1990, and latterly until retirement from the Cabinet as senior minister in 2011), Lee was known to espouse absolutist views on maintaining the 'purity'

[157] *Yong Vui Kong v Attorney-General* [2011] SGCA 9, [177], [180]; 'A List of Death Row Inmates in Singapore Who Were Granted Clemency' (2005).

[158] See further Chapter 2.

[159] Lee (1991) 141; Singapore Ministry of Communications and Information (2015).

[160] Interview with London-based death penalty lawyer; interview with Singaporean NGO staff #3.

[161] Interview with Singaporean NGO staff #4. As first noted in Chapter 2, in jurisdictions where a large number of clemency petitions pass before the executive, particular presumptions or 'rules of thumb' will be needed to manage the caseload (Hawkins (1992) 39).

[162] Interview with Singaporean law professor and Singaporean NGO staff #5. See also Jayakumar (2011) 155, reiterating the importance of these ministers' views, along with the Minister for Foreign Affairs for foreign defendants.

of deterrence in death penalty cases,[163] and his opinions on this policy and others are likely to have carried significant weight within Cabinet.[164] The prediction of one interviewee—echoing the views of death penalty scholars Johnson and Zimring—that the Singapore government's position on the need for an absolute 'purity' of deterrence might change after Lee's departure from a senior decision-making role[165] appears to have been vindicated after the legislative changes announced in 2012 came into force.

Third, the Cabinet appears to be significantly influenced by the constitutionally mandated recommendation on clemency by the Attorney-General,[166] the appointed state legal adviser, who, as described earlier, concurrently performs the role of Singapore's public prosecutor. As first articulated in Chapter 2, in jurisdictions which rely on a written recommendation on capital clemency from the prosecuting authority, professional pride and bureaucratic inertia generally conspire against any mitigation.[167] Indeed, Singaporean opponents of the death penalty have labelled this constitutional arrangement a 'conflict of interest', a 'farce', or a breach of natural justice.[168] Given that prosecutorial discretion is available to reduce the charge to a non-capital one if the case exhibits significant mitigating circumstances, why would the Attorney-General suggest a reduction at the clemency phase? We Believe in Second Chances, an anti-death penalty NGO from Singapore, has neatly summarized the dilemma:

> After charging the offender, prosecuting him at trial, then fighting against his appeal, just how likely is [it that] the AG [is] going to say, 'You know what, I was wrong to demand the death penalty in court, this person doesn't deserve to die after all, let's pardon him'?[169]

163 Interview with London-based death penalty lawyer; statement by former Singaporean politician; Erlanger (1989).

164 Statement by former Singaporean politician; Quah (2001) 291–2.

165 Interview with London-based death penalty lawyer; Johnson and Zimring (2009) 419.

166 Interview with Singaporean criminal defence lawyer #2; We Believe in Second Chances (2011); Lee (2006) 460–1, 477; Ravi (2005) 79.

167 Abramowitz and Paget (1964) 171; Barkow (2009) 156.

168 Ravi (2005) 79; Trembat (2005); We Believe in Second Chances (2011). The Singapore Court of Appeal has denied that this procedure creates a legal conflict of interest: *Yong Vui Kong v Attorney-General* [2011] SGCA 9, [110].

169 We Believe in Second Chances (2011).

If the prisoner's circumstances were to change after a long period spent on death row, this may be one foreseeable scenario for a recommendation in favour of commutation to be made by the case prosecutor. However, defendants in Singapore's ultra-efficient criminal justice system rarely possess the luxury of pleading for clemency as 'redemption',[170] which links to a fourth and final observation.

The clemency outcomes in Singaporean death penalty cases are also a reflection of the culture of efficiency found within the three branches of government. From arrest through to trial, appeal, and the determination of clemency, the usual time a capital prisoner spends in detention in Singapore ranges from one year to eighteen months.[171] As observed in Chapter 2, the expeditious processing of death penalty cases through the criminal justice system will reduce possible justifications for clemency. There will be little time for new mitigating circumstances to arise (such as psychiatric illness or old age). The same holds true in Singapore.[172] With no little sarcasm, Hor summarizes: 'there is no death row phenomenon in Singapore because executions are carried out with wonderful efficiency.'[173]

Clemency's Arbitrariness

Successful clemency applications in Singapore have been so few and far between that it has been possible to list them in their entirety in this chapter. In none of the other jurisdictions under study is it possible to do the same. The apparent conclusion is that the Singapore Cabinet, already constrained by its own restrictive decision-making processes, actively seeks to avoid

[170] See Chapter 2. The one exception here may have been the case of Mohamad Kunjo Ramalan, whose grant of clemency was recommended by the Privy Council on the basis of (only) two years spent on death row (see *Ramalan v Public Prosecutor* [1978] 2 WLR 130 (Privy Council), 136).

[171] Interview with Singaporean criminal defence lawyer; interview with Singaporean criminal defence lawyer #2; Johnson (2013) 43. Delays caused by judicial appeals were longer in the pre-1994 period, due to the prospect of Privy Council appeals (interview with Singaporean criminal defence lawyer).

[172] Interview with international human rights NGO staff #4; interview with Singaporean criminal defence lawyer #2; interview with Singaporean NGO staff #2.

[173] Hor (2004) 115. See also Novak (2014) 87.

granting clemency in as many cases as possible. However, this is not to say that Singapore's criminal justice system, which incorporates the mandatory death penalty for murder, drug trafficking, and firearms offences, lacks any form of compassionate discretion. For the PAP government, authorizing regular grants of executive clemency in capital cases would invite allegations that the state's uncompromising approach to the rule of law was being undermined, and that Singapore's politicians were becoming 'soft' in their stance on drug trafficking. Instead, it is clear that the preferred means of taking into account individual mitigating circumstances, as well as any political imperative to reduce execution rates, has been through prosecutorial discretion—at least until the 2012 legislative changes allowed for limited judicial discretion. Through prosecutorial discretion, capital charges are reduced behind closed doors, before a trial takes place, without outwardly compromising either the general deterrence of capital crimes or the political imperative (and historical tradition) to maintain the mandatory death penalty for crimes deemed the most serious by the Singapore government.

Given the Singapore Cabinet's clear aversion to clemency, and the existing means to exercise leniency through prosecutorial discretion, the final question to ask is why any clemency grants have been made *at all* during Singapore's independent history. This question is the exact opposite to the one I considered in relation to Thailand during the previous chapter. Singapore's six successful clemency cases, described in detail earlier in this chapter, provide clues. First, terminal illness as a mitigating factor would not yet have been diagnosed during the charging process.[174] If it were, it is unlikely that the suspect would be sentenced to death in the first place.[175] Second, two of the three prisoners possibly granted clemency for assisting police and prosecutors in their accomplices' cases were arrested long before Singaporean prosecutors began to bring lesser charges in exchange for cooperation.[176] Third, some cases with particularly deserving mitigating features may

[174] See the cases of Koh Swee Beng and Sim Ah Cheoh. Terminal illness only became relevant in Sim Ah Cheoh's case once her death sentence had already been commuted to life imprisonment.

[175] See note 75.

[176] See note 136, and the cases of Siti Aminah Jaafar and Sim Ah Cheoh.

also have 'slipped through the cracks' during the prosecutorial discretion phase.

Yet it is also likely that many cases with very similar features to those involving Mohamad Kunjo Ramalan, Bobby Chung Hua Watt, Siti Aminah Jaafar, Sim Ah Cheoh, and Mathavakannan Kalimuthu have resulted in the defendants being executed, rather than charged with non-capital offences and imprisoned. Arbitrariness has clearly played a major role in sparing some defendants through clemency, but not others. As with executions in discretionary death penalty jurisdictions such as the United States and India,[177] in Singapore clemency forms part of a 'lethal lottery' within the administration of the mandatory death penalty. The key difference is that in Singapore, death is the overwhelmingly likely outcome once a capital defendant is brought to court, rather than any lesser punishment.

[177] Amnesty International AI Index ASA 20/006/2008, 1; Steiker and Steiker (2016) 2.

5

Federation of Malaysia

[T]he state gets its perceived deterrent benefit of the threat of mandatory death, but is spared both much of the difficulty of administering it and the international embarrassment of too many executions.

Sidney L Harring, commenting on Malaysia's mandatory death penalty in 1991[1]

Inherited from the British colonial administration, the death penalty by hanging has occupied a prominent place in Malaysia's criminal justice system since Malayan independence in 1957.[2] From 1960 to the beginning of 2011, 441 prisoners were executed (an average of 8.5 per year), with drug trafficking the most prominent capital offence.[3] Within Southeast Asia, the only retentionist region in which a majority of death sentences are passed on drug traffickers,[4] Malaysia's drug laws were once the most punitive of all, characterized by the mandatory death penalty applying to all traffickers[5] and a 'no mercy' policy towards drug convicts applying for clemency from 1983 to the early 1990s.[6]

[1] Harring (1991) 404.

[2] The Federation of Malaya incorporated modern-day peninsular Malaysia, and became independent from the United Kingdom in 1957. Malaysia was formed in 1963 after Singapore, Sabah, and Sarawak were added to the Federation. Singapore was expelled and became an independent state in 1965.

[3] Hector (2012).

[4] See Amnesty International AI Index ASA 01/003/2007.

[5] Dangerous Drugs Act 1952 (Malaysia), s 2, 39B. The definition of 'trafficking' here was expanded in 1977 to include 'manufacturing, importing, exporting, keeping, concealing, buying, selling, giving, receiving, storing, administering, transporting, carrying, sending, delivering, procuring, supplying or distributing any dangerous drug' (Dangerous Drugs (Amendment) (No 2) Act 1977 (Malaysia), s 2).

[6] During his second reading speech to Parliament before the 1983 mandatory death penalty amendment was passed, Prime Minister Mahathir Mohamad

Last Chance for Life: Clemency in Southeast Asian Death Penalty Cases. First Edition. Daniel Pascoe. Published 2019 by Oxford University Press.

Nevertheless, given the Malaysian government's reliance on the mandatory death penalty to denounce and deter drug offences, firearms offences, and murder, it is curious that members of the Malaysian monarchy and relevant state governors approved clemency for capital prisoners in approximately 55–63 per cent of finalized cases between 1991 and 2016. A concerted push to lower execution rates from the mid-1990s[7] provides only part of the explanation. At least where reasons are ascertainable, most clemency grants over the period of study reflect individual case characteristics rather than broader policy goals.[8]

In contrast with its neighbour Singapore, the Malaysian experience suggests that legislating for a mandatory death penalty across a variety of offences and propagating a public image of government ruthlessness against crime is not necessarily inconsistent with the widespread use of clemency. Although academic investigation of Malaysia's death penalty and clemency policies is significantly hampered by the prevailing government secrecy over executions and clemency decisions,[9] this chapter analyses the possible factors that have led to Malaysia's moderately high clemency rate over the period of study, despite notable structural obstacles to mercy.

described drug traffickers as 'cruel, mercenary killers, "traders in death, destruction and traffickers in suffering", and added that such persons were completely undeserving of forgiveness and compassion' (Tan and Harn (2007)). By 1992, 'Almost all convicted drug traffickers' appeals for clemency to Malaysian pardons boards [had] been rejected', whether from Malaysians or foreigners ('Rocky Man to Hang' (1992); Baker (1992)). Talib (1989, at 109) recorded one grant of clemency and thirty-nine executions for drug trafficking from 1983 to 1986 across the Federation, whereas the news agency Reuters reported in 1991 that no commutation or pardon had ever been granted in a federal drug trafficking case ('Indonesian Lawyers Seek Mercy for Condemned Drug Offenders' (1991)).

[7] See Appendix (Malaysia).

[8] There has been a small increase in clemency frequency since the 1980s, but not large enough to account entirely for the precipitous decline in executions. Compare Talib (1989, at 118) (49+ grants from 1975 to 1986) with Palansamy (2015) (127 grants from 1998 to 2015). See also Donoghue (2013) 236, 239.

[9] Of the four nations under study, Malaysia's state secrecy in death penalty cases is the most pervasive. Throughout Malaysia's history, comprehensive death penalty statistics and information have proven difficult to come by, and no official figures are published by the federal government (Harring (1991) 400 n225; UN Office of the High Commissioner for Human Rights (2014) 25). Detailed information on the use of capital punishment generally only appears in the public domain after a question by an opposition member of parliament (Interview with

Death Penalty and Clemency Practice 1991–2016

Death sentences and executions

Malaysia's modern death penalty story begins in 1975, well before the period under analysis. It was from this year that the government's now well-documented campaign against drugs began, with capital punishment introduced as a discretionary penalty for drug traffickers.[10] Although opium use had a long history among the ethnic Chinese population in Malaysia, the use of the country's seaports and airports as transit points for Golden Triangle heroin en route to the West from the 1970s, together with 'the arrival of a western-type, youth-culture drug problem' in domestic markets, prompted the government of Prime Minister Abdul Razak to pass legislative amendments to the Dangerous Drugs Act 1952, making trafficking a capital offence for the first time.[11] The year 1975 also saw radical new trial procedures enacted for the various mandatory and discretionary firearms, explosives, and ammunition offences (known as 'security offences') created by the Internal Security Act 1960, to ensure a higher conviction rate.[12] Here, the Razak government's stated justification was to counter the low-level insurgency waged by the Malayan Communist Party.[13] However, the Internal Security Act and other 'emergency' laws also allowed the Barisan Nasional government[14] to strengthen its own semi-authoritarian rule over the decades.

international human rights NGO staff #2; interview with Malaysian human rights lawyer). As for clemency decisions, Hector (2015) observes:

> Information about the whole process of application for pardon is not easily available to the public. Neither are the principles or the considerations that are relevant in making or considering such application.

[10] Dangerous Drugs (Amendment) Act 1975 (Malaysia), s 39B; Harring (1991) 365. Under the original Dangerous Drugs Act 1952 (Malaysia), the maximum penalty for trafficking was five years imprisonment.

[11] Harring (1991) 365, 368–9, 379; Schwarz (1987).

[12] Lent (1984) 444–5; Penna (1987) 109–10. These new trial procedures were imposed pursuant to the Essential (Security Cases) Regulations 1975. Regulation 2 defines 'security offences' as those present within ss 57–62 of the Internal Security Act 1960 (Malaysia).

[13] Lent (1984) 444.

[14] At a federal level, the UMNO (United Malays National Organization) political party held power as part of a coalition government (called the Barisan

As Baxstrom observes, in Malaysia 'the threat of communism is now widely regarded as a straw man in contemporary political debates'.[15]

Thereafter, following inconsistent sentencing practices in drug-trafficking cases from 1975,[16] in 1983 the Malaysian parliament made the death penalty mandatory for trafficking in scheduled drugs, and reduced the weight threshold required to presume trafficking to 15 grams for pure heroin or morphine, 40 grams for cocaine, and 200 grams for cannabis or cannabis resin.[17] From this point forward, Malaysia had proclaimed itself as having the world's toughest drug laws.[18] Throughout the remainder of the 1980s and through to the mid-1990s, the government of Prime Minister Dr Mahathir Mohamed (in power from 1981 to 2003) saw drug crime as the country's premier security concern, eclipsing the threat of domestic communist insurgency and the mass influx of refugees fleeing the communist regime in Vietnam.[19] In keeping with this heightened concern, Malaysian authorities hanged more than 120 prisoners convicted of capital drug offences from 1983 to 1992.[20]

Overall, in Malaysia, as in neighbouring Singapore, drug-trafficking and security offences add to the mandatory death penalty in force for murder since the British colonial period, to constitute the three major categories of capital crimes leading to executions after independence. From 1960 to 2011, 52 per cent of executions in Malaysia were for drug offences, 29 per cent were for firearms/explosives/ammunition offences, and 18 per cent were for murder. The handful of remaining executions were carried out

Nasional, or 'National Front', since 1973) from Malayan independence in 1957 until the coalition's first election loss in May 2018.

[15] Baxstrom (2010) 62. See also Human Rights Watch (2006) 1–2; Farrar (2013) 242.

[16] Kamariah (1988) 149; Shafee Abdullah (1/11/2012).

[17] Dangerous Drugs (Amendment) Act 1983 (Malaysia), s 37(da), 39B.

[18] Harring (1991) 371; Swain (1988); Schwarz (1987).

[19] Sodhy (1987) 1075, 1081; Amnesty International (1989) 18; Sulong (1986). The peak of Malaysia's campaign against drugs arrived in 1987, when Prime Minister Mahathir was elected Chair of the Vienna International Conference on Drug Abuse and Illegal Trafficking (Sodhy (1981) 1081).

[20] 'ASEAN to Impose Death Penalty for Drug Crimes'. The first person sentenced to death under the 1983 amendments may not have been executed until 1985. See Amnesty International AI Index ACT 51/02/95, 53.

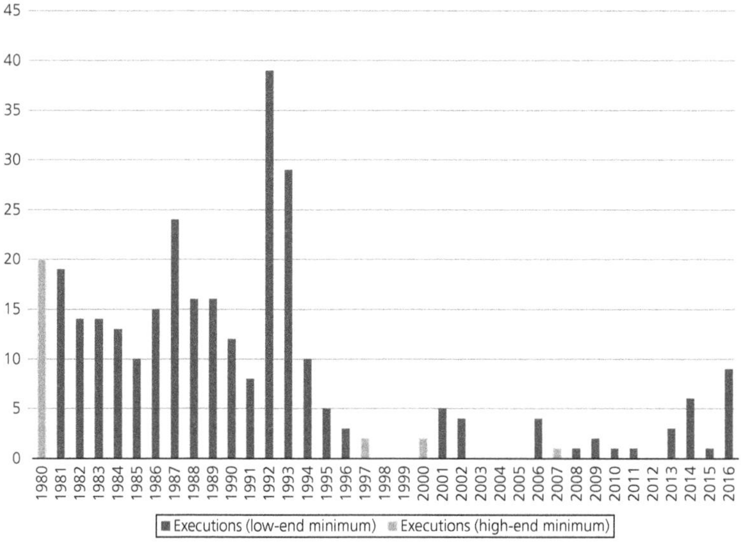

Figure 4 Executions in Malaysia 1980–2016

Sources: Johnson and Zimring (2009) and Amnesty International Annual Reports (1981–91) (for 1980–90); Appendix (Malaysia) (for 1991–2016)

for treason and kidnapping.[21] However, with drug trafficking becoming a discretionary death penalty offence only in 1975, and then a mandatory death penalty offence in 1983, drug offences have provided a higher proportion of executions during the period under analysis from 1991 to 2016, perhaps approaching the proportion of drug convicts on Malaysia's death row in 2011 (69 per cent)[22]—a similar proportion to neighbouring Singapore.

Given the historical context, the most prominent recent feature of Malaysia's capital punishment practice is the significant decline in executions since the mid-1990s (depicted in Figure 4), foreshadowing Singapore's stark death penalty decline a decade later.[23] Malaysia's execution totals fell from an average

[21] Shankar (2011).

[22] Hector (2012). According to the most recent set of official figures from 2011, 69 per cent of 696 prisoners then on death row were convicted of drug offences, 29 per cent were convicted of murder, and 2 per cent were convicted of firearms/explosives/ammunition offences.

[23] See Appendix (Singapore).

of 15+ to 16+ per year from 1980 to 1996, to only 2+ per year between 1997 and 2016.[24] There were no executions recorded at all in 1998, 1999, 2003–5, 2012, and possibly several other years.[25]

Any reduction in serious crime levels can only go so far in explaining such significant declines. The Malaysian government's shifting policies on drugs and security offences are likely to have had the greatest effect. The authorities' main means of reducing executions, in addition to a small increase in successful clemency petitions,[26] consisted of public prosecutors bringing non-capital charges,[27] trial and appeal judges creatively employing 'discretion' to circumvent the mandatory death penalty,[28] and, in some cases, diversion away from the courts altogether, using administrative detention laws.[29] These mechanisms are explained in further detail below.

Yet despite the significant decline in executions since the mid-1990s, the death penalty is still very much entrenched in Malaysia's statute books. Death sentences may be passed by a judge of the High Court at trial, by the Court of Appeal on appeal, or by the highest appeal court in Malaysia: the Federal Court.[30] In 2016, six offence categories were punishable with the mandatory death penalty: drug trafficking, certain firearms offences, murder, certain types of treason, terrorism causing death, and hostage taking causing death.[31] The discretionary death penalty, on the other

[24] Sources: Johnson and Zimring (2009); Amnesty International Annual Reports (1981–92); Amnesty International AI Index ASA 03/01/97 (1980–96); Appendix (Malaysia) (1991–2016).

[25] See Appendix (Malaysia).

[26] See note 8.

[27] Interview with Malaysian member of parliament; interview with Malaysian human rights lawyer; interview with former Malaysian Federal Court judge.

[28] Harring (1991) 400–1; 'A Peculiar Purgatory' (2008); Amnesty International AI Index ASA 03/01/97, 13.

[29] US Department of State (2009). The 2012 repeal of the Internal Security Act 1960 (Malaysia) presumably also had a small impact on annual death sentence and execution totals, given there are now fewer firearms offences available to public prosecutors.

[30] Majid (1995) 364. From 1985 to 1994, after appeals to the Privy Council were abolished, there was only one level of criminal appeal: from the High Court to the Supreme Court, subsequently renamed the Federal Court (see Federal Court of Malaysia (2004) 1, 15–16).

[31] See Dangerous Drugs Act 1952 (Malaysia), s 39B (drug trafficking); Firearms (Increased Penalties) Act 1971 (Malaysia), s 3, 3A (discharging firearms with intent during scheduled offence; being an accomplice thereto); Penal Code 1997 (Malaysia), ss 121A (treason), 130C, 130I, 130N, 130O, 130QA, 130ZB (terrorist

hand, was available in 2016 in cases of kidnapping, abduction, arms trafficking, arms manufacturing, other categories of treason, providing false evidence in a death penalty case, abetting mutiny, various military offences, rape causing death, abetting the suicide of a child or an insane person, attempted murder by a life sentence prisoner, gang robbery where murder results, and water contamination causing death.[32]

As noted, executions have declined significantly in Malaysia since the mid-1990s. Official figures released by the Malaysian government list only thirty-three executions from 1998 to 2015.[33] Total death *sentences*, however, have not declined at all, and may even have increased over the period under analysis. Based on the available data, depicted in Figure 5, in all but five years since 1991 (namely 1994 and the period 1996–9), at least ten death sentences have been passed annually by Malaysian courts, either at first instance level or on appeal.[34] Moreover, recently released government data reveal that between 2010 and 2016, 829 death

offences), 302 (murder), 374A (hostage taking). The Internal Security Act 1960 (Malaysia), which made possession of, or demanding/collecting/receiving/providing, firearms, explosives or ammunition mandatory capital offences (via ss 57(1), 59(1), 59(2), and 59(3)), was repealed in 2012.

Limited prospective-only exceptions to the mandatory death penalty for drug offences are provided by the Dangerous Drugs (Amendment) Act 2017 (Malaysia), which came into force on 15 March 2018. The amending act (s 2(b)) provides that judges may sentence a drug trafficker to life and at least fifteen strokes of the cane, rather than death, if the defendant provides assistance to law enforcement authorities in disrupting drug trafficking activities, and (a) there was no evidence of buying or selling the drug; (b) there was no involvement of an agent provocateur, or (c) the defendant's involvement was limited to transporting, carrying, sending, or delivering a dangerous drug.

[32] See Kidnapping Act 1961 (Malaysia), s 3 (kidnapping); Penal Code 1997 (Malaysia), s 121 (treason), 132 (abetting mutiny), 194 (false evidence), 305 (abetting suicide), 307, 307(2) (attempted murder), 364 (kidnapping/abduction), 376(4) (rape causing death), 396 (gang robbery with murder); Firearms (Increased Penalties) Act 1971 (Malaysia), s 7(1) (trafficking firearms); Arms Act 1960 (Malaysia), s 14(1) (manufacturing firearms); Armed Forces Act 1972 (Malaysia), s 38(1), 41(1), 47(1), 48, 88(3) (military offences); Water Services Industry Act 2006 (Malaysia), s 121(2) (water contamination). As above, the Internal Security Act 1960 (Malaysia), which made consorting with a person in possession of firearms, explosives, or ammunition a discretionary capital offence (s 58(1)), was repealed in 2012.

[33] Palansamy (2015).

[34] Appendix (Malaysia). See note 30 and associated text.

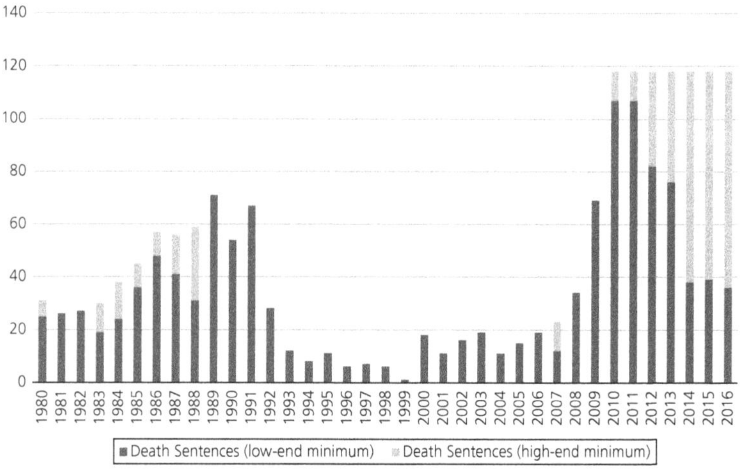

Figure 5 Death sentences passed in Malaysia 1980–2016

Sources: Talib; Amnesty International Annual Reports (1984, 1986, 1987, 1990, 1991); Amnesty International (1983); Amnesty International (1989) (for 1980–90); Appendix (Malaysia) (for 1991–2016). Note the 118 yearly average for 2010–16

sentences were passed—an average of 118 per year.[35] While the data for all years consist of incomplete 'minimum' totals, available figures suggest that from 1997 to 2016 death sentences were passed at an even higher rate than during the 1980s and early 1990s, when the Mahathir government's anti-drugs rhetoric was at its peak.[36] As executions have become rarer, the result is a ballooning death row population, rising from 245 prisoners in 1996, to 696 in 2011, to 1043+ in 2016.[37] With neither acquittals on appeal nor clemency being granted as often as is needed to reduce the size of death row, the present pattern for most condemned prisoners is indefinite delay.

[35] Appendix (Malaysia).

[36] Based on available data, the 'highest minimum' total for death sentences from 1983 to 1996 was 542, or thirty-nine per year (Talib (1989); Amnesty International Annual Reports (1989–97)). From 1997 to 2016, the 'highest minimum' total for death sentences was 1078+, approximately fifty-four per year, albeit with a higher variation from year to year compared with the 1980s (see Appendix (Malaysia)). These averages should be treated with caution, as the figures for most years are unofficial, counted from media reports by Amnesty International.

[37] Appendix (Malaysia).

Clemency procedures in death penalty cases

Before an execution may take place, clemency in a Malaysian death penalty case is automatically considered by the State and Federal Pardons Boards established under the 1957 Constitution,[38] together with a special Federal Pardons Board for Security Offences established by subordinate legislation in 1981.[39] Each Board consists of the Federal Attorney-General or his delegate, the relevant State Chief-Minister (or the Minister of Federal Territories in federal cases), and up to three appointed members of the public,[40] and considers cases from within its own jurisdiction. The fifteen different Pardons Boards make recommendations to the Malay hereditary rulers (state sultans, *Raja*, and *Yang di-Pertuan Besar*) within nine states, who are commonly referred to as the 'rulers';[41] to the four appointed state governors (*Yang di-Pertua Negeri*—in states without a ruler);[42] or the Malaysian king (the *Yang di-Pertuan Agong*—in federal and security cases).[43] The rulers, the

[38] Constitution of Malaysia 1957, art 42(1); Criminal Procedure Code 2006 (Malaysia), s 281(c); Talib (1989) 62–3. The State and Federal Pardons Boards not only hear from prisoners sentenced to death, but also from petitioners serving long-term sentences of imprisonment (Prisons Regulations 2000 (Malaysia), reg 54).

[39] See Essential (Security Cases) Amendment Regulations 1981 (Malaysia), reg 29(2). Security offences were once defined as sections 57–62 of the Internal Security Act 1960 (Malaysia). Security offences now constitute offences within Chapters VI and VIa of the Penal Code 1997 (Malaysia) (dealing with offences against the state, and terrorism), pursuant to the Security Offences (Special Measures) Act 2012 (Malaysia), sch 1.

[40] Constitution of Malaysia 1957, art 42(5); Penna (1987) 109; Harring (1991) 381–2 n110; Essential (Security Cases) Amendment Regulations 1981 (Malaysia), reg 29(2). The lay members must not be Members of State or Federal Parliament (Constitution of Malaysia 1957, art 42(7)). Moreover, Butler and Low (1991, at 220–1) assert that the three members are normally representatives from the major racial groups making up Malaysian society: Malay, Chinese, and Indian.
Hashim (1976, at 42) and Harding (1996, at 70) observe that the Attorney-General's normal practice is to delegate this power to the State Legal Advisor, as permitted by the Constitution of Malaysia 1957, art 42(5).

[41] The Malay hereditary rulers are the monarchs of the nine Malay States: Johor, Kedah, Kelantan, Negeri Sembilan, Pahang, Perak, Perlis, Selangor, and Terengganu. In Perlis the ruler is the *Raja* and in Negeri Sembilan the ruler is the *Yang di-Pertuan Besar*; the remaining seven states are ruled by a Sultan.

[42] These are Penang, Malacca, Sabah, and Sarawak.

[43] Constitution of Malaysia 1957, art 42(1), 42(4)(b); Singh (2004) 92; Talib (1989) 30–1, 39. In a unique constitutional system, the title of *Yang di-Pertuan Agong* as head of state rotates between the nine Malay rulers every five years (Funston (2001a) 172). In military cases, the *Yang di-Pertuan Agong* is not advised

governors, and the *Agong*, while not obliged to follow the Boards' recommendations,[44] do so in the majority of cases,[45] particularly as they preside over these meetings themselves as chairmen.[46] The true extent of their decision-making discretion is discussed later in this chapter.

Relevant materials before the Board relating to each capital case under consideration include:

- the prisoner's (optional) written petition, outlining the reasons why clemency should be granted;[47]
- the evidence notes from the prisoner's trial, and a reasoned recommendation from the sentencing judge as to whether or not the death sentence imposed should be carried out;[48]
- the record of proceedings in any appeal to the Federal Court, and an optional report from the Federal Court on the appeal;[49]
- police, psychologist, and Prisons Department files on the case;[50]
- the Federal Attorney-General's written opinion on the case.[51]

A grant of clemency made by the rulers, governors, or *Agong* may convert a death sentence to life imprisonment (which nominally stands at twenty years, but often results in conditional release after two thirds of the sentence);[52] a 'natural life' term; immediate release through a full pardon, or at the very minimum will authorize a temporary reprieve from execution.[53]

by a Pardons Board, but by the Cabinet or a minister acting under the Cabinet's authority (Lee (2017) 72).

[44] Faruqi (2008); Addruse (1986) 2. Contrast Talib (1989) 3, who asserts that 'the advice of the various State Pardons Boards are binding upon the Rulers and *Yang di Pertua Negeri*, but theoretically not so on the *Yang di Pertuan Agong*'. See the section entitled 'The rulers, governors, and *Agong* as final decision makers'.

[45] Sharif and Veera (1997a); Crook (1986) 203; Addruse (1986) 1–2.

[46] Constitution of Malaysia 1957, art 42(8); Penna (1987) 109; Talib (1989) 40, 65.

[47] Prisons Regulations 2000 (Malaysia), rr 113–14.

[48] Criminal Procedure Code 2006 (Malaysia), s 281(b).

[49] Criminal Procedure Code 2006 (Malaysia), s 281(b).

[50] Amnesty International (1983) 4; 'Perak Pardons Board Denies Backlog of Cases' (2001); Damis (11/2004); interview with Malaysian criminal defence lawyer; Tan (2010).

[51] Constitution of Malaysia 1957, art 42(9).

[52] Sharif and Veera (1997a).

[53] Criminal Procedure Code 2006 (Malaysia), s 281(c)–(d); Damis (11/2004); Talib (1989) 67.

Importantly, there is no legal time limit within which the rulers, governors, or *Agong* must come to a final decision on a clemency petition, and no upper time limit within which an execution must be carried out.[54] Again, this point will be discussed later in the chapter, as it has affected the proportion of prisoners granted clemency overall.

Calculating Malaysia's clemency 'rate'

The most straightforward method of calculating Malaysia's clemency rate during the 1990s, 2000s, and 2010s only takes into account data from 1998 to 2015, thereby excluding the period 1991–7 and the year 2016. The Malaysian Prisons Department has released official execution and clemency statistics for the period 1998–2015 revealing that 127 prisoners received clemency and 33 executions were carried out over that eighteen-year timeframe,[55] resulting in a clemency rate of 79 per cent, firmly within the 'high' categorization identified in Chapter 1. If unofficial data relating to 2016 are also included, the rate becomes 77–81 per cent.[56]

However, this calculation method is far from satisfactory, and as first stated in Chapter 1, I do not use 77–81 percent as Malaysia's final clemency rate. Relying only upon the 1998–2015 figures excludes the first seven years of the period under study, thereby reducing the comparability of Malaysia's clemency practice with Thailand's, Singapore's, and Indonesia's.[57] Even more significantly, excluding the years from 1991 to 1997 artificially increases Malaysia's final clemency rate. As described previously, the period 1983–96 saw a high volume of executions as part of the Mahathir government's 'war on drugs'. The execution rate from the excluded years (1991–7) is approximately 13+ to 14+ per year, compared with just 2+ per year thereafter. Indeed, the 39+ executions in 1992 represent the highest minimum total Amnesty

[54] Tan (2010); *Husin v Lembaga Pengampunan Negeri Pahang* [2001] 3 MLJ 458, 466–7.

[55] Appendix (Malaysia). The split between commutations and pardons is unknown.

[56] See Appendix (Malaysia).

[57] See Appendix (Thailand, Singapore, Indonesia).

International has ever recorded in one year in Malaysia.[58] While it is possible that clemency grants were commensurately more numerous during the early 1990s, this is unlikely, given the Mahathir government's stated 'no mercy' policy for drug traffickers covering this period.[59]

There are two possible remedial measures, both imperfect, as they assume that annual clemency totals remain stable over time (whereas in reality they fluctuate, alongside other death penalty metrics). Given the known 'low-end minimum' and 'high-end minimum' execution totals for 1991 to 1997, the associated clemency rate can be calculated using an average estimate for clemency grants from publicized official figures covering the years between 1998 and 2015. At slightly more than seven clemency grants per year, this method assumes that there were forty-nine commutations and pardons from 1991 to 1997, and therefore an overall clemency rate of 58–63 per cent over the entire period of study (1991 to 2016). Alternatively, the most detailed source providing clemency aggregates from 1975 to 1986 suggests a yearly average of approximately 4.5+ clemency grants over this period.[60] If this average is extrapolated to cover the period 1991 to 1997 (thirty-one clemency grants), then the total clemency rate from 1991 to 2016 falls slightly, to 55–61 per cent. I combine these two methods to produce a final clemency range of 55–63 per cent.

None of the calculation methods depicted in Figure 6 are ideal, but what they do suggest is that: (a) Malaysia's post-1991 clemency rate most likely falls within the 'high' category identified in Chapter 1, yet (b) a clemency rate approaching 80 per cent is probably overstated. Although execution and clemency figures from non-official sources (such as non-governmental organization (NGO) reports and news media articles) confound attempts at reaching firm conclusions,[61] it is likely that, in Malaysia, slightly more clemency grants have been made than executions carried out over the period of study.

[58] Amnesty International AI Index ASA 03/01/97, 11.

[59] See note 6.

[60] Talib (1989) 118.

[61] See note 9.

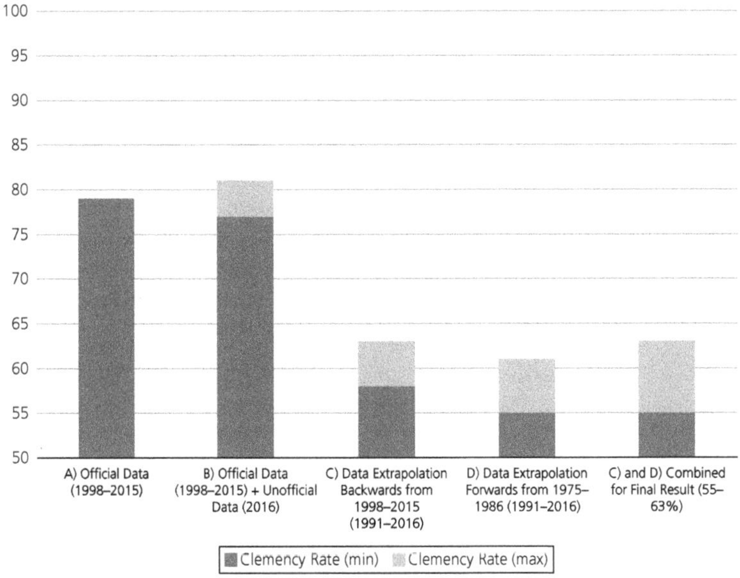

Figure 6 Malaysia clemency rate 1991–2016: calculation method

Sources: Appendix (Malaysia); Talib (1989)

Features of cases where clemency was granted

Although the justification behind a capital clemency grant (or rejection) is rarely made public in Malaysia,[62] it is nonetheless possible to speculate on and narrow down the range of factors that have proved consistently influential. Commentators have generally seen *extralegal* factors as being of greatest importance to the decision-making of the State and Federal Pardons Boards.[63] This appears consistent with the Malaysian Constitution, which sees the *Agong* as a 'fountain of mercy' in granting clemency, rather than as a final judicial adjudicator.[64] Nevertheless, the existing literature's focus on extralegal matters may simply reflect greater media exposure of 'public interest' death penalty cases, rather than

[62] Interview with international human rights NGO staff #3; interview with Malaysian criminal defence lawyer; Roy (1986).

[63] Talib (1989) 31; 'Death or Life: Decision on Penang Pair "This Weekend"' (1986); 'Insults Could See Convicted Men Hang: Lawyer' (1986); Aisbett (2001); Azlan Shah (1986) 86–7; interview with Malaysian prosecutor.

[64] 'Other Important Duties of the Yang di-Pertuan Agong' (2003); *Public Prosecutor v Soon Seng Sia Heng* [1979] 2 MLJ 170, 171.

the more mundane petitions of murderers and drug couriers pardoned for retributivist or redemptive reasons. As two Malaysian lawyers observed in interview, there are many cases where clemency has been granted by the State and Federal Pardons Boards, the precise details of which remain unknown to the public.[65]

In all likelihood, the State and Federal Pardons Boards consider both case-based circumstances and broader societal and political goals in assessing clemency petitions. Writing in 1968, former Malaysian Attorney-General Abdul Kadir Yusuf (who served in that capacity from 1963 to 1977) confirmed as much, in stating that the members of each Pardons Board

> have to consider very carefully all aspects of the case in the national and public interest, the nature and gravity of the offence, the circumstances in which the offence was committed and all grounds submitted by their counsel [i.e. the Federal Attorney-General] before making their decision.[66]

Indeed, academic sources, media reports, and 'elite' interviews suggest that retributive justifications for clemency in previous cases have included the prisoner's youth or criminal inexperience;[67] cases in which a complete or partial defence, while argued by defence lawyers at trial, could not be proven;[68] and other cases in which pressing legal criteria demanding commutation, including evidential flaws, have emerged during trial.[69]

Many prisoners in lower-profile, unreported cases have also been awarded *redemptive* pardons or commutations where they 'showed remorse, had repented and apologized, and promised good behavior and not to repeat the offence'.[70] Moreover, the long

[65] Interview with Malaysian criminal defence lawyer; statement by Malaysian human rights lawyer.

[66] Talib (1989) 173.

[67] Interview with Malaysian prosecutor. The normal practice of the Pardons Boards was to commute the sentence of those minors (under eighteen years) sentenced to death to life imprisonment, before the death penalty was completely abolished for juvenile offenders in firearms/explosives/ammunition cases in 2001 (Child Act 2001 (Malaysia), s 97(1)). See Ngui (2005); Sharif and Veera (1997a); Sharif and Veera (1997b).

[68] Interview with former Malaysian Federal Court judge; interview with Malaysian prosecutor.

[69] Interview with Malaysian criminal defence lawyer; Soong (1986) 6.

[70] Tan (2010); Talib (1989) 183. For example: Khairulrijal (2015); 'Rehabilitation Is Our Top Priority, Says Prisons D-G' (1997); 'Johor Sultan Pardons Eight Prisoners'

intervals between Pardons Board sittings in some Malaysian jurisdictions significantly aid redemptive justifications for clemency.[71] Although there is no firm evidence to prove it, most of the 127 clemency grants made in capital cases from 1998 to 2015[72] may have been based on good behaviour, religious piety, and expressed remorse over the course of a long period spent on death row. Grants made for other reasons simply do not occur frequently enough to dominate official totals of this size.

The remaining group of prisoners granted commutations and pardons, whose cases tend to be most widely reported in the media, are next described in chronological order. These are primarily, but not exclusively, cases where the prisoner/s have received clemency for *utilitarian* or *political* reasons.

- Various foreign prisoners from neighbouring nations Indonesia and the Philippines have been granted commutations or pardons to safeguard Malaysia's relationship with their countries of origin.[73] Nevertheless, in numerous other cases the executions of foreign nationals have proceeded.[74]
- In 1994, the *Agong* stayed Tan Kim Guan's execution for drug trafficking. Tan's death sentence was subsequently commuted in January 1995. The *Agong* had reportedly been impressed by the prisoner's bravery in making a guilty plea on a mandatory death penalty offence so that his wife could escape the gallows on a joint drug-trafficking charge.[75]
- In 2003, Liu observed that a number of UMNO politicians had received clemency (for capital and non-capital offences) in the

(2012); Yesuiah (2017); 'Sultan Gives Death Row Convicts One More Chance' (2015); 'Perak Sultan Pardons Two Drug Offenders on Death Row' (2017).

[71] See section entitled 'Long stays on death row'.

[72] Palansamy (2015).

[73] Amnesty International AI Index 03/01/97, 13; Osman (2010); 'Menuju Tiang Gantung Malaysia' (2010); 'Capital Sentence against Indon Worker in M'Sia Aborted' (2004); Fauziyah (2015) 56 (on Indonesian citizens); 'Malaysia Commutes Death Sentence of Filipina to Life' (2015); 'Malaysia Lowers Sentences of 3 Death Throw [sic] Pinoys' (2012) (on Filipino citizens).

[74] Johnson and Zimring (2009) 306 n11.

[75] Donoghue (2013) 235–6. One interviewee stated that 'self-sacrifice' was a criteria taken into account by the Pardons Boards (interview with former Malaysian Federal Court judge).

past.[76] The best known case, although outside the period of study, is that of Mokhtar Hashim, a former government minister found guilty of murdering an UMNO colleague in 1983. Hashim's death sentence was commuted to life imprisonment by the *Agong* in 1984 and he was released from prison in 1991.[77]

- In 2006, the Sultan of Kedah commuted Chu Tak Fai's death sentence to natural life imprisonment. Chu was a British national born in Hong Kong, who argued that he was forced to smuggle drugs into Malaysia from Thailand by a money-laundering group to whom his family owed a significant debt. The British Foreign and Commonwealth Office kept a close watch on Chu's case.[78]
- In 2008, the *Agong* commuted to life imprisonment the death sentence of property developer Kenneth Lee Fook Mun, the grandson of Malaysia's first finance minister. Lee was convicted of murder for shooting dead a woman after a car crash.[79] One significant factor here may have been the RM 550,000 (approximately GBP 90,000) civil award paid by Lee to his victim's family, although the family did not take kindly to the commutation.[80] The failure to prove a defence of diminished responsibility or self-intoxication at trial may also have been an influential factor in the commutation.[81] Lee's case was considered in further detail in this book's Introduction.

[76] Liu (2003). One interviewee stated that stated that 'service to the country' was a criteria taken into account by the Pardons Boards (interview with former Malaysian Federal Court judge). A recent example of this practice at the time of writing was the May 2018 pardon granted to Anwar Ibrahim, a former deputy prime minister imprisoned for sodomy in 2015 ('Anwar Ibrahim Freed from Prison after Royal Pardon from Malaysian King' (2018)).

[77] Bass (1983) 167; 'Beneath Malaysia's High-Profile Murder Cases, What Lies Beyond The Killers' Minds?' (2015). See *Hashim v Public Prosecutor* [1983] 2 MLJ 232.

[78] 'Hong Kong Citizen Loses Bid to Revise Federal Court Decision' (2006); Reprieve (2013); Amnesty International AI Index ASA 28/014/01.

[79] Hands Off Cain, 'Malaysia' (2008).

[80] 'Family Aghast after King Pardons Killer' (2008); Babulal and Mokhtar (2008). One interviewee stated that 'philanthropy' was a criteria taken into account by the Pardons Boards (interview with former Malaysian Federal Court judge).

[81] Interview with Malaysian prosecutor; interview with Malaysian criminal defence lawyer.

Several patterns emerge from this list. Liu's observations, together with Mokhtar Hashim's earlier precedent and Kenneth Lee Fook Mun's case in 2008, all suggest that, over the period under analysis, political connections to the Barisan Nasional government increased a prisoner's chances of death sentence commutation. Chu Tak Fai and Kenneth Lee Fook Mun's cases reiterate the importance of arguable, yet ultimately unsuccessful, defences for retributive clemency. The Indonesian and Filipino cases, together with that of British citizen Chu Tak Fai, also hint at mercy being applied selectively in cases involving foreign nationals. This represents a notable shift in policy from the 1980s and early 1990s, when the Malaysian government deemed it essential that local and foreign prisoners were treated with absolute equality within the judicial and royal pardons systems.[82] As Datuk Than Tai Hing, an official from the Malaysian Ministry of Foreign Affairs, confirmed to the media in 2010, 'there have been cases where appeals for clemency by foreign governments were entertained by Malaysia'.[83] The context of the quote reveals that by 'entertained', Datuk Than meant that diplomatic representations had proven successful in obtaining clemency.

Finally, within the forthcoming section explaining the reasons for Malaysia's moderately high clemency rate, I also refer to clemency cases that potentially fit within the 'mercy from the sovereign' paradigm first described in Chapter 2. These are cases where clemency primarily benefits the Malay rulers within the nine Malay states, even if the rulers make their final decision after considering the Pardons Boards' advice and the written clemency materials.

The rulers' own vested interests in granting clemency, the often long intervals between Pardons Board sittings, and the judicial discretion constrained by the mandatory death penalty together operate to ensure that a majority of clemency petitions have succeeded in Malaysian capital cases since 1991. Admittedly, in Malaysia, as with Singapore, the public prosecutor occupies a central role on the State and Federal Pardons Boards, thereby directly influencing clemency proceedings. Moreover, as with Singapore, cases initially deemed undeserving of execution are filtered away through lenient discretion at earlier stages, thereby limiting the potential

[82] Pillai (1990); Sulong (1986); Aisbett (2001); Deans (1990).
[83] Than (2010). See also Hector (2015).

role of executive discretion at the 'back end' of the criminal justice system. However, these two structural factors which potentially limit clemency are countered by the rulers' own preferences, together with favourable written reports from the trial judge, prison authorities, and the petitioner him or herself. While the Malaysian rulers, governors, and *Agong* may not grant capital clemency with the same inevitability as Thailand's late King Bhumibol did over the period of study, neither does Malaysia's practice resemble that of its neighbour Singapore. Even if a prisoner's death sentence 'survives' prosecutorial discretion, trial, and appeal,[84] over the entire period under analysis it has still proven more likely than not that a commutation or pardon will follow.

Explaining the High Clemency Rate in Malaysia

Discretion at earlier stages

The Malaysian government has typically justified retaining the mandatory death penalty for murder, drug trafficking, and firearms offences by reference to the sentencing philosophies of retribution, deterrence, and incapacitation. In addition, there is an implicit assumption that the death penalty enables the government to exercise continuing control over Malaysian citizens.[85] However, not every eligible case must proceed to execution in order to achieve these aims. By the late 1980s, the *symbolic* value of retaining and widely publicizing the existence of mandatory capital offences was seen by the Mahathir government as a more humane and internationally tolerable method of deterring drug trafficking in particular, in place of frequent executions.[86] By the 2000s, the Malaysian government had acknowledged privately the ineffectiveness of the mandatory death penalty in curbing drug trading and addiction,[87] and provided increased funding to harm reduction efforts.[88] In 2012, the mandatory death penalty's

[84] However, see notes 36–37 and associated text on Malaysia's growing death row population. At least since the year 2000, an outcome even more probable than either execution or clemency is indefinite delay.

[85] Harring (1991) 383; Soong (1990) 30; Novak (2014) 85.

[86] Harring (1991) 403–4; interview with Malaysian prosecutor; interview with Malaysian member of parliament.

[87] US Department of State (2009); Lines (2007) 14; interview with Malaysian member of parliament.

[88] Human Rights Watch (2009).

ineffectiveness was even publicly acknowledged by the Home Minister in Parliament.[89] However, despite these shifting sentiments, it took until November 2017 for the Malaysian Parliament to propose (albeit limited) exceptions to the mandatory death penalty for drug offences.[90] As with Singapore's PAP governments since 1975, in Malaysia frequent government statements since 1983 had proclaimed that 'drug dealers deserve death'—propaganda which had backed UMNO into a public relations corner and had long prevented any public steps toward abolition.[91]

To lower execution rates, the Malaysian government has devised three solutions to address capital cases before they ever reach the State and Federal Pardons Boards. By each method, a proportion of defendants who might otherwise receive mandatory capital convictions are instead detained in prison, or even released. First, the suspect may be detained indefinitely under administrative detention laws, instead of facing capital charges in court.[92] Second, the public prosecutor may proceed with a non-capital charge. Third, judges in narcotics cases have creatively used judicial 'discretion' to circumvent the dual presumption of trafficking in capital drugs cases.[93] Each move potentially affects Malaysia's final clemency rate in its own way.

The first opportunity for the authorities to filter cases away from death is through long-term administrative detention. Detention without trial was, for most of the twenty-six-year period under study, authorized by the Dangerous Drugs (Special Preventive Measures) Act 1985 (for renewable periods of up to two years), the Emergency (Public Order and Crime Prevention) Ordinance 1969 (indefinite detention, subsequently repealed in 2012), and

[89] Buang (2017).

[90] Dangerous Drugs (Amendment) Act 2017 (Malaysia), s 2(b). See note 31.

[91] Interview with Malaysian member of parliament; US Department of State (2009); Lines (2007) 14.

[92] Administrative detention has also been used to detain narcotics or firearms/explosives/ammunition defendants after acquittal in the courts (interview with Malaysian criminal defence lawyer; Gallahue and Lines (2010) 30; Lent (1984) 445).

[93] The two presumptions created by the Dangerous Drugs Act 1952 (Malaysia), s 37(d) and 37(da) operate to: (1) presume a defendant who has custody or control of anything containing a scheduled 'dangerous drug' as being in possession of the drug and of knowing its nature; (2) presume a defendant who is in possession of a traffickable quantity of drugs to be trafficking in those drugs. The defendant may bring evidence to rebut these presumptions.

the Internal Security Act 1960 (indefinite detention, also repealed in 2012). The Security Offences (Special Measures) Act 2012 and the Prevention of Crime Act 1959 (as amended in 2013) are now also used to detain criminal suspects, in the former case for twenty-eight days and in the latter case for a potentially indefinite period. Detention without trial, whether for an indefinite period or not, has enabled the Malaysian government to pre-emptively punish, incapacitate, and deter drug-trafficking and firearms/explosives/ammunition offence suspects,[94] without risking the international criticism that high execution rates would inevitably attract.[95] Strikingly, these measures had become so common by 2009 that a majority of drug-trafficking suspects were confined to preventive detention rather than being charged for offences under the Dangerous Drugs Act 1952.[96]

Next, during the pre-trial stage, the public prosecutor may bring a non-capital charge on his or her own initiative, given compelling mitigating factors or a lack of evidence.[97] The police may also drop charges altogether if the defendant assists with more important ongoing investigations,[98] or, as two sources alleged, if bribes are paid to investigating officers.[99] Nevertheless, as several interviewees acknowledged, despite the availability of charging discretion there are still 'some very bad cases which [the prosecutor] cannot do anything about', which must then proceed to trial on capital charges.[100] According to one Malaysian criminal defence lawyer, if the requisite amount of trafficked drugs in a narcotics case is confirmed by chemists then prosecutors will have no choice but to bring the case as a capital prosecution,[101] unlike the '14.99 charge' which has proven so successful in reducing executions in Singapore.

[94] Interview with international human rights NGO staff #3; Harring (1991) 405; Freedom House (2002b); US Department of State (2009).

[95] Harring (1991) 403–5.

[96] US Department of State (2009).

[97] Interview with Malaysian member of parliament; interview with Malaysian human rights lawyer; interview with former Malaysian Federal Court judge.

[98] Harring (1991) 401.

[99] Donoghue (1990) 157; interview with Malaysian member of parliament.

[100] Interview with former Malaysian Federal Court judge. Also: interview with Malaysian criminal defence lawyer; statement by Malaysian human rights lawyer #2.

[101] Interview with Malaysian criminal defence lawyer.

Finally, if the case nonetheless proceeds to trial on mandatory death penalty charges or onwards to appeal, the Malaysian judiciary has developed several legal devices that avoid the need to send defendants to the gallows. One of the most prominent is a finding of 'possession' rather than 'trafficking' in a drugs case,[102] which only draws a maximum sentence of five years' imprisonment plus a fine.[103] Despite the operative double presumption enacted to make convictions easier,[104] and the wide legislative definition of 'trafficking',[105] convictions for capital drug-trafficking offences now appear restricted to 'cases where there is absolute, corroborated proof of the actual event of a drug *transaction*'.[106] In non-drugs cases, the courts may likewise convict for non-capital culpable homicide on a murder charge, or may convict for a non-capital firearms offence on a mandatory death penalty firearms charge.[107] The other option available to judges is acquittal. Notably, the percentage of outright acquittals on the basis of insufficient evidence is much higher in Malaysia than in neighbouring Singapore, with 50–60 per cent of defendants in all capital cases being discharged.[108]

All three procedures just described have the potential to affect death penalty clemency rates, albeit in different ways. One hypothesis holds that, if employed in the very worst cases, administrative detention without trial may in fact make clemency *more* likely among the less serious cases which remain. However, there is no guarantee that any 'residual' lenient discretion will be exercised as clemency, rather than at the prosecutorial or judicial phases. A more convincing explanatory link is that if discretion is utilized as a 'safety valve' at an earlier stage, by prosecuting for non-capital crimes, or where a judge considers the evidence presented and 'commutes' a potential mandatory death sentence by substituting a non-capital conviction, the prisoner will have

[102] Harring (1991) 404; Amnesty International AI Index ASA 03/01/97, 13; interview with former Malaysian Federal Court judge.

[103] Dangerous Drugs Act 1952 (Malaysia), ss 6, 9, 12.

[104] See note 93.

[105] See note 5.

[106] Cornell Center on the Death Penalty Worldwide, 'Malaysia' (2017) emphasis added.

[107] Novak (2014) 78.

[108] Interview with former Malaysian Federal Court judge; interview with Singaporean human rights lawyer. See also Novak (2014) 82.

fewer available arguments to make for clemency before the State and Federal Pardons Boards. The only exceptions will be utilitarian/political and redemptive grounds for clemency, as well as any mitigating circumstances which were not known to the prosecutor before trial.

Similar considerations apply where the Malaysian government has sought to reduce executions for policy reasons alone since the mid-1990s. Clemency has been displaced as a potential 'back-end' policy tool to limit execution totals, by administrative detention, non-capital charges, and even judicial devices such as acquittals and convictions on alternative charges.[109] Yet even the widespread exercise of lenient discretion at earlier stages has not stopped clemency flourishing in Malaysian mandatory death penalty cases. When granted by the *Agong*, rulers, or governors, clemency still performs important retributive, redemptive, and merciful functions that lenient discretion at earlier stages does not capture.

State and Federal Pardons Boards—composition and materials

The State and Federal Pardons Boards were established in order to provide advice to the rulers, governors, and *Agong* on the exercise of their prerogative power to reduce or abrogate criminal sentences. Such 'advice' is interpreted in different ways by the various final decision makers, leading to wide provincial variation in clemency practice. However, the constitutionally and legislatively mandated *composition* of and *materials* before each Board impact heavily the kind of advice passed to the rulers, governors, and *Agong*, thereby influencing the final decision itself. The role played by the Federal Attorney-General is especially notable here.

First of all, despite the official position being that 'the Federal Government has no say in the power of pardon',[110] the implicitly or overtly political representatives serving on the Pardons Boards

[109] Although the courts are formally independent from the executive government in Malaysia, trial and appeal judges who have found creative means of bypassing the mandatory death penalty for drug trafficking and security offences may be following executive policy in doing so. Although there is no 'smoking gun' pointing to political interference, Novak (2014, at 82) notes: 'The government has not criticized the high acquittal rate [in drug-trafficking cases], suggesting some equilibrium has been reached'.

[110] Hashim (1976) 42; interview with Malaysian human rights lawyer.

(the Federal Attorney-General, the local Chief Minister,[111] and perhaps even politically sympathetic lay members)[112] are usually in a position to guarantee recommendations to the ruler, governor, or *Agong* that suit the government's agenda, whether these recommendations are in favour of clemency or, as is more likely, against it.[113] Echoing Hashim's milder assertion that federal government influence on these constitutional advisory bodies 'may be brought to bear only *indirectly* through the good offices of the Attorney-General',[114] Harding has more bluntly argued that the Federal Pardons Board, at least, has been subjected to unconstitutional governmental pressure from time to time.[115]

The Malaysian Constitution provides that before making a decision, the Pardons Board '*shall* consider any written opinion which the Attorney-General may have delivered thereon',[116] presumably originally in reference to the Attorney-General's opinion on the legal (rather than political) reasons for either carrying out or commuting the death sentence.[117] While the prisoner has no formal procedural right to make oral submissions to members of the Pardons Board,[118] and must primarily rely on a written petition,[119] the Attorney-General's written representations *must* be considered. As one interviewee noted, the Attorney-General is the only author physically present at the meeting who can defend his

[111] At the end of 2016, Barisan Nasional-backed Chief Ministers or *Menteri Besar* held power in ten of the thirteen states. By comparison, the pro-establishment figure in in 1991 was eleven of thirteen.

[112] The lay members of the Pardons Boards are appointed by the ruler or governor of the relevant state (Constitution of Malaysia 1957, art 42(5)).

[113] Interview with Malaysian prosecutor. Two interviewees observed that being 'tough on crime' has significantly boosted UMNO's political appeal (interview with Australian academic expert on Thailand; interview with Australian academic expert on Indonesia). However, in particular cases, government input in the clemency process may enable prisoners with political connections to *receive* clemency. This remains an unverified possibility for the cases of Mokhtar Hashim and Kenneth Lee Fook Mun.

[114] Hashim (1976) 42, emphasis added.

[115] Harding (1996) 70 n58.

[116] Constitution of Malaysia 1957, art 42(9), emphasis added.

[117] Talib (1989) 43–4, 184.

[118] Penna (1987) 126–7; Amnesty International (1983) 4. However, informal representations through legal counsel are often possible (interview with Malaysian prosecutor; interview with Malaysian criminal defence lawyer).

[119] Prisons Regulations 2000 (Malaysia), rr 113–14.

tendered written report on the case.[120] Unsurprisingly, then, it is the Attorney-General (or his delegate) whose written and verbal opinion has the most influential effect on all the Board members present.[121]

The Federal Attorney-General—the Malaysian Federal Government's chief legal adviser—doubles as Malaysia's chief public prosecutor, and has often been accused of lacking independence from the elected government in the exercise of this function.[122] As the Malaysian Bar observed as far back as 1983:

> If an accused person is apprehended after an offence has been committed the Attorney General has the following discretionary powers: to charge him, if so the type of charge, to issue a certificate to bring the case under the emergency legislation [on security offences], to transfer the case to the High Court, to appear in person at the trial, to appeal to the Federal Court against acquittal and to apply for the remand of the accused until the disposal of the appeal, *to give a written opinion to the Pardons Board if the accused is convicted and to sit on the Pardons Board when the pardon is considered* ... The powers of the Attorney General make nonsense the doctrine of separation of powers.[123]

As first described in Chapter 2, in jurisdictions where the case prosecutor must be consulted before a decision to grant clemency or pardon is made, grants of clemency will usually be rarer.[124] Why would the Federal Attorney-General recommend commutation after devoting significant resources to a prosecution? As with the situation in Singapore, if a new case exhibits mitigating factors that justify a lesser punishment than death, or if the government simply seeks fewer executions for policy reasons, a decision not to bring a capital prosecution in favour of administrative detention or a non-capital charge can be made within the Attorney-General's Chambers at the earliest possible opportunity, rather than at the final stage of clemency deliberations.

Nevertheless, exceptions can arise for factors which only appear during trial and appeal hearings, or as a result of long-term

[120] Interview with Malaysian prosecutor.

[121] Interview with Malaysian prosecutor; interview with Malaysian member of parliament; interview with Malaysian criminal defence lawyer.

[122] Amnesty International AI Index ASA 28/03/97; Farrar (2013) 16; Whiting (2013) 36; interview with Malaysian member of parliament.

[123] 'The Attorney General—The Most Powerful Person in Malaysia?' (1983), emphasis added.

[124] Abramowitz and Paget (1964) 184–5; Barkow (2009) 156.

incarceration. Here, the Attorney-General's recommendation on clemency may be influenced,[125] or even contradicted, by written submissions from: (a) the trial and appeal judges, (b) the Prisons Department, and (c) the petitioner him or herself. Although the Attorney-General undoubtedly possesses the most powerful voice on the Board, his opinion as public prosecutor and government legal adviser is not the only criteria relevant to the Board's decision-making. Also relevant are the trial and appeal judges' reports before the Board, as well as the impact of long stays on death row for prisoners' reported rehabilitation.

For matters first arising during trial and appeal, it is common for the presiding judge to write in favour of mitigation,[126] recommending clemency for circumstances that cannot be considered in sentencing, due to the mandatory penalty on conviction.[127] The late Karpal Singh, Malaysia's best known criminal defence lawyer, always made a plea in mitigation before the trial judge in a mandatory death penalty case, to ensure that the court possessed 'all relevant information before it, in the event of an appeal being lost'.[128] The very fact that Malaysia's Criminal Procedure Code legally *requires* the trial judge to write a report on the case, making a recommendation as to whether the death sentence should be carried out or not,[129] forces trial judges (as well as federal court appeal judges, should they also choose to write) to at least open their minds to the possibility of clemency. Given the moral burden

[125] Two interviewees viewed the Attorney-General's advice as being presented *after* the Attorney-General had considered other written reports (interview with Malaysian member of parliament; interview with Malaysian criminal defence lawyer), as with the constitutional procedure in Singapore (see Chapter 4). However, in Malaysia, there is no explicit constitutional or legislative guidance on this matter.

[126] Talib (1989) 63; Amnesty International (1983) 4; interview with Malaysian prosecutor. Although the trial and appeal judges' confidential reports are only addressed to the Pardons Boards, occasionally definitive recommendations for pardon do come into the public domain within a written judgment on a case or via a media report. Three examples here are: *Public Prosecutor v Yee Kim Seng* [1983] 1 MLJ 252 (for an Internal Security Act offence); 'Ex-Cop Goes Back on Death Row' (2009) (in a murder case); 'Dadah Man, 84, Loses Appeal' (1994) (in a drug trafficking case).

[127] Interview with Malaysian prosecutor; interview with Malaysian criminal defence lawyer.

[128] Donoghue (2013) 191.

[129] See Criminal Procedure Code 2006 (Malaysia), s 281(b).

inherent in pronouncing a mandatory death sentence, it is not surprising that trial judges often prefer to 'delegate' their sentencing discretion in capital cases to the Pardons Board, and it is equally unsurprising that the Pardons Board considers these judicial recommendations influential.[130] Several of the reported examples of capital clemency provided previously may have originated in judicial recommendations, although there is no direct evidence available to prove this.[131]

The rulers, governors, and Agong *as final decision makers*

In making their final decisions on clemency, the Malay hereditary rulers usually follow the relevant Pardons Board's recommendation.[132] However, they are under no formal legal or conventional obligation to do so.[133] This decision-making process is at odds with the traditional role of a constitutional monarch, whereby prerogative powers (such as the power to pardon) are only exercised in a ceremonial fashion, *on advice* from the elected government. Although the drafting of the Malaysian Constitution's power to pardon was significantly influenced by the royal prerogative of mercy as practised in pre-abolition Britain,[134] the nine Malay hereditary rulers had been exercising their traditional power to pardon well before British possession of Penang, Malacca, and Singapore in 1825, and as far back as the sixteenth century.[135] The late Azlan Shah (a former Malaysian Chief Justice and himself the Sultan of Perak from 1984 to 2014) portrayed the Malay rulers in a manner that suggests they frequently exercised clemency in the form of 'mercy from the sovereign', as described in Chapter 2: 'A Malay Sultan during the Malacca period [1402–1511 AD] held absolute power and his subjects gave him absolute loyalty … The Sultan declared war, decided on life and

[130] Amnesty International (1983) 4; Interview with former Malaysian Federal Court judge.

[131] See the cases of Tan Kim Guan, Chu Tak Fai, and Kenneth Lee Fook Mun.

[132] Interview with former Malaysian Federal Court judge; interview with Malaysian criminal defence lawyer.

[133] See note 44.

[134] Lee (2017) 71.

[135] Talib (1989) 21–4; Harding (1986) 364.

death of his subjects, administered justice, and maintained law and order.'[136]

Even relatively recent pardons have been granted in conjunction with rulers' birthdays, coronations, and the first day of Ramadan (although it is unclear whether the festivities were the reason for the grants, or simply affected the timing of grants decided by other criteria).[137] Whether in continuation of a historical practice associated with the pre-colonial Malay sultanates and with Islam,[138] from a desire to re-assert traditional royal powers after the enactment of the Constitution (Amendment) Act 1994,[139] or simply by force of personality, a number of modern rulers (particularly the sultans of Johor, Selangor, and Perak) have demonstrated their independent discretion in constitutional matters over the period of study.[140] In politically contentious death penalty cases, the Barisan Nasional executive may have still been able to influence the outcome by making a strong recommendation through the Attorney-General and/or the relevant State Chief Minister;[141] however, the rulers are also empowered to authorize what would be politically unpopular pardon grants.[142]

A number of interview and archival sources suggest that the dynamics of the Pardons Board will differ depending on whether the Board is chaired by one of the nine Malay Rulers with

[136] Azlan Shah (1986) 77.

[137] For example: 'Perak Sultan Grants Four Prisoners Royal Pardon' (2000); New (2016); 'Johor Sultan Pardons Eight Prisoners' (2012); 'Pardon Unlikely for Malaysian Opposition Leader' (2015); Hands Off Cain, 'Malaysia' (2015); 'Sultan Gives Death Row Convicts One More Chance' (2015).

[138] The Malay rulers are the constitutional guardians of Islam in their jurisdictions (Azlan Shah (1986) 78–9; Bari (2003) 60). Chapter 2 observed that the use of lenient discretion in death penalty cases falls within the spirit of Islamic law, at least in certain circumstances.

[139] Interview with Australian academic expert on Malaysia. The 1994 amendments to the Malaysian Constitution removed many of the legal immunities previously enjoyed by the rulers, and legally compelled the *Yang di-Pertuan Agong* to act on the advice given in matters beyond his personal discretion under the Constitution. These amendments were the culmination of a long campaign by Prime Minister Mahathir Mohamad to restrict the residual royal prerogatives (Kershaw (2001) 160).

[140] Interview with Australian academic expert on Malaysia; interview with international human rights NGO staff #2; interview with Malaysian prosecutor.

[141] Winchester (1986); Harding (1996) 70 n58; Lim (1985); Hashim (1976) 42.

[142] Addruse (1986) 2; Interview with international human rights NGO staff #2.

a long collective history of granting pardons, or by one of the four government-appointed *Yang di-Pertua Negeri* (state governors). The latter, being appointed by the *Agong* on the political advice of the State Chief Minister,[143] have generally demonstrated less independence from Barisan Nasional policy in their decision-making.[144]

With relevance for federal, military, and security cases, the *Yang di-Pertuan Agong* holds a rotating throne created by the Malaysian Constitution only in 1957,[145] rather than a standalone hereditary title hundreds of years old. The *Agong*'s decision-making discretion on clemency has therefore been subject to intense constitutional debate.[146] Suh and Oorjitham quote a senior lawyer's view that may reflect the *Agong*'s largely ceremonial role in relation to pardons: 'The decision is exclusively his'; however, the king 'will not see it as his function to take a different view from that advised. He's the head of state, not a political leader.'[147]

Conversely, Bari contrasts the *Agong* with the Malay rulers: 'the rulers are likely more able to assert their influence as they, unlike the *Yang di Pertuan Agong*, practically reign for life. This enables the rulers to influence the administration of [their] states.'[148]

Notably, all drug-trafficking and murder cases that are committed outside Malaysia's Federal Territories of Kuala Lumpur, Putrajaya, and Labuan, together with firearms/explosives/ammunition offences *not* governed by the (now repealed) Internal Security Act 1960, fall within the rulers' and governors' prerogative, rather than the *Agong's*.[149] As previously described, the rulers

[143] Ibrahim (1992) 519; Azlan Shah (1986) 76; Harding (1996) 63 n16.

[144] Interview with Australian academic expert on Malaysia; interview with international human rights NGO staff #2; Talib (1989) 3. Since 1991, each state governor has been a Barisan Nasional appointee, even though Penang has been governed by the opposition Democratic Action Party since 2008.

[145] Constitution of Malaysia 1957, art 32(1), 32(3).

[146] The Constitution of Malaysia 1957 is ambiguous on the decision-making independence of the *Yang di-Pertuan Agong* in pardons cases. It is unclear whether or not art 40(1A), inserted in 1994 in order to *compel* the *Agong* to act in accordance with 'advice' when given, applies to arts 40(3) and 42(4)(a), describing the Federal Pardons Board as a forum for 'consultation' with or 'recommendation' to the *Agong* (rather than a body to dispense 'advice').

[147] Suh and Oorjitham (1999).

[148] Bari (2003) 60, emphasis added.

[149] Constitution of Malaysia 1957, art 42(1); Essential (Security Cases) Amendment Regulations 1975 (Malaysia), reg 2(1), 32(1).

in particular will be free to make up their own mind on the merits of granting clemency, irrespective of the federal government's view conveyed through the Federal Attorney-General. Unlike the President of Singapore, the Malay rulers' power to pardon is not automatically exercised 'on advice', as per the Westminster tradition. The rulers' own particular incentives to grant pardons, described previously, together with their ultimate discretion to do so, thereby constitute a key factor helping to explain Malaysia's 'high' clemency rate over the period of study.[150]

Long stays on death row

One further consequence of the power over the clemency process exercised by the rulers, governors, and *Agong* is the extremely long wait on death row for condemned prisoners. Over the period of study, in state cases it was common for prisoners sentenced to death in Malaysia to wait for around ten years for a decision by the relevant Pardons Board, due to the infrequency of their meetings,[151] although the precise interval between sittings varied between the individual Boards.[152] A meeting of each Pardons Board must be initiated by the Attorney-General requesting an audience with the respective ruler or governor,[153] but it is entirely within the latter's discretion as to when (or whether) the meeting will take place,[154] with no legal time limit within which clemency appeals must be heard.[155] The logistical difficulties in requiring all six Board members to meet face to face, in addition to the alleged

[150] Although a statistical breakdown of capital prosecutions by state and territory is unavailable, one crude measure of the rulers' influence is population. Approximately two-thirds of Malaysia's population live in the nine Malay States.

[151] Shafee Abdullah (2/11/2012); 'Some Pardons Boards Have Not Met for Years' (2006). See generally Aziz (2001); 'Dead Wait' (2006); Habib (2009).

[152] 'Review Parole System and Pardons Board' (2009); interview with Malaysian prosecutor. Hands Off Cain has recently reported a fall to a two-year average interval and a ten-year maximum (Hands Off Cain, 'Malaysia' (2017)).

[153] Talib (1989) 64; interview with Malaysian prosecutor; interview with Malaysian member of parliament.

[154] New (2016); interview with Malaysian human rights lawyer.

[155] New (2016). Although the Prisons Regulations 2000 (Malaysia), reg 54, mandate that prisons authorities prepare a report every four years on each long-term prisoner for consideration by the State and Federal Pardons Boards, there is no guarantee that the Boards will meet every four years, as the legislation anticipates.

low priority accorded to Pardons Board meetings by the nine Malay rulers have, in the past, caused multiple-year delays before each meeting.[156] Malaysia's past practice therefore more closely resembles Thailand's five- to ten-year wait for the disposal of petitions for individual royal pardon,[157] rather than Singapore's ultra-efficient death penalty regime.

Prior to delays in convening the Pardons Boards, the judicial process itself can also take up to ten years.[158] This means that death row prisoners in Malaysia have often faced an interminable wait to be heard. In 2006, the *New Straits Times* reported that the two prisoners on death row in Malaysia for the lengthiest periods had been imprisoned for twenty-two years (for drug trafficking) and twenty-five years (for firearms possession), with their cases yet to be considered by the relevant State Pardons Boards.[159] In 2012, the same newspaper reported one case whose resolution took thirty-eight years.[160] In recent years, the rulers do appear to have taken their responsibilities to convene Pardons Boards more seriously, forming one possible explanation for the comparatively high number of recent clemency grants (ninety-five between 2010 and 2016).[161] Nevertheless, prominent lawyer Muhammad Shafee Abdullah has observed that when judicial appeals and Pardons Board delays are added together, a condemned prisoner's total time spent incarcerated before either execution or clemency typically extends to 13.5 years: almost exactly the same as a 'life' sentence subject to a one-third remission for good behaviour.[162]

[156] Interview with Malaysian human rights lawyer; interview with international human rights NGO staff #2. The rulers may have different motivations for failing to convene Pardons Boards meetings. For example, two interviewees speculated whether some rulers had actively sought to establish a de facto moratorium on executions in their states (interview with Malaysian human rights lawyer; interview with international human rights NGO staff #2).

[157] See Chapter 3.

[158] Interview with Malaysian human rights lawyer; '121 Convicts in "Death Row"' (2003); Human Rights Commission of Malaysia (2004) 5; Hands Off Cain, 'Malaysia' (2008). Shafee Abdullah asserts a 'minimum period of about six years' (Shafee Abdullah (2/11/2012)).

[159] 'Some Pardons Boards Have Not Met for Years' (2006); 'A Peculiar Purgatory' (2008). See also 'Dead Wait' (2006) and Shafee Abdullah (2/11/2012).

[160] Shafee Abdullah (2/11/2012).

[161] Appendix (Malaysia); Pascoe (2017c) 11.

[162] Shafee Abdullah (2/11/2012).

As first described in Chapter 2, whether the situation arises through simple negligence, by design as a de facto moratorium on executions, or as a deliberate form of additional punishment, lengthening the time a prisoner spends on death row actually increases the chances of clemency being eventually granted. In common with other retentionist jurisdictions, very long stays on death row provide prisoners in Malaysia ample time to rehabilitate themselves and to demonstrate remorse for their crimes. Although their cases are not usually mentioned in the media by name, from 1991 to 2016 there were several reports of death row prisoners whose sentences were commuted or who were released outright following good behaviour, among other criteria.[163] Moreover, rehabilitation in prison has been explicitly confirmed by the Attorney-General's Chambers as one of the most important criteria for clemency considered by the rulers and governors in capital cases.[164]

The end result is a direct link between the tardiness of Malaysia's judicial process, certain rulers' alleged inattention to their Pardons Boards, and the proportion of finalized cases eventually granted clemency. By the time that a State Pardons Board convenes to consider a list of pending capital cases—many years after the petitioners were first arrested—potential retributive justifications for clemency deriving from the trial,[165] together with the Attorney-General's views on the case as public prosecutor and as a conduit for elected government interests, may well hold lesser importance. It is possible that, given such a long delay, both the Attorney-General and other Board members may instead accord greater prominence to Prisons Department reports detailing the way the convict has spent his or her time incarcerated, the convict's own written plea for mercy, and what a senior Malaysian lawyer labelled the Board's own collective 'guilty conscience' in prolonging the prisoner's stay on death row in the first place.[166]

[163] See note 70. Natural life sentence prisoners (i.e. those who were sentenced never to be released) have also seen their sentences commuted by the State and Federal Pardons Boards as a result of time served and good behaviour (Damis (12/2004)).

[164] Tan (2010).

[165] See the section entitled 'Discretion at earlier stages'.

[166] Interview with Malaysian prosecutor.

The Symbolic Value of the Mandatory Death Penalty

Systemic features of the Pardons Boards' decision-making processes, in particular the role played by the Malay rulers in State cases, mean that in all likelihood more death sentences have been commuted by clemency than have been carried out in Malaysia since 1991. The role of the Malay rulers, together with written submissions from trial and appeal judges, the Prisons Department, and even condemned prisoners themselves, all have a significant countervailing effect in overcoming factors that would otherwise minimize the possibility of clemency for retributive, redemptive, or purely merciful reasons. These purportedly restrictive factors are the Federal Attorney-General's central role on each Pardons Board, and the various available means to exercise lenient discretion at stages prior to clemency.

One remaining mystery is why the *Agong*, rulers, and governors have publicly approved clemency for several foreign nationals over the period of study (it is unclear exactly how many) in order to safeguard Malaysia's international relations with both retentionist and abolitionist countries.[167] In order to preserve a valued economic relationship, or even to prompt reciprocal leniency to Malaysian citizens sentenced to death abroad,[168] it would have been possible to take nationality into account behind closed doors at the prosecutorial discretion phase, as is most likely now done in Singapore. One distinct possibility is that, although administrative, prosecutorial, and judicial discretion operate to filter away certain cases before they ever reach the State and Federal Pardons Boards, the foreign governments concerned did not make formal or informal representations to the Malaysian government at these earlier stages, for fear of infringing national sovereignty.[169] Knowing that the rulers, governors, and *Agong* grant clemency reasonably frequently for extralegal reasons, the diplomatic and political representatives of some nations may only have sought to intervene at the final procedural stage, leading to their

[167] See the section entitled 'Features of cases where clemency was granted'.

[168] Anti-Death Penalty Asia Network (2012); statement by Malaysian human rights lawyer #2.

[169] Statement by Malaysian human rights lawyer #2.

success there. Available evidence, albeit limited, from media reports appears to support this theory.[170]

The overall impact of leniency exercised by police, prosecutors, judges, and clemency decision makers is that mandatory death penalty laws have more of a symbolic rather than a practical value within Malaysia's criminal justice system, at least since the decline of Malaysia's 'war on drugs' in the mid-1990s. The large and growing gap between legislation and enforcement calls into question the Malaysian government's motivations in retaining mandatory capital sentencing. Of the offences prosecuted with any frequency since 1991, mandatory capital murder is largely retained for historical reasons,[171] the repealed Internal Security Act's weapons offences were directed at a Communist insurgency that ended in 1989, and there is little empirical evidence to suggest that the more punitive narcotics laws enacted in 1983 have led to lower rates of drug supply or addiction.[172] Moreover, the Firearms (Increased Penalties) Act 1971 incorporated the mandatory death penalty at a time when Malaysia faced law and order problems far more serious than is the case today.[173] Yet even if Malaysia completely abolishes mandatory capital sentencing for murder, drug trafficking, or remaining firearms offences, clemency

[170] Although little is known about the effectiveness of diplomatic representations before trial, foreign governments have certainly been successful with interventions at the clemency phase. Consider the following examples: Osman (2010) (Indonesian government representatives seeking a meeting with the *Agong*); Fauziyah (2015) 55–6 (Indonesian government representatives sending letters to the *Agong* and meeting with the Malaysian Minister for Home Affairs; Indonesian Ambassador and Consulate-General sending a letter to the Sultan of Johor); 'Malaysia Lowers Sentences of 3 Death Throw [sic] Pinoys' (2012) (Philippines Ambassador sending a letter to the Governor of Sabah); Clapano (2003) (correspondence between the Philippines president and the Malaysian deputy prime minister).
Fauziyah (2015, at 55, 70) notes that Indonesian government representatives have also sent diplomatic notes to Malaysian courts in the past. Moreover, Indonesian president Susilo Bambang Yudhoyono (in power from 2004 to 2014) sent letters to the Malaysian government asking for judicial acquittals. It is unclear whether these approaches ultimately proved successful in helping to obtain more lenient sentences.

[171] Mehat (1991) x; Amnesty International (1989) 171.

[172] Harring (1991) 403; Amnesty International AI Index ASA 03/01/97, 12; Amnesty International AI Index ACT 51/02/95, 56; Firdaws (2017).

[173] Interview with former Malaysian Federal Court judge; interview with Malaysian human rights lawyer.

will no doubt continue to play a role in the future administration of a discretionary death penalty regime. As with Thailand, Malaysia's slow judicial process, together with the constitutional role accorded to Malaysia's traditional monarchs suggests that this will be the case, at least in the nine Malay states.

6

Republic of Indonesia

> *Indonesia has reached a crossroads as far as capital punishment is concerned. With almost twice as many people on death row as have been executed in the past 30 years, either it will soon have to conduct a lot more executions, or it will have to commute many or all of these sentences.*
>
> Dave McRae, writing for *Inside Indonesia* in 2008, foreshadows future developments[1]

The modern history of Indonesia encompasses two distinct political regimes: the 'New Order' period (1967–98) under the military autocrat Suharto, and the period known as *Reformasi*, or Indonesia's 'Reform Era' (1999–present).[2] Death penalty developments during the Suharto era were dominated by repercussions from a single event: the failed coup that took place on 30 August and 1 September 1965, subsequently attributed to members and associates of the Partai Komunis Indonesia (Indonesian Communist Party, or 'PKI'). The failure of the coup allowed then General Suharto to claim the Indonesian presidency from Sukarno and institute a crackdown on PKI members, sympathizers, and Suharto's own political opponents, resulting in an estimated half a million people imprisoned and up to one million massacred during the following few years.[3] Around sixty PKI members and associates labelled most responsible for the coup attempt were

[1] McRae (2008).

[2] The administration of Indonesia's third president, BJ Habibie (May 1998–October 1999), is considered a transitional period here. Habibie was the author of a number of democratic reforms but came from Suharto's GOLKAR party and was an unelected president.

[3] Amnesty International AI Index ASA 21/43/96; Cribb (2002) 557–9; Smith (2001) 77. Lev (2011, at 223) asserts that 'calculating how many died is nearly impossible because of the lack of hard evidence; the figure of 500,000 commonly

Last Chance for Life: Clemency in Southeast Asian Death Penalty Cases. First Edition. Daniel Pascoe. Published 2019 by Oxford University Press.

sentenced to death in 'show' trials in military and civilian courts in the late 1960s and 1970s.[4]

The fate of many of these detainees remained undecided for decades. The most recent executions of these prisoners took place in 1990 (marginally outside the period of study);[5] however, between four and ten coup-related prisoners remaining on death row were pardoned and released in 1999.[6] When added to the twelve coup-related prisoners granted commutations in 1980,[7] it is greatly significant that the majority of publicly reported capital clemency grants over Indonesia's past fifty years can be tied to the events of 30 August and 1 September 1965, and their aftermath.

Following Suharto's resignation in May 1998 (and the subsequent resignation of his former deputy and immediate successor, BJ Habibie, in October 1999),[8] Indonesia's four recent democratically elected leaders have pursued a more overtly populist criminal justice policy, with drug crimes emerging, and Islamic terrorism re-emerging, as crimes demanding a lethal response from the state.[9] During the *Reformasi* era, death penalty clemency has been granted reasonably rarely, at least in publicly reported cases. Media and NGO reports suggest that clemency was only granted in a single capital case during the administrations of Abdurrahman Wahid (October 1999–July 2001) and Megawati

referred to is simply midway between low and high estimates'. Hunt has acknowledged that:

> The abortive coup of 30 September 1965, including the eventual replacement of Sukarno by General Suharto and the repression of communists or communist sympathisers throughout Indonesia, were, as Edwards has described, 'a major turning-point in the politics of Indonesia and all of Southeast Asia'. (Hunt (2017) 199, quoting Edwards (2014) 132)

[4] Amnesty International (1988a) 2; Lev (2011) 233–4, 346; Amnesty International AI Index ASA 21/33/85. TAPOL quotes at least sixty-six death sentences (TAPOL (1980) 1–2) while Southwood and Flanagan (1983, at 156) list seventy-four sentences.

[5] KontraS (2010).

[6] See Appendix (Indonesia).

[7] Amnesty International (1988a) 9; Glasius (1999) 95.

[8] See note 2.

[9] Perry (2009). Between 1983 and 1991, at least six alleged Muslim terrorists were executed after being convicted of subversion or murder (KontraS (2010)). Both Murray (1991) and Glasius (1999, at 98–9) suggest that Suharto sought to strike a balance between executions of 'extreme right' Muslim prisoners and 'extreme left' PKI prisoners, to satisfy the domestic audience.

Sukarnoputri (July 2001–October 2004).[10] Under Susilo Bambang Yudhoyono (October 2004–October 2014) and Joko Widodo (October 2014–present), clemency has become more frequent, with 13+ confirmed grants by May 2016, but so too have executions,[11] thereby limiting the clemency rate to a 'medium' level over the period of study from 1991 to 2016.

The challenge in conducting research on capital punishment in Indonesia is therefore to document common trends that span what are two very different political eras—autocratic and democratic. In no other Southeast Asian jurisdiction is this problem so apparent. Of the four jurisdictions under study, Indonesia's clemency practice is also the most irregular, seemingly defined more by ad hoc case-based factors and immediate political considerations than by long-term, consistent policies on particular crime and offender categories. As documented in detail in this chapter, the inconsistency of clemency over time and between cases is in itself the notable trend in Indonesia.

Death Penalty and Clemency Practice 1991–2016

Death sentences and executions

Indonesia inherited the death penalty as a criminal punishment, together with the firing squad as a method of execution, from the Netherlands, the colonial power from which Indonesia declared independence in 1945.[12] Despite the country's large population (260 million in 2016), at least up until Joko Widodo's presidency from October 2014, Indonesia had always carried out capital punishment sporadically. Until Widodo came to power, Indonesia's death penalty practice was characterized by low annual totals for

[10] Appendix (Indonesia). See also Imparsial (2004) 13. Although there are no affirmative reports of President Wahid granting clemency in a death penalty case, overall Wahid granted clemency 72 times and rejected 151 petitions. President Megawati granted clemency 33 times and rejected 116 petitions (Deliani (2011) 166).

[11] Appendix (Indonesia).

[12] Imparsial (2010) 4, 8. See Sahetapy (1979) 45–51, for an account of clemency practices in death penalty cases during the Dutch colonial era.

death sentences, and unpredictable 'stops and starts' in execution practice.[13]

From 1945 through to 2016, a wide variety of crimes contained within sixteen different legislative and executive instruments attracted the death penalty as a discretionary punishment,[14] although in practice the set of crimes for which death sentences have been passed and executions conducted is substantially smaller, historically limited to subversion against the Suharto regime, premeditated murder, terrorism, and drugs offences.[15] Death sentences imposed by district courts (*Pengadilan Negeri*) may be appealed to a provincial High Court (*Pengadilan Tinggi*) and from there to the Indonesian Supreme Court (*Mahkamah Agung*) by cassation appeal.[16] A High Court or the Supreme

[13] Johnson and Zimring (2009) 313–14, 323 n28; Lindsey and Nicholson (2016) 106.

[14] See Reza (6/2016) for the current list of all thirteen death penalty laws, which excludes the now repealed Anti-Subversion Law (Presidential Decree 11/1963 on the Eradication of Anti-Subversive Activities (Indonesia), incorporated into law by Law 5/1969 on Subversion (Indonesia)), Law 9/1976 on Narcotics (Indonesia), and Law 22/1997 on Narcotics (Indonesia). See Amnesty International (1988a, at 4) for an equivalent list of capital offences in 1985. Executions are prohibited for defendants under eighteen at the time the crime was committed and are delayed for pregnant women (Cornell Center on the Death Penalty Worldwide, 'Indonesia' (2017)).

[15] KontraS (2010); Lindsey and Nicholson (2016) 103. The relevant offences are set out in the Criminal Code 1918 (Indonesia), art 340 (premeditated murder); Law 15/2003 on Eradicating Criminal Acts of Terrorism (Indonesia); Law 9/1976 on Narcotics (Indonesia) (now replaced); Law 5/1997 on Psychotropic Drugs (Indonesia); Law 22/1997 on Narcotics (Indonesia), replaced by Law 35/2009 on Narcotics (Indonesia); and Presidential Decree 11/1963 on the Eradication of Anti-Subversive Activities (Indonesia), incorporated into law by Law 5/1969 on Subversion (Indonesia), but subsequently repealed.For murder cases, the criteria for passing a death sentence are that the killing:

> is [first] clearly unnatural, sadistic ... Second, the culprit does not show remorse or has a criminal record. Third, there is more than one victim. Fourth, his acts have caused social unrest. [Fifth] Can the culprit be reformed or not? (Haryoso (1997))

For narcotics crimes, the type and quantity of drugs seized, the accused's purported knowledge of the package's contents (Bampton (2006) 6; Bachelard (2012)), the accused's seniority within the trafficking syndicate (interview with Indonesian NGO staff), and the accused's antecedents (interview with Indonesian Supreme Court judge) are the important factors relevant to capital sentencing.

[16] Lindsey and Nicholson (2016) 93. Other than coup-related subversion trials at the Extraordinary Military Tribunal (*Mahmillub*) from 1966 to 1978, after

Court may increase a prison sentence to a death sentence on appeal.[17]

To illustrate Indonesia's historical ambivalence towards capital punishment, only three executions took place under Indonesia's first president, Sukarno (in power from 1945 to 1967), resulting from an attempt to assassinate the President in 1957.[18] Death sentences were not passed on a regular basis until the trials of alleged PKI conspirators in the late 1960s and the 1970s.[19] In fact, following independence, no prisoner was executed for premeditated murder until 1978.[20] Local NGO KontraS lists the following executions conducted under Suharto from 1991 to 1998 (see Figure 7):

- premeditated murder: 4;
- subversion (due to Islamic terrorism): 1;[21]
- drug offences: 1.[22]

Of those sentenced to death in the period from Suharto's resignation in May 1998 through to mid-2016, 57 per cent had committed narcotics offences, 40 per cent had committed premeditated murder, and 3 per cent were convicted of terrorist offences.[23] A compilation of NGO data reveals executions for the following offences from 1999 to 2016 (see Figure 7):

- drug offences: 25;
- premeditated murder: 17;
- terrorism (relating to the 2002 Bali bombing): 3.[24]

which prisoners held no right to appeal (Presidential Decree 16/1963 on the Extraordinary Military Tribunal (Indonesia), art 7(2); Lev (2011) 419 n29), death sentences imposed by military courts may be appealed to a military appeal tribunal, and thereafter to the Indonesian Supreme Court (Law 6/1950 on Criminal Procedure (Indonesia), arts 7–9).

[17] McRae (2012) 6; Amnesty International AI Index ASA 21/2434/2015, 18.

[18] Amnesty International (1988a) 2. These executions were performed in 1960 (Amnesty International AI Index 21/27/87, 1).

[19] Amnesty International (1988a) 2.

[20] Amnesty International AI Index ASA 21/01/83, 5; Amnesty International (1979) 4. Local NGO Imparsial counts eighty-four judicial executions conducted since the early 1960s (Imparsial (2017) 1).

[21] See note 9.

[22] KontraS (2010).

[23] Reza (6/2016).

[24] KontraS (2013); Reza (8/2016); Amnesty International (2013).

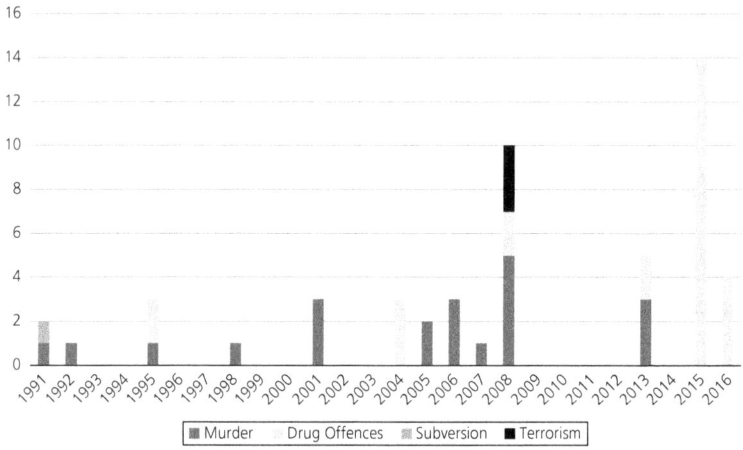

Figure 7 Executions in Indonesia 1991–2016

Sources: Appendix (Indonesia); KontraS (2010); Amnesty International AI Index ACT 50/001/2014; Amnesty International AI Index ACT 50/3487/2016; Amnesty International AI Index ACT 50/5740/2017

Although historical statistics are not nearly as complete on death sentences and death row prisoners as they are for executions, taking cumulative figures from all available sources it is striking that from 1991 to 2016, approximately 6–7 times as many prisoners were sentenced to death (294+ to 367+) as were executed (51).[25] Explanations for this wide discrepancy include successful judicial appeals, the extraordinary case re-opening procedure before the Indonesian Supreme Court, grants of presidential clemency, and Indonesia's ever expanding death row of pending cases.

Executions, historically rare and irregularly spaced in comparison with death sentences (see Figure 7), are typically timed for political benefit.[26] One illustrative trend is that during the period under study the majority of executions conducted have taken place in two distinct blocks—between 2004 and 2008 (nineteen executions) and during the years 2015 and 2016 (eighteen executions)—which together account for more than 70 per cent of the total from

[25] See Appendix (Indonesia).

[26] Interview with Australian academic expert on Indonesia #3; Interview with Indonesian human rights activist; Sabdo (forthcoming).

1991 onwards.[27] Both Brummitt and McRae have argued that the ten executions approved or acquiesced to by President Yudhoyono in 2008 alone came in response to 'mounting pressure to prove he is tough on crime', given the impending presidential election in 2009.[28] Moreover, since Joko Widodo's election as Indonesia's seventh president in October 2014, Indonesia has become one of the ASEAN region's fiercest advocates of executions for drug offences,[29] whereas narcotics executions in neighbouring states have declined since the early 2000s. During 2015 and 2016, eighteen drug prisoners were executed in Indonesia,[30] with the Jakarta-based Attorney General's Office ('AGO')[31] having budgeted for up to thirty more in 2017.[32]

While capital drug offences date back to 1976, during the New Order period,[33] the *Reformasi* governments' recent enforcement of these laws represents a marked development.[34] Commentators have speculated that in a large and disorganized state such as Indonesia, the move to acknowledge drug trafficking as an issue of state security and the consequent tightening of the judicial process took much longer than in neighbouring Malaysia and Singapore. President Suharto and his successors considered developments in the wider region during the 1970s and 1980s and eventually wanted Indonesia to be seen as a 'legally responsible partner' in

[27] See Appendix (Indonesia).

[28] Brummitt (2008); McRae (2008). Arguably, the same applies for the three narcotics executions leading up to the 2004 elections, in which the incumbent Megawati Sukarnoputri was defeated by Susilo Bambang Yudhoyono (interview with Australian academic expert on Indonesia #2; interview with Indonesian human rights activist).

[29] Lindsey and Nicholson (2016) 107.

[30] Reza (8/2016).

[31] The Jakarta-based Attorney General's Office functions as the state prosecutor, as well as head of the government department that administers judicial executions (McRae (2012) 12–13; ASEAN Law Association (2005) 90).

[32] Eddyono et al (2016) 2. By the end of the year, the AGO was unable to meet this 'target', largely due to the legal uncertainty created by Indonesian Constitutional Court Decisions No 107/PUU-XII/2015 and No 34/PUU-XI/2013, as well as differing political priorities.

[33] See Law 9/1976 on Narcotics (Indonesia), art 23(4)–(5).

[34] Only four death sentences were passed for drug trafficking in the decade after Law 9/1976 on Narcotics (Indonesia) was enacted (Amnesty International AI Index ASA 21/27/87, 5; Sakti (1986)).

the fight against trafficking.[35] Indonesia's first execution for drug trafficking took place in 1995,[36] and from the 2000s onwards the dominant political perception was that drug trafficking and abuse were threatening the viability of political, community, and religious institutions.[37] As in Malaysia during the 1980s and early 1990s, and Singapore during the entire period of study, drug trafficking is now seen as one of the premier law and order concerns in Indonesia, alongside pervasive corruption.[38]

Clemency procedures in death penalty cases

Since independence, the Indonesian president as head of state has always possessed the constitutional power to grant clemency. Article 14(1) of the 1945 Constitution grants the president the power to grant clemency (*grasi*), by commuting a sentence to a lesser punishment or by releasing a prisoner through a pardon.[39] Indonesia's Federal Constitution of 1949 and Provisional Constitution of 1950 also contained a presidential clemency power,[40] before the 1945 Constitution was re-established by President Sukarno in 1959. There is no constitutional or legislative requirement that condemned prisoners apply for clemency only after all judicial appeals are exhausted, although prisoners desperate to maintain their innocence during remaining appeal

[35] Interview with Australian academic expert on Indonesia; Lindsey and Nicholson (2016) 47.

[36] Amnesty International AI Index ACT 51/02/95, 42.

[37] US Department of State (2009); Lindsey and Nicholson (2016) 136.

[38] Interview with Indonesian human rights activist; interview with Australian academic expert on Indonesia; McRae (2008). A death sentence for corruption has never been handed down during the *Reformasi* period, despite there being a legislative basis to do so during periods of national crisis pursuant to Law 31/1999 on the Eradication of Criminal Acts of Corruption (Indonesia), art 2(2).

[39] See Law 22/2002 on Clemency (Indonesia), art 4(2). Under the Constitution of Indonesia 1945, art 14(2), the president may also issue *amnesti* (amnesty) to groups of prisoners sentenced to any judicial punishment. Although amnesty is included within this book's definition of clemency, never has an amnesty grant by the Indonesian president benefited a prisoner sentenced to death (see Indonesian Ministry of Law and Human Rights (2016)).

[40] Constitution of Indonesia 1949, art 160; Constitution of Indonesia 1950, art 107.

stages rarely apply for clemency prematurely,[41] given that clemency is implicitly seen as forgiveness for guilt.[42]

Despite the president's ever present constitutional prerogative, the operational specifics of the clemency process in Indonesia have changed a number of times through legislative and executive intervention. The Indonesian legislature has enacted three clemency laws to further regulate the broad clemency power found in the 1945 Indonesian Constitution.[43] Law 3/1950, promulgated under Sukarno, was replaced by Law 22/2002 during the presidency of Megawati, whereas under Yudhoyono, Law 5/2010 amended Law 22/2002 without repealing it.

Law 3/1950 first allowed for the defendant 'or another party' to request clemency from the Indonesian president by written petition. Law 22/2002 explicitly expanded this right to the defendant's family in a death penalty case.[44] Under the 1950 statute there was a thirty-day time limit for clemency appeals,[45] whereas no time limits were initially prescribed in the 2002 law. However, under either law, an execution could not be performed until a presidential decree (*Keputusan Presiden*) was issued rejecting clemency.[46] Until the 2002 law was passed (fixing a limit of three months),[47] there was no time limit for the president to issue the required decree once armed with the Supreme Court's mandatory recommendation on the case.[48] Nevertheless, the three-month deadline has been regularly contravened by Indonesian presidents since 2002.[49]

Under the 1950 law, there were also no restrictions on the number of times that a prisoner could request clemency.[50] Similarly, from 2002, if a capital prisoner's first petition was rejected and yet

[41] Amnesty International (1988b) 6; Bampton (2006) 24.

[42] See Law 22/2002 on Clemency (Indonesia), elucidation; Pascoe (2017a) 325–30.

[43] Indonesia's wartime clemency regulations, Government Regulation 7/1947 on Clemency in the Present Situation (Indonesia), and Government Regulation 67/1948 on Clemency (Indonesia), fall outside the temporal limits of this study.

[44] Law 3/1950 on Clemency (Indonesia), art 1; Law 22/2002 on Clemency (Indonesia), art 6(1), 8(1).

[45] Law 3/1950 on Clemency (Indonesia), art 2(1), 2(2).

[46] Law 22/2002 on Clemency (Indonesia), art 13; Law 3/1950 on Clemency (Indonesia), art 2(3).

[47] Law 22/2002 on Clemency (Indonesia), art 11.

[48] Constitution of Indonesia 1945, art 14(1).

[49] Lindsey and Nicholson (2016) 105.

[50] Fidrus (2003); Hands Off Cain, 'Indonesia' (2014).

he or she was not executed within a two-year period, as was most often the case, Law 22/2002 allowed a second or subsequent application, and again, the death sentence could not be carried out until the president had rejected the prisoner's new petition.[51] The practical effect of the latter provision was that executions needed to be carried out within two years of the president refusing clemency (on a first or subsequent occasion). For the AGO, tasked with organizing executions, this proved difficult to achieve with regularity, unless an individual case was given high priority and rushed through the system.[52]

The state's inability to conduct regular executions pursuant to the 1950 and 2002 clemency laws then led the Indonesian legislature to revise and streamline the clemency procedure via Law 5/2010 on Clemency, enacted on 23 August 2010. The 2010 law amended the 2002 clemency law in the following important ways:

- The Minister of Law and Human Rights is now entitled to unilaterally apply for clemency on a prisoner's behalf, where the prisoner or prisoner's family does not do so (article 6A).[53]
- Upon enactment in 2010, prisoners initially had a time limit of one year to apply for clemency from the date the conviction attained 'permanent legal force' ('*kekuatan hukum tetap*') (article 7(2)). However, in June 2016 this provision was struck out by the Indonesian Constitutional Court, as it was deemed to clash with death row prisoners' human right to apply for clemency, and the Indonesian president's unlimited prerogative to grant it.[54]
- The prisoner's right to launch a second or subsequent clemency appeal after two years has been removed (article 2(3)).

[51] Law 22/2002 on Clemency (Indonesia), art 2(3), 13.

[52] One example arose in 2006, when three Christian militants convicted for murder were promptly executed after their first round of clemency petitions was rejected (Sijabat (2006)). Another example was the 2008 executions of the Bali bombers: Imam Samudra, Amrozi Nurhasyim, and Ali Ghufron (McRae (2012) 7).

[53] This provision is designed to ensure that all prisoners have their death sentences considered for clemency, whether or not they apply for it. It is not designed to expedite a prisoner's execution. See notes 168–169 and associated text.

[54] See Constitutional Court Decision No 107/PUU-XII/2015 (Indonesia), 11, 19, 21, 22, 37, 78–9.

Furthermore, transitional provisions outlined in the 2010 law mandated that all outstanding clemency petitions made under the 2002 law should have been be ruled on by 22 October 2012.[55] Death row prisoners who had not yet submitted clemency petitions under the 2002 law had one year to do so, from the enactment of the amendment on 23 August 2010 through to 23 August 2011.[56]

Agencies that have regularly advised Indonesia's presidents on whether to grant clemency include the Jakarta-based AGO, which processes a prisoner's formal appeal before it reaches the president,[57] and the Ministry of Justice (known from the Yudhoyono administration onwards as the Ministry of Law and Human Rights),[58] together with the police, prison authorities, and, during the *Reformasi* era, the National Narcotics Board (Badan Narkotika Nasional or 'BNN') in drugs cases.[59] Nevertheless, the president's most important clemency advisers have always been justices from the Indonesian Supreme Court's criminal chambers, pursuant to the requirements of Law 3/1950, Law 22/2002, and article 14(1) of the 1945 Constitution.[60] Significantly, the Supreme Court is the only advisory body mentioned in the 1945 Constitution, with the president mandated to 'have regard to' ('*memperhatikan*') such advice but not necessarily to follow it. One interviewee asserted that Indonesia's first president, Sukarno, usually followed the Supreme Court's advice on clemency.[61] Suharto, in his

[55] Law 5/2010 on Clemency (Indonesia), art 15A(1).

[56] Law 5/2010 on Clemency (Indonesia), art 15A(2).

[57] Law 3/1950 on Clemency (Indonesia), art 8; Elda (2009) 89; interview with Australian academic expert on Indonesia #2; interview with Indonesian deputy minister. Law 3/1950 on Clemency (Indonesia), art 8 also gave an advisory role to the local prosecutor who brought the case and to the District Court which tried the case.

[58] Law 3/1950 on Clemency (Indonesia), art 8; Elda (2009) 89; interview with Australian academic expert on Indonesia #2; interview with Indonesian deputy minister. From October 1999 to August 2001 the minister's title was 'Minister of Law and Legislation', whereas from August 2001 to October 2004 the minister's title was 'Minister of Justice and Human Rights'.

[59] Marszalek (2013); interview with Indonesian deputy minister; Salna (2013).

[60] Law 22/2002 on Clemency (Indonesia), art 4(1), 10, 11; Law 3/1950 on Clemency (Indonesia), art 8; Constitution of Indonesia 1945, art 14(1). The Chief Justice will choose a single judge from within the Supreme Court's criminal chambers to make the formal recommendation to the president (interview with Indonesian Supreme Court judge).

[61] Interview with Indonesian human rights lawyer.

autobiography, also stated that he usually followed the advice of the Supreme Court in either affirming or commuting the death sentence,[62] and various sources suggest that President Yudhoyono likewise heeded the Supreme Court's advice in most cases, in addition to advice given by his Cabinet ministers.[63] There are so far no reports on President Widodo's treatment of the Supreme Court's advice in capital cases, although Widodo's stated blanket denial of clemency in drugs cases from December 2014 onwards[64] is a politically motivated decision that will surely clash with the legal opinion of the Supreme Court in a current or future case.[65]

Even after considering the Supreme Court's advice and rejecting a petition, the president retains some control over the timing of executions.[66] The AGO does not usually proceed to arrange an execution unless the serving president has given informal approval.[67] Anecdotal evidence suggests that behaviour in prison (including attempted bribery, escape, and dealing narcotics), the prisoner's nationality, and the political and public prominence of the case will operate to expedite the executions of some prisoners ahead of others.[68] There is often no relationship between the order in which clemency petitions are disposed of and the order

[62] Soeharto (1991) 337; see also Sya'ban (1985) 82. However, a leading Indonesian human rights lawyer from the New Order period acknowledged that such advice was usually tendered by a subservient Supreme Court based on a prediction of what Suharto wanted to hear (interview with Indonesian human rights lawyer).

[63] Kencana (2012); Yudhoyono (2011); 'Presiden Tidak Beri Grasi Penjahat Narkoba' (2006); interview with Indonesian human rights lawyer; interview with Indonesian human rights lawyer #2. Deliani (2011, at 173) found that, in capital and non-capital cases from 2004 to 2010, Yudhoyono followed the Supreme Court's advice on 86 per cent of clemency petitions.

[64] Aritonang and Susanto (2014). See also note 142 and associated text.

[65] Nonetheless, the Indonesian NGO Institute for Criminal Justice Reform has asserted that Jokowi received advice on this mass clemency rejection from several Cabinet ministers, the Attorney-General's Office, the Head of the Indonesian National Police, and the Supreme Court itself (Institute for Criminal Justice Reform (2017) 224–5).

[66] McRae (2017) 15.

[67] Interview with Indonesian human rights lawyer #2; McRae (2015) (during *Reformasi*); Glasius (1999) 105 (under Suharto).

[68] Interview with Australian academic expert on Indonesia #2; Hands Off Cain, 'Indonesia' (2008); McRae (2008); McRae (2012) 7; Amnesty International (1988b) 3.

and frequency of executions. Instead, executions are usually timed for maximum political benefit, as described earlier.

Features of cases where clemency was granted

Based on publicly available data, Indonesia's 1991–2016 clemency rate fits firmly within the 'medium' category identified in Chapter 1, at 26–33 per cent.[69] While taking this range at face value reveals that clemency is not uncommon in Indonesian death penalty cases, it does not on its own provide a truly accurate picture of the incidence of capital clemency over Indonesia's recent history.

From 1991 to 2016, different Indonesian presidents prioritized different types of cases for either clemency or execution. When classifying capital clemency according to the type of crime committed, from 1991 to 2016, prisoners guilty of subversion received pardon in 4–10 cases (depending on the sources consulted) and murder convicts received clemency in 9+ reported cases, whereas the sentences of drug traffickers have been commuted in only 6+ reported cases.[70] However, these are unofficial aggregates only. Particularly in murder cases, there are likely to have been further unreported grants of capital clemency since 1991 not documented by media, NGO, academic, and interview-based sources.[71] If so, 26–33 per cent may well be an underestimation of Indonesia's clemency rate, given that complete execution totals are available for the period under study.[72]

The most prominent group of prisoners to have received presidential clemency over the period of study were all sentenced to death for their role in orchestrating the alleged PKI coup in 1965. On 17 March 1999, as part of Indonesia's political transition from authoritarianism to democracy, the ten remaining coup-related prisoners were released by President Suharto's successor, BJ Habibie. Between four and ten of the prisoners released were still under sentence of death more than thirty years after first

[69] See Appendix (Indonesia).
[70] Appendix (Indonesia).
[71] Interview with Indonesian human rights lawyer; interview with Indonesian deputy minister; interview with Indonesian Supreme Court judge.
[72] Appendix (Indonesia).

being convicted.[73] Given the historical significance of their cases, the coup-related prisoners are discussed in a separate section later in this chapter.

Next, murderers have been granted clemency more consistently than prisoners sentenced to death for other types of crimes during recent Indonesian history, primarily for rehabilitative reasons. During the New Order era, President Suharto developed an unofficial 'remissions' policy to quietly reprieve certain well-behaved prisoners sentenced to death, most likely for murder.[74] While there is no public record of which individual prisoners benefited, Amnesty International researchers, an academic expert on Indonesian law, and even President Suharto himself (in his autobiography) have all confirmed that presidential clemency commonly reduced death sentences to life imprisonment during the New Order era, without any formal publication by the media or the State Secretariat.[75] Although these sources primarily refer to 1980s practices, it is possible that Suharto continued his death row 'remissions' policy from 1991 through to his resignation in May 1998. After all, remissions (*Remisi*) in non-death penalty cases occur on a regular basis, to celebrate Indonesia's Independence Day and religious holidays each year.[76]

Suharto's 'remissions' policy may also have been continued by democratically elected Indonesian leaders since 1999, via reported and unreported grants of clemency in murder cases. First, in 2003, President Megawati Sukarnoputri commuted the death sentence

[73] Appendix (Indonesia); 'Coup Plotter to Be Freed after Years of Failed Efforts' (1999).

[74] Amnesty International (1988a) 5; Amnesty International AI Index ASA 21/27/87, 5. These unreported commutations are likely to have predominantly benefited murder convicts, given that (a) the cases of the accused PKI prisoners as well as Islamic terrorists convicted under the Anti-Subversion Law were all reasonably well documented by the Indonesian and international media, and (b) other than for the aforementioned crimes, drug traffickers provided the only other group of prisoners sentenced to death during the Suharto era, and these cases were relatively rare (see notes 34-36 and associated text).

[75] Amnesty International (1988a) 5; statement by Australian academic expert on Indonesia #5; Amnesty International AI Index ASA 21/27/87, 5; Soeharto (1991) 337.

[76] Lindsey and Nicholson (2016) 108–9. The unofficial 'remissions' policy should be interpreted as clemency for redemptive purposes rather than as 'mercy from the sovereign' under the military autocrat Suharto. This is because the grants were made quietly, away from the public eye.

of convicted murderer Harnoko Dewantoro, who had been 'sentenced to death [extra-territorially] in 1997 for killing three people … in Los Angeles, California, between 1991 and 1992'. Dewantoro was granted clemency when reports of his psychiatric problems surfaced,[77] and following ten years' good behaviour in prison.[78] Significantly, Megawati announced the commutation in conjunction with a sentence remission for around 37,000 inmates to celebrate the Islamic holy day Eid al-Fitr.[79] Next, in 2013, President Yudohoyno granted at least one petitioner clemency following a death sentence for murder, although his reasons for doing so remain unknown.[80] Then, between October 2014 and May 2016, President Widodo granted at least seven condemned murderers clemency,[81] even as he concurrently vowed to reject all clemency appeals from drug traffickers. No official reasons for the commutations have been publicly provided, although media articles have speculated on possible rehabilitative and retributive justifications.[82]

[77] Unidjaja (2003). Mental disorder at the time the crime was committed is an exculpatory factor in Indonesia (Criminal Code 1918 (Indonesia), art 44(1)), but a mental illness developed on death row does not legally prevent execution.

[78] 'Hukuman Mati Terhadap Oki, Jaksa Tunggu Keputusan Grasi' (2017).

[79] Hands Off Cain, 'Indonesia' (2003); 'Indonesia's Megawati Grants Muslim Holy Day Amnesties' (2003). However, a conflicting report from Indonesian NGO KontraS stated that Dewantoro was still on death row as of 2010, with his first clemency appeal having been rejected (KontraS (2010)). A media report from 2013 suggested that Dewantoro was still seeking clemency ('5 Pembunuh Kejam Ini Menanti Eksekusi Mati' (2013)).

[80] McRae (2017) 7; Lingga (2015).

[81] Mulyana (2016); 'Jokowi Berikan Grasi Dua Terpidana Mati Asal Sumut' (2016). The first source (Mulyana (2016)) does not list the crimes that the first five prisoners committed. However, given (a) the very small number of terrorism suspects on death row (see KontraS (2016)), and (b) Widodo's stated approach to reject all petitions from narcotics convicts (Aritonang and Susanto (2014)), by deduction these grants must have been made for murder. Subsequently, in May 2016 Widodo granted clemency to two more murder convicts—Ronald Sagala and Nasib Purba ('Jokowi Berikan Grasi Dua Terpidana Mati Asal Sumut' (2016)).

[82] At least one of the prisoners spared, Dwi Trisna Firmansyah, received a favourable recommendation for clemency from prison authorities, although this may not have been the sole justification. Firmansyah may also have been a lesser participant in the crime, and may have acted out of desperation to feed his family ('Dapat Grasi, Ini Curhat Terpidana Mati Pembunuhan Sadis ke Jokowi' (2015)). One of the other prisoners to benefit may have been provoked into killing ('Dua Terpidana Mati Dapat Grasi dari Presiden Jokowi' (2016)).

In drug-trafficking cases, Indonesia's first reported clemency grant came in 1998, during the final days of Suharto's presidency. Kamjai Kong Thavorn,[83] a sailor, was arrested in August 1987 in East Kalimantan

> after Indonesian customs officials conducting a routine inspection discovered 17.76 kilograms of heroin in his cabin. Evidence which emerged *after his trial* suggested strongly that Kamjai Kong Thavorn was either innocent or else a very minor actor in a large drug smuggling operation. According to defence lawyers, two men questioned by Thai police in June 1991 admitted that they had placed a bag containing 20 packages of heroin in Kamjai Khong Thavorn's cabin on instruction from a Japanese national.[84]

President Yudhoyono also granted clemency to four drug traffickers during 2011 and 2012.[85] In granting the four commutations, despite a promise in 2006 not to do so for narcotics convicts,[86] Yudhoyono and his spokespersons cited to the media the prisoners' demonstrated remorse,[87] their family circumstances,[88] and their status as drug 'mules' rather than large-scale traffickers.[89] The clemency grants may also have been an attempt to influence clemency decision makers for Indonesian citizens on death row in other retentionist nations,[90] notably Malaysia, Saudi Arabia, and China.[91] Finally, Yudhoyono made a further grant in 2013, reducing a marijuana trafficker's sentence from death to twenty years.[92] Although no reasons for this commutation have

[83] Imparsial (2004) 18; Amnesty International AI Index ASA 21/040/2004, 9.

[84] Amnesty International AI Index ASA 21/040/2004, 9, emphasis added.

[85] McRae (2013). These were Merika Franola, Rani Andriani, Indra Bahadur Tamal, and Deni Setia Maharwan (Saragih (2012)).

[86] The four traffickers on death row to benefit were part of a group of nineteen capital and non-capital drug convicts to receive clemency, who had all submitted their petitions to Yudhoyono between 2004 and 2011 (Sagita (2012)).

[87] Deni Setia Maharwan and Rani Andriani (Sumarno (2014)).

[88] Deni Setia Maharwan (Saragih (2012); Sagita (2012)).

[89] All four clemency recipients (Sagita (2012)).

[90] McRae (2017) 13; Amnesty International AI Index ASA 21/2434/2015, 16; Kencana (2012).

[91] Mulya Lubis (2015) 17.

[92] 'Lolos Hukuman Mati, Cong Roib Abdikan Diri Menjadi Guru Ngaji' (2017).

been publicly revealed, a similar logic as for the 2011 and 2012 prisoners is likely to apply.

Explaining the Medium Clemency Rate in Indonesia

As with the previous chapter on Malaysia, the approach I take in analysing the reasons for Indonesia's 'medium' clemency rate is to first outline factors that, throughout recent Indonesian history, have worked to *minimize* the incidence of presidential clemency. These two factors are lenient discretion exercised at earlier stages of potential capital cases, and Indonesia's 'rule of law' politics during democratization. The first factor is a feature of Indonesia's death penalty practice that both the Suharto and *Reformasi* eras have in common, whereas by definition the second factor only arose after the fall of the New Order regime. Two more considerations then follow to explain, despite the aforementioned constraints, why up to one third of Indonesian capital prisoners were nonetheless granted clemency between 1991 and 2016 rather than being executed. The first of these enabling factors involves the historically unique circumstances of one group of prisoners granted pardons: those accused of directing and participating in the alleged coup of 1965. The second enabling factor is excessive time on death row: a systemic feature of Indonesia's death penalty landscape, both pre- and post-*Reformasi*, which has served to promote capital clemency within both reported and unreported cases.

Leniency at earlier stages

Put simply, leniency exercised at the early stages of capital cases in Indonesia, whether at the pre-trial stage, before sentencing judges, or on appeal, operates to reduce the value of executive clemency as a final remedy for prisoners and as a political tool for Indonesia's presidents. Within the present section, I consider the impact of corruption and nepotism on capital cases, Indonesia's discretionary death sentence laws, and the *peninjauan kembali* case re-opening procedure. Arguably, each reduce clemency's importance and therefore incidence in capital cases.

First, corruption and nepotism. While the democratic reforms that have taken place since the fall of Suharto have aided transparency, on a historical level corruption and nepotism within the

Indonesian criminal justice system have been endemic.[93] As a result, prisoners with sufficient money and connections often escape a death sentence long before the case ever comes to the Indonesian president for clemency consideration.[94] Although it is possible that political and business connections, together with outright bribery, favourably determined a number of clemency petitions during the Suharto era,[95] throughout the period under analysis corruption and nepotism have usually changed the outcome of potential capital cases at earlier stages, such as during police investigations, prosecutors' handling of the case, and judicial adjudication.[96] To illustrate, in 2012, Butt described a host of systemic corruption problems in the criminal justice sector:

> Police, prosecutors and judges are often criticised for seeking illicit payments from suspects and defendants and their families, sometimes using their lawyers as 'go-betweens'. Bribes are said to be commonly extorted or paid to police to avoid or delay arrest, investigation and detention; and to alter, remove or supplement statements or evidence in the case file ... Some prosecutors allegedly seek payment in return for indicting a suspect under a lesser charge or seeking a lesser sentence before the court.[97]

How do corruption and nepotism affect the frequency of capital clemency in Indonesia? While in other retentionist jurisdictions political or military ties, foreign nationality, or wealth alone are non-legal factors that may help a death row prisoner mitigate his

[93] Lindsey and Nicholson (2016) 135; Lynch (2009) 558; Butt and Lindsey (2011) 189–90; Mulya Lubis (2015) 22.

[94] Interview with Australian academic expert on Indonesia; Lev (1999) 185.

[95] Interview with Australian academic expert on Asian Studies; interview with Australian academic expert on Indonesia. In one well-known case, murderer Kusni Kasdut, executed in 1979, reportedly withdrew his clemency appeal after being told that Rp 200,000 (at the time, approximately GBP 160) would be required to ensure its success ('Perjalanan Grasi Kusni Kasdut' (1979)).
During the more transparent Yudhoyono presidency, it seems unlikely that corruption and nepotism alone could have consistently altered the result of clemency applications. However, a 2013 newspaper article reported a prison rumour that death row convicts 'could bribe their way to a life sentence for Rp 1 billion [GBP 55,000]', although it is unclear whether this fee was to secure clemency or judicial leniency on appeal (Pasandaran and Sihombing (2013)).

[96] Fidrus (2006); Hands Off Cain, 'Indonesia' (2007); Langit (2004); Michelmore (2008); Lynch (2009) 558.

[97] Butt (2012) 23. See also Lev (1999, at 186), confirming the same kinds of practices during the Suharto era.

or her sentence at the executive clemency phase,[98] in Indonesia it is less likely that such a case will proceed all the way through the death penalty system in the first place. Lev, writing at the end of the Suharto period, described corruption and nepotism's practical effect in criminal cases: 'Political or social prominence, for example, is on the face of it exculpatory. Murder is not an indictable offense, or at least not subject to conviction, if committed by members of well-connected, well-known, or well-heeled families.'[99]

Several well-known cases provide possible examples of bribery and nepotism at earlier stages in potential capital cases. These include cases of murders committed or narcotics trafficking engaged in by members of the Indonesian military;[100] the cases of Hanky Gunawan and Hillary Chimezie (where the death penalty for drug trafficking was inexplicably commuted to a lesser penalty by the Indonesian Supreme Court);[101] the murder trial of President Suharto's youngest son, Tommy Suharto (who was sentenced to fifteen years' imprisonment, rather than death, for ordering the killing of a judge);[102] the cases of the co-defendants of condemned British drug trafficker Lindsay Sandiford (sentenced to between one and six years' imprisonment);[103] and several further occasions where capital defendants' lawyers were offered lesser punishments in exchange for payment, but they refused.[104]

Next, whereas corruption and nepotism demand that death sentences be avoided at earlier stages for non-legal reasons, less insidious *retributive* justifications for clemency are also foreclosed by prior lenient discretion in Indonesia. Unlike in common law Singapore and Malaysia, in Indonesia the death penalty has always

[98] See Chapter 2.

[99] Lev (1999) 185.

[100] Interview with Australian academic expert on Indonesia. For example, in 2013 a military court sentenced Serma Supriadi (a member of the Indonesian military's Strategic Intelligence Body) to seven years' imprisonment plus a fine of Rp 1.5 billion for involvement in Freddy Budiman's importation of 1.4 million ecstasy tablets (Erdianto (2016)). Budiman was sentenced to death for this crime in 2012 and was executed in 2016 (Kurniawati (2016)).

[101] Butt (2014) 135.

[102] Aglionby (2002).

[103] 'Lindsay Sandiford—What Price a Life?' (2016).

[104] 'Lindsay Sandiford—What Price a Life?' (2016) (mentioning the cases of Australian nationals Andrew Chan and Myuran Sukumaran, and Nigerian Silvester Obiekwe Nwolise); Cornell Center on the Death Penalty Worldwide, 'Indonesia' (2017) (mentioning the case of Malawian Adami Wilson).

been a discretionary punishment for all capital crimes,[105] which is a reflection of Indonesia's Dutch civil law heritage.[106] This means that the Indonesian judiciary may take into account mitigating factors during sentencing deliberations, rather than leaving these to prosecutors (as in Singapore) or the ultimate clemency decision maker (as in many Malaysian cases).

As noted previously, the Indonesian Constitution provides for a mandatory recommendation on clemency from the Supreme Court to the president. Given the Court's power to alter an excessive sentence on appeal, it is unsurprising that the majority of such clemency recommendations are negative.[107] Although it is never made public,[108] presumably the Supreme Court's advice to the president covers retributive, rather than non-legal, justifications for clemency. In a discretionary death penalty setting such as Indonesia, clemency will most likely be granted where the executive decision maker finds novel redemptive, political or utilitarian, justifications for doing so. Yet, as described earlier, presidents Sukarno, Suharto, and Yudhoyono each claimed to have followed the Supreme Court's advice in a majority of cases. In other words, the Supreme Court has little incentive to recommend clemency in a discretionary death penalty setting, whereas Indonesian presidents tend to follow the Court's advice as a means of avoiding political fallout over clemency decisions.[109] The result is relatively infrequent clemency grants.

The third discretion-based explanation for clemency's relative scarcity is the growth in popularity of the *Peninjauan Kembali* ('PK') procedure, which enables the Supreme Court to re-open a case after the cassation stage. A PK may overturn a judicial finding, after the discovery of new evidence that could have resulted in acquittal or lesser punishment if known at the time of trial, where contradictory evidence has been given in another case, or where a judge at an earlier stage has made a clear mistake.[110]

[105] Lindsey and Nicholson (2016) 103.

[106] Lindsey and Kingsley (2006).

[107] Lindsey (2015); McRae (2012) 7; interview with Indonesian Supreme Court judge.

[108] Interview with Australian academic expert on Indonesia #2; interview with Indonesian human rights lawyer #2.

[109] Interview with Indonesian human rights lawyer #2; statement by Indonesian human rights lawyer.

[110] Law 8/1981 on Criminal Procedure (Indonesia), art 263(2). See also Law 14/1985 on the Supreme Court (Indonesia), art 67.

It is not uncommon for the Supreme Court to reverse the trend of all previous judicial decisions on the case,[111] although much will depend on the composition of the bench hearing the appeal and a reduction in penalty cannot automatically be assumed.[112]

The PK procedure has evolved in importance since the Suharto era, and is now a common feature of serious criminal cases.[113] It provides Supreme Court judges with a further avenue through which to exercise their lenient discretion to reduce a death sentence to a lesser punishment, usually before the prisoner applies for presidential clemency. Although it was originally intended to operate as an extraordinary remedy only, PK has since become the 'final stage of appeal' for criminal defendants, as Indonesia's judicial structure has gradually evolved from three tiers to four.[114] Although this remains unsubstantiated, a leading Indonesian human rights lawyer also asserts that the PK procedure forms a key conduit within the judicial process for political considerations or corrupt practices, both under Suharto and throughout the *Reformasi* era.[115] Whether lenient discretion here is commonly exercised for legalistic, retributive purposes or else in a corrupt or politically partial manner is largely inconsequential. The key point is that it partially usurps the need for the president to consider either at the final phase—that is, clemency. The PK procedure adds a further layer of discretion not present in the other three jurisdictions under study, discretion that by law may only reduce the severity of a sentence (to death from life) and not increase it (from life to death).[116] In effect, PK leaves capital defendants in Indonesia with three judicial opportunities to escape the death sentence, following appeals to the provincial High Courts and the Indonesian Supreme Court.[117] In Malaysia and Thailand there are

111 Lindsey et al (2005); Conway (2006).

112 Statement by Australian academic expert on Indonesia #5; interview with Indonesian human rights lawyer.

113 Butt and Lindsey (2012) 89; Lindsey and Nicholson (2016) 85.

114 Pompe (2005) 246; Butt and Lindsey (2012) 89; interview with Indonesian human rights lawyer #2.

115 Interview with Indonesian human rights lawyer.

116 Law 8/1981 on Criminal Procedure (Indonesia), art 263, 266(3). See notes 16–17 and associated text.

117 Lindsey and Nicholson (2016) 93; Law 8/1981 on Criminal Procedure (Indonesia), art 268. Since 2014, there has been legal debate over whether prisoners may file for PK more than once. Constitutional Court Decision No 34/PUU-XI/2013 (Indonesia) held that restricting petitioners to only one case

now two levels of appeal in capital cases, whereas in Singapore there is only one.[118]

Democratization and Indonesia's 'rule of law' politics

With the resignation of Suharto and the beginning of the *Reformasi* era in Indonesian politics, strengthening the 'rule of law' became an important priority for national leaders.[119] As with the contemporary leaders of Singapore,[120] from 1999 successive democratically elected Indonesian presidents have interpreted adherence to the rule of law as requiring strict deference to court-imposed sentences in capital cases, precluding clemency in all but the most exceptional circumstances.[121] As first described in Chapter 2, a modern, democratic state whose leaders proclaim the need for non-arbitrary decision-making and for equality of all citizens before the law will generally not support frequent clemency grants. In these circumstances, mercy as a form of executive discretion can carry 'strong overtones of inevitable arbitrariness, favouritism, and potential corruption. Acknowledging discretion [can be] seen as abandoning the "impersonal" ideal of the state and its "rule of law".'[122]

Political statements by Indonesian presidents in the *Reformasi* era bear out this trend. Langit reports that when President Megawati rejected the clemency appeals of three death row prisoners in 2004, her decision was 'significantly influenced by the country's social and political atmosphere and the *public perception that the government was weak in enforcing laws*'.[123] More recently, in a 2011 speech President Yudhoyono justified his decision to refuse a majority of clemency petitions in both capital and non-capital cases, stating that he would refuse appeals if this was necessary to uphold justice and the rule of law in Indonesia, and

re-opening could cause injustice. However, until 2016, the Indonesian Supreme Court refused to allow second PK petitions (Lindsey and Nicholson (2016) 87–8).

118 See Chapter 3; Chapter 4; Chapter 5.

119 Langit (2004); Suhadji (2006).

120 See Chapter 3 on Singapore.

121 McDonald (2006); Amnesty International AI Index UA-064-2006; Bampton (2006) 26.

122 Nelken (2002) 194.

123 Langit (2004), emphasis added.

that every decision his administration made must be justifiable, in accordance with applicable rules and systems.[124] This interpretation was confirmed late in Yudhoyono's second term by a deputy minister, during interview.[125] Suhadji summarizes the prevailing mood in Indonesian politics during the 2000s:

> To stamp out corruption and uphold the law in Indonesia, there must be transparency from its governments and society ... By granting clemency and pardons, it is going to weaken these efforts—an image that Indonesia believes it cannot afford to have.[126]

Statistically, excluding the historically unique circumstances of the 1965 coup prisoners, discussed in further detail later in this chapter, the overall clemency rate in *Reformasi*-era Indonesia stands at approximately 22–24 per cent.[127] The reluctance of *Reformasi*-era Indonesian presidents to grant clemency does not approach Singapore's level of frugality, but nor is clemency the expected outcome in a finalized case, as in Thailand. Clemency was also granted in a very similar proportion of finalized capital cases (21 per cent) in another retentionist democracy between 1999 and 2016—the United States.[128] In both countries, clemency operates as an exceptional remedy via petition for condemned prisoners, albeit one that most elected politicians are noticeably uncomfortable with. The key difference is that the United States' death penalty clemency rate reaches a 'medium' classification largely due to collective commutations issued by outgoing state governors personally opposed to capital punishment or the way that it is administered, or else as a retrospective measure once the state legislature abolishes the death penalty.[129] Indonesia's *Reformasi* clemency grants, deriving from the central government in Jakarta

[124] See Yudhoyono (2011).

[125] Interview with Indonesian deputy minister.

[126] Suhadji (2006).

[127] Appendix (Indonesia). The equivalent rate for the entire Suharto period is unavailable due to a lack of data.

[128] Death Penalty Information Center (2017a; 2017b). As with clemency data shortcomings in the Indonesian case, the US figure may also be an underestimate, as the Death Penalty Information Center's data only includes clemency grants for 'humanitarian' reasons, rather than clemency granted for judicial expediency, for example to avoid retrials. See further Chapter 1.

[129] See Death Penalty Information Center (2017a). Without these collective commutations, the combined US capital clemency rate from 1999 to 2016 drops from 21 per cent to a mere 5 per cent.

rather than from provincial governors, instead reflect individual case-based retributive and rehabilitative considerations, as well as the protection of Indonesian citizens abroad (a political factor President Yudhoyono saw as outweighing rule of law primacy).

One of the primary consequences of moves towards greater transparency and consistency in discretionary decision-making is that the Indonesian president (as opposed to police, prosecutors, and judges, discussed earlier) can no longer be seen to favour foreign prisoners over locals, rich or powerful prisoners over the poor,[130] or women over men in the clemency process.[131] Although pressure from international NGOs and western governments may have been able to influence Suharto's decisions regarding condemned political prisoners to a certain extent,[132] with democratization and true accountability at the ballot box for the first time since the mid-1950s, the domestic costs of bending to international pressure are now significantly higher.[133] During the Suharto era, only one foreigner (Malaysian drug trafficker Chan Tian Chong) was judicially executed, possibly in retaliation for

[130] Bampton (2006) 6, 26; Lindsey and Kingsley (2006); interview with Australian academic expert on Asian Studies.

[131] Interview with Australian academic expert on Indonesia #4; Unmacht (2005). Indonesia's first judicial execution of a woman took place in 2005. See 'Woman Executed in Indonesia, 1st in Country's Judicial History' (2005).

[132] Fealy (1995) 12–13; Glasius (1999) 134; interview with Indonesian human rights activist. For example, in 1990, six alleged PKI prisoners were taken from their cells to be executed but did not face the firing squad, 'apparently due to international pressure' (Murray (1991)).

[133] Unmacht (2005); Hargreaves (2004); interview with Australian academic expert on Indonesia #3. An important exception to Indonesia's general disregard for western governments' opinions on domestic criminal justice issues relates to Islamic terrorism, which re-emerged as a security issue in Indonesia during the 2000s, executions of alleged terrorists having first been carried out in the 1980s under Suharto (see note 9). Since the terrorist attacks of 11 September 2001 in the United States, Indonesia has become a key partner in the US-led 'War on Terror' (Lynch (2009) 578; Chew (2005)), with one result being that the death penalty was included as a punishment within Indonesia's first dedicated anti-terrorism statute: Law 15/2003 on Eradicating Criminal Acts of Terrorism (Indonesia). In 2004, Hargreaves argued that granting clemency to Islamic terrorists would be interpreted as a weakness in Indonesia's resolve to tackle extremism, a prediction borne out by the executions of the three Bali bombers in 2008, despite appeals from international NGOs, Islamic and Christian groups, and even some of the family members of victims (Sheridan and Taher (2008); 'Survivors, Families Mourn Bali Lost Ones' (2008); Zwartz (2008)).

Malaysia's earlier execution of an Indonesian citizen.[134] Whether or not executive clemency was responsible for the dearth of executions of foreigners under Suharto is unclear, given limited clemency data. But as with the effect of nepotism and corruption, it is instead likely that political intervention took place at earlier stages of the criminal justice process, to prevent death sentences ever being passed on foreign nationals in the first place.[135] However, since *Reformasi*, the various democratically elected Indonesian presidents have had no such hesitation in approving the execution of foreign citizens.[136]

Since the fall of Suharto, convicts from Nigeria (ten), Malawi (two), Thailand (two), Australia (two), Brazil (two), India, Vietnam, and the Netherlands have been executed,[137] and from 1999 to 2010, 46 per cent of death sentences were passed on foreign nationals.[138] By July 2016, at least 40 per cent of Indonesia's 165+ death row population were foreign citizens.[139] Lindsey and Nicholson even assert that Indonesian courts now consider foreign nationality an aggravating circumstance in trials for narcotics offences, with foreigners more likely to receive the death penalty when charged with exactly the same offence.[140] Only one foreign national sentenced to death has reportedly been granted clemency during the *Reformasi* era: Indra Bahadur Tamal, a Nepalese drug trafficker whose sentence was commuted by President Yudhoyono.[141]

With twenty-one foreigners executed since 1999 and only a single commutation, impartiality to national origin at the clemency phase is a crucial feature of Indonesia's new rule of law politics

[134] Imparsial (2010) 119–31; KontraS (2010); Bremboo (2016).

[135] Interview with Indonesian human rights lawyer.

[136] Recent increases in the number of foreigners sentenced to death may not only have arisen as a result of policy changes during *Reformasi*, but also simply because more foreigners visited Indonesia from the late Suharto period onwards (interview with Indonesian human rights lawyer; interview with Indonesian Supreme Court judge).

[137] Combined sources: KontraS (2013); Amnesty International (2013); 'Indonesia Executes 6 Drug Convicts, Including 5 Foreigners' (2015); Whiteman et al (2015); 'Indonesian and Three Nigerians Executed for Drug Crimes' (2016).

[138] Imparsial (2010) 45, 167.

[139] Lamb (2016).

[140] Lindsey and Nicholson (2016) 4.

[141] Saragih (2012); Appendix (Indonesia). See notes 85–91 and associated text.

that has lowered the overall clemency rate during the period of study. Recent events suggest this trend will continue in the near future. Shortly after coming to power in October 2014, President Widodo asserted that he would never commute the sentence of any drug convict sentenced to death, and that he would reject the petitions of all sixty-four drug traffickers then on Indonesia's death row.[142] Among the prisoners so far executed under Widodo are Andrew Chan (Australian), Myuran Sukumaran (Australian), and Ang Kim Soe (Dutch), the first westerners to be executed in independent Indonesia. Earnest appeals from their home governments failed to lead to clemency or to prevent the executions.[143]

I next consider two factors that largely explain Indonesia's 'medium' clemency rate from 1991 to 2016, despite the aforementioned restrictions brought on by the politics of democratization, and the existing structural opportunities to mitigate penalties at earlier stages of the criminal justice process. The second factor discussed below (time on death row) reflects a common pattern across both the Suharto and *Reformasi* eras, as well as within the three other nations under study, whereas the following factor is historically unique, and again reflective of Indonesia's transition from autocracy to democracy within the period of study.

The collective pardon of 1965 'coup' prisoners

In a historically low-execution jurisdiction such as Indonesia, it will only take a couple of isolated cases of *collective* commutation or pardon grants to reach a 'medium' (5–50 per cent) or 'high' (above 50 per cent) clemency rate classification.[144] It is not necessary for clemency to be granted in a regular, institutionalized manner such as in the constitutional monarchies of Thailand and Malaysia. Accordingly, the 1965 coup cases are considered separately here, as together they have contributed up to 40 per cent of Indonesia's documented capital clemency grants since 1991.[145]

Although the judicial executions of accused PKI prisoners from the early 1970s to 1990 fulfilled an important justificatory function

[142] 'Bali Nine: Indonesian President Rules Out Clemency for Inmates on Death Row' (2014); Sajarwo (2014).

[143] See note 137; interview with Indonesian human rights activist.

[144] See Chapter 1.

[145] Appendix (Indonesia).

for the Suharto regime,[146] up to one third of the political prisoners sentenced to death during the late 1960s and early 1970s were also spared execution through presidential clemency.[147] Initially, twelve coup-related prisoners were removed from death row in 1980 after the Indonesian government claimed they had exhibited good behaviour and had shown remorse for their actions.[148] These prisoners may also have escaped execution as a mark of respect for their surviving family members,[149] and to placate international criticism over their continued detention on death row.[150]

The pardoning of all remaining 1965 coup prisoners by President Habibie in 1999, less than a year after Suharto's resignation, must instead be understood in the context of Indonesia's democratization.[151] During his sixteen months in office, Habibie released up to 230 political detainees (including imprisoned separatist leaders from East Timor, West Papua, and Aceh), in an attempt to signal a break from the New Order regime.[152] The March 1999 release from prison of accused PKI members or sympathisers Bungkus,[153] Marsudi,[154] Asep Suryaman, and Sri Rahardjo,[155] possibly among a larger group still under sentence of death,[156] was part of this ongoing democratization process. The pardons granted to these prisoners could also be interpreted as a natural consequence of Habibie's repeal of Presidential Decree

[146] Amnesty International AI Index 21/017/1994, 104; Elson (2001) 244; interview with Australian academic expert on Indonesia.

[147] See notes 3–7 and associated text.

[148] Glasius (1999) 95; Amnesty International AI Index 21/27/87, 9.

[149] Elson (2001) 243, 347 n30.

[150] Interview with Australian academic expert on Indonesia; interview with London-based Indonesian human rights activist.

[151] 'President Grants Clemency to 10 More Political Prisoners' (1999); interview with Indonesian human rights lawyer.

[152] Smith (2001) 109; 'Indonesia Frees Two Political Prisoners' (1998); Singh (2000) 167.

[153] Also spelt Boengkoes.

[154] Also spelt Marzuki.

[155] Also spelt Sri Suhardjo. See 'President Grants Clemency to 10 More Political Prisoners' (1999); TAPOL (1999) 17. See the Introduction for further detail on Asep Suryaman's case.

[156] England (1999) reports that of ten prisoners released from long-term detention, all but one were still under sentence of death. The International Commission of Jurists (1999, at 97) asserts that all ten were under sentence of death. Other reports listed Isnanto as the fourth prisoner, instead of Sri Rahardjo/Sri Suhardjo (TAPOL (1998) 16; Amnesty International AI Index ASA 21/58/98, 11).

11/1963 on the Eradication of Anti-Subversive Activities, under which they were originally convicted; however, the pardons actually pre-dated the repeal by two months.[157]

Rather than individualized grants of clemency issued for primarily retributive or redemptive reasons, as have occurred in several murder and drug-trafficking cases since 1991, Habibie's presidential decrees that collectively released both capital and non-capital political prisoners are examples of an amnesty for political prisoners after a change of regime, as has occurred in numerous transitional justice contexts.[158] Capital clemency exercised in this manner falls within the 'political advantage or utilitarian' paradigm described in Chapter 2, and has a particularly significant impact on clemency rates given its collective exercise. When analysed comparatively, Indonesia is in a unique position among the four jurisdictions under analysis, as it is the only country that has undergone a complete political transition from autocracy to democracy during the period 1991–2016.[159] Democratization and its aftermath are sufficient to explain up to 40 per cent of the publicly reported commutation and pardon grants reported over the period of analysis.[160]

Clemency procedure and long stays on death row

Finally, Indonesia's procedural framework for clemency is perhaps the most protracted among Southeast Asia's retentionist jurisdictions, thereby indirectly enabling certain prisoners to 'earn' clemency through rehabilitation, among other justifications. To

[157] See Law 26/1999 on the Annulment of the Anti-Subversion Law (Indonesia); England (1999); International Commission of Jurists (1999) 98–9.

[158] McEvoy (2007) 426; Fitzpatrick (1995) 716–17. Nonetheless, the 1999 pardons were also justified on the basis of humanitarian considerations such as 'good behaviour, advanced age and bad health' ('Coup Plotter to Be Freed after Years of Failed Efforts' (1999)).

[159] During the period under study, Thailand experienced military coups in 1991, 2006, and 2014. The first two of these were followed by a temporary resumption of electoral democracy, although the military retained significant power as part of a 'parallel state' (Chambers and Waitoolkiat (2016) 426–7). Given its long history and legitimizing function for the Thai monarchy, the ongoing practice of individual or collective royal pardon in death penalty cases appears to have been largely unaffected by Thailand's frequent military coups and democratic restorations. See further Chapter 3 on Thailand, and Appendix (Thailand).

[160] See Appendix (Indonesia).

reiterate, three separate legislative enactments regulated executive clemency over the period of study: Law 3/1950, Law 22/2002, and Law 5/2010. Each provides its own loopholes that have elongated the clemency process.

First, although Law 3/1950 set a legal time limit of thirty days to apply for clemency,[161] the law did not specify the consequences of failing to submit a petition within that time, and also required a petition to be affirmatively rejected before any prisoner was executed.[162] Thereafter, from the enactment of Law 22/2002 through to its substantial amendment via Law 5/2010, if a prisoner's first clemency petition was rejected and yet he or she was not executed within a two-year period, Law 22/2002 allowed the prisoner to restart the process and petition the president again.[163] Prisoners often chose to submit their first or second clemency petition only as their impending execution date approached, in order to gain more time within which to prepare the appeal, and also to deliberately stall the process.[164]

Law 5/2010 subsequently amended Law 22/2002 by abolishing a prisoner's right to petition for clemency a second time, and by imposing a strict one-year time limit on clemency petitions after the death sentence reached 'final and binding' status.[165] Between 2010 and 2016, the cases of capital prisoners could therefore be finalized more rapidly. However, a 2016 Constitutional Court decision then declared the one-year time limit unconstitutional, striking it out of the legislation.[166] Although the legal impact of the Constitutional Court's recent decision is still being debated, prisoners are again likely to enjoy an open-ended period within which to prepare their requests for presidential clemency.

As a result, whether their cases were governed by Law 3/1950, by Law 22/2002, or now under the Constitutional Court's new interpretation of Law 5/2010, there are many reports of death row prisoners refusing to seek clemency for a first or subsequent time for fear that their appeal will be rejected, paving the way for

[161] Law 3/1950 on Clemency (Indonesia), art 2(1).

[162] Law 3/1950 on Clemency (Indonesia), art 2(2), 2(3).

[163] See Law 22/2002 on Clemency (Indonesia), art 2(3).

[164] Interview with Australian academic expert on Indonesia #2; interview with Indonesian human rights lawyer.

[165] Law 5/2010 on Clemency (Indonesia), art 7(2).

[166] Constitutional Court Decision No 107/PUU-XII/2015 (Indonesia).

their prompt execution.[167] Suharto tried to deal with the impasse created by the 1950 law by enacting a separate decree in 1986, which mandated that a first clemency petition be submitted on a prisoner's behalf by the District Court judge who had originally passed the death sentence, if the prisoner would not do so himself.[168] Similarly, in other pre- and post-*Reformasi* cases, prison officials have even forged or forced the signatures of death row prisoners so as to apply for clemency, in order to expedite their executions.[169]

The overall stagnation in the appeals process has been further exacerbated by the lack of time limits on the filing of a PK application.[170] From 1985 onwards, notification of an 'intent to file' for case re-opening within 180 days of the final judgment has been the only procedural step required to stop an impending execution.[171] In 2015 the Chief Justice of the Indonesian Constitutional Court stated that, as with their clemency petitions, death row prisoners often stalled their PK applications as a pretext to delay execution indefinitely.[172]

The end result of this convoluted legal regime has been, inevitably, very long stays on death row for condemned prisoners, even before taking into account the fact that President Suharto deliberately delayed the execution of some political prisoners and 'common criminals' to ensure their later execution would provide

[167] For example, Amnesty International AI Index ASA 21/017/1994, 103; Amnesty International AI Index ASA 03/01/97, 10; Eksa (2016). See generally Law 22/2002 on Clemency (Indonesia), elucidation; Law 5/2010 on Clemency (Indonesia), elucidation. Once the petition's outcome is conveyed to the prisoner, only three days' notice are required before the prisoner may be executed (Amnesty International AI Index ASA 21/040/2004, 2).

[168] Supreme Court Decree 1/1986 on Clemency (Indonesia); Fidrus (2003); Dean and Aleksander (1995). It remains unknown how many prisoners were refused clemency on this basis, or why this provision was not used to force clemency applications on those alleged PKI prisoners eventually released by pardon in 1999.

[169] Amnesty International AI Index ASA 21/040/2004, 9; Amnesty International AI Index ASA 21/016/2001; Amnesty International AI Index 21/017/1994, 103, 106.

[170] Lindsey and Nicholson (2016) 7.

[171] Cornell Center on the Death Penalty Worldwide, 'Indonesia' (2017); Law 14/1985 on the Supreme Court (Indonesia), art 69.

[172] Adzkia (2015).

greater political impact.[173] Towards the end of Suharto's rule, the United Nations Special Rapporteur on Extrajudicial, Summary or Arbitrary Executions reported that a number of prisoners had been on death row for more than twenty years.[174] In 2009, Elda listed the following range of incarceration lengths for capital prisoners following conviction at first instance: fifty-four prisoners for fewer than five years; forty-one prisoners for five to ten years; ten prisoners for ten to twenty years, and one prisoner for more than twenty years.[175] As of mid-2016 the two longest serving narcotics prisoners on Indonesia's death row had been sentenced to death in 2001, whereas the three longest serving murder convicts had been sentenced to death in 1987 (one prisoner) and 1988 (two prisoners).[176] According to Indonesian NGO KontraS' 2016 data, among the group of 35+ prisoners whose judicial appeals had been exhausted, the average time spent incarcerated since first conviction was approximately thirteen years.[177] Time spent on remand adds to this figure.

How do these significant loopholes and delays shape Indonesia's 1991 to 2016 clemency rate? As first observed in Chapter 2, in Indonesia as elsewhere, many years spent on death row provide a prisoner ample time to demonstrate remorse for having committed the crime, and to rehabilitate him or herself so as to be considered a law-abiding citizen.[178] Moreover, as two interviewees observed, in a Muslim-majority state such as Indonesia, commutation may be more likely for prisoners who are able to demonstrate a strong sense of religious piety in prison, given the Islamic religion's concept of redemption.[179] Both during the New Order and the *Reformasi* eras, murder convicts have often been 'forgotten' by the Indonesian media and public after spending 10–20 years on death row. In selected cases, the president could quietly commute their death sentences without weakening the death penalty's perceived general deterrence and denunciatory functions. Because

[173] Johnson and Zimring (2009) 323 n28; 'Death Us Don't Part' (2008); Imparsial (2004) 11; Amnesty International AI Index 21/017/1994, 104.

[174] Ndiaye (1996) 60.

[175] Elda (2009) 102, 106.

[176] KontraS (2016).

[177] KontraS (2016).

[178] See Chapter 2.

[179] Interview with Australian academic expert on Indonesia #4; interview with Australian academic expert on Indonesia. See generally Chapter 2 on conceptions of mercy in Islam.

public indignation is generally less pronounced in Indonesia for clemency in a murder case,[180] the political cost of granting capital clemency is far lower compared with offences thought to threaten Indonesia's national security, such as subversion and drug trafficking. A recent example is the relative domestic media silence on President Widodo's seven clemency grants in murder cases from 2014 to 2016, compared with the public backlash against President Yudhoyono's four clemency grants in narcotics cases in 2011 and 2012.[181]

President Widodo's seven commutations (to date) add to President Megawati's single grant in 2003 and a further grant by Yudhoyono in 2013, to total at least nine confirmed occasions on which condemned murderers have been reprieved by Indonesian presidents during the *Reformasi* era, primarily to reward rehabilitation. Furthermore, as noted earlier, under President Suharto clemency was granted on an unreported basis to reward good behaviour by murder convicts on death row, possibly to coincide with *remisi* (sentence remissions) celebrating important national and religious holidays. As Suharto himself confirmed in his autobiography: 'There have been cases when I have granted a pardon to someone sentenced to death ... All of these cases were determined without much publicity.'[182]

It is unclear if Suharto's policy has been explicitly or implicitly maintained by Indonesia's *Reformasi* presidents. Still, clues exist suggesting that long-term rehabilitation has affected their clemency decision-making. As with annual sentence remissions in non-capital cases, recommendations to commute death sentences are made by prison governors on the basis of good behaviour, or where the crime committed is no longer regarded as particularly serious.[183] President Megawati's sole reported grant of capital clemency was partially justified by more than ten years of

[180] McRae (2008).

[181] Lindsey and Nicholson (2016) 106; McRae (2013).

[182] Soeharto (1991) 337, emphasis added. Given the complete figures for executions available over the period 1991–2016 (Appendix (Indonesia)), even publicly unreported commutations in murder cases have an observable statistical effect, by 'taking the place' of potential executions in certain cases, and therefore increasing the overall clemency rate.

[183] Interview with Australian academic expert on Indonesia; 'Bali Nine Prisoners on Death Row Recommended for Lesser Sentences' (2014). See also Law 22/2002 on Clemency (Indonesia), art 8.

good behaviour in prison, whereas President Yudhoyono's four clemency grants to narcotics prisoners were also partially brought about by demonstrated remorse, after at least three of the four prisoners concerned spent more than a decade on death row.[184] Likewise, a deputy minister in Yudhoyono's government has confirmed that rehabilitation was a criterion that the president took into account in ruling on petitions.[185] In a more streamlined death penalty regime such as Singapore's, the prisoners to benefit in these circumstances may already have been executed, considering the ten or more years taken to resolve their cases. In Indonesia, the significant delays caused by the clemency appeal process instead allow capital prisoners much more time within which to rehabilitate, display remorse and religiosity, and become 'forgotten' by the public.

Neither Here Nor There

There are few, if any, statutory guidelines regulating the Indonesian president's broad power to grant pardon or commutation for any reason he or she sees fit.[186] Clemency has been awarded during the period of study for justifications as varied as wrongful conviction, lesser culpability, rehabilitation and remorse, aiding democratization efforts, and attempts to obtain better outcomes for Indonesian citizens on death row abroad. Furthermore, there are likely to have been additional clemency grants between 1991 and 2016, primarily to reward prisoner rehabilitation, which have not been reported by the media or by NGO sources. Of the four nations under study, Indonesia remains the jurisdiction with the most irregular and ad hoc clemency practice, which by itself provides a key explanation for the overall clemency prevalence settling firmly within the 'medium' category first defined in Chapter 1.

Two of the opposing explanations for Indonesia's clemency rate are structural (leniency at earlier stages and long stays on death row), whereas the remaining two explanations (rule of

184 KontraS (2010).

185 Interview with Indonesian deputy minister.

186 See Law 5/2010 on Clemency (Indonesia), elucidation. Lindsey and Nicholson (2016, at 105) observe: 'In recent decisions, the [Jakarta] Administrative Court has held that the President's exercise of his wide discretion in clemency cases cannot be reviewed by that court.'

law politics and the release of the 1965 coup-related prisoners) arise directly as a result of Indonesia's democratization process from 1998 onwards. Reflecting Indonesia's 'medium' clemency classification, at least one of these factors reappears in ultra low-clemency Singapore (rule of law politics), whereas another (long stays on death row) is found in both Thailand and Malaysia, which are high-clemency jurisdictions. Other than the evidently consistent role of prisoner rehabilitation across the Suharto and *Reformasi* eras, it is inconsistency and contradiction which characterize Indonesia's clemency practice from 1991 to 2016. This in itself constitutes the key trend setting Indonesia apart from the other three jurisdictions under study. Six different Indonesian presidents since 1991 have used (or have refused to use) the clemency mechanism in noticeably different ways.

7

What Accounts for Southeast Asia's Diverse Clemency Practice?

[L]ike so much in legal scholarship, debates about what factors influence clemency decisions within the death penalty context often take place without the benefit of data.

Michael Heise, on shortcomings in the academic literature[1]

In the preceding four chapters, I described in significant detail the 1991–2016 clemency laws and practice for each of the four jurisdictions under study: Thailand, Singapore, Malaysia, and Indonesia. For comparative analysis, the most important components of those case studies are: (a) the list of known commutation or pardon cases and the reasons for those grants;[2] (b) the jurisdiction's clemency rate, whether 'low', 'medium', or 'high'; and (c) the list of factors that operate as plausible determinants of that clemency rate. Southeast Asia ultimately proves a regional exemplar of substantial global clemency variation among retentionist states.[3] The key puzzle, then, is why such wide variation exists, particularly among near neighbours who each use the death penalty to punish similar crimes.

Recalling the discussion in Chapter 1, the category of prisoner receiving clemency, the nature and role of the decision maker, and the reasons for which clemency is granted all help greatly to explain *how many* prisoners receive clemency overall. Accordingly, this chapter begins with a comparison of

[1] Heise (2003) 262.

[2] In Chapter 3 I noted that it is more useful in the Thai context to identify those prisoners denied clemency and subsequently executed, given that the overwhelming presumption in Thai death penalty cases is in favour of clemency, either by individual royal pardon or collective royal pardon.

[3] See Pascoe (2019b).

clemency decision makers and recipients in individual cases and moves thereafter towards an empirically informed account of clemency incidence in retentionist Southeast Asia, addressing the book's central research question. The preliminary findings outlined in this chapter ultimately suggest a three-part clemency hypothesis, which may have broader application beyond the ASEAN region and outside the 1991–2016 timeframe chosen for study.

Clemency Decision Makers

The first set of comparative findings that helps to inform an ASEAN-wide explanation for clemency frequency pertains to the clemency actors themselves. Based on the case studies set out in Chapters 3–6, Table 2 presents Southeast Asia's *formal* (constitutional) and *actual* decision makers on executive clemency in capital cases. Over the period of analysis from 1991 to 2016, regardless of the changes that have occurred in clemency practice, both the constitutionally designated and actual regional decision-makers on clemency have remained reasonably consistent over time. As far as constitutional provisions, legislation, 'elite' interviews, and the secondary literature reveal, political shocks such as three military coups in Thailand (1991, 2006, 2014) or the fall of Suharto in Indonesia (1998) appear to have made little difference to prevailing decision-making structures, even though the personnel within those structures may have changed as a result.

As Table 2 makes clear, the national or provincial head of state, who is the formal constitutional decision maker in each jurisdiction, is not always the *actual* decision maker on clemency. The advisory role of other parties vis-à-vis the head of state often pre-empts the latter's formal decision-making power. In Thailand and Malaysia, this phenomenon may be understood in the context of a worldwide shift from absolute to constitutional monarchy during the nineteenth and twentieth centuries, such that the prerogative powers once synonymous with royal rule are now exercised on the advice of elected leaders or bureaucrats.[4] Nonetheless, it appears that the Malay rulers (in Malay state cases) and the king of Thailand can act, and occasionally have acted, contrary to

[4] Sebba (1977b) 111–15; Sebba (1977a) 221.

Table 2 Capital clemency decision makers in Southeast Asia

National jurisdiction	System of government	Formal constitutional decision maker/s	Actual decision maker/s
Thailand	Constitutional monarchy	King	Ministry of Justice/Ministry of Interior/Department of Corrections/Cabinet/King[a]
Singapore	Parliamentary republic	President	Cabinet[b]/Attorney-General
Malaysia	Federal constitutional monarchy	Malay rulers/State governors (state cases)/*Yang di-Pertuan Agong* (federal, military, security cases)	Federal Attorney-General/ Pardons Boards (state, federal, security cases)/ Cabinet (military cases)/Malay rulers (Malay state cases)
Indonesia	Presidential republic	President	President/Supreme Court's Criminal Chambers

[a]Chapter 3 observed that King Bhumibol's personal role in adjudicating petitions for individual royal pardon probably declined over the years of his reign, with the Cabinet and the civil service bureaucracy playing a more important role since the 2000s. Moreover, for collective royal pardons, the rate of royal assent to government proposals for a decree approached 100 percent under King Bhumibol.

[b]As described in Chapter 4, within Singapore's 16–20 minister Cabinet over the period of analysis, the most influential voices were probably former prime minister Lee Kwan Yew (who remained a Cabinet minister until 2011) and the Ministers of Law and Home Affairs.

political and bureaucratic recommendations on clemency petitions.[5] Strictly speaking, clemency still falls within their discretionary remit, rather than being a prerogative power exercised only 'on advice'.

Of the two republics in the study, the Singaporean president's purely ceremonial powers on clemency are a reflection of the parliamentary system of government enshrined in the 1965 Constitution.[6] The change to direct election of the president from 1993 onwards has not in any way enhanced the head of

[5] Interview with Thai law professor; interview with Thailand Department of Corrections staff; Handley (2006) 375; interview with former employee of the Thailand Department of Corrections (for Thailand). Addruse (1986) 2; Bari (2003) 60; interview with Australian academic expert on Malaysia; interview with international human rights NGO staff #2; interview with Malaysian prosecutor (for Malaysia).

[6] Constitution of Singapore 1965, arts 23–4; Tey (2008) 610–11.

state's authority in clemency decision-making.[7] By contrast, the Indonesian president's continuing authority over clemency outcomes is a reflection of Indonesia's unitary, presidential system, with relatively few constitutional constraints on executive power. Indeed, when it was drafted in 1945, Indonesia's present constitution was the second shortest in the world,[8] and it has been described as a 'dictator's dream'.[9] Tellingly, through a 1959 decree, President Sukarno revoked Indonesia's short-lived parliamentary republic (1950–9) under the 1950 Interim Constitution, favouring a return to the powerful executive presidency that the 1945 Constitution had provided.[10] Although available sources suggest that Indonesian presidents typically follow the recommendations of the Supreme Court in granting or refusing clemency, there are numerous historical examples of presidents ignoring these recommendations to make their own decisions, or to rely on the advice of other agencies.[11]

If Southeast Asia's heads of state do not always decide clemency outcomes, it is worth considering who does. In three of the four nations under study, senior civil servants play an influential role. In Singapore and Malaysia, the role of the Attorney-General as government legal adviser and state prosecutor reflects these countries' shared legal heritage. In Thailand, officials from the Ministry of Interior, the Ministry of Justice, and the Department of Corrections (the latter an agency of the Ministry of Justice) all play key roles in making recommendations to the king.

Within the same three jurisdictions, elected political representatives or their agents also possess a key decision-making role. In Thailand and Singapore, this body is the Cabinet itself. In Malaysia, the Attorney-General acts as a conduit for the federal government's political views on clemency, whereas the relevant State Chief-Minister represents local political interests on the State Pardons Boards. In federal and security cases, the Malaysian

[7] Interview with Singaporean NGO staff #3; interview with Singaporean human rights lawyer; interview with Singaporean law professor and Singaporean NGO staff #5.

[8] Butt and Lindsey (2012) i.

[9] 'Paint It Black' (2014); 'Indonesia' (2010).

[10] Lindsey and Santosa (1999) 8–9.

[11] Interview with Indonesian Supreme Court judge; Lindsey and Nicholson (2016) 104; interview with Australian academic expert on Indonesia #2; interview with Indonesian deputy minister; Deliani (2011) 173.

government has a direct representative on the Pardons Board in the form of the Minister for Federal Territories, whereas in military cases a Cabinet minister is the primary decision maker.

Indonesia is the only example where the judiciary plays a key decision-making role. Although in Singapore and in Malaysia the trial judge passing the death sentence provides a written opinion on the case, available evidence suggests that this report is merely taken into account by the final decision maker/s, rather than being determinative.[12] The Indonesian Supreme Court's long historical role in advising the president on commutations and pardons, together with its primacy in the 1945 Constitution's clemency provision,[13] explains the Court's current predominance over the Indonesian president's other institutional clemency advisers, such as the Ministry of Law and Human Rights and the Attorney General's Office.[14]

The Four Models of Clemency

Following the above comparison of clemency decision makers, this section considers comparative clemency reasoning and recipients. Table 3 contains a summary of findings from the four national case studies, based on the four models of clemency practice first identified in Chapter 2:

- mercy from the sovereign;
- retributivist clemency;
- redemptive clemency;
- clemency for political advantage or utilitarian reasons.

None of the four jurisdictions under study fit perfectly within any one of these four categories, based on their clemency practice from 1991 to 2016. The findings set out in this chapter are only indicative of broad clemency trends over the period of study, and in particular whether there exists a consistent pattern of clemency

[12] See Chapter 4 and Chapter 5. In Thailand, although Department of Corrections staff add court documents to the clemency papers for decision (interview with former employee of the Thailand Department of Corrections; interview with Thai criminal defence lawyer and Thai NGO staff), there is no evidence that these court documents contain recommendations on clemency from the sentencing or appeal judges (Thailand Department of Corrections (2008)).

[13] Constitution of Indonesia 1945, art 14(1).

[14] See Chapter 6.

Table 3 Clemency models in Southeast Asia from 1991 to 2016

Jurisdiction	Mercy from the sovereign	Retributivist clemency	Redemptive clemency	Utilitarian/Political advantage clemency
Thailand	Yes[a]	Yes[b]	Yes[c]	Yes[d]
Singapore	No	No	No	No[e]
Malaysia	Yes[f]	Yes[g]	Yes[h]	Yes[i]
Indonesia	No	Yes[j]	Yes[k]	Yes[l]

[a]Individual and collective royal pardons granted as part of a 1,000-year-old royal tradition. Moreover, clemency granted to maintain the prestige of the monarchy as a revered Buddhist institution.

[b]Gender, old age, youth, terminal illness.

[c]Rehabilitation in prison; admitting to the crime and showing remorse; employment in the civil service or the military.

[d]Foreign nationality; assisting ongoing police investigations.

[e]Although only limited evidence is available, the most common justification for capital clemency in Singapore since 1965 may have been assisting investigations and prosecutions in accomplices' cases (for three prisoners). However, incidences of clemency in Singapore have historically arisen in only miniscule numbers, with no category of prisoner consistently benefiting over the decades.

[f]Clemency grants justifying the status of the Malay rulers.

[g]Youth, criminal record, arguable yet unproven defences, evidential flaws.

[h]Remorse and repentance, good behaviour in prison, religious piety, UMNO political connections.

[i]Foreign nationality.

[j]Although no two cases are the same, there are previous examples of clemency granted for wrongful conviction, psychiatric illness, lesser participation in the offence, arguable defences, and family circumstances. These cases span from the Suharto to the Widodo presidencies.

[k]Rehabilitation in prison and expressed remorse, also possibly rewarded through an unofficial 'remissions' policy.

[l]Political prisoners released as a democratizing measure. It is unclear whether President Yudhoyono's clemency grants to assist Indonesian prisoners on death row abroad were a one-off move or part of a more consistent pattern. Without further evidence, I assume the former.

decision-making that follows one of the four justificatory paradigms. In the case of Singapore, despite three prisoners avoiding execution as a result of presidential clemency since 1991 and six prisoners receiving clemency since 1965, as an extremely low-clemency jurisdiction, the only predominant trend is the rarity or absence of presidential discretion altogether. However, in the remaining three jurisdictions (Thailand, Malaysia, Indonesia), state practice over many years confirms that clemency tends to be granted to particular categories of defendants and for particular case-based, utilitarian, or politically self-serving reasons. While arbitrariness may ultimately determine which individual prisoners live and die in any particular jurisdiction, there are undoubtedly case attributes, redemptive behaviours, and prevailing political conditions that appear to make capital clemency far more likely.

Several interesting conclusions follow from this comparative data. First is the fact that, in addition to the overall rarity of clemency in Singapore, each of the other three jurisdictions' clemency rates appear to correlate with greater or lesser *variety* in their clemency practice. Indonesia, with its medium-clemency classification, sees consistent patterns of retributivist clemency, redemptive clemency, and clemency for utilitarianism or political advantage, but no evidence of clemency granted as 'mercy from the sovereign'. Thailand and Malaysia, as jurisdictions with clemency rates greater than 50 per cent, see clemency granted pursuant to all four paradigms.

The broader implication, albeit coming from a very small sample of jurisdictions, is that clemency as 'mercy from the sovereign' is a necessary condition for, or at least a major contributor to, high clemency rates. In other words, countries are unlikely to achieve clemency rates of more than 50 per cent if clemency is not granted as a role-enhancing measure by autocrats, monarchs, or other unelected decision makers, such as the king of Thailand and Malaysia's nine Malay rulers. As a theory, this appears logical. In any retentionist jurisdiction where death sentences are passed consistently, it will be difficult to find retributive, redemptive, and utilitarian circumstances to mitigate punishment in more than half of finalized cases.[15] Retentionist democracies, or at least popularly elected clemency decision makers in retentionist nations (such as Indonesia's elected presidents and Singapore's elected Cabinet ministers), are unlikely to grant clemency at high rates. Clemency's self-legitimizing feature is largely superfluous for these decision makers and in these societies.

Nevertheless, even in the study's two high-clemency jurisdictions with clemency frequently granted as 'mercy from the sovereign', other justifications also appear significant. Although they do not form an absolute majority, many of the death penalty

[15] Possible exceptions are mass amnesties granted after one-off political upheavals such as civil wars or a transition to democracy, or an amnesty granted as a prelude to death penalty abolition for all crimes or a subset of crimes. See further Chapter 2.

commutations in Thailand over the period of study were made as individual royal pardons, for case-based reasons such as good behaviour in prison and foreign nationality, rather than as collective royal pardons.[16] In Malaysia, clemency grants are made not only for self-justifying reasons by the Malay rulers, but also in response to rehabilitation in prison, religious piety, retributive justifications which emerge at trial, foreign nationality, and political connections, among other explanations.[17] The overall conclusion is that those Southeast Asian jurisdictions which grant clemency most frequently tend to grant it for a variety of reasons, rather than to serve a single aim.

Factors Contributing to Clemency Incidence

The one remaining interpretive challenge is to analyse the position of each of the four Southeast Asian nations on a clemency-use continuum from 0 to 100 percent of finalised death penalty cases. As first described in Chapter 1, based on available execution and clemency data covering the years from 1991 to 2016, actively retentionist Southeast Asia contains a jurisdiction with an extremely low rate of clemency (Singapore: 0.6 per cent), a jurisdiction with a medium rate of clemency (Indonesia: 26–33 per cent or more), and two jurisdictions with high rates of clemency (Malaysia: 55–63 per cent and Thailand: more than 95 per cent). Although the *reasons* for which clemency has typically been granted in each of these four jurisdictions since 1991 find strong regional parallels, as described previously, the basic numerical discrepancy in clemency rates remains extraordinary.

In the case studies within Chapters 3–6, a variety of plausible explanations were suggested for clemency frequency in each jurisdiction. For Thailand (Chapter 3) and Singapore (Chapter 4), with their respective clemency rates falling at extreme ends of the 0–100 spectrum, the explanations described were unidirectional. In these jurisdictions, over the period of study, the interests of criminal justice actors and the structures within which they operated were reasonably consistent in either promoting (Thailand) or inhibiting (Singapore) capital clemency. In Malaysia (Chapter 5) and in Indonesia (Chapter 6), where the clemency picture is more

[16] See Appendix (Thailand); Chapter 3.
[17] See Chapter 5.

nuanced, I identified factors with contradictory effects: some enabled clemency, whereas others restricted it. State practice in these two jurisdictions is far more difficult to interpret.

Malaysia and Indonesia exhibit significant longitudinal variation in clemency practice, greater data shortcomings than for Thailand and Singapore, and opposing interests among criminal justice actors. Other than to acknowledge that there are conflicting forces affecting clemency practice in both nations, without quantitative analysis it is difficult to be categorical about the influence exerted by each individual factor. More accurate scientific explanations would require multivariate regression-based testing, a topic addressed in the book's Conclusion. In the meantime, I have proposed plausible explanations for clemency frequency within each of the four case studies, through a close analysis of state practice, backed by relevant theoretical literature and the collective opinions of interviewees. Table 4 summarizes the factors suggested as potentially influential in shaping death penalty clemency rates within the four national case studies.

Taken together, Tables 2, 3, and 4 begin to describe several patterns which span the set of actively retentionist ASEAN nations (minus Vietnam), which may or may not extend to capital clemency in other parts of the world. Yet even a cursory glance at the findings outlined in Table 4 reveals that potential explanations for clemency frequency are complex and often specific to each jurisdiction. How then might comparative criminal justice scholars make sense of Southeast Asia's diverse death penalty clemency practice?

Here, it is appropriate to adopt Lijphart's sensible recommendations on qualitative comparative studies involving few jurisdictions, by combining two or more potential explanations that 'express an essentially similar underlying characteristic' and moreover by 'simplifying a set of several categories into a dichotomy'.[18] Lijphart's method helps to clarify the suggested contributing factors, without selectively 'ignoring' uncorroborated or unexpected findings. Nevertheless, underdetermination of causal factors is a common danger in the social sciences.[19] Identifying several potential explanations and framing these at the correct level of generality are important steps, to guard against comparative criminologists' tendency to

[18] Lijphart (1971) 687. See also Anckar (2007) 53.
[19] Garland (1990) 125.

Table 4 Factors enabling and inhibiting capital clemency in Southeast Asia

Jurisdiction	Plausible factors *enabling* clemency	Plausible factors *inhibiting* clemency
Chapter 3: Thailand (high rate)	1. King Bhumibol and Thailand's tradition of Buddhist monarchy 2. Pardoning process and associated long stays on death row 3. Extrajudicial killings 4. International relations affecting foreign prisoners' cases	(None Listed)
Chapter 4: Singapore (low rate)	(None listed)	1. Rule of law and the Singapore 'brand name' 2. Public justifications for the mandatory death penalty 3. Maximizing deterrence in drug cases 4. Prosecutorial discretion 5. Cabinet dynamics/ Attorney-General's role/ efficient case processing
Chapter 5: Malaysia (high rate)	1. Trial and appeal judges' reports to the Pardons Boards 2. The Malay rulers' ultimate discretion in state cases 3. Long stays on death row	1. Lenient discretion exercised at earlier stages 2. Federal Attorney-General's role on the Pardons Boards
Chapter 6: Indonesia (medium rate)	1. Collective pardon of 1965 'coup' prisoners as a democratizing measure 2. Clemency procedure and associated long stays on death row	1. Leniency exercised at earlier stages 2. Democratization and Indonesia's rule of law politics

explain penality in terms of any single causal principle or functional purpose, be it 'morals' or 'economics', 'state control' or 'crime control'. Instead of searching for a single explanatory principle, we need to grasp the facts of multiple causality, multiple effects, and multiple meaning ... The aim of analysis should always be to capture that variety of causes, effects, and meaning and trace their interaction, rather than to reduce them all to a single currency.[20]

Accordingly, based on the findings set out in Table 4, this study's preliminary conclusions are that in the four countries under analysis, and based on the data available from 1991 to 2016, the proportion of finalized cases granted clemency is largely determined by three overlapping legal and political factors, each supported to some extent by the prior academic literature:[21]

1. The extent to which clemency operates as a form of *lenient discretion*, given the relative 'attrition rate' of capital cases at earlier stages through the criminal justice system;
2. The extent to which granting clemency enhances or detracts from *political power* for the final decision maker;
3. The usual *length of time prisoners spend on death row* before their clemency petitions are answered.

Each of these three factors may be expressed dichotomously, such that as its presence increases, clemency becomes more important as a remedial measure or political tool. Conversely, where the factor is largely absent from the jurisdiction's death penalty practice, clemency rates tend to fall. Within the following three sections, these regional patterns are considered in greater detail and factual and counterfactual examples are provided from the four jurisdictions under study.

Clemency and lenient discretion

The first explanation for clemency frequency concerns clemency's role as a form of lenient discretion. Southeast Asian practice from

[20] Garland (1990) 280. See also Gay (1985) 187.

[21] For lenient discretion, see for example Colgate Love (2010) 39; Novak (2015) 36; Sebba (1977a) 230–1. For clemency as political power, see for example Novak (2015) 12; Thurschwell (2009) 278; Botsman (2007) 45–9. For clemency after excessive time spent on death row, see for example Acker et al (2010) 195; Abramowitz and Paget (1964) 153, 168.

1991 to 2016 suggests that, among other factors, the proportion of finalized cases which result in commutation or pardon rather than in execution is directly related to how much lenient discretion is exercised at earlier stages of the criminal justice system. Clemency is an executive branch solution at the 'back end' of the system, where state authorities within the relevant jurisdiction lack other mechanisms to individualize punishments or to keep the annual number of executions at a politically manageable level. The greater the capital case 'attrition rate' through the criminal justice system, the less need there is for clemency.

Of the four countries under analysis, pertinent examples here are the 'show trials' of coup-related prisoners during the early Suharto period in Indonesia,[22] and the regular processing of death penalty cases through Thailand's criminal justice system. In the former case, Chapter 6 observed that up to 40 percent of Indonesia's confirmed clemency grants from 1991 to 2016 relate to the 1965 coup prisoners. For the coup prisoners convicted and sentenced to death in the *Mahmillub* (Extraordinary Military Tribunal), there was no right of appeal, other than to President Suharto for clemency.[23] Furthermore, convictions upon charges being laid were universal: not one prisoner was acquitted in either military or civil trials relating to the events of 1965,[24] although it appears that death sentences were at least reduced to lesser punishments on appeal in the civil courts.[25]

As described in Chapter 6, between four and ten prisoners convicted of coup-related crimes were eventually pardoned and released from prison as part of Indonesia's democratization in 1999. Had those 4–10 prisoners been afforded a realistic opportunity to overturn their conviction or mitigate their punishment in the courts, at least some of the death sentences passed on these prisoners would not have come before President Habibie for decision 25–30 years later. In other words, with opportunities for leniency at earlier stages, these death sentences may have been overturned on retributive grounds long before they were ever reduced

[22] Lev (2011) 233.

[23] Presidential Decree 16/1963 on the Extraordinary Military Tribunal (Indonesia), art 7(2); Lev (2011) 239.

[24] Lev (1999) 187; Lev (2011) 233.

[25] Amnesty International AI Index ASA 21/30/85, 2.

as a democratization measure in 1999. Several of these prisoners would still have been released by President Habibie, possibly from life sentences (as with army colonel Abdul Latief and trade unionists Alexander Warouw and Pudjo Prasetyo, all pardoned and released in 1998 and 1999),[26] rather than as prisoners still under sentence of death.

Clemency as lenient discretion is prompted in Thailand, on the other hand, by the country's status as one of the 'world capital[s] of overcharging'[27] and the 1991–2016 average figure of seventy-four prisoners remaining on death row who had exhausted two judicial appeals.[28] While some leniency for retributive reasons, as well as due to corruption, is undoubtedly exercised at earlier stages by Thai police, prosecutors, and judges, this is not sufficient to reduce annual execution totals to a symbolic and politically manageable level, given that capital punishment's main purpose is to highlight the state's lack of tolerance for a particular form of crime and to make an example of the offender for others.[29] More than 100 death sentences were passed at first instance in at least fourteen of the twenty-six years under analysis,[30] whereas only limited mitigating circumstances exist to reduce a death sentence to a lesser punishment on appeal.[31] Grants of individual and collective royal pardon by the Thai king operate to fill the breach (among their other purposes).

The converse situation arises where lenient discretion is frequently exercised at earlier stages, due to pervasive corruption (particularly in Indonesia), to individualize punishments, or to keep execution totals to politically tolerable levels. Such discretion includes decisions by police and prosecutors to reduce charges or to discontinue prosecution altogether, acquittal and sentencing discretion at the trial and appeal stages in court, and in

[26] 'Coup Plotter to Be Freed after Years of Failed Efforts' (1999); Amnesty International AI Index ASA 21/84/98. See further Image 4.

[27] Interview with American academic expert on the death penalty; Appendix (Thailand).

[28] See Appendix (Thailand).

[29] Interview with Australian academic expert on Thailand; interview with Singaporean criminal defence lawyer #2; interview with Thai human rights activist (2012).

[30] See Appendix (Thailand).

[31] Penal Code 1956 (Thailand), s 78; Union for Civil Liberty (2011) 9.

Indonesia the further 'extraordinary' case re-opening procedure at the Supreme Court level (*peninjauan kembali*).

The death penalty system operates in this manner in Singapore (using prosecutorial discretion), Malaysia (using police, prosecutorial, and judicial discretion), and Indonesia (using police, prosecutorial, and judicial discretion, with the exception of the coup-related cases previously referred to). In each of these three jurisdictions, the practical effect of discretion exercised at earlier stages is that by the time an application for clemency reaches the head of state or other government decision maker, most relevant exculpatory and mitigating factors have already been considered and therefore few case-related reasons remain to stop the execution proceeding. Even clemency's utility to lower potential execution totals to politically manageable levels is compromised, where much the same is achieved at the prosecutorial discretion phase, behind closed doors.

Southeast Asia's most obvious procedural mechanism to negate executive clemency in these circumstances is a written recommendation by the case prosecutor or presiding trial or appeal judge forwarded to the final clemency decision maker. Prosecutors or judges in capital cases usually have little incentive to recommend commutation or pardon. They have their own opportunity to exercise lenient discretion at earlier phases of the process and may well consider a subsequent grant of clemency on retributive grounds as an affront to their assessment of the case, wasting the time and public money required to secure a capital conviction. In Singapore and Malaysia, archival research and 'elite' interviews confirmed that the Attorney-General's written report or oral views on the case had a significant influence on the final clemency decision maker.[32] And the likelihood is that, in both nations, most prosecutorial recommendations on clemency over the period of study were negative.[33]

Of course, the exception to this general rule on clemency advice is where the *mandatory* death penalty robs judges of their

[32] Interview with Singaporean criminal defence lawyer #2; We Believe in Second Chances (2011); Lee (2006) 460–1, 477; Ravi (2005) 79 (Singapore); interview with Malaysian prosecutor; interview with Malaysian member of parliament; interview with Malaysian criminal defence lawyer (Malaysia).

[33] We Believe in Second Chances (2011); interview with Singaporean NGO staff #3 (Singapore); Donoghue (2013) 79; interview with Malaysian prosecutor; interview with Malaysian member of parliament (Malaysia).

sentencing discretion. In Malaysia, as described in Chapter 5, reports by trial and appeal judges to the State and Federal Pardons Boards have proven influential in securing death penalty commutations in mandatory death penalty cases.[34] Indeed, the Malaysian Criminal Procedure Code provides that the trial judge must explicitly provide in his or her report an 'opinion [on] whether there are any reasons, and, if any, what reasons there are, why the sentence of death should or should not be carried out'.[35] In Singapore, less is known about the trial and appeal judges' reports forming part of the Singapore Cabinet's constitutional 'clemency materials', but their main function appears to be to inform the more influential Attorney-General's report on the case.[36] Moreover, unlike in Malaysia, there is no explicit requirement in the Constitution of Singapore that the trial judge's report explicitly addresses whether the death sentence should be carried out or not.[37] Singapore's situation is similar to that of Thailand, whereby court documents placed before decision makers on individual royal pardon do not appear to include judicial recommendations on clemency.[38]

In Indonesia, as described in Chapter 6, the clemency advice to the president customarily includes a report from the Jakarta-based Attorney-General (whose responsibilities as government legal adviser include prosecutions) and will always contain an opinion from the Supreme Court, pursuant to constitutional requirements. The high level of discretion enjoyed by prosecutors and judges in Indonesia's civil law system makes consistent recommendations in favour of clemency unlikely. Importantly, as previously observed, presidents Suharto and Yudhoyono typically followed the Supreme Court's advice on clemency.[39] As with prosecutors in Singapore and Malaysia, the advice given by the Indonesian Supreme Court is usually negative.[40]

[34] Amnesty International (1983) 4; interview with former Malaysian Federal Court judge.

[35] Criminal Procedure Code 2006 (Malaysia), art 281(b).

[36] Constitution of Singapore 1965, art 22P(2); Lee (2006) 472.

[37] Constitution of Singapore 1965, art 22P(2).

[38] See note 12.

[39] Soeharto (1991) 337; Sya'ban (1985) 82 (for Suharto); interview with Indonesian human rights lawyer; interview with Indonesian human rights lawyer #2; Deliani (2011) 173 (for Yudhoyono).

[40] Lindsey (2015); McRae (2012) 7; interview with Indonesian Supreme Court judge.

Finally, the prevalence of *extrajudicial* sanctions may also have an effect upon clemency as lenient discretion, although the results of the present study are inconclusive on this point. The two countries under study where potential capital crimes have instead been frequently dealt with by extrajudicial means since 1991 are Thailand (extrajudicial killings of drug traffickers)[41] and Malaysia (administrative detention of drug traffickers and security offences suspects, empowered by legislation).[42] In these two jurisdictions, extrajudicial sanctions may have a contrary effect to lenient discretion exercised at earlier phases of the criminal justice system, described previously. Instead of allowing gradual case 'attrition' through the system, extrajudicial sanctions represent the opposite approach: a presumption of guilt and the immediate infliction of (sometimes deadly) punishment, thereby filtering out what are perceived as some of the most serious cases *prior to* prosecution. Within the less serious cases which remain, the executive may proceed to grant clemency to reward good behaviour in prison, to maintain international comity, or for any other case-based or political reason, all the while ensuring that its crime control and security aims remain fulfilled through extrajudicial means.

In Chapter 3, I observed that this 'residual leniency' typically manifests as individual and collective royal pardons in Thailand, to maintain the king's enduring image as a benevolent God-like figure. In Malaysia it is unclear whether such residual leniency necessarily manifests as executive clemency, rather than as prosecutorial or even judicial discretion in the cases that remain. Moreover, suggesting a correlative relationship between extrajudicial sanctions and clemency makes sense only if the *very worst* cases are those diverted from trial using administrative detention, leaving behind cases capable of attracting sympathy at the clemency phase. For Malaysia this is a working assumption, but it is not (yet) backed by available empirical data.

[41] See Chapter 3.

[42] See Chapter 5. Here, I do not include Singapore's own administrative detention laws. On the basis of the information available, since 1991 administrative detention in Singapore appears to have been used primarily when there was insufficient evidence available to conduct a prosecution (interview with Singaporean human rights lawyer; '366 Criminal Law Detentions in Five Years' (2009); Erlanger (1989)). If those indefinitely detained are not potential capital defendants, it cannot be said that administrative detention, no matter how widespread, has any impact on the prevailing capital clemency rate.

In Indonesia, the evidence is also equivocal on whether President Suharto's state-sponsored extrajudicial killing policy for common criminals such as murderers or drug traffickers[43] continued after 1990, or even into the *Reformasi* era after 1998. There is some evidence of terrorism suspects being extrajudicially targeted under *Reformasi* presidents,[44] but it is unclear whether such a state policy extended to suspects accused of the far more common capital offences of murder and drug trafficking over the period of study.[45] Given these current uncertainties, further research may be required to test any potential correlation between extrajudicial punishments and clemency incidence. Death penalty scholars have identified the similar relationship between judicial and extrajudicial killing as theoretically important, yet, largely due to data shortcomings, it has proven a consistently elusive empirical research topic.[46]

Clemency and the final decision maker

The second explanation for capital clemency frequency in the four nations under study is clemency's role in enhancing or alternatively reducing political power for the final decision maker.[47] Based on observations from the four case studies, commutation and pardon are more often granted where the final decision maker, bearing ultimate political responsibility for clemency, is *not* popularly elected. In these circumstances the unelected decision maker (as a monarch or autocrat) may utilize clemency, in conjunction with executions, as a strategy to rule by benevolence, or as a demonstration of state power over life and death.[48] Similarly, selective

[43] Asian Human Rights Commission (2012) 12; Bourchier (1988) 10; van den Berg (2001) 263.

[44] Interview with Australian academic expert on Indonesia #2; interview with Indonesian human rights lawyer #2.

[45] However, by the end of 2017, Indonesian president Joko Widodo had authorized a 'shoot on sight' policy for law enforcement officers dealing with narcotics suspects ('55 Dead in Indonesia's War on Drugs with "Shoot-on-Sight" Policy' (2017)).

[46] Johnson and Zimring (2009) 450; Miethe et al (2005) 120–1; Hood and Hoyle (2015) 4.

[47] By 'final clemency decision maker', here I refer to the most senior clemency decision maker with any actual authority over clemency outcomes. See Table 2.

[48] Strange (1996) 7; Botsman (2007) 49; interview with American academic expert on the death penalty.

or wholesale mercy for foreign nationals (or for locals in response to foreign pressure) is a means by which an unelected clemency decision maker may gain greater international legitimacy, particularly among abolitionist nations.

The most pertinent examples are the long established and religiously influenced traditions to exercise the power to pardon by Thailand's kings and Malaysia's nine rulers in the Malay States. As described in Chapters 3 and 5, each of these leaders receive multiple recommendations on each clemency petition within the framework of constitutional monarchy, yet, unusually, they also retain the absolute discretion to grant or withhold pardon as they see fit. Exercising royal prerogative in death penalty cases concurrently portrays the traditional ruler as religiously pious, as taking a close interest in the welfare of his constituents, as maintaining good relations with abolitionist nations, and generally helps maintain the relevance and popularity of the monarchy as an institution within the constitutional scheme, where elected politicians determine state policy in other fields. Likewise, in Indonesia, the shoring up of domestic and international legitimacy at a moment of democratization helps to explain the actions taken in 1998 and 1999 by President Habibie, Suharto's unelected successor, in revoking the death and prison sentences handed down on numerous political prisoners during the New Order regime.[49]

A practical feature of the 'mercy from the sovereign' and 'political or utilitarian' clemency paradigms first identified in Chapter 2 is that, regardless of each individual petition's relative merits, clemency to boost power, prestige, and the public good is often granted in aggregate form. Within the study, relevant examples include regular collective royal pardons in Thailand, President Habibie's pardons of Indonesian political prisoners at the end of the New Order era, and also in some cases the results of Malaysian Pardons Board meetings (although the explanation for multiple simultaneous grants in Malaysia may be more to do with the long intervals between sittings, rather than a desire to maximize the political impact of clemency). Collective grants such as these have the potential to distort and dominate cumulative clemency totals and therefore have a disproportionate influence over the relevant jurisdiction's aggregate clemency rate.

[49] Liddle (1999) 13; 'Indonesia Frees Two Political Prisoners' (1998).

Conversely, the national case studies suggest that commutations and pardons tend not to be granted on a widespread scale where the final clemency decision maker/s are popularly elected and form part of a government promoting the rule of law as a criminal justice priority. Here, death penalty clemency (at least where reported publicly) is usually a significant political liability, rather than being of political benefit. The decision makers concerned gain domestic and international legitimacy not through royal benevolence, but through popular election and the gradual improvement of living standards.

The study's two most relevant examples are the People's Action Party Cabinet in Singapore (during the entire period of study) and the administrations of Indonesia's four democratically elected presidents from 1999 to 2016: Megawati Sukarnoputri, Abdurrahman Wahid, Susilo Bambang Yudhoyono, and Joko Widodo.[50] In the former case, the rule of law has formed an essential part of Singaporean political identity, stretching back to independence in 1965.[51] People's Action Party politicians commonly believe that the rule of law being made a political priority is a key reason for Singapore's prosperity and attractiveness to foreign investment.[52] In the second counterfactual example, Indonesia's four democratically elected presidents have embraced the same principle to distance their administrations from those of autocratic President Suharto,[53] and relatedly as a means of combating public perceptions of endemic political and judicial corruption.[54]

In practical terms, in both jurisdictions this has meant a publicly even-handed treatment *at the clemency phase* of women and men, rich and poor, young and old, and—perhaps most controversially—foreign nationals and local citizens. Even-handed treatment at the clemency phase has had its greatest impact in drug-trafficking cases.[55] A much higher proportion of those

[50] Malaysia's 'no mercy' policy, under Prime Minister Mahathir's early Barisan Nasional government, also fits within this conception. However, as I described in Chapter 5, this policy fell into disuse by the early 1990s.

[51] Silverstein (2008) 77; Chan (2012) 209–10; Rajah (2012) 285.

[52] Silverstein (2008) 77; Rajah (2012) 285; Tey (2011) 100.

[53] Lindsey (2006); Lindsey and Butt (2013) 169; Lynch (2009) 554.

[54] Suhadji (2006); Lynch (2009) 554; Agustin (2017).

[55] In Singapore, a strong belief in general deterrence also explains low clemency in drug-trafficking cases, in addition to the 'rule of law' as an overarching political philosophy.

sentenced to death for drug-trafficking offences in Southeast Asia are foreign nationals, women, or young people,[56] when compared with equivalent cohorts of capital prisoners convicted of murder, political crimes, or firearms offences. In post-Suharto Indonesia, as in Singapore throughout the period of study, foreign nationality has been noticeably ignored as a mitigating characteristic in narcotics cases, at least at the clemency phase. In Singapore since 1991, as in Indonesia since the fall of Suharto in 1998, clemency has not been awarded after diplomatic representations from foreign governments in any single known case.[57] This stands in sharp contrast with the clemency practice of Thailand and Malaysia over the equivalent period, whereby foreign nationals have been regularly spared in order to maintain good international relations. The monarchical decision makers in the latter two jurisdictions may commute death sentences in this manner without compromising their political futures, given that they inherit power by birth, rather than being elected by the public.

Clemency and time spent on death row

The third and final conception of clemency that the four case studies appear to support is clemency as a response to excessive time spent on death row. Based on state practice in Thailand, Malaysia, and Indonesia, commutation and pardon are more commonly granted if loopholes in the precise legal procedures for clemency operate to frustrate the elected government's desire to increase the processing pace and volume of executions. Within the three aforementioned jurisdictions, the slow pace of investigations, trials, judicial appeals, and clemency proceedings often extends to ten years, and sometimes to more than twenty. When

[56] International Federation for Human Rights (2015) 13–14; Shelley and Metz (2017) xii.

[57] The only foreign national granted capital clemency in either jurisdiction over these timeframes was Indra Bahadur Tamal, a Nepalese drug trafficker whose sentence was commuted by President Yudhoyono alongside the death sentences of three others during 2011 or 2012 (see Saragih (2012)). Yudhoyono was reportedly motivated by the prisoner's status as a drug 'mule' (Sagita (2012)), and by an opportunity to help Indonesia's many citizens on death row abroad (McRae (2017) 13; Amnesty International AI Index ASA 21/2434/2015, 16; Kencana (2012)), rather than any intervention from the Nepalese government.

the length of time an offender spends in prison on remand, during judicial appeals, and while awaiting a clemency ruling begins to be measured in decades rather than in years, it becomes less likely (and may even be perceived as unconscionable) for an executive decision maker to deny clemency and authorize execution after such a long delay.

State practice in Thailand, Malaysia, and Indonesia reveals that death sentences have been commuted to lesser punishments, or prisoners released outright, after prisoners have remained on death row for excessive lengths of time. Many of the prisoners eventually spared by Malaysia's State and Federal Pardons Boards, Thailand's system of individual and collective royal pardons, Indonesia's publicly reported presidential clemency grants, and President Suharto's unofficial remissions procedure during the New Order era spent many years incarcerated after first being arrested. Singapore's death penalty practice, on the other hand, reveals only one case where time spent on death row influenced the Cabinet in granting commutation.[58] Prima facie, it is unclear whether Southeast Asian prisoners' long stays on death row are a side effect of prevailing legal structures, or instead arise from political ambivalence over executions. However, clues may be found in individual cases. In many instances, excessive time spent by prisoners on death row before a clemency decision is reached has a procedural explanation or, at worst, results from severe negligence. Few prisoners are left languishing on death row in Southeast Asia through indecision alone. Indeed, where national jurisdictions retain capital punishment in law but their leaders remain politically ambivalent over executions, the petitions of death row prisoners should, in theory, be favourably addressed as soon as is practicable.

The precise legal and political mechanisms that have frustrated elected governments' desire to carry out executions more quickly over the period of study are described in Chapters 3, 5,

[58] See *Ramalan v Public Prosecutor* [1978] 2 WLR 130 (Privy Council), 136. The Cabinet's exact reasoning in this case is unknown. However, if commutation was granted in accordance with the Privy Council's explicit recommendation, then cruelty or the 'death row effect', rather than the defendant's good behaviour, would have been the justification.

and 6. In Malaysia, the slow pace of judicial appeals together with infrequent sittings of the Pardons Boards in a number of states left prisoners incarcerated for up to twenty-five years before their petitions were ruled upon, with thirteen and a half years the approximate median figure.[59] In Thailand, the slow judicial appeal process combined with the bureaucratic clemency appeal process for individual royal pardons, exacerbated by the ill health of King Bhumibol during the 2000s, also resulted in indeterminate stays in detention for many prisoners convicted of capital crimes. While a period of incarceration of ten to twenty years following arrest was once typical before King Bhumibol ruled on an individual royal pardon petition,[60] the late king's worsening health problems meant that many petitions remained entirely unanswered during the 2000s and 2010s, further slowing the process.[61] Collective royal pardons, granted to celebrate important royal events as part of a long tradition, routinely benefited prisoners whose individual royal pardon petitions were still pending.[62]

Importantly, for both types of Thai royal pardon, demonstrated rehabilitation in prison is an important criteria.[63] In Malaysia there are also several examples of capital clemency granted to reward rehabilitation,[64] and the Attorney-General's Chambers has explicitly confirmed the importance of rehabilitation for clemency decision-making.[65] Furthermore, in both nations, there is evidence to suggest that prisoners were granted clemency, on an individual basis, after the relevant decision makers considered their one or two decades spent on death row as sufficient 'punishment' for the

[59] Shafee Abdullah (2/11/2012).

[60] See Chapter 3 on Thailand (five to ten years for judicial appeals, plus five to ten years awaiting a decision on individual royal pardon).

[61] Interview with Thai human rights activist (2012); interview with Thailand Department of Corrections staff.

[62] Pouaree (1999a); International Federation for Human Rights (2005) 27; interview with Thai prison caseworker.

[63] 'Amnesty for Drug Offenders Reflects King's Generosity' (1996); interview with Thailand Department of Corrections staff; Pouaree (1999a); Jaruboon (2006) 87; interview with Thai criminal defence lawyer and Thai NGO staff.

[64] Khairulrijal (2015); 'Rehabilitation Is Our Top Priority, Says Prisons D-G' (1997); 'Johor Sultan Pardons Eight Prisoners' (2012); Yesuiah (2017); 'Sultan Gives Death Row Convicts One More Chance' (2015); 'Perak Sultan Pardons Two Drug Offenders on Death Row' (2017).

[65] Tan (2010).

crime committed.[66] Prisoners in Thailand and Malaysia might have enjoyed none of these opportunities if their executions were procedurally possible within several years of first arrest.

In Indonesia, as observed in Chapter 6, the loopholes in the 1950 and 2002 clemency laws allowed prisoners ample time within which to submit their clemency petitions, if they did so at all. In practice, Law 3/1950 allowed prisoners an indefinite period within which to file, whereas Law 22/2002 allowed for a second petition two years after the prisoner's first petition was rejected. Likewise, Law 14/1985 allows, in practice, an unlimited time within which to file an application for *peninjauan kembali* (case re-opening),[67] which has become a regular part of the criminal appeal process since the fall of Suharto. Under all three statutes, prisoners often waited as long as possible to seek legal redress, or did not do so at all, for fear that rejection by the president or the Indonesian Supreme Court would pave the way to a speedier execution. Unsurprisingly, a stay on death row of ten or more years has proven common in Indonesian cases, from the New Order era to the present day. Again, although inordinate delays under a sentence of death are known to lead to a range of physical and mental health afflictions,[68] prisoners in Indonesia have ultimately benefited from long delays by receiving clemency. During both the New Order and the *Reformasi* eras, case data reveal that rehabilitation on death row and expressed remorse have proven prominent justifications for presidential clemency.

As first described in Chapter 2, the academic literature suggests that the longer procedural complications or other sources of delay extend a prisoner's stay on death row, the greater the opportunity for the prisoner to demonstrate attributes making him or her worthy of commutation or pardon. Demonstrated rehabilitation, religious piety, and expressed remorse may be the most recognizable explanations which find parallels in Southeast Asian state practice, yet less obvious are assisting ongoing police investigations, psychiatric or terminal illness, old age, reconciliation with victims, opportunities to bribe clemency advisers, diminishing public indignation, and (as the Indonesian example demonstrates)

66 Handley (2006) 375; interview with Malaysian prosecutor.

67 See Cornell Center on the Death Penalty Worldwide, 'Indonesia' (2017).

68 Hood and Hoyle (2015) 212–18.

an eventual change to a more liberal regime.[69] These are all factors created or made more likely by the passing of time, which will greatly improve a prisoner's chances of leaving death row alive.

Returning to the one counterfactual example within the study, in Singapore the available data point to precisely the opposite conclusion. Chapter 4 revealed that the sole explicit constitutional ground for clemency—providing information in the cases of accomplices[70]—may have been completely usurped by prosecutors, and is now considered before trial rather than after the case is finalized. In Singapore, clemency has historically been granted for case-based retributive factors such as youth or first offence, provocation, or lesser involvement in the crime,[71] whereas the delays required for time-based commutations simply do not occur. In stark contrast to the other three jurisdictions under analysis, the total time a capital prisoner normally spends in detention in Singapore, from arrest through to execution, usually ranges from twelve to eighteen months.[72] Redemption, as one of four clemency paradigms, is almost entirely ruled out if prisoners have no realistic opportunity to convince decision makers that they recognize the harm their crime caused—that they have changed and deserve another chance.[73] Likewise, changes in political or societal conditions that might justify clemency as utilitarianism or for political gain rarely develop over such a short timeframe. In Singapore's mandatory death penalty regime, this means that (aside from rare acquittals on appeal, or a retrospective change in the law, as with the 2012 legislative reforms),[74] a defendant's fate is largely sealed the moment the Singapore High Court pronounces its guilty

[69] See generally Table 3.

[70] Constitution of Singapore 1965, art 22P(1)(a).

[71] As noted in Chapter 4, even when granted on a retributive basis, capital clemency in Singapore has been tainted by arbitrariness. There have undoubtedly been many other cases resembling the six grants since 1965 where clemency has been rejected and the prisoner executed.

[72] Interview with Singaporean criminal defence lawyer; interview with Singaporean criminal defence lawyer #2; Johnson (2013) 43.

[73] The exception is redemption created by circumstances arising before conviction, such as significant national service (see Moore (1989) 204; Kobil (2003) 222). However, within the four jurisdictions under study, this version of clemency as redemption ultimately proves far less common, compared with redemption as rehabilitation, remorse, or religious piety.

[74] See Amnesty International AI Index ACT 50/7158/2017, 5.

verdict. The same can hardly be said for defendants in Thailand, Malaysia, and Indonesia, with post-arrest factors proving significant in justifying clemency.

Factors Not Previously Discussed

Aside from the three explanations for clemency incidence just described, there are several other plausible factors which appear in single jurisdictions only, or within the prior academic literature outlined in Chapter 2. While each may appear logical within particular contexts, and worthy of further empirical investigation in the future, these factors do not appear to be supported by comparative state practice within actively retentionist Southeast Asia. The structural and cultural attributes in this category, together with the reasons why they do not seem to adequately explain death penalty clemency across the four jurisdictions under study, are described here. Ultimately, this study bears negatively on their theoretical prospects of explaining clemency incidence across a larger range of retentionist jurisdictions.

Separation of powers

Within Chapter 2, reference was made to the strong overlap of this political factor with that of another: the type of political regime granting clemency. Chapter 2 observed that retentionist democracies typically only allow for infrequent clemency grants, as part of a 'checking' exercise between government branches. Autocracies, on the other hand, more often bear witness to judicial power being 'usurped' by the executive through mass or frequent clemency grants. To a large extent, the type of political regime (autocratic or democratic) also correlates with the status of the final clemency decision maker (elected or unelected), and hence whether clemency enhances or detracts from political power. Accordingly, this factor is already indirectly considered, under the section of this chapter entitled 'Clemency and the final decision maker'.

Mandatory death penalties

This is one of the study's more surprising findings. Despite strong theoretical arguments to the contrary in Chapter 2, no overwhelming link has been found between mandatory death penalties and the frequency of capital clemency grants in Southeast Asia. Malaysia and Singapore, which both retain and utilize the mandatory death penalty for an almost identical set of crimes (and were once both part of the same Federation of Malaya), demonstrate vastly different clemency rates over the period 1991–2016. On the other hand, Thailand's purported mandatory death penalty laws are not really mandatory at all. A defendant pleading guilty at the earliest possible opportunity will usually be sentenced to a term of imprisonment, rather than to death. Moreover, mitigating circumstances particular to the offender may also reduce a purportedly mandatory death sentence to a lesser punishment.[75] As such, Thailand's mandatory death penalty works more like a starting point, rather than a fixed sentence.

What the Malaysian and Singaporean (and even the Thai) cases instead suggest is that restricting judicial discretion through the mandatory death penalty will ensure that a greater degree of leniency is granted at some other procedural stage—but not *necessarily* the clemency phase. In Singapore, this is exemplified by the '14.99 charge' brought by prosecutors in narcotics cases, or by charging culpable homicide rather than murder. In Malaysia, restricted judicial sentencing discretion manifests as clemency, but also as prosecutorial discretion, and even as an increased number of acquittals or convictions on lesser charges within the judicial stage itself. Thailand is, of course, one example where a very large number of death sentences imposed at first instance lead directly to a very large number of commutations by the king at the 'back end' of the process.

Single decision makers or politically insulated boards

This factor was briefly discussed in Chapter 4, which suggested that the Singapore Cabinet's consensual decision-making process, or alternatively the views of Lee Kuan Yew as a senior minister and minister mentor from 1990 to 2011, help to explain Singapore's clemency scarcity, set alongside several other factors.

Regarding the impact of decision-making structures, the predominantly American literature summarized in Chapter 2 suggests that a politically insulated clemency board or a single

[75] See Chapter 3.

decision maker is most likely to grant clemency. On first impressions, Singapore's clemency decision-making pattern appears consistent with this theoretical model. Clemency is rarely granted by the Singapore Cabinet, which is a collective, consensual decision-making body that is directly politically accountable. Moreover, although the views of Lee Kuan Yew as Singapore's founding prime minister undoubtedly proved influential from 1990 through to his retirement from the Cabinet in 2011, it is unlikely that Lee could be considered the sole decision maker on clemency over this period, given the prominence of views tendered by the Ministers of Law and Home Affairs.

Nevertheless, upon closer inspection, the American decision-making model fails to 'fit' precisely any of the Southeast Asian nations under study. As Chapter 2 initially foreshadowed, in all of the jurisdictions under analysis, including Singapore, there exists a well-developed system of bureaucratic and political advice on a clemency petition before it reaches the final decision maker. As Table 2 suggests, in none of the four Southeast Asian jurisdictions under analysis is there a genuinely lone decision maker on clemency, nor is the final decision made solely by a politically insulated board, and yet clemency frequency still varies widely between the jurisdictions. The grants of clemency commonly issued by single rulers—the king of Thailand; Malaysia's hereditary rulers, governors, and *Yang di-Pertuan Agong*; and the president of Indonesia—tend to confirm (or, less often, repudiate) advice from judicial, political, prosecutorial, and civil service sources.

Unavailable criminal law defences

This factor is now mainly of historical relevance. Even in jurisdictions where clemency has been granted due to a condemned prisoner's lesser culpability for the crime, the law of these jurisdictions also provides for an equivalent range of partial and complete legal defences. Indeed, successful clemency cases within this category mainly involve situations where there is insufficient evidence to found a complete or a partial defence available in law. Examples from Chapters 3–6 are provocation, intoxication, duress and sudden fight (Singapore), duress, diminished responsibility and intoxication (Malaysia), and duress (Indonesia).

Automatic clemency appeals

In all four jurisdictions under analysis, death row prisoners must be considered for clemency before they are executed, either as a matter of law or as a matter of practice. This means that, at least formally speaking,[76] the American phenomenon of death row 'volunteers' does not exist in retentionist Southeast Asia.

(No) time limits

There is, however, significant variation among the four jurisdictions with regard to application time limits for clemency. In Thailand, prisoners have sixty days to file a request for individual royal pardon;[77] in Singapore the time limit to petition the president is approximately three months;[78] and in Malaysia, subordinate legislation permits a petition 'as soon as is practicable',[79] which presumably must only be filed in the period before the next meeting of the relevant State or Federal Pardons Board—in practice, a period ranging from several months to more than ten years. In Indonesia, Law 3/1950 imposed a thirty-day time limit on clemency applications, whereas Law 22/2002 abolished this and allowed an unlimited period for filing. Thereafter the one-year time limit imposed by Law 5/2010 was in force for several years, before being constitutionally invalidated in June 2016.[80]

In one sense, none of these time restrictions prevent prisoners being considered for clemency before being executed, given the mandatory clemency appeals previously described. Application time limits do, however, prevent a prisoner compiling and presenting substantial evidence of rehabilitation, remorse, and reconciliation with victims, and if strictly enforced may also prevent a prisoner from submitting a petition based on retributive grounds. Nevertheless, it is unlikely that the variation in state practice here affects Southeast Asia's clemency rates in any significant way. Thailand, with by far the highest rate of clemency, limits filing

[76] Nonetheless, in any of the jurisdictions under analysis, in practice a prisoner may reduce his or her chances of receiving commutation or pardon by failing to file an individualized petition.

[77] Criminal Procedure Code 1934 (Thailand), s 262.

[78] *Yong Vui Kong v Attorney-General* [2011] SGCA 9, [114].

[79] Prisons Regulations 2000 (Malaysia), reg 113(1).

[80] Constitutional Court Decision No 107/PUU-XII/2015 (Indonesia).

times to sixty days; Singapore allows prisoners a longer time for filing but hardly grants capital clemency at all. In a minor way, strict filing deadlines may help to restrict clemency for time spent on death row (described previously), but are a poor predictor of overall clemency rates. A prisoner's total time spent incarcerated before petitioning appears as readily affected by the judicial process and any bureaucratized system of clemency advice as by filing deadlines alone.

(No) victim notification or consent; (no) requirement for reasons

Provisions mandating victim notification or consent to clemency are found in no Southeast Asian jurisdiction. Likewise, none of the four jurisdictions under study require their final clemency decision makers to give reasons for rejecting or accepting petitions.

(No) outright prohibitions on clemency

Furthermore, none of the jurisdictions under analysis have ever banned clemency for particular death penalty offences either by constitutional or legislative means. In fact, formal prohibitions on clemency for capital offences are exceedingly rare worldwide, outside of Muslim-majority jurisdictions which strictly incorporate Sharia into their positive criminal laws.[81] Former Thai prime minister Thaksin Shinawatra's attempt to ban drug traffickers from receiving individual royal pardon in 2001 was stymied by the constitutional and legislative rights of drug prisoners to be considered for clemency.[82] Indonesian President Joko Widodo's blanket rejection of clemency for drug traffickers announced in December 2014 has so far proven more effective for his administration, surviving a legal challenge and paving the way for a record number of executions in a single year in Indonesia (fourteen executions in 2015).[83] However, Widodo's 'no mercy' policy is best considered as a counterfactual example of clemency *refusals*

[81] See Pascoe (2019b).

[82] Interview with Thai law professor; interview with Thai human rights lawyer.

[83] See Cassrels (2017); Zhang (2015); KontraS (2010); 'Bali Nine Duo's Challenge to Deny Clemency Heard by Jakarta Court' (2015).

boosting political power for the final decision maker rather than as a *legal* prohibition on mercy, which it is not.

Public opinion

Chapter 2 also identified the peripheral impact of public opinion on clemency granted as 'political power'. Popularly elected decision makers such as US state governors will often take into account public opinion before acting on clemency.[84] Conversely, popular opinion will not prove as relevant a decision-making criterion for autocrats or other unelected clemency arbiters. This logic suggests that, within retentionist democracies at least, the general extent of the public's support for capital punishment has a bearing on how often the head of state commutes death sentences. In the Southeast Asian context the major flaw with this argument is that within all four jurisdictions under study (whether democracies or not), death penalty retention enjoys robust public support.[85] Clemency rates cannot possibly turn on differences of public opinion in Southeast Asia, where none can be found.

A Three-Part Hypothesis

Within the limitations of an exploratory study dealing with a topic often shrouded in official secrecy, it is nonetheless possible to reach several conclusions about the primary contributing factors to clemency rates in Southeast Asian nations that continue to practise capital punishment. While the constitutionally sanctioned prerogative to commute and pardon criminal punishments, as with any other source of political power, is not always exercised in a consistent, principled fashion,[86] the empirical data collected suggest three plausible explanations for Southeast Asian capital clemency incidence during the period 1991–2016.

Clemency and lenient discretion

The proportion of finalized death sentences commuted or pardoned is partially determined by the extent to which lenient

[84] Breslin and Howley (2002) 253; Sullivan (1993); Bedau (1990–1) 260, 268.
[85] Delaney (2013); Hood (2012) 9; McRae (2012) 7.
[86] Schabas (2002) 132.

discretion can be, and is, exercised at earlier points in the criminal justice system, be that by police, prosecutors, at trial, on appeal, or by an extraordinary case re-opening procedure. The more death-eligible cases that are filtered away at earlier stages, the less importance clemency possesses as a remedial and political measure. Conversely, it is also possible that the widespread use of extrajudicial punishments (such as administrative detention or extrajudicial killings) at earlier stages impacts capital clemency rates in precisely the opposite manner. If the very worst cases are filtered out of the system altogether, clemency rates increase for those cases which remain.

Clemency and the final decision maker

The proportion of finalized death sentences commuted or pardoned is partially determined by the political status of the final clemency decision maker. An unelected final decision maker (such as a monarch or autocrat) stands to gain power and legitimacy by alternating executions with recurrent and collective clemency grants. In contrast, an elected final decision maker (such as a cabinet or president) whose government's criminal justice agenda emphasizes the 'rule of law' will instead gain political traction by rejecting clemency petitions in an even-handed manner.

Clemency and time spent on death row

Finally, the proportion of finalized death sentences commuted or pardoned is partially determined by the usual length of time prisoners spend in detention before their clemency petitions are ruled upon. Clemency tends to be granted more often where, for procedural reasons, prisoners remain in detention for 10–20 years or more after arrest. Conversely, a jurisdiction with a maximally efficient criminal justice bureaucracy and no procedural loopholes will quickly proceed to execute the vast majority of convicted prisoners, after rejecting their judicial and clemency appeals.

As discussed throughout this chapter, each of these three factors help to explain clemency incidence within all four jurisdictions under study. Notably, the country in which the criminal justice and political system supports clemency in none of these three forms—Singapore—has an extremely low overall clemency rate. Conversely, the country where clemency fulfils all three functions—Thailand—has an extremely high clemency rate. Malaysia and Indonesia, with clemency rates in between these two extremes, share mixed results. Overall, a cumulative three-part model largely appears to predict Southeast Asian state practice, as Table 5 indicates.

The cumulative model proposed is admittedly far from perfect: it suffers from significant data shortcomings, as described in detail in Chapter 1 and throughout the country case studies in Chapters 3–6. Moreover, it is unclear whether the three explanatory factors should be weighed equally, or whether one is more important than others in each case. Nevertheless, bearing in mind these caveats, at least for the four Southeast Asian jurisdictions under study, the model does a serviceable job in explaining the

Table 5 Preliminary test of the three-part hypothesis for clemency rates

Characteristic	Thailand	Singapore	Malaysia	Indonesia
Limited lenient discretion	✓	X	✓[a] X[b]	✓[c] X[d]
Unelected final decision maker	✓	X	✓[e] ?[f]	✓[g] X[h]
Excess time on death row	✓	X	✓	✓
Clemency rate prediction	*Common*	*Rare*	*Mixed*	*Mixed*
Clemency rate observed	High (95+%)	Low (0.6%)	High (55–63%)	Medium (26–33+%)

[a]Judicial recommendations for clemency in mandatory death penalty cases. Administrative detention in lieu of prosecution has an unclear effect on Malaysia's clemency rate.

[b]Police, prosecutorial, and judicial leniency.

[c]Coup-related prisoners surviving to the end of the Suharto presidency only. Possible extrajudicial executions from 1991 onwards.

[d]Non-coup-related cases.

[e]Cases in the nine Malay states, adjudicated by the relevant Malay ruler.

[f]Cases from Malacca, Penang, Sabah, and Sarawak, where the official decision maker is the *Yang di-Pertua Negeri* (governor), and federal cases, where the official decision maker is the *Yang di-Pertuan Agong* (king). In these jurisdictions, the final decision makers in practice are both elected (State Chief Ministers, Minister for Federal Territories) and unelected (Malaysian Federal Attorney-General).

[g]Coup-related cases pardoned by President Habibie only.

[h]*Reformasi*-era presidents.

relative incidence of capital clemency, according to theoretically relevant explanations. The model is also notable for the many theoretical explanations for clemency incidence it excludes, which were described earlier in this chapter. Despite its limitations, it is a significant advance on previous empirical research on both clemency incidence, and the comparative death penalty in Southeast Asia. In the next chapter, the final question to be addressed is what these findings mean for policy makers, practitioners, and future scholarship.

Conclusion: Clemency's Place

In a system marked by such arbitrariness, perhaps only the arbitrary power of clemency provides a route to justice.

Austin Sarat, *Mercy on Trial: What It Means to Stop an Execution*[1]

In this final chapter, I discuss the practical and scholarly implications of the comparative findings set out in Chapter 7. As the first transnational study of executive clemency using empirical methods, the potential applications of this research are several. For scholars, the results suggest a future research agenda to fill existing gaps in knowledge on Southeast Asia, and to test the purported determinants of capital clemency frequency on a broader range of retentionist jurisdictions. The findings also suggest possible modifications to existing theoretical understandings of clemency's place within death penalty scholarship.

For practitioners and policymakers dealing with Southeast Asian capital cases, this study identifies certain legal and political conditions which make clemency more or less likely in death penalty cases, and, where possible, the means by which to bring about those conditions. For supporters of death penalty abolition, increasing prevailing clemency rates brings any retentionist jurisdiction closer to de facto abolitionist status,[2] although from there it may prove a longer struggle to abolish the death penalty altogether.[3] For criminal defence lawyers on the ground in Southeast Asia, who may or may not be abolitionists themselves,

[1] Sarat (2005) 134.

[2] Parliament of Australia (2016) 130.

[3] Hood and Hoyle (2015) 20–1; Cornell Law School (2016) 32; Nicholson (2017) 5–6. Prominent examples in Southeast Asia are Brunei, Laos, and Mynamar, each of which have failed to conduct an execution for more than twenty-five years, yet still retain capital punishment in law.

Last Chance for Life: Clemency in Southeast Asian Death Penalty Cases. First Edition. Daniel Pascoe. ©Daniel Pascoe 2019. Published 2019 by Oxford University Press.

the findings of this study have particular resonance as they try to save the lives of individual clients on death row. While life imprisonment or a twenty-year sentence in Southeast Asia's jails may be a grim prize to aim for,[4] life is infinitely preferable to death, not least because it maintains hope of eventual release through parole, remission, or a further act of commutation.[5] Nevertheless, even if activists and practitioners attempt concerted interventions to force the issue in individual cases, Southeast Asian clemency incidence appears set to decline overall in the medium term. For abolitionists, the associated good news is that, alongside clemency, executions themselves are also likely to become ever rarer, as fewer capital cases are prosecuted in the first place and fewer that are prosecuted survive appellate scrutiny.

Implications for Future Scholarship

Filling the gaps in coverage

Before any suggestion of what the findings presented here mean for future research on death penalty clemency and in other areas, this book's existing shortcomings are, in themselves, a potential target for future data collection and analysis. This study's interview and archival-based fieldwork, presented alongside data systematically collected from news media and NGO sources, undoubtedly expands existing understanding of the use of the death penalty in Southeast Asia. Yet data limitations are still evident from the four tables in the Appendix, as well as within each narrative case study in Chapters 3–6. Here, there are a number of gaps that future

[4] See Cornell Center on the Death Penalty Worldwide, 'Singapore' (2017); Cornell Center on the Death Penalty Worldwide, 'Thailand' (2017); Cornell Center on the Death Penalty Worldwide, 'Malaysia' (2017), and Cornell Center on the Death Penalty Worldwide 'Indonesia' (2017), on prison conditions in the four countries under study.

[5] See Chapter 2. In each of the four jurisdictions under study, commutation and pardon may be granted to prisoners serving life or fixed terms of imprisonment. On the prospects of release from a life sentence through other methods, see Lindsey and Nicholson (2016, at 112–13) on sentence remissions in Indonesia; Heng (1998, at 104–5 n3) on conditional release from a life sentence in Singapore, and Sharif and Veera (1997a) and Oxford Pro Bono Publico (2016, at 61–2) on conditional release from a life sentence in Malaysia. Other than through clemency, there is no possibility of release from a *natural* life sentence in Malaysia (Sithambaram (2005)).

scholarship (or indeed investigative journalism) may seek to fill, once the national governments themselves release further quantitative data, or through qualitative means such as interviews with key decision makers. Answers to the following questions would allow for an even deeper public understanding of Southeast Asia's death penalty and clemency practices.

First are notable statistical shortcomings. Missing from existing coverage is Thailand's complete list of collective royal pardons during the reign of King Bhumibol, including how many condemned prisoners benefited,[6] together with complete yearly totals for individual royal pardons.[7] Also absent are Singapore's complete yearly death sentence totals and death row prisoner numbers for most of the years under study. In Singapore, publicly known execution totals substantially outnumber known death sentence totals from 1991 to 2016 (466 to 197+),[8] a patently absurd result given the typically short period from arrest to execution. In Malaysia, the jurisdiction where data has proven hardest to come by overall, this study's empirical research failed to obtain complete Malaysian execution and clemency statistics for the years 1991–7,[9] just as the Mahathir government's 'no mercy' campaign targeting drug traffickers drew to a close.[10] Likewise, Malaysia's annual death sentence totals throughout the period under analysis (1991–2016) remain incomplete.[11] In Indonesia, official clemency statistics from the late Suharto and early *Reformasi* eras,[12] which are held on file by the State Secretariat,[13] are presently unavailable to researchers and do not form part of the data presented here.

[6] Thereby extending the lists provided by Boriboonthana (1999) and Barrow (2017) (covering collective royal pardons from 1977 to 1996 and 1999 to 2007, respectively).

[7] See Appendix (Thailand).

[8] See Appendix (Singapore).

[9] See Appendix (Malaysia).

[10] See Chapter 5.

[11] See Appendix (Malaysia). The historic triumph of the Malaysian opposition in the May 2018 general election has brought new hope that such elusive data will soon be released to the public.

[12] See Appendix (Indonesia). McRae's assertion that only one clemency petition was granted from at least thirty-six pleas from 1990 to 2012 is not based upon official government records but instead upon NGO datasets, supplemented by media articles (McRae (2012) 4).

[13] See Chapter 1. An employee of the Ministry of Law and Human Rights refused to provide these figures when asked by the author in 2016.

Moreover, the precise number of condemned prisoners who benefited from Suharto's unofficial 'remissions' policy during the New Order period, possibly continued by Indonesia's *Reformasi* presidents,[14] is also unclear and may even never be publicly known.

Beyond the numbers, there are also several notable shortcomings in this study's summary of case-by-case reasoning on clemency petitions that future scholarship might target. In Singapore, future research may uncover whether, as I suspect, assisting investigations and prosecutions in the cases of accomplices was a key criteria in Cabinet decision-making in the cases of Siti Aminah Jaafar, Sim Ah Cheoh, and Mathavakannan Kalimuthu.[15] In Malaysia, although questions tabled in parliament by an opposition lawmaker revealed that there were 127 clemency grants made in capital cases from 1998 to 2015,[16] only sporadic official justifications for any of these grants have been provided in the media. Moreover, it is unclear which foreign nationals, other than prisoners from Indonesia, the Philippines, and the United Kingdom,[17] have benefited at the clemency phase in Malaysian cases, given that foreign nationality has been explicitly confirmed by the Malaysian Ministry of Foreign Affairs as an important mitigating factor before the State and Federal Pardons Boards.[18] Finally, over the period under analysis it is uncertain exactly how many capital clemency grants have been made *arbitrarily* in Malaysia, primarily to boost the prestige, religiosity, and legitimacy of the nine Malay rulers, rather than where the case evinces decisive individual mitigating features. Perhaps the only way to uncover this information would be through first-hand sources such as the written proceedings of Pardons Board meetings, or through interviews with the rulers themselves.

In Indonesia, data from the State Secretariat could quite readily reveal whether four, ten, or any intermediate number of coup-related prisoners were released by President Habibie from death (as opposed to life) sentences in 1999.[19] If the relevant documentation from the Suharto period exists, further archival research

[14] See Chapter 6.
[15] See Chapter 4.
[16] Palansamy (2015).
[17] See Chapter 5.
[18] Than (2010).
[19] See Chapter 6.

may also reveal why these prisoners (a) were not part of the group whose death sentences were commuted by Suharto in 1980, yet contrastingly (b) were also not executed during the late 1980s and early 1990s, after Supreme Court Decree 1/1986 purportedly removed any procedural barrier to doing so.[20] Most recently, during the presidency of Joko Widodo, it remains puzzling why Widodo commuted the death sentences of at least seven murderers from 2014 to 2016 but has refused to do the same for any convicted drug traffickers. Given the lack of explanation by the president himself, clues might be found in the Supreme Court's (secret) recommendation on commutation in each of the murder cases, as well as advice given by the Attorney-General's Office and the Ministry of Law and Human Rights.

Moreover, although it has helped to clear away some of the opacity involved, this study has not completely revealed Southeast Asia's clemency decision-making structures and patterns over the entire period from 1991 to 2016. Major shortcomings are as follows. In Thailand, the extent to which King Bhumibol personally contributed to clemency outcomes in individual royal pardon claims during his reign remains partially unclear. At the very least, Bhumibol acceded to the vast majority of recommendations from civil servants, politicians, the king's Principal Private Secretary, and the Privy Council,[21] although it would be interesting to know the kinds of cases which did not fit this pattern, before health problems significantly curtailed the king's role during the 2000s. In Singapore, the extent to which other Cabinet ministers deferred to Lee Kuan Yew's views on petitions until Lee's political retirement in 2011 remains similarly unknown, as does the frequency of cases in which the Cabinet reached a decision contrary to the written recommendation provided by the Attorney-General.[22]

In Malaysia, the role of the Malay rulers in clemency proceedings remains of great interest. Although they are legally entitled to rule on petitions in any way they wish,[23] practically speaking,

[20] See Chapter 6. Here, Sabdo suggests that, during the Suharto era, 'bureaucratic inaction [formed] part of the regime's intimidation' toward enemies in selected cases (Sabdo, forthcoming).

[21] Interview with Thailand Department of Corrections staff; interview with former employee of the Thailand Department of Corrections.

[22] See Chapter 4.

[23] Constitution of Malaysia 1957, art 42(1); Criminal Procedure Code 2006 (Malaysia), s 281(c); interview with Malaysian human rights lawyer.

how often have the Malay rulers disregarded the opinion of the federal Attorney-General? Beyond the assertiveness shown by the rulers of Johor, Perak, and Selangor in recent decades,[24] what decision-making disparity exists among the nine Malay States themselves, and as between the States and the federal jurisdiction? Moreover, what role do the three lay members on the State and Federal Pardons Boards play, beyond ensuring racial equity?[25] For example, are their votes ever determinative over the Pardons Boards' final recommendations, or do they merely defer to the opinion of the federal Attorney-General or the chair of the Board?[26] In Indonesia, although empirical research revealed Sukarno, Suharto, and Yudhoyono's usual preference for following the Supreme Court's mandatory advice on clemency,[27] the attitude towards the Supreme Court taken by *Reformasi* presidents Wahid, Megawati, and Widodo—beyond populist calls to reject drug traffickers' petitions—remains unknown.

Generalizing the findings

Based on the comparative case studies in Chapters 3–6, the three-part hypothesis for Southeast Asian clemency frequency set out in Chapter 7 is the most plausible comparative finding currently possible. However, although lenient discretion at earlier stages, the political status of the final decision maker, and time spent on death row each appear to impact clemency frequency in Thailand, Singapore, Malaysia, and Indonesia, it remains unclear which, if any, of these three factors exerts a greater influence in each jurisdiction. The traditional methodological means of answering this question would be through multivariate regression analysis, going from qualitative to quantitative methods in an attempt to crystallize a new theoretical model.[28] However, given the data shortcomings just identified, it is presently all but impossible to test the three explanatory factors on a quantitative basis within Southeast

[24] Interview with Australian academic expert on Malaysia; interview with international human rights NGO staff #2; interview with Malaysian prosecutor.

[25] Butler and Low (1991) 220–1.

[26] One interviewee argued that the three lay members' views carried little weight (interview with Malaysian prosecutor), whereas another interviewee disagreed (interview with former Malaysian Federal Court judge).

[27] See Chapter 6.

[28] Neuman (2005) 76–7; Babbie (2004) 410; Blaikie (2010) 212.

Asia. Continuous measures for key variables, such as the extent of police and prosecutorial discretion exercised before cases reach the courts, the average (or median) time which capital prisoners spend incarcerated before a clemency decision is reached, and even the precise clemency-to-execution ratio itself (in Thailand, Malaysia, and Indonesia), each remain unavailable to researchers.

The broader question, however, is whether the comparative trends presented here reflect the reality of death penalty practice outside of the four nations under study. In other words, does the three-part hypothesis set out at the end of Chapter 7 explain clemency rates solely across these four Southeast Asian jurisdictions, or also elsewhere within the retentionist world?

There are several potential sites for further regional comparison. Using an extended timeframe, the other Southeast Asian jurisdictions now classified as abolitionist de facto (abolitionist in practice) or indeed as abolitionist de jure (in law) could form one sample. All Southeast Asian nations have executed prisoners and have granted executive clemency at some point during the twentieth century. The remaining ASEAN member states not considered in this study are Vietnam (still actively retentionist), the Philippines (abolitionist for all crimes since 2006, albeit with a first period of abolition from 1987–93),[29] Myanmar (abolitionist de facto, last execution in 1993), Laos (abolitionist de facto, last execution in 1989), and Cambodia (abolitionist for all crimes since 1989, last execution in 1988).[30] Brunei's last execution, although the Sultanate has not yet abolished capital punishment in law, occurred in 1957.[31] A qualitative investigation of death penalty and clemency practice in these jurisdictions covering the period from, say, 1975 to 1990 would help to test the patterns identified within this book, and may suggest further modifications and refinements to a regional theory of clemency in Southeast Asian death penalty

[29] The Philippines is one of only two national jurisdictions worldwide to have reinstated capital punishment, and resumed executions, after previously abolishing it. The other is The Gambia (Hood and Hoyle (2015) 20).

[30] Johnson and Zimring (2009) 103; World Coalition against the Death Penalty (2014). Of the two ASEAN Observer States, Timor-Leste was an occupied territory administered by retentionist Indonesia from 1975 to 1999 (Hands Off Cain, 'East Timor' (2017)), whereas Papua New Guinea last conducted an execution in 1954 (Cornell Center on the Death Penalty Worldwide, 'Papua New Guinea' (2017)).

[31] World Coalition against the Death Penalty (2011).

cases. However, even employing the same qualitative comparative case study approach, data availability problems are likely to persist, given (a) the limited availability and memory of interview subjects on pre-1990 cases; (b) patchy and non-digitized news media sources, and (c) the staunchly authoritarian power structures in place in the region during the 1970s and 1980s.

An alternative approach would be to assess the suggested clemency hypothesis within other predominantly retentionist world regions such as the Caribbean, the Middle East, or East and Northeast Asia. Again, problems in collecting sufficient quantitative data within secretive and semi-secretive jurisdictions,[32] particularly on the amount of lenient discretion exercised at earlier stages during potential capital prosecutions,[33] may well undermine the potential for rigorous quantitative analysis. As with Southeast Asia's own retentionist states, in-depth qualitative analysis involving only a few jurisdictions at a time may be the only feasible way forward for future transnational research on this topic.[34] Nevertheless, clemency's practical importance as the last procedural hope for condemned prisoners, together with its theoretical significance as a prominent symbol of state sovereignty, together demand further efforts from comparative death penalty scholars, no matter the precise methodology adopted.

Beyond capital clemency rates

Subject to future quantitative or qualitative testing in other parts of the retentionist world, the findings presented in this study have several broader theoretical implications. Each of the three

[32] See Pascoe (2016b) 197–8.

[33] One potential, albeit crude, proxy measure of lenient discretion exercised at earlier stages is a comparison between murder rates and the number of prisoners on death row who have exhausted all judicial appeals, each assessed on a per capita basis. However, this comparison problematically assumes that (a) murder is the jurisdiction's sole death-eligible crime, which is often not the case in Asia and the Middle East; (b) police detection rates are equivalent across jurisdictions, and (c) 'death eligible' murder is defined exactly the same way across retentionist states.

[34] One alternative possibility is to test the three-part hypothesis for clemency frequency on US state jurisdictions. As of April 2017, twenty US states had carried out executions in the previous ten years (Death Penalty Information Center (2017c)).

elements of the hypothesis set out in Chapter 7 is partially supported by the previous academic literature on clemency frequency. Indeed, this is what helps to make the model a plausible one in the first place.[35] However, the trends documented in Chapter 7 also reveal several surprising findings, each suggesting possible modifications to existing theoretical understandings of clemency's role and function in modern criminal justice systems, both in capital and non-capital cases. Beyond explaining clemency rates, the three-part hypothesis also suggests new research agendas in the criminal justice field more generally.

Turning to the model's first explanation for capital clemency frequency, restricted lenient discretion at earlier stages, this study's most surprising finding is that enacting a mandatory death penalty for all or selected capital crimes does not automatically increase clemency as a lenient remedy at the 'back end' of the system. Eliminating discretion at an intermediate phase simply shifts discretion to another phase of case processing, whether earlier or later. Several scholars have previously hinted at this outcome, without reaching a firm conclusion on the mandatory death penalty's true impact on lenient discretion.[36]

This finding, if replicated on a broader scale, compromises not only the purported relationship between mandatory death sentences and capital commutation rates,[37] but potentially also that between any type of mandatory minimum sentence and executive clemency. This study suggests that mandatory minimum sentences may shift lenient discretion not only to clemency decision makers, but also to police, to prosecutors, to judges (if acquittals become more common), and even to parole boards and remissions procedures, much later in the process. Future research may seek to explore these relationships in different national and comparative contexts.

Restricted lenient discretion as an explanation for capital clemency also counterfactually hints at a relationship between the use of extrajudicial punishments and the amount of leniency exercised

[35] Kohli et al (1995) 5, 47; Parsons (1938) 15.

[36] Hawkins (1992) 32, 36; Acker et al (2010) 193; interview with Canadian academic expert on the death penalty.

[37] On the purported relationship, see Novak (2015) 20–1; Fitzgerald (2011); interview with London-based death penalty lawyer #2; interview with British academic expert on the death penalty.

in the remaining cases that are prosecuted. Again, future research may examine this relationship not only within the death penalty context but also when considering non-lethal judicial punishment. Johnson and Zimring have previously suggested a correlative relationship between extrajudicial and judicial killings in the Asian context, with authoritarian government being the common causal factor for both types of sanctions.[38] In contrast, the present study suggests a substitution effect, albeit involving non-lethal as well as lethal punishments, in line with Black's theoretical account of an inverse relationship between informal and formal social control.[39] This finding tentatively suggests that the widespread use of extrajudicial punishments (both lethal and non-lethal) in potential capital cases may open the door for proportionally greater leniency in remaining cases, when compared with jurisdictions with a stricter focus on formal legality.

Nevertheless, this finding relies on an assumption that it is only the *very worst* cases which are dealt with by extrajudicial means, thereby altering the remaining sample of death-eligible cases which are processed through the criminal justice system. The conclusion would be different if the cohort of persons subject to extrajudicial penalties were instead chosen by the authorities because they were the most vulnerable targets (as with murderers, petty thieves, and drug dealers extrajudicially killed in Indonesia during the Suharto era, for example)[40] or because they were unlikely to be convicted or sentenced to death in court (as with administrative detainees in Singapore).[41]

For the second element of the hypothesis, clemency and the final decision maker, the contribution this study makes is to suggest the need for a much closer look at actual decision-making power on clemency in each jurisdiction, rather than making any simplistic assertion that authoritarianism and clemency frequency are causally connected, in the same way that execution rates and authoritarian government seem to be.[42] This study suggests that the

[38] Johnson and Zimring (2009) 450–1.

[39] Black (2010) 123–4.

[40] Bourchier (1988) 10; van den Berg (2001) 263; Amnesty International AI Index ASA 03/01/87; Asian Human Rights Commission (2012) 12.

[41] Interview with Singaporean human rights lawyer; '366 Criminal Law Detentions in Five Years' (2009); Erlanger (1989).

[42] Johnson and Zimring (2009) 289–90; Bae (2007) 12; Hood (1989) 50; Johnson (2010) 338.

structural feature producing capital clemency as a tool of governance is not *necessarily* authoritarianism, but rather the unelected status of the final decision maker (as the person or group with ultimate power over petitions). Malaysia and Thailand, both semi-authoritarian constitutional monarchies whose political leaders have been directly elected on several occasions during the period of study,[43] still vest final discretion over individual clemency petitions (but not much else) in their traditional hereditary rulers. Singapore, as a republic and another semi-authoritarian nation,[44] commutes death sentences at a much lower rate than Thailand and Malaysia, in part because Singapore's directly elected Cabinet is the final arbiter on petitions, rather than any unelected leader.[45] This finding is also likely to extend to clemency in non-capital cases in both retentionist and abolitionist jurisdictions. Using executive commutation or pardon to reduce or abrogate a prison sentence is, in theory, an equally valid means of demonstrating domestic and international legitimacy, benevolence, and religiosity, alongside dispensing mercy in capital cases.

For the third element of the hypothesis, clemency and time on death row, this study's broader contribution is to expand the list of potential time-based justifications which may convince executive decision makers to show leniency. Assisting ongoing or future police investigations, psychiatric or terminal illness, old age, opportunities for bribery, and regime change are all factors that aid clemency over time, in addition to the more commonly recognized capacity to rehabilitate, find religion, and show remorse in prison.[46] In other words, time spent incarcerated before a clemency decision is made aids not only clemency

[43] NGO Freedom House classified Malaysia as 'Partly Free' in each of the twenty-six years from 1991 to 2016. Thailand has a more variable record, being classified 'Partly Free' fifteen times, 'Free' seven times, and 'Not Free' four times over the same period (Freedom House (2016)).

[44] As with Malaysia, NGO Freedom House classified Singapore as 'Partly Free' in each of the twenty-six years from 1991 to 2016 (Freedom House (2016)).

[45] The president of Singapore was first elected by the public in 1993, although as noted in Chapter 7, this appears to have made little difference to prevailing clemency practice. The president always follows the advice of the Cabinet, having no discretion to make an individual decision (*Yong Vui Kong v Attorney-General* [2011] SGCA 9, [126], [150], [175], [180]).

[46] See Chapter 7.

as *redemption*, but also clemency for *retributive* and *political/utilitarian* reasons.

Again, this finding may well extend to clemency granted in non-capital cases, and to leniency shown by other criminal justice actors. For example, are prison sentences imposed at trial shorter (taking into account time spent on remand) in systems where prisoners take longer to be sentenced, due to procedural inefficiencies? Given the same head sentence, are parole boards more generous when the time interval between parole sittings is longer? Do prosecutors in systems tainted by inefficient investigatory practices offer more leniency than do prosecutors in more efficient systems? If the answer to such questions is yes, then why is this so? What are the time-based mitigating and exculpatory factors that emerge to sway the relevant decision makers? These are some of the questions the time-based element of the clemency hypothesis presented here prompts for future scholarship.

Finally, the third element of the three-part clemency hypothesis also tentatively suggests that the usual point at which time incarcerated becomes important as a mitigating factor is, at the very most, *thirteen to fifteen years* after arrest in retentionist Southeast Asia. This is the average time interval before a prisoner's clemency petition is answered in Thailand, Malaysia, and Indonesia: all jurisdictions where rehabilitation on death row (as well as other time-based justifications) happen to be important decision-making criteria that have previously led to commutations.[47] It is an open question whether this finding might be replicated in non-capital cases in Southeast Asia, or in capital and non-capital cases in other

[47] In Thailand, individual royal pardons in capital cases were typically resolved 10–20 years after arrest during King Bhumibol's later reign (see Chapter 3). Here, I take fifteen years as a mid-point estimate. In Malaysia, in 2012, the average time spent in prison before the State and Federal Pardons Boards disposed of a prisoner's petition stood at 13.5 years (Shafee Abdullah (2/11/2012)). In Indonesia, 2016 data revealed a thirteen-year average period spent incarcerated, not including time on remand, for prisoners who had exhausted judicial appeals (KontraS (2016)). The latter group included prisoners whose clemency appeals had been resolved and prisoners whose clemency appeals had not.

Nevertheless, no case study within this book considered the treatment of prisoners incarcerated for average periods of between eighteen months (as in Singapore, where there is little or no clemency as 'redemption') and ten years (Thailand's minimum figure). It is possible that, in other Southeast Asian and global jurisdictions, time incarcerated becomes an important decision-making factor well before ten years have elapsed.

parts of the world.[48] It seems relatively uncontroversial to state that lengthening the time before a clemency decision is reached increases a prisoner's odds of escaping execution (or of attaining freedom altogether). What is more uncertain is *how long* this delay needs to be in each jurisdiction, before it becomes determinative over the retributive, deterrent, and incapacitating justifications for continued incarceration or death penalty enforcement. Again, this is an important line of inquiry for future empirical scholarship.

Implications for Practitioners and Policymakers

Within this section, it is appropriate to begin with a general warning about prediction. Steinmo and Garland have both cautioned against using the results of comparative studies as a tool to predict future developments in politics, sociology, or other social science fields. For Steinmo, the very subjects of such studies, namely human beings and human institutions,

> adapt and are affected by history itself. Prediction and the related conception of ['hard'] science imply a linear analysis of variables that can be distinguished from one another and which react to one another in predictable ways … For many social scientists, such analysis denies the realities of the world in which we live.[49]

According to Garland:

> The fact that we have been able—through empirical research and theoretical reflection—to discern the kinds of determinants and functional requirements which tend to shape punishment, does not mean that we can predict, in any particular instance, how penal developments will turn out.[50]

Even if quantitative regression analysis were to vindicate Chapter 7's three-part hypothesis on clemency frequency in Southeast Asia or anywhere else in the retentionist world, great care should be taken before attempting to use the model to predict future clemency developments. Qualitative socio-scientific studies are most useful to explain past observations, rather than

[48] Fitzgerald (2011) notes vastly differing worldwide standards for what counts as an 'inhumane' time spent on death row: from two years in some Commonwealth cases, up to two decades in the United States.

[49] Steinmo (2008) 134.

[50] Garland (1990) 285.

as a means of predicting the future.[51] It is trite knowledge that academic researchers cannot double as fortune-tellers.

Nevertheless, abolitionist and capital defence strategies must begin somewhere, and it is better that these be based on prior empirical data rather than on hunches and preconceptions,[52] particularly for practitioners turning their attention to unfamiliar jurisdictions. Relayed here are a number of possible practical lessons deriving from the four comparative case studies, as human rights activists and policymakers seek to boost national clemency rates as a means of inching closer to abolition, and as criminal defence lawyers and diplomats seek to secure individual reprieves for their clients and national citizens, respectively. Importantly, the recommendations set out are distinct from (and sometimes contradictory to) the campaigning strategies employed in pursuing constitutional or legislative abolition of capital punishment altogether. Instead, they represent an evidence-based response to the plight of individual defendants currently facing execution in Thailand, Singapore, Malaysia, and Indonesia, and potentially elsewhere in Asia and the retentionist world. On the assumption that capital punishment is retained in the medium term among the most punitive retentionist states in Southeast Asia and elsewhere,[53] clemency remains vital as a condemned prisoner's final procedural hope for life. Significant arbitrariness within clemency decision-making, especially in those jurisdictions with clemency rates at either end of the 0–100 per cent spectrum, means that even well-thought-out strategies are no guarantee of success in individual cases. Yet this study suggests several steps which may make executive clemency more likely in present and future cases.

The value of clemency as precedent

The first lesson comes not from the comparative findings within Chapter 7, but rather from the data on previous clemency grants in capital cases set out within each national case study in Chapters 3–6. Clemency, defined here as discretionary political leniency by the executive branch,[54] is not restricted by precedent, even in common

[51] Anckar (2004) 102.

[52] Hubert (2013); Laurin (2015) 328.

[53] This is the pessimistic view. Contrast Schabas (2013) 25–6, and Hood and Hoyle (2009) 9–10.

[54] See Introduction.

law jurisdictions such as Singapore and Malaysia.[55] Although, as Chapters 3–6 reveal, the process for granting clemency is often heavily regulated by constitutional and legislative provisions, in most modern political systems the executive decision maker ultimately retains the authority to grant commutations and pardons for any reason that he or she sees fit, in keeping with clemency's origins as a monarchical privilege.[56]

The value, then, of empirical research which compiles a list of previous clemency successes in each jurisdiction is that 'clemency supporters' may utilize these as templates and points of leverage when making formal or informal submissions before the relevant decision maker. Here, the defendant's clemency supporters may include friends and family, legal representatives, civil society personnel, foreign diplomats, and even opposition politicians in the jurisdiction concerned. Each of these individuals or groups, whether in drafting a formal clemency petition to the chief executive, in making informal representations through personal channels, or when acting indirectly through the media, may draw upon the prior practice summarized in Chapters 3–6 as examples of clemency successes in retentionist Southeast Asia. Although previous clemency grants or refusals are not binding on present decision makers, the academic literature first described in Chapter 2 suggests that, when confronted by a large caseload of petitions, decision makers frequently abide by 'rules of thumb' in order to dispose of cases more efficiently.[57] Where the condemned prisoner's case falls within a frequently established exception to death penalty enforcement, especially before the same final decision maker, group of clemency advisers, or political party in power, continuing the existing practice will often prove the path of least resistance.[58]

Furthermore, irrespective of whether certain clemency justifications have historically appeared frequently (for example, prisoner rehabilitation in Malaysia, or foreign nationality in Thailand) or rarely (for example, arguable defences in Singapore, or protecting nationals sentenced to death abroad in Indonesia), newly

[55] Abramowitz and Paget (1964) 176; Rapaport (2001) 1001.

[56] Abramowitz and Paget (1964) 139–40; Morison (2006) 2. However, see Novak (2015, ch 8) on the trend towards judicial review of clemency decisions in common law jurisdictions.

[57] For example, Hawkins (1992) 39.

[58] Rapaport (2001) 1001.

installed government decision makers may be surprised to learn that historical precedents for certain kinds of clemency grants already exist within their jurisdiction. In seeking to persuade elected governments with an ideological posture favouring the 'rule of law', such as the People's Action Party in Singapore and consecutive *Reformasi* presidents in Indonesia, helpful analogous cases relayed within individual clemency petitions or oral representations may act as historical reminders that an elected government's political agenda based on 'law and order', the 'rule of law', or the 'separation of powers' will not be undermined beyond repair merely because capital prisoners are spared from death in infrequent cases. It is perfectly feasible to maintain a capital punishment regime for serious offences while simultaneously commuting death sentences where significant mitigating or political factors so demand. Indeed, this was the model contemplated for retentionist states by the International Covenant on Civil and Political Rights in 1966,[59] long before its Second Optional Protocol (furthering the cause of abolition) was created in 1989.[60]

Maximizing clemency as lenient discretion

In Chapter 7 I observed that lenient discretion is exercised at various points as death penalty cases are processed through Southeast Asia's criminal justice systems. After a death-eligible crime is detected by police, leniency that prevents an eventual execution may arrive at the pre-trial phase (when exercised by police or prosecutors), the judicial phase (as an acquittal, as sentencing leniency, or as a successful appeal), or the executive phase (as commutation or pardon). Even in jurisdictions where executive clemency is limited for political reasons (such as in Singapore and in *Reformasi*-era Indonesia), relevant government authorities still commonly show leniency to capital detainees at earlier, and often less visible, stages of proceedings.

There are three potential implications for practitioners and policymakers. First, in Southeast Asia it is notable that high-profile legal counsel are often only sought or appointed as a case

[59] International Covenant on Civil and Political Rights, art 6(2), 6(4); Schabas (2002) 57.

[60] Second Optional Protocol to the International Covenant on Civil and Political Rights, art 1.

proceeds towards execution. The results of this study suggest a more effective strategy by briefing experienced legal counsel at the earliest possible phase (that is, as soon as possible after arrest).[61] Examples where quality legal representation at an early stage may make a difference to a capital suspect's eventual fate include making representations to prosecutors to reduce murder charges to (non-capital) culpable homicide in Singapore;[62] advising a client to plead guilty on a capital charge at the earliest possible opportunity in Thailand, thereby avoiding a death sentence;[63] arguing for a conviction for non-capital possession rather than for capital trafficking in a Malaysian drugs trial;[64] and navigating Indonesia's notoriously corrupt investigatory processes and judicial system.[65] In jurisdictions and in situations such as these, the most effective defence strategy is not to let a potential death sentence reach the clemency phase in the first place.

Second, in capital cases, diplomatic representations by the home governments of foreign nationals are often mostly strongly made during the clemency phase, on the basis that governments do not wish to be seen to be interfering in the judicial systems of other countries. Yet representations for leniency made by foreign governments possess their greatest chances of success when they are made at multiple stages of case processing, and especially before prosecutors first lay charges.[66] This point becomes even more critical given the reluctance of the Singaporean and *Reformasi*-era Indonesian governments to reprieve foreign prisoners at the clemency phase, for fear of compromising political platforms, angering

[61] Although it is not always fully observed in practice, Indonesian and Singaporean laws afford suspects the right to consult a lawyer as soon as possible after arrest on a capital charge. See Criminal Code 1918 (Indonesia) arts 54–5; Constitution of Singapore 1965, art 9(3); Lindsey and Nicholson (2016) 88–9, 179. In Thailand, capital defendants have the right to consult a lawyer before making a plea (Criminal Procedure Code 1934 (Thailand), s 173), but again, the quality of representation is often low (Cornell Center on the Death Penalty Worldwide, 'Thailand' (2017)). In Malaysia, the right to legal representation is enshrined in the Federal Constitution (Constitution of Malaysia 1957, art 5(3)), but this right is not always respected in practice (Cornell Center on the Death Penalty Worldwide, 'Malaysia' (2017)).

[62] See Chapter 4.

[63] See Chapter 3.

[64] See Chapter 5.

[65] See Chapter 6.

[66] Reprieve (2014) 28–9.

domestic constituents, and inviting allegations of racial and economic favouritism. In Malaysia and Indonesia, where recent practice suggests that some foreign emissaries wait until the clemency phase before making direct representations for leniency based on reciprocity and shared economic interests,[67] prisoners' lives are being risked to maintain diplomatic protocol.

Finally, if, despite the manoeuvres previously suggested, a death sentence remains intact all the way through the judicial phase, clemency as a form of lenient discretion suggests that the prisoner's lawyers and supporters ought to focus their time and attention on justifications *not already considered* at earlier phases, by police, prosecutors, and judges. Given that clemency partially operates as an extension of lenient discretion found elsewhere in the criminal justice system, at the final stage of 'appeal' before the political executive, novel arguments would appear to hold the greatest chance of success. Examples from the four jurisdictions under analysis include redemptive clemency based upon prior service to the nation, in addition to good behaviour, remorse, and religious practice over many years spent incarcerated (Thailand, Malaysia, Indonesia); arguable yet unsuccessful defences first raised at trial (Singapore, Malaysia, Indonesia); assisting investigations and prosecutions in the cases of accomplices (Singapore, Thailand); exacerbated mental illness on death row (Indonesia); and terminal illness (Thailand, Singapore).[68]

Maximizing clemency before unelected and elected final decision makers

The key policy implication of clemency bolstering the political power of unelected decision makers is that, once a case proceeds past the judicial appeal phase and onto clemency deliberations, criminal defence counsel and foreign diplomats ought to direct their written or oral representations to the decision maker most likely to benefit from approving leniency (the king, sultan, autocratic leader, and so forth). Adding to the 'novel arguments' strategy just described, such representations might include appeals to the executive decision maker's benevolence, compassion,

[67] See Chapter 5 on Malaysia; Byrnes (2015); Department of Foreign Affairs and Trade (Australia), 5.

[68] See Chapter 7.

political legitimacy, and religiosity, in preference to retributive arguments already pursued at earlier stages. In the case of foreign nationals sentenced to death, appeals to unelected final decision makers in Southeast Asia should ideally be backed by the highest levels of the prisoner's home government (e.g. the head of state, the head of government, and the minister of foreign affairs), to serve as a mark of respect and international legitimacy for the individual serving as ultimate clemency arbiter. These strategies remain the same whether the appeal is made directly to the final decision maker or whether the petition is processed within various bureaucratic or political channels before reaching the unelected head of state.

By contrast, in jurisdictions where directly elected leaders are the final decision makers (e.g. the Singapore Cabinet, the president of Indonesia, or Malaysian Cabinet ministers in federal, military, and security cases), political benefit typically derives from rejecting capital clemency petitions, rather than from acceding to them. Of course, whether the final clemency decision maker is elected or unelected is not something over which outsiders have any control. Yet there are still potentially helpful steps that clemency supporters may take.

In these circumstances, in addition to ensuring that all prior prosecutorial and judicial outlets for lenient discretion are explored and exhausted, and then focusing on relevant novel arguments at the clemency phase (as just described), petitioners and their supporters might also engage directly with influential clemency *advisers* who do not bear the political cost of granting commutations or pardons. The case studies in Chapters 4–6 suggest that final decision makers such as the Singapore Cabinet, the President of Indonesia, or the Malaysian Minister of Federal Territories may be more amenable to granting capital clemency upon a positive recommendation from the Attorney-General (in Singapore and Malaysia) or a Justice of the Supreme Court's Criminal Chambers (in Indonesia). Although legal and diplomatic convention dictates that clemency petitions should be addressed to the head of state as the *formal* decision maker in each case, if this is the only clemency strategy petitioners and their supporters pursue, they may be acting too late. In circumstances where the final decision maker sees little to gain politically from making clemency grants, influential advisers earlier in the process may hold the key to realising the condemned prisoner's hope for leniency.

Maximizing clemency for time spent on death row

The final clemency-maximizing strategy that the results of this study suggest is to artificially extend the length of time a prisoner remains on death row before a clemency decision is made, or even after clemency has been rejected and before execution. A deliberate strategy of delay, especially after all judicial appeals are exhausted, may help a variety of time-based justifications for clemency to emerge, as documented in detail in Chapters 2 and 7.[69] Moreover, simply by staying alive, all death row prisoners retain some hope, however small, that capital punishment will eventually be abolished for all crimes, or at least for the crimes that they have committed. In these circumstances, the prisoners affected will usually receive retrospective commutation grants,[70] or might even be freed altogether through pardons or amnesties (similar to Indonesia's surviving coup-related prisoners, who were released in 1999, shortly before the Indonesian legislature repealed the Anti-Subversion Law of 1963).[71]

In adopting such tactics, clemency supporters must balance the prisoner's existing quality of life in jail,[72] and the inherent cruelty in prolonging uncertainty,[73] with improvements in the prisoner's chances of departing death row alive. For example, where an acquittal or a sentence reduction within the judicial process appears likely, or where a pardon at the clemency stage due to wrongful conviction is a realistic prospect, defence advocates ought to press

[69] Many of these time-based justifications for clemency are, to a certain extent, within the control of prisoners. Four prominent examples are rehabilitation and remorse, finding religion, testifying against accomplices, and attempts at reconciling with the victim's family in a murder case. Other clemency justifications, such as democratization and death penalty reductionism, fall outside a prisoner's sphere of influence.

[70] One example, albeit outside this study's geographical scope, is presidential amnesty or clemency granted to prisoners in Vietnam, as the number of death-eligible offences has been gradually reduced over time (Hands Off Cain, 'Viet Nam' (2000); Hands Off Cain, 'Vietnam' (2009)).

[71] Law 26/1999 on the Annulment of the Anti-Subversion Law (Indonesia), repealing Presidential Decree 11/1963 on the Eradication of Anti-Subversive Activities (Indonesia).

[72] See note 4.

[73] See Hood and Hoyle (2015) 205: 'Various socio-psychological studies have described the reactions of prisoners who have experienced a long period of uncertainty about their fate, as well as the problems posed for humane prison management.'

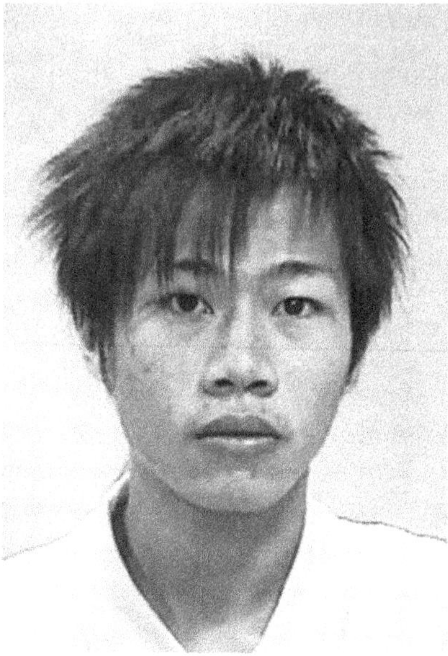

Image 6 Yong Vui Kong

Source: savevuikong.blogspot.com (reprinted with permission)

ahead with the legal process in an effort to free their client as soon as possible. However, if exoneration remains unlikely, then defence advocates' tactics such as legal and constitutional challenges to death penalty laws and procedures (preferably right from the very beginning of the case) and achieving temporary delays to clemency processing and execution protocols—even if these do not have much chance of permanent legal success[74]—are critical in enabling time-based justifications to emerge as an intended side effect.

Although he did not receive executive clemency from the President of Singapore, a prominent recent beneficiary of this approach is Malaysian citizen Yong Vui Kong (Image 6), arrested

[74] This may conflict with advocates' ethical responsibilities to pursue only matters that have a reasonable chance of success. Consider Sarat (1998) 332–5:

> [One] lawyer ... told me that his practice was like 'throwing sand in the machine'. For him, as for the others who respond to the hostile political and legal environment by stretching ethical limits, the contemporary political

in Singapore for trafficking in 47.27 grams of heroin in 2007, and sentenced to the mandatory death penalty in 2008.[75] Vui Kong first received a temporary stay of execution in order to file an appeal against conviction out of time, and thereafter his case served as a platform to challenge the constitutionality of the mandatory death penalty for drug trafficking in 2010, the clemency decision-making process in 2011, and finally the Singapore Public Prosecutor's decision to discontinue prosecution against Vui Kong's alleged drug supplier and 'mastermind' in 2012. Each of these legal manoeuvres proved ultimately unsuccessful.[76] However, in November 2013, following the landmark legislative amendments to Singapore's death penalty laws documented in Chapter 4 of this book, Vui Kong's death sentence was lifted by the Singapore High Court and replaced with life imprisonment and fifteen strokes of the cane, as the prisoner was deemed a mere courier and was certified as a 'justice collaborator' by the public prosecutor.[77] By the time he was re-sentenced Vui Kong had been imprisoned for six years and five months,[78] only a medium-length term on death row by regional standards but still far longer than the Singaporean average of 12–18 months.[79] Vui Kong largely owes his life to the work of his legal counsel at the latter stages of his case, Ravi Madasamy.[80]

In jurisdictions other than Singapore, after an elongated stay on death row, the same opportunity for leniency might arise through executive clemency, rather than through a one-off re-sentencing scheme brought about by legislative change. For example, in Indonesia, opportiunities to advocate for time-based clemency have recently improved with the Constitutional Court's abolition of clemency filing deadlines in June 2016.[81] Although at

battle seems to have been lost, and the courts seem intent only on moving people forward toward execution.

[75] *Yong Vui Kong v Public Prosecutor* [2010] SGCA 20, [2].

[76] *Yong Vui Kong v Public Prosecutor* [2010] SGCA 20, [3]; 'Vui Kong's Journey' (2010).

[77] *Yong Vui Kong v Public Prosecutor* [2010] SGCA 20, [5].

[78] 'Everything You Need to Know about Malaysian Drug Courier Yong Vui Kong in 60 Seconds' (2013).

[79] See notes 47-48 and associated text.

[80] 'Drug Courier Spared Death Now Challenges Caning Sentence' (2014).

[81] Constitutional Court Decision No 107/PUU-XII/2015 (Indonesia), 11, 19, 21, 22, 37, 78–9.

the time of writing the Attorney-General's Office is still grappling with the effects of the Constitutional Court's decision,[82] prisoners are now likely to enjoy a longer timeframe within which to prepare their petitions. In Thailand, petitioners for individual royal pardon whose circumstances have changed materially after excessive delay already enjoy the opportunity to resubmit personal information to the Department of Corrections.[83] In Malaysia, the length of the clemency process remains the most arbitrary among the four jurisdictions under study, being largely determined by the discretionary prerogative of the Malay rulers and state governors.[84] Yet even before the Malay rulers there may be an opportunity for legal advocates and foreign diplomats to privately encourage informal death penalty moratoria, given that certain state hereditary leaders have *deliberately* refused to convene meetings for this purpose.[85] The longer the time interval between the sittings of Pardons Boards, the more likely it is that prisoners will receive time-based clemency when these boards next meet, plus the more likely it is that the Malaysian parliament will have passed legislation restricting the death penalty's scope in the meantime.[86]

If substantial legislative change is possible in Singapore, a state often considered the spokesperson for death penalty retentionists in international fora,[87] then maximizing delay appears a painful yet viable option for capital defendants and their supporters within Indonesia, Malaysia, Thailand, and elsewhere in the retentionist world. In addition to the possibility of legislative reductionism, delay creates case-by-case conditions for various types of retributive, redemptive, and utilitarian clemency grants. Collectively, the

[82] 'AGO Waits for Supreme Court Decision on Pardon for Death Penalty Execution' (2017).

[83] Interview with Thailand Department of Corrections staff.

[84] New (2016); interview with Malaysian human rights lawyer; interview with Malaysian Human Rights Commissioner.

[85] Interview with Malaysian human rights lawyer; interview with international human rights NGO staff #2. However, an unwanted side effect of moves to extend the time intervals between sittings of State Pardons Boards is that petitioners with valid claims for clemency in non-death penalty cases will be left without recourse. In previous cases, it has not been uncommon for non-capital prisoners to serve the entire length of their sentences by the time that the relevant State Pardons Board next convened ('Anwar Seen as Admitting Guilt in Sodomy with Pardon Petition—Political Analysts' (2015)).

[86] See Hood (2013) 3.

[87] Hood and Hoyle (2015) 41–2, 113; Tan (2016).

problem for petitioners and their supporters is that, unless clemency decision makers in Indonesia, Malaysia, and Thailand begin to treat time-based arguments far more generously, it may take as much as 13–15 years of delay and uncertainty before a death sentence is lifted on this basis,[88] and even then there are no guarantees.

Looking Forward, Looking Back

As I first described in Chapter 2, the existing literature provides some sense of why capital clemency has declined across the world over time, both from an absolute point of view and also as a ratio compared with executions.[89] Nevertheless, within the ASEAN region and elsewhere in the retentionist world, my assumption is that, so long as the formal clemency power survives on paper, capital clemency *practice* will also survive. In other words, it is too early to forecast the total demise of executive clemency.[90] No legal system is entirely free of error, no government is entirely devoid of compassion for rehabilitated inmates on death row, and few leaders would wish to do away entirely with the inherent flexibility and political benefits provided by occasional grants of commutation or pardon.

If the immediate past is any indication of future practice,[91] then capital clemency will continue to be exercised at different levels of frequency within the four Southeast Asian jurisdictions under study, albeit with an overall downward trajectory. In Thailand, unless and until the incumbent military government moves decisively to abolish capital punishment, under the recently crowned King Maha Vajiralongkorn individual and collective royal pardons will continue to diminish and periodically empty Thailand's death row in displays of royal benevolence. Non-western prisoners whose offence categories are excluded from certain collective royal pardons remain at some risk of execution.[92] In Singapore, the landmark 2012 legislative changes enabling limited judicial discretion for capital murder and drug-trafficking offences will likely make clemency even rarer than it already is, as judicial officers and

[88] See note 47 and associated text.
[89] Strange (1996) 14–15; Novak (2015) 2, 5, 166; Sebba (1977a) 234.
[90] Sebba (1977a) 234–6.
[91] However, see notes 49–51 and associated text.
[92] See Agerholm (2018) on Thailand's recent resumption of executions.

prosecutors use their new discretionary powers to divert select cases away from death.

In Malaysia, a death row numbering more than 1,000 prisoners (including more than 400 foreign nationals) as of May 2016[93] will keep the State and Federal Pardons Boards busy as the Malaysian government considers how to balance its diplomatic and law enforcement interests. If, as has been mooted since 2011,[94] the mandatory death penalty is abolished for all crimes or for particular crimes, it is possible that hundreds of prisoners will be retrospectively 're-sentenced' to lesser punishments, following the precedent established in neighbouring Singapore.[95] As with Singapore, clemency's overall utility will likely decline in a system allowing judges sentencing discretion for the most serious crimes.

Finally, in Indonesia, if the proposed draft Criminal Code passes through the national legislature without significant amendments, the sentences of capital prisoners may be commuted to life imprisonment upon good behaviour during the first ten years spent on death row.[96] This procedure, resembling China's 'suspended death sentence',[97] may result in clemency for redemptive purposes becoming ever rarer, as rehabilitation and remorse are rewarded under the new statutory scheme, rather than by presidential prerogative shortly after the prisoner has exhausted all judicial appeals.[98] President Widodo's established preference for commuting

[93] 'Kasthuri: Cabinet Shifting Goal Post on Death Penalty' (2016). At the time of writing, the most recent report from June 2018 suggested that 1,267 persons remain under sentence of death, with 442 of these having exhausted judicial appeals (Bedi (2018)).

[94] Hood (2013) 3.

[95] The alternative would be a mass commutation of death sentences through executive clemency (Hector (2017)), or perhaps any new legislation only to apply prospectively, as with the November 2017 legislation that abolished the mandatory death penalty for drug trafficking in limited circumstances ('Malaysia Scraps Mandatory Death Sentence for Drugs' (2017); Dangerous Drugs (Amendment) Act 2017 (Malaysia)).

[96] Draft Criminal Code 2013 (Indonesia), art 91(2); Draft Criminal Code 2018 (Indonesia), art 111(3). See Tilemann (2016) and Pascoe (2019a) for further analysis.

[97] Criminal Law 1997 (China), art 48.

[98] Draft Criminal Code 2013 (Indonesia), art 91(2); Draft Criminal Code 2018 (Indonesia), art 111(3). Articles 92 (2013 draft) and 112 (2018 draft) of the same legislation also appear to provide the president an opportunity to reconsider a capital clemency rejection if the prisoner concerned is not executed in the course of the next ten years, for whatever reason.

only the death sentences of murder convicts and denying all petitions from condemned drug traffickers will (at least partially) make way for a fairer, less politicized balance between law enforcement and incentivized rehabilitation.

In the Introduction to this book, I observed that care should be taken before attempting to extrapolate the findings from the present study to other parts of the retentionist world. Chapter 7's three comparative trends from Southeast Asia have the potential to inform a 'global' theory of capital clemency incidence, and in time, quantitative testing and more widespread qualitative research may—or may not—achieve this result. However, what the present study has already accomplished is to shed light on a previously understudied phenomenon (clemency), in an understudied world region (Southeast Asia) within the comparative criminal justice field. In the broader context of capital punishment research, the data contained within this study go a small way towards rectifying the dearth of academic studies on the operational similarities and differences of death penalty practice within retentionist regions, as opposed to global studies contrasting the characteristics of retentionist and abolitionist states.[99] Moreover, the information contained within each case study from Chapter 3 to Chapter 6, the comparative findings in Chapter 7, and the present Conclusion have the potential to assist defence lawyers, civil society, and policymakers in their quest to remove from individuals or groups of defendants the threat of execution.

At first glance, clemency represents an entirely arbitrary, unprincipled, and irregular exercise of executive power, yet the prior academic literature, combined with empirical data from retentionist Southeast Asia, suggests that commutations and pardons are nonetheless granted pursuant to recurring patterns and justificatory paradigms. However, uncovering capital clemency grants in Southeast Asia and the likely reasons for them remains a work in progress given clemency's inherent opacity, especially within partially closed criminal justice systems. The more information that is revealed about the way the power to commute or pardon is exercised, the more clarity scholars and practitioners will have over the practice of capital punishment in general, given clemency's status as the final source of hope for a condemned prisoner: the last procedural obstacle separating life and death.

[99] See Chapter 2.

Appendix
Thailand Death Penalty Statistics 1991–2016

Year	Death Sentences	Death Row Prisoners (Exhaused Judicial Appeals)	Individual Royal Pardon (Full Release)	Collective Royal Pardon	Executions[i]
1991	7[ii]		2+[iii]	0[iv]	0
1992	2+[v]	108[vi]	1+[vii]	50[viii]	0
1993	8+[ix]	285(70)[x]		0[xi]	0
1994	5+[xii]	100+[xiii]	10+[xiv]	0[xv]	0
1995	4+	100[xvi] to 270+[xvii]		0[xviii]	0
1996	10,[xix] 97[xx]	c.100[xxi] to 197[xxii]		75,[xxiii] 120+,[xxiv] 127[xxv]	1
1997	37,[xxvi] 103[xxvii]	c.100[xxviii] to c.105[xxix]			2
1998	13,[xxx] 107[xxxi]	52+[xxxii] to 158[xxxiii]	50 (1994–8)[xxxiv]		2
1999	109[xxxv]	73[xxxvi] to 148;[xxxvii] (16)[xxxviii] to (53)[xxxix]		30+[xl]	16
2000	205[xli]	130[xlii]		0[xliii]	1
2001	303[xliv]	212[xlv] to 371,[xlvi] (19)[xlvii] to (100)[xlviii]	22(10)[xlix]	0[l]	11

Year	Death Sentences	Death Row Prisoners (Exhaused Judicial Appeals)	Individual Royal Pardon (Full Release)	Collective Royal Pardon	Executions[i]
2002	447[li]	318[lii] to 690,[liii] (21)[liv] to (55)[lv]	42(10)[lvi]	0[lvii]	11
2003	310[lviii]	c.950[lix] to c.1000,[lx] (31)[lxi] to (68)[lxii]	65(2),[lxiii] 97 (2001–3)[lxiv]		4
2004	270[lxv]	874(68)[lxvi] to 971[lxvii]	78(2)[lxviii]	+[lxix]	0
2005	311[lxx]	955(95)[lxxi] to c.1000(65)[lxxii]	98(0)[lxxiii]		0
2006	304[lxxiv]	848(91)[lxxv] to 1000+[lxxvi](124) [lxxvii]		+[lxxviii]	0
2007	6+,[lxxix] 7+[lxxx]	c.900[lxxxi] to 1000+[lxxxii]	+[lxxxiii]	85[lxxxiv]	0[lxxxv]
2008	57[lxxxvi]	c.850[lxxxvii] to 1000+[lxxxviii]			0[lxxxix]
2009	7+[xc]	743[xci] to 857,[xcii] (32)[xciii] to (127)[xciv]	0[xcv]		2[xcvi]
2010	87,[xcvii] 392[xcviii]	708(65)[xcix] to 832(127)[c]	0[ci]		0[cii]
2011	10,[ciii] 40[civ]	610(81)[cv] to 759(87),[cvi] (16)[cvii]	0[cviii]	83+[cix]	0[cx]
2012	189[cxi]	622[cxii] to 728,[cxiii] (21)[cxiv] to (88)[cxv]	0[cxvi]	57,[cxvii] 58[cxviii]	0[cxix]
2013	294[cxx]	678[cxxi] to 706[cxxii], (48)[cxxiii] to (112)[cxxiv]			0[cxxv]
2014	55+[cxxvi]	609(238)[cxxvii] to 687+[cxxviii]			0[cxxix]
2015	7+[cxxx]	413[cxxxi] to 649,[cxxxii] (253)[cxxxiii]		+[cxxxiv]	0[cxxxv]
2016	216[cxxxvi]	427[cxxxvii] to 454[cxxxviii]		213+[cxxxix]	0[cxl]

i Johnson and Zimring (2009) 403 (1991–2006 execution data).
ii Amnesty International Annual Report (1992) 251–2.
iii Amnesty International Annual Report (1992) 251–2.
iv Boriboonthana (1999) 358.
v Amnesty International Annual Report (1993) 280.
vi Amnesty International Annual Report (1993) 280.
vii Amnesty International Annual Report (1993) 280.
viii Amnesty International Annual Report (1993) 280.
ix Amnesty International Annual Report (1994) 286.
x Amnesty International Annual Report (1994) 286.
xi Boriboonthana (1999) 358.
xii Amnesty International Annual Report (1995) 282–3.
xiii Amnesty International Annual Report (1995) 282–3.
xiv Amnesty International Annual Report (1995) 282–3.
xv Boriboonthana (1999) 358.
xvi Amnesty International Annual Report (1996) 295.
xvii Amnesty International AI Index ASA 39/04/95, 1.
xviii Boriboonthana (1999) 358.
xix Amnesty International Annual Report (1997) 307–8.
xx Johnson and Zimring (2009) 402.
xxi Amnesty International Annual Report (1997) 307–8.
xxii 'Murderer First Convict to Be Executed in Eight Years' (1996).
xxiii UN Economic and Social Council (2000) 24.
xxiv Amnesty International AI Index ASA 39/002/1997, 5; Amnesty International Annual Report (1997) 307–8.
xxv Brooke (1996).
xxvi Amnesty International, 'Amnesty International Report 1998—Thailand' (1998).
xxvii Johnson and Zimring (2009) 402.
xxviii Amnesty International AI Index ASA 03/01/97, 20.
xxix Amnesty International AI Index ASA 39/002/1997, 5.
xxx Amnesty International Annual Report (1999) 328.
xxxi Johnson and Zimring (2009) 402.
xxxii Amnesty International Annual Report (1999) 328.
xxxiii Amnesty International AI Index ASA 39/01/98, 1.
xxxiv Hood and Hoyle (2008) 261.
xxxv Johnson and Zimring (2009) 402.
xxxvi Hands Off Cain, 'Thailand' (1999).
xxxvii Traisophon (1998).
xxxviii Amnesty International AI Index ASA 39/07/99, 1.
xxxix Amnesty International AI Index ASA 39/01/99, 7.
xl Amnesty International Annual Report (2000) 233.
xli Johnson and Zimring (2009) 402.
xlii 'Executions, Prison Overcrowding Mars Thai Rights Record: Amnesty' (2001).
xliii Barrow (2017).
xliv Johnson and Zimring (2009) 402.
xlv Amnesty International AI Index ASA 39/005/2001, 2.
xlvi Hands Off Cain, 'Thailand' (2002).
xlvii Amnesty International AI Index ASA 39/001/2001, 1.
xlviii Kwhankhom (2001).
xlix Union for Civil Liberty (2011) 17.
l Barrow (2017).
li Johnson and Zimring (2009) 401.
lii Hands Off Cain, 'Thailand' (2002).
liii Hands Off Cain, 'Thailand' (2002).
liv 'Drug Busts Put Record Number of Thai Inmates on Death Row' (2002).
lv Union for Civil Liberty (2011) 18.
lvi Union for Civil Liberty (2011) 17.
lvii Barrow (2017).
lviii Johnson and Zimring (2009) 402.
lix Bonner (2003).
lx Hands Off Cain, 'Thailand' (2005).
lxi Thongpao (2007).
lxii Hands Off Cain, 'Thailand' (2003).
lxiii Union for Civil Liberty (2011) 17.
lxiv Johnson and Zimring (2009) 404 n10.
lxv Johnson and Zimring (2009) 402.

lxv Malakunas (2004).
lxvi International Federation for Human Rights (2005) 27.
lxviii Union for Civil Liberty (2011) 17.
lxix International Federation for Human Rights (2005) 27.
lxx Johnson and Zimring (2009) 402.
lxxi Levett (2005).
lxxii Hands Off Cain, 'Thailand' (2005).
lxxiii Union for Civil Liberty (2011) 17.
lxxiv Johnson and Zimring (2009) 402.
lxxv 'Latest Statistics on Death Penalty in Thailand' (2006).
lxxvi Hands Off Cain, 'Thailand' (2006).
lxxvii Hands Off Cain, 'Thailand' (2008).
lxxviii Hands Off Cain, 'Thailand' (2006).
lxxix Amnesty International AI Index ACT 50/001/2008, 7.
lxxx Hands Off Cain, 'Thailand' (2007).
lxxxi Thongpao (2007).
lxxxii Hands Off Cain, 'Thailand' (2007).
lxxxiii Hands Off Cain, 'Thailand' (2007): 'chosen prisoners'. Unclear whether the data suggests individual or collective royal pardons.
lxxxiv Thamnukasetchai (2007).
lxxxv Johnson and Zimring (2009) 35.
lxxxvi Union for Civil Liberty (2011) 14.
lxxxvii Union for Civil Liberty (2011) 18.
lxxxviii Hands Off Cain, 'Thailand' (2008).
lxxxix Johnson and Zimring (2009) 405.
xc Hands Off Cain, 'Thailand' (2009).
xci 'When the Killing Hour Arrives' (2009).
xcii Statement by Thai human rights activist.
xciii Kowitwanij (2009).
xciv Thamnukasetchai (2009).
xcv Breen (2013).
xcvi Thamnukasetchai (2009).
xcvii Finch and Tangprasit (2012).
xcviii Junlakan et al (2013) 314.
xcix Amnesty International AI Index ACT 50/001/2011, 11, 23.
c Hands Off Cain, 'Thailand' (2010).
ci Breen (2013).
cii Cornell Center on the Death Penalty Worldwide, 'Thailand' (2017).
ciii Hands Off Cain, 'Thailand' (2011).
civ Amnesty International AI Index ACT 50/001/2012, 7.
cv Amnesty International AI Index ACT 50/001/2012, 27.
cvi 'Death Penalty in Thailand' (2011).
cvii Chanprasert (2012) 2.
cviii Breen (2013).
cix Hands Off Cain, 'Thailand' (2015).
cx Cornell Center on the Death Penalty Worldwide, 'Thailand' (2017).
cxi 'Newly Published Statistics on Death Penalty Sentencing in Thailand' (2015).
cxii 'Death Row for Women in Thailand Is Empty' (2012).
cxiii 'Update, Thailand Death Penalty Statistics' (2012).
cxiv 'Current Statistics of Prisoners Condemned to Death' (2012).
cxv Chanprasert (2012) 2.
cxvi Breen (2013).
cxvii 'Current Statistics of Prisoners Condemned to Death' (2012).
cxviii 'Death Penalty—Facts from Figures' (2013).
cxix Cornell Center on the Death Penalty Worldwide, 'Thailand' (2017).
cxx UN Office of the High Commissioner for Human Rights (2014) 34.
cxxi Amnesty International AI Index ACT 50/001/2014, 27.
cxxii 'Thailand Does Not Execute Women' (2013).
cxxiii 'Death Penalty Thailand Statistics' (2013).
cxxiv 'Death Penalty in Thailand' (2013).
cxxv Cornell Center on the Death Penalty Worldwide, 'Thailand' (2017).
cxxvi Amnesty International AI Index ACT 50/001/2015, 39. June to December figures.
cxxvii 'Statistics of Prisoners Condemned to Death, 31st October 2014' (2014).
cxxviii Hands Off Cain, 'Thailand' (2014).
cxxix Cornell Center on the Death Penalty Worldwide, 'Thailand' (2017).
cxxx Amnesty International AI Index ACT 50/3487/2016, 7.

cxxxi Amnesty International AI Index ACT 50/3487/2016, 41.

cxxxii Cornell Center on the Death Penalty Worldwide, 'Thailand' (2017).

cxxxiii 'Death Penalty Statistics' (2015).

cxxxiv King Bhumibol Adulyadej, 'Pardon Decree' (Thailand Government Gazette, 30 March 2015).

cxxxv Cornell Center on the Death Penalty Worldwide, 'Thailand' (2017).

cxxxvi Amnesty International AI Index ACT 50/5740/2017, 41.

cxxxvii Sander (2018) 35.

cxxxviii 'Statistics of Those Condemned to Death in Thailand: September 2016' (2016).

cxxxix Constant (2016); Amnesty International AI Index ACT 50/5740/2017, 26.

cxl Cornell Center on the Death Penalty Worldwide, 'Thailand' (2017).

Appendix
Singapore Death Penalty Statistics 1991–2016

Year	Death Sentences	Death Row Prisoners (Exhausted Judicial Appeals)	Clemency (Pardons)[i]	Executions[ii]
1991	3+[iii]		0	6
1992	7+[iv]		2(0)	21
1993	26+[v]		0	7
1994	10+[vi]	93[vii]	0	76
1995	34+[viii]		0	73
1996	19+[ix]		0	50
1997	8+[x]		0	15
1998	5+[xi]		1(0)	28
1999	3+[xii]		0	43
2000	5[xiii]		0	21
2001	7[xiv]		0	27
2002	3[xv]		0	28

Year	Death Sentences	Death Row Prisoners (Exhausted Judicial Appeals)	Clemency (Pardons)[i]	Executions[ii]
2003	4[xvi]		0	19
2004	5[xvii]		0	8
2005	4[xviii]	8+[xix]	0	8
2006	7[xx]		0	8
2007	3[xxi]		0	3
2008	5,[xxii] 6[xxiii]	(5+)[xxiv]	0	6
2009	6+[xxv]		0	5
2010	9+[xxvi]	9+[xxvii]	0	0
2011	4[xxviii]		0	4
2012	3[xxix]	32[xxx] to 35[xxxi]	0	0
2013	1+[xxxii]	26+[xxxiii] to 34+[xxxiv]	0	0
2014	3[xxxv]	22[xxxvi] to 23[xxxvii]	0	2
2015	5+[xxxviii]	23+[xxxix]	0	4[xl]
2016	7+[xli]	25+[xlii] to 38+[xliii]	0	4[xliv]

[i] Chan (2016) 200 (clemency data 1991–2016).
[ii] Chan (2016) 183 (execution data 1991–2014).
[iii] Amnesty International Annual Report (1992) 231.
[iv] Amnesty International Annual Report (1993) 257.
[v] Amnesty International Annual Report (1994) 261.
[vi] Amnesty International Annual Report (1995) 260.
[vii] 'Show Mercy Mr Ong' (1994)
[viii] Amnesty International AI Index ASA 03/01/97, 17.
[ix] Amnesty International Annual Report (1996) 281.
[x] Amnesty International Annual Report (1998) 301.
[xi] Amnesty International Annual Report (1999) 300.
[xii] Amnesty International Annual Report (2000) 212.
[xiii] Hands Off Cain, 'Singapore' (2000).
[xiv] Hands Off Cain, 'Singapore' (2001).
[xv] Hands Off Cain, 'Singapore' (2002).
[xvi] Hands Off Cain, 'Singapore' (2003).
[xvii] Hands Off Cain, 'Singapore' (2004).
[xviii] Hands Off Cain, 'Singapore' (2005).
[xix] Hands Off Cain, 'Singapore' (2009).
[xx] Hands Off Cain, 'Singapore' (2006).
[xxi] Hands Off Cain, 'Singapore' (2007).
[xxii] Amnesty International AI Index ACT 50/003/2009, 13.
[xxiii] Hands Off Cain, 'Singapore' (2008).
[xxiv] Amnesty International Annual Report (2009) 290.
[xxv] Amnesty International Annual Report (2010) 286.
[xxvi] Amnesty International AI Index ASA 36/002/2010, 5.
[xxvii] Cornell Center on the Death Penalty Worldwide, 'Singapore' (2017).
[xxviii] Hands Off Cain, 'Singapore' (2011).
[xxix] Hands Off Cain, 'Singapore' (2012).
[xxx] 'Death and the City: The Death Penalty in Singapore' (2013).
[xxxi] Au (2012).
[xxxii] Amnesty International AI Index ACT 50/001/2014, 8, 16, 26.
[xxxiii] Amnesty International (7/2014).
[xxxiv] Hands Off Cain, 'Singapore' (2013).
[xxxv] Hands Off Cain, 'Singapore' (2014).
[xxxvi] UN Office of the High Commissioner for Human Rights (2014) 33.
[xxxvii] Hands Off Cain, 'Singapore' (2014).
[xxxviii] Amnesty International AI Index ACT 50/3487/2016, 7.
[xxxix] Amnesty International AI Index ACT 50/3487/2016, 40.
[xl] Singapore Prison Service (2017) 10.
[xli] Amnesty International AI Index ACT 50/5740/2017, 5.
[xlii] International Federation for Human Rights (2016) 12.
[xliii] Amnesty International AI Index ACT 50/5740/2017, 17.
[xliv] Singapore Prison Service (2017) 10.

Appendix
Malaysia Death Penalty Statistics 1991–2016

Year	Death Sentences	Death Row Prisoners (Exhausted Judicial Appeals)	Clemency (Pardons)	Executions
1991	67+[i]			8[ii]
1992	28+[iii]			39+[iv]
1993	12+[v]			29+[vi]
1994	8+[vii]			10+[viii]
1995	11+[ix]			5+[x]
1996	6+,[xi] 43+ (1993–6)[xii]	245[xiii]		3+[xiv]
1997	7+[xv]	(13+)[xvi]		0,[xvii] 2+[xviii]
1998	6+[xix]			0[xx]
1999	1+[xxi]			0[xxii]
2000	18+[xxiii]	212[xxiv]		2,[xxv] 0[xxvi]
2001	11+[xxvii]	159[xxviii]		5[xxix]
2002	16+[xxx]			4[xxxi]

Year	Death Sentences	Death Row Prisoners (Exhausted Judicial Appeals)	Clemency (Pardons)	Executions
2003	19+[xxxii]	121[xxxiii] to 159[xxxiv]		0[xxxv]
2004	11+[xxxvi]			0[xxxvii]
2005	15+[xxxviii]			0[xxxix]
2006	19+[xl]	159[xli]		4[xlii]
2007	12,[xliii] 23+[xliv]	c.300[xlv]		0,[xlvi] 1[xlvii]
2008	34+[xlviii]	c.300[xlix]	9(0)[l] (2003–8)	1+[li]
2009	69+[lii]		14(2)[liii] (2000–9)	2[liv]
2010	107,[lv] 114+[lvi]	300[lvii]		1[lviii]
2011	107,[lix] 108+[lx]	696[lxi] to 860(150)[lxii]		1+[lxiii]
2012	82[lxiv]	860[lxv] to 930+[lxvi], (205)[lxvii]	41(2)+ (2001–12)[lxviii]	0[lxix]
2013	76+[lxx]	930+[lxxi] to 992[lxxii]		3+[lxxiii]
2014	38+[lxxiv]	975,[lxxv] (255) [lxxvi]		6[lxxvii]
2015	39+[lxxviii]	975+[lxxix] to 1043[lxxx]	127 (1998–2015)[lxxxi]	1,[lxxxii] 33 (1998–2015)[lxxxiii]
2016	36+,[lxxxiv] 829 (2010–16)[lxxxv]	1041[lxxxvi] to 1043+,[lxxxvii] (393)[lxxxviii]	95 (2010-2016)[lxxxix]	9+[xc]

[i] Amnesty International Annual Report (1992) 179.
[ii] Amnesty International Annual Report (1992) 179.
[iii] Amnesty International Annual Report (1993) 200.
[iv] Amnesty International AI Index ASA 03/01/97, 11.
[v] Amnesty International Annual Report (1994) 204.
[vi] Amnesty International AI Index ASA 03/01/97, 12.
[vii] Amnesty International Annual Report (1995) 204.
[viii] Amnesty International AI Index ASA 03/01/97, 12.

ix Amnesty International Annual Report (1996) 217.
x Amnesty International AI Index ASA 03/01/97, 12.
xi Amnesty International Annual Report (1997) 224.
xii Amnesty International AI Index ASA 03/01/97, 11.
xiii Amnesty International AI Index ASA 03/01/97, 11.
xiv Amnesty International AI Index ASA 03/01/97, 11.
xv Amnesty International Annual Report (1998) 243.
xvi Amnesty International AI Index ASA 28/12/97, 1.
xvii Johnson and Zimring (2009) 18.
xviii Amnesty International Annual Report (1998) 243.
xix Amnesty International Annual Report (1999) 242.
xx Johnson and Zimring (2009) 18.
xxi Amnesty International Annual Report (2000) 165.
xxii Johnson and Zimring (2009) 18.
xxiii Hands Off Cain, 'Malaysia' (2000).
xxiv Hands Off Cain, 'Malaysia' (2000).
xxv Hands Off Cain, 'Malaysia' (2000).
xxvi Johnson and Zimring (2009) 18.
xxvii Hands Off Cain, 'Malaysia' (2001).
xxviii '159 Left Hanging on Death Row' (2001).
xxix Hands Off Cain, 'Malaysia' (2001).
xxx Hands Off Cain, 'Malaysia' (2002).
xxxi Hands Off Cain, 'Malaysia' (2002).
xxxii Hands Off Cain, 'Malaysia' (2003).
xxxiii Hands Off Cain, 'Malaysia' (2005).
xxxiv 'The Executioners' (2005).
xxxv Johnson and Zimring (2009) 18.
xxxvi Hands Off Cain, 'Malaysia' (2004).
xxxvii Johnson and Zimring (2009) 18.
xxxviii Hands Off Cain, 'Malaysia' (2005).
xxxix Johnson and Zimring (2009) 18.
xl Hands Off Cain, 'Malaysia' (2006).
xli Johnson and Zimring (2009) 305.
xlii Hands Off Cain, 'Malaysia' (2006).
xliii Amnesty International AI Index ACT 50/001/2008, 7.
xliv Hands Off Cain, 'Malaysia' (2007).
xlv Johnson and Zimring (2009) 19.
xlvi Johnson and Zimring (2009) 35.
xlvii UN Economic and Social Council (2009) 21.
xlviii Hands Off Cain, 'Malaysia' (2008).
xlix Kuppusamy (2008).
l Hands Off Cain, 'Malaysia' (2008). It is unclear whether these figures only relate to the Federal Pardons Board, or all of Malaysia's Pardons Boards.
li UN Economic and Social Council (2009) 21.
lii Hands Off Cain, 'Malaysia' (2009).
liii '14 Death-Row Prisoners Get Pardon, Says Hishamuddin' (2010).
liv Hood (2013) 2.
lv Hands Off Cain, 'Malaysia' (2010).
lvi Amnesty International AI Index ACT 50/001/2011, 5.
lvii Hands Off Cain, 'Malaysia' (2010).
lviii Hood (2013) 2.
lix Hands Off Cain, 'Malaysia' (2011).
lx Amnesty International AI Index ACT 50/001/2012, 7.
lxi Amnesty International AI Index ACT 50/001/2012, 23.
lxii Hands Off Cain, 'Malaysia' (2015).
lxiii Cornell Center on the Death Penalty Worldwide, 'Malaysia' (2017).
lxiv Hands Off Cain, 'Malaysia' (2012).
lxv Leechaianan and Longmire (2013) 133.
lxvi Hands Off Cain, 'Malaysia' (2012).
lxvii Hands Off Cain, 'Malaysia' (2012).
lxviii Hands Off Cain, 'Malaysia' (2012). Figures to August 2012.
lxix Amnesty International AI Index ACT 50/001/2015, 34.
lxx Amnesty International AI Index ACT 50/001/2014, 51.
lxxi Hands Off Cain, 'Malaysia' (2013).
lxxii Amnesty International AI Index ACT 50/001/2014, 24.
lxxiii Mayberry (2015).
lxxiv Amnesty International AI Index ACT 50/001/2015, 23.
lxxv Amnesty International AI Index ACT 50/001/2015, 33.

[lxxvi] Hands Off Cain, 'Malaysia' (2014).
[lxxvii] Surach (2017).
[lxxviii] Amnesty International AI Index ACT 50/3487/2016, 7.
[lxxix] Hands Off Cain, 'Malaysia' (2015).
[lxxx] Gallahue and Lines (2015) 15.
[lxxxi] Palansamy (2015).
[lxxxii] Surach (2017).
[lxxxiii] Palansamy (2015). Figures to October.
[lxxxiv] Amnesty International AI Index ACT 50/5740/2017, 17.
[lxxxv] Surach (2017).
[lxxxvi] '1041 Criminals Appealing Death Sentence' (2016).
[lxxxvii] Kulasegaran (2016).
[lxxxviii] Surach (2017).
[lxxxix] New (2016).
[xc] Amnesty International AI Index ACT 50/5740/2017, 17. Figures to September.

Appendix
Indonesia Death Penalty Statistics 1991–2016

Year	Death Sentences	Death Row Prisoners (Exhausted Judicial Appeals)	Clemency (Pardons)[i]	Executions
1991	0,[ii] 4[iii]	33+(8)[iv]	0	1[v]
1992	2,[vi] 3+[vii]	34+[viii]	0	1[ix]
1993	1,[x] 2[xi]	32+[xii]	0	0[xiii]
1994	3[xiv]	35[xv]	0	0[xvi]
1995	4[xvii]	26+[xviii]	0	3[xix]
1996	2[xx]	26+[xxi]	0	0[xxii]
1997	6,[xxiii] 7[xxiv]	26+[xxv] to 33[xxvi]	0	0[xxvii]
1998	5[xxviii]	30+[xxix]	1(0)[xxx]	1[xxxi]
1999	2[xxxii]	16[xxxiii] to 27+(16)[xxxiv]	(4+),[xxxv] (9+),[xxxvi] (10+)[xxxvii]	0[xxxviii]
2000	10[xxxix]	16[xl] to 34[xli]	0	0[xlii]
2001	19[xliii]	16(9+)[xliv]	0	3[xlv]
2002	11[xlvi]	16[xlvii]	0	0[xlviii]

Year	Death Sentences	Death Row Prisoners (Exhausted Judicial Appeals)	Clemency (Pardons)[i]	Executions
2003	13[xlix]	55[l] to 57[li]	0, 1+(0)[lii]	0[liii]
2004	12,[liv] 14+[lv]	c.30[lvi] to 65,[lvii] (33+)[lviii]	0	3[lix]
2005	10,[lx] 14+[lxi]	54+[lxii] to 82[lxiii]	0	2[lxiv]
2006	21[lxv]	60+[lxvi] to 134[lxvii]	0	3[lxviii]
2007	14,[lxix] 15+[lxx]	90+[lxxi] to 134[lxxii]	0	1[lxxiii]
2008	13,[lxxiv] 15[lxxv]	92[lxxvi] to 116+,[lxxvii] (7)[lxxviii] to (57)[lxxix]	0	10[lxxx]
2009	1[lxxxi]	109[lxxxii] to c.132[lxxxiii], (31)[lxxxiv]	0	0[lxxxv]
2010	9[lxxxvi]	102 to 120[lxxxvii]	0	0[lxxxviii]
2011	7[lxxxix]	87[xc] to 118[xci]		0[xcii]
2012	15[xciii]	87+[xciv] to 133,[xcv] (23)[xcvi]	4+(0) (2011–12)[xcvii]	0[xcviii]
2013	25[xcix]	130[c] to 149+[ci]	2+(0)[cii]	5[ciii]
2014	10[civ]	130+[cv] to 140[cvi]		0[cvii]
2015	48,[cviii] 76[cix]	120[cx] to 191+[cxi], (60)[cxii]		14[cxiii]
2016	31,[cxiv] 60+[cxv]	115[cxvi] to 215+,[cxvii] (35+)[cxviii] to (64)[cxix]	7+(0) (2014–16)[cxx]	4[cxxi]

[i] McRae (2012) 4, 19, unless otherwise noted.
[ii] Imparsial (2010) 132–3.
[iii] Amnesty International Annual Report (1992) 141.
[iv] Amnesty International Annual Report (1992) 141.
[v] Imparsial (2004) 18–21; Amnesty International Annual Report (1992) 141.
[vi] Imparsial (2010) 132–3.
[vii] Amnesty International AI Index ASA 21/03/93, 24.
[viii] Amnesty International AI Index ASA 21/03/93, 24.
[ix] KontraS (2010).
[x] Imparsial (2010) 132–3.
[xi] Amnesty International Annual Report (1994) 160.
[xii] Amnesty International Annual Report (1994) 160.

[xiii] KontraS (2010).
[xiv] Imparsial (2010) 132–3.
[xv] Amnesty International Annual Report (1995) 160.
[xvi] KontraS (2010).
[xvii] Imparsial (2010) 132–3.
[xviii] Amnesty International Annual Report (1996) 175.
[xix] KontraS (2010).
[xx] Imparsial (2010) 132–3.
[xxi] Amnesty International Annual Report (1997) 181.
[xxii] KontraS (2010).
[xxiii] Amnesty International Annual Report (1998) 196, 199.
[xxiv] Imparsial (2010) 132–3.
[xxv] Amnesty International AI Index ASA 03/01/97, 8.
[xxvi] Amnesty International Annual Report (1998) 196, 199.
[xxvii] KontraS (2010).
[xxviii] Mulya Lubis and Lay (2009) 439.
[xxix] Amnesty International Annual Report (1999) 195.
[xxx] Imparsial (2010) 120.
[xxxi] KontraS (2010).
[xxxii] Reza (6/2016).
[xxxiii] Hands Off Cain, 'Indonesia' (1999).
[xxxiv] Amnesty International Annual Report (2000) 131.
[xxxv] 'President Grants Clemency to 10 More Political Prisoners' (1999); TAPOL (1999) 17; Amnesty International AI Index ASA 21/58/98, 11.
[xxxvi] England (1999).
[xxxvii] International Commission of Jurists (1999) 97.
[xxxviii] KontraS (2010).
[xxxix] Imparsial (2004) 18–21.
[xl] Hands Off Cain, 'Indonesia' (2000).
[xli] Hood (2002) 48.
[xlii] KontraS (2010).
[xliii] Reza (6/2016).
[xliv] Hands Off Cain, 'Indonesia' (2001).
[xlv] KontraS (2010).
[xlvi] Reza (6/2016).
[xlvii] Hands Off Cain, 'Indonesia' (2002).
[xlviii] KontraS (2010).
[xlix] Reza (6/2016).
[l] Amnesty International AI Index ASA 21/040/2004, 1.
[li] Hands Off Cain, 'Indonesia' (2003).
[lii] Hands Off Cain, 'Indonesia' (2003); 'Indonesia's Megawati Grants Muslim Holy Day Amnesties' (2003).
[liii] KontraS (2010).
[liv] Reza (6/2016).
[lv] Hands Off Cain, 'Indonesia' (2004).
[lvi] Khalik (2004).
[lvii] Hands Off Cain, 'Indonesia' (2005).
[lviii] Imparsial (2004) 2, 16, 22.
[lix] KontraS (2010).
[lx] Reza (6/2016).
[lxi] Hands Off Cain, 'Indonesia' (2005).
[lxii] Unmacht (2005).
[lxiii] Amnesty International Annual Report (2006) 140.
[lxiv] Kontras (2010).
[lxv] Reza (6/2016).
[lxvi] Hands Off Cain, 'Indonesia' (2009).
[lxvii] 'Indonesian Court to Rule on Legality of Death Penalty for Drugs' (2007).
[lxviii] KontraS (2010).
[lxix] Reza (6/2016).
[lxx] Hands Off Cain, 'Indonesia' (2007).
[lxxi] Soedarjo (2007).
[lxxii] National Human Rights Commission of Indonesia (2007) 28.
[lxxiii] KontraS (2010).
[lxxiv] Reza (6/2016).
[lxxv] Imparsial (2010) 166.
[lxxvi] Hands Off Cain, 'Indonesia' (2008).
[lxxvii] Amnesty International Annual Report (2009) 172.

lxxviii Johnson and Zimring (2009) 323 n28.
lxxix Amnesty International AI Index ASA 21/010/2008.
lxxx Reza (6/2016).
lxxxi Imparsial (2010) 166.
lxxxii Hands Off Cain, 'Indonesia' (2009).
lxxxiii KontraS (2010).
lxxxiv 'Time Running Out for 109 Death Row Inmates' (2009).
lxxxv KontraS (2010).
lxxxvi Reza (6/2016).
lxxxvii Amnesty International AI Index ACT 50/001/2011, 20.
lxxxviii Amnesty International AI Index ACT 50/001/2011, 20.
lxxxix Reza (6/2016).
xc Hands Off Cain, 'Indonesia' (2011).
xci UN Human Rights Committee (2012) 16.
xcii Amnesty International AI Index ACT 50/001/2012, 18.
xciii Reza (6/2016).
xciv Hands Off Cain, 'Indonesia' (2012).
xcv Cornell Center on the Death Penalty Worldwide, 'Indonesia' (2017).
xcvi 'Who Deserves Clemency' (2012).
xcvii McRae (2013).
xcviii Amnesty International AI Index ACT 50/001/2013, 20.
xcix Reza (6/2016).
c KontraS (2013).
ci Amnesty International AI Index ACT 50/001/2014, 23.
cii Lingga (2015); 'Lolos Hukuman Mati, Cong Roib Abdikan Diri Menjadi Guru Ngaji' (2017).
ciii Amnesty International AI Index ACT 50/001/2014, 23.
civ Reza (6/2016).
cv Amnesty International AI Index ACT 50/001/2015, 31.
cvi Hands Off Cain, 'Indonesia' (2014).
cvii Amnesty International AI Index ACT 50/001/2015, 5.
cviii Reza (6/2016).
cix Sihombing (2016).
cx Linggasari (2016).
cxi Amnesty International AI Index ASA 21/2434/2015, 22.
cxii Lindsey and Nicholson (2016) 107.
cxiii Amnesty International AI Index ACT 50/3487/2016, 6.
cxiv Reza (6/2016).
cxv Amnesty International AI Index ACT 50/5740/2017, 5.
cxvi Eddyono et al (2016) 33.
cxvii Amnesty International AI Index ACT 50/5740/2017, 17.
cxviii KontraS (2016).
cxix 'Kaji Ulang Terpidana Mati' (2016).
cxx Mulyana (2016); 'Jokowi Berikan Grasi Dua Terpidana Mati Asal Sumut' (2016).
cxxi Amnesty International AI Index ACT 50/5740/2017, 5.

References

'10,000 Inmates Released under Royal Pardon' *Pattaya Mail* (Pattaya, 16 August 2012) <http://www.pattayamail.com/thailandnews/10000-inmates-released-under-royal-pardon-15729> accessed 26 August 2017

'1041 Criminals Appealing Death Sentence' *Free Malaysia Today* (17 May 2016) <http://www.freemalaysiatoday.com/category/nation/2016/05/17/1041-criminals-appealing-death-sentence/> accessed 14 December 2017

'121 Convicts in "Death Row"' *Bernama Daily Malaysian News* (Kuala Lumpur, 11 November 2003)

'14 Death-Row Prisoners Get Pardon, Says Hishamuddin' *Bernama Daily Malaysian News* (Kuala Lumpur, 22 June 2010)

'159 Left Hanging on Death Row' *The Sun Daily* (Petaling Jaya, 14 June 2001)

'17 Persons Executed and Sentenced to Death during April and May' (1982) 6(2) Human Rights in Thailand Report

'31 Were Sentenced to Death' (1982) 6(4) Human Rights in Thailand Report 27

'366 Criminal Law Detentions in Five Years' *Today Online* (Singapore, 10 February 2009) <http://eresources.nlb.gov.sg/newspapers/Digitised/Article/today20090210-2.2.4.9> accessed 22 September 2018

'5 Pembunuh Kejam Ini Menanti Eksekusi Mati' *detik News* (Pekanbaru, 18 May 2013) <https://news.detik.com/berita/2249592/5-pembunuh-kejam-ini-menanti-eksekusi-mati/6> accessed 25 September 2017 [in Indonesian]

'55 Dead in Indonesia's War on Drugs with "Shoot-on-Sight" Policy' *The Straits Times* (Singapore, 14 August 2017) <http://www.straitstimes.com/asia/se-asia/55-dead-in-indonesias-war-on-drugs-with-shoot-on-sight-policy> accessed 15 January 2018

'A List of Death Row Inmates in Singapore Who Were Granted Clemency' *Associated Press Newswires* (New York, 2 December 2005)

'A Peculiar Purgatory' *New Straits Times* (Kuala Lumpur, 28 January 2008)

'A Royal Occasion' (*Worldhop.com Journal*, 5 December 1996) <http://www.worldhop.com/Journals/J5/ROYAL.HTM> accessed 11 December 2017

'Activities of CGRS' (1983) 7(1) Human Rights in Thailand Report

'AGO Waits for Supreme Court Decision on Pardon for Death Penalty Execution' (*Netral News*, 29 September 2017) <http://www.

en.netralnews.com/news/currentnews/read/12149/ago.waits.for.supreme.court.decision.on.pardon.for.death.penalty.execution> accessed 27 November 2017

'American Given Life for Trafficking in Heroin' *The Sunday Courier* (Brisbane, 17 October 1995)

'Amnesty for Drug Offenders Reflects King's Generosity' *Bangkok Post* (18 February 1996)

'Anwar Ibrahim Freed from Prison after Royal Pardon from Malaysian King' (*Channel News Asia*, 16 May 2018) <https://www.channelnewsasia.com/news/asia/anwar-ibrahim-freed-from-prison-royal-pardon-malaysia-10237840> accessed 20 September 2018

'Anwar Seen as Admitting Guilt in Sodomy with Pardon Petition—Political Analysts' *Bernama Daily Malaysian News* (Kuala Lumpur, 25 February 2015)

'ASEAN to Impose Death Penalty for Drug Crimes' *Inter Press Service* (Rome, 28 September 1992)

'Bali Nine Duo's Challenge to Deny Clemency Heard by Jakarta Court' (*News.com.au*, 7 April 2015) <http://www.news.com.au/national/bali-nine-duos-challenge-to-deny-clemency-heard-by-jakarta-court/news-story/bb6172561a8a5800acd44497fd48dd6b> accessed 11 December 2017

'Bali Nine: Indonesian President Rules Out Clemency for Inmates on Death Row' *The Guardian* (London, 9 December 2014) <http://www.theguardian.com/world/2014/dec/10/bali-nine-indonesian-president-rules-out-clemency> accessed 26 August 2017

'Bali Nine Prisoners on Death Row Recommended for Lesser Sentences' *The Guardian* (London, 17 August 2014) <https://www.theguardian.com/world/2014/aug/17/bali-nine-prisoners-on-death-row-recommended-for-lesser-sentences> accessed 25 September 2017

'Beneath Malaysia's High-Profile Murder Cases, What Lies beyond the Killers' Minds?' (*Malaysian Digest*, 28 May 2015) <http://malaysiandigest.com/opinion/555381-beneath-malaysia-s-high-profile-murder-cases-what-lies-beyond-the-killers-minds.html> accessed 17 September 2017

'Capital Punishment Called into Question' *The Nation* (Bangkok, 23 November 1998)

'Capital Sentence against Indon Worker in M'Sia Aborted' *Antara* (Jakarta, 6 January 2004)

'Captain the Only One to Admit to Drug Trafficking' *Sing Tao Daily* (26 March 2005) [in Cantonese]

'Chavalit Honours Anti-Drug Efforts' *The Nation* (Bangkok, 26 June 2001)

'Clemency Plea to Sheares by Man Sentenced to Die' *Straits Times* (Singapore, 6 January 1978)

'Coup Plotter to Be Freed After Years of Failed Efforts' *Kyodo News* (Tokyo, 29 March 1999)

'Current Statistics of Prisoners Condemned to Death' (*Death Penalty Thailand*, 29 October 2012) <http://deathpenaltythailand.blogspot.com/2012/10/current-statistics-of-prisoners.html> accessed 26 August 2017

'Dadah Man, 84, Loses Appeal' *New Straits Times* (Kuala Lumpur, 9 March 1994)

'Dapat Grasi, Ini Curhat Terpidana Mati Pembunuhan Sadis ke Jokowi' (*detik News*, 14 March 2015) <https://news.detik.com/berita/2858599/dapat-grasi-ini-curhat-terpidana-mati-pembunuhan-sadis-ke-jokowi> accessed 25 September 2017 [in Indonesian]

'Dead Wait' *The Times* (London, 4 July 2006)

'Death and the City: The Death Penalty in Singapore' (*Death Penalty News*,16 October 2013) <https://deathpenaltynews.blogspot.hk/2013/10/death-and-city-death-penalty-in.html> accessed 14 December 2017

'Death or Life: Decision on Penang Pair "This Weekend"' *The Advertiser* (Adelaide, 19 June 1986)

'Death Penalty—Facts from Figures' (*Death Penalty Thailand*,22 January 2013) <http://deathpenaltythailand.blogspot.hk/2013/01/death-penalty-facts-from-figures_22.html> accessed 14 December 2017

'Death Penalty in Thailand' (*Death Penalty Thailand*, 11 April 2011) <http://deathpenaltythailand.blogspot.hk/2011/04/current-death-penalty-statistics-for.html> accessed 14 December 2017

'Death Penalty in Thailand' (*Death Penalty Thailand*, 9 October 2013) <http://deathpenaltythailand.blogspot.hk/2013/10/death-penalty-in-thailand.html> accessed 14 December 2017

'Death Penalty Should Be Abolished' *Bangkok Post* (11 February 1996)

'Death Penalty Statistics' (*Death Penalty Thailand*, 30 January 2015) <http://deathpenaltythailand.blogspot.hk/2015/01/death-penalty-statistics_56.html> accessed 14 December 2017

'Death Penalty Thailand Statistics' (*Death Penalty Thailand*, 21 March 2013) <http://deathpenaltythailand.blogspot.hk/2013/03/death-penalty-thailand-statistics.html> accessed 14 December 2017

'Death Row for Women in Thailand Is Empty' (*Death Penalty Thailand*, 13 February 2012) <http://deathpenaltythailand.blogspot.hk/2012/02/death-row-for-women-in-thailand-is.html> accessed 27 November 2017

'Death Sentences' (1983) 7(1) Human Rights in Thailand Report

'Death Sentence for Canadian Father, Son' *Hamilton Spectator* (Ontario, 19 February 1993)

'Death Us Don't Part' *The Canberra Times* (15 November 2008)

'Drug Busts Put Record Number of Thai Inmates on Death Row' *ABC News* (Australia, 17 July 2002)

'Drug Courier Spared Death Now Challenges Caning Sentence' *The Straits Times* (Singapore, 28 April 2014) <http://www.straitstimes.com/singapore/courts-crime/drug-courier-spared-death-now-challenges-caning-sentence> accessed 29 November 2017

'Drug Trafficker Was Given Second Chance but She Blew It' *Straits Times* (Singapore, 22 November 2001)

'Drugs Hanging' *Daily Mail* (London, 19 June 1993)

'Dua Terpidana Mati Dapat Grasi dari Presiden Jokowi' (*Seruu*, 12 May 2016) <https://article.wn.com/view/2016/05/12/Dua_Terpidana_Mati_Dapat_Grasi_dari_Presiden_Jokowi/> accessed 30 November 2017 [in Indonesian]

'Eks Tapol PKI Minta Nyoblos' *Jawa Pos* (Jakarta, 30 March 1999) [in Indonesian]

'Everything You Need to Know about Malaysian Drug Courier Yong Vui Kong in 60 Seconds' (*Mothership*, 15 November 2013) <https://mothership.sg/2013/11/malaysian-drug-courier-yong-vui-kong-60-seconds/> accessed 29 November 2017

'Ex-Cop Goes Back on Death Row' *New Straits Times* (Kuala Lumpur, 10 September 2009)

'Executions, Prison Overcrowding Mars Thai Rights Record: Amnesty' *Agence France Presse* (Paris, 31 May 2001)

'Ex-Police Officer Executed' *Bangkok Post* (31 October 1998)

'Family Aghast after King Pardons Killer' *The New Paper* (Singapore, 30 January 2008)

'First Brush with Crime Nearly Sent Mum to Gallows' *Straits Times* (Singapore, 25 March 1992)

'HK Men on Drug Charges in Bangkok' *The Standard* (Hong Kong, 23 March 2006)

'Hong Kong Citizen Loses Bid to Revise Federal Court Decision' *Bernama Daily Malaysian News* (Kuala Lumpur, 9 November 2006)

'Hukuman Mati Terhadap Oki, Jaksa Tunggu Keputusan Grasi' (*Hukum Online*, 22 September 2004) <http://www.hukumonline.com/berita/baca/hol11201/hukuman-mati-terhadap-oki-jaksa-tunggu-keputusan-grasi> accessed 25 September 2017 [in Indonesian]

'Human Rights Situation' (1988) 13(2-4) Human Rights in Thailand Report 2

'Human Rights—US Document Cites Abuses in Thailand' *Bangkok Post* (1 February 1997)

'Indonesia Executes 6 Drug Convicts, Including 5 Foreigners' *USA Today* (New York, 17 January 2015) <https://www.usatoday.com/story/news/world/2015/01/17/indonesia-drug-executions/21933547/> accessed 25 September 2017

'Indonesia Frees Two Political Prisoners' *BBC News* (London, 26 May 1998) <http://news.bbc.co.uk/2/hi/events/indonesia/latest_news/100266.stm> accessed 17 November 2017

'Indonesia' (*Timelines of History*, 2010) <http://www.timelinesdb.com/listevents.php?subjid=83&title=Indonesia> accessed 17 November 2017

'Indonesian and Three Nigerians Executed for Drug Crimes' *BBC News* (London, 29 July 2016) <http://www.bbc.com/news/world-asia-36920293> accessed 25 September 2017

'Indonesian Court to Rule on Legality of Death Penalty for Drugs' *Agence France-Presse* (Paris, 30 October 2007)

'Indonesian Lawyers Seek Mercy for Condemned Drug Offenders' *Reuters* (London, 25 September 1991)

'Indonesia's Megawati Grants Muslim Holy Day Amnesties' *Kyodo News* (Tokyo, 25 November 2003)

'Insults Could See Convicted Men Hang: Lawyer' *The Advertiser* (Adelaide, 14 January 1986)

'Johor Sultan Pardons Eight Prisoners' *The Malaysian Insider* (Kuala Lumpur, 18 July 2012)

'Joint Stakeholders' Report on the UPR of Indonesia (Third Cycle)—On Issues Relating to the Death Penalty' (*upr-info*, 2016) <https://www.upr-info.org/sites/default/files/document/indonesia/session_27_-_may_2017/js23_upr27_idn_e_main.pdf> accessed 13 December 2017

'Jokowi Berikan Grasi Dua Terpidana Mati Asal Sumut' (*Inilah Medan*, 12 May 2016) <http://www.inilahmedan.com/2016/05/jokowi-berikan-grasi-dua-terpidana-mati.html> accessed 25 September 2017 [in Indonesian]

'Kaji Ulang Terpidana Mati' *Pontianak Post* (West Kalimantan, 1 May 2016) [in Indonesian]

'Kasthuri: Cabinet Shifting Goal Post on Death Penalty' (*Free Malaysia Today*, 11 July 2016) <http://www.freemalaysiatoday.com/category/nation/2016/07/11/kasthuri-cabinet-shifting-goal-post-on-death-penalty/> accessed 17 September 2017

'Keep Death Penalty but Allow Leeway' *The Sunday Times* (Singapore, 11 October 2009)

'Kenneth Lee Sentenced to Death' *Bernama Daily Malaysian News* (Kuala Lumpur, 26 March 2005)

'King's Pardon Application' (*Foreign Prisoner Support Service*, 5 August 2016) <https://web.archive.org/web/20160805162150/www.phaseloop.com/foreignprisoners/transfer-uk.html> accessed 11 December 2017

'Labourer Gets Death for Killing Man Who Beat Up "Foster Father"' *Straits Times* (Singapore, 21 April 1990)

'Latest Statistics on Death Penalty in Thailand' (*Death Penalty Thailand*, 16 September 2006) <http://deathpenaltythailand.blogspot.hk/2006/09/latest-statistics-on-death-penalty-in.html> accessed 13 December 2017

'Legality of Pardon Move Doubted' *The Nation* (Bangkok, 30 June 2009)

'Lindsay Sandiford—What Price a Life?' (*opentrial*, 27 July 2016) <http://opentrial.info/index.php?title=Lindsay_Sandiford_-_What_price_a_life%3F&oldid=2019> accessed 15 January 2018

'Lolos Hukuman Mati, Cong Roib Abdikan Diri Menjadi Guru Ngaji' (*Kumparan*, 9 December 2017) <https://kumparan.com/wartabromo/lolos-hukuman-mati-cong-roib-abdikan-diri-menjadi-guru-ngaji> accessed 22 September 2018 [in Indonesian]

'Malaysia Commutes Death Sentence of Filipina to Life' *Manila Bulletin* (2 July 2015)

'Malaysia Lowers Sentences of 3 Death Throw [sic] Pinoys' (*philstar.com*, 30 May 2012) <http://www.philstar.com/pinoyworldwide/ofw-news/2012/05/30/811966/malaysia-lowers-sentences-3-death-throw-pinoys> accessed 18 August 2017

'Malaysia Scraps Mandatory Death Sentence for Drugs' *Kyodo News* (Tokyo, 1 December 2017)

'Menuju Tiang Gantung Malaysia' *Viva News* (Jakarta, 27 August 2010) <http://www.bobbyinside.yolasite.com/sorot/menuju-tiang-gantung-malaysia> accessed 17 November 2017 [in Indonesian]

'Murderer Escapes Gallows after President's Pardon' *Straits Times* (Singapore, 15 May 1992)

'Murderer First Convict to Be Executed in Eight Years' *Bangkok Post* (30 January 1996)

'Nathan Grants Zero Presidential Pardon during His 2 Terms' *The Independent* (27 August 2016) <http://www.theindependent.sg/nathan-grants-zero-presidential-pardon-during-his-2-terms/> accessed 11 September 2017

'Newly Published Statistics on Death Penalty Sentencing in Thailand' (*Death Penalty Thailand*, 13 October 2015) <http://deathpenaltythailand.blogspot.hk/search?q=statistics> accessed 13 December 2017

'Nigeria: Five Foreigners Executed in Thailand' *Daily Trust* (Abuja, 18 January 2002) <http://allafrica.com/stories/200201180099.html> accessed 3 September 2017

'Of Amnesties and Royal Pardons' *The Nation* (Bangkok, 7 November 2008)

'Other Important Duties of the Yang di-Pertuan Agong' (*Perpustakaan Negara Malaysia*, 2003) <https://web.archive.org/web/20120526135132/http://www.malaysianmonarchy.org.my/malaysianmonarchy/?q=en/duties> accessed 11 December 2017

'Paint It Black' *The Economist* (London, 21 June 2014)

'Pardon for Drug Convicts Possible' *Bangkok Post* (6 December 1994)

'Pardon Unlikely for Malaysian Opposition Leader' *Turkish Weekly* (Ankara, 18 February 2015)

'Pardoned Inmates "Must Serve at Least 25 Years"' *Bangkok Post* (9 October 1995)

'Perak Pardons Board Denies Backlog of Cases' *Bernama Daily Malaysian News* (Kuala Lumpur, 28 March 2001)
'Perak Sultan Grants Four Prisoners Royal Pardon' *New Straits Times* (Kuala Lumpur, 18 April 2000)
'Perak Sultan Pardons Two Drug Offenders on Death Row' (*Malay Mail Online*, 1 November 2017) <http://www.themalaymailonline.com/malaysia/article/perak-sultan-pardons-two-drug-offenders-on-death-row#hw8MpFeexBARycI3.97> accessed 17 November 2017
'Perjalanan Grasi Kusni Kasdut' *Tempo* (Jakarta, 27 October 1979) [in Indonesian]
'Persons Detained by Special Orders and Condemned to Death' (1983) 7(1) Human Rights in Thailand Report 5
'Presiden Tidak Beri Grasi Penjahat Narkoba' *TEMPO Interaktif* (Jakarta, 30 June 2006) [in Indonesian]
'President Grants Clemency to 10 More Political Prisoners' *ANTARA* (Jakarta, 24 March 1999)
'President Grants Clemency to Mum on Death Row' *Straits Times* (Singapore, 23 March 1992)
'Presidential Pardon Saves Death Row Man from Gallows' *Straits Times* (Singapore, 14 May 1992)
'Prison Inmates Pay Last Respects' *Bangkok Post* (26 October 2017) <https://www.bangkokpost.com/news/general/1348886/prison-inmates-to-pay-their-last-respects> accessed 11 December 2017
'Prisoner Suffering from Cancer Granted Clemency' *Straits Times* (Singapore, 16 February 1995)
'Prisons to Free 15,000 under Amnesty' *Bangkok Post* (5 November 1990)
'Public Prosecutorial Discretion Exercised Carefully' *Channel News Asia* (Singapore, 20 January 2012)
'Rehabilitation Is Our Top Priority, Says Prisons D-G' *New Straits Times* (Kuala Lumpur, 14 September 1997)
'Review Parole System and Pardons Board' (*The Star Online*, 1 October 2009) <http://www.thestar.com.my/news/nation/2009/10/01/review-parole-system-and-pardons-board/> accessed 17 September 2017
'Rocky Man to Hang' *Courier-Mail* (Brisbane, 13 May 1992)
'Row at UN over Call by EU for Moratorium on Death Penalty' *Agence France-Presse* (Paris, 4 November 1999)
'Royal Pardon to Mark Bicentennial' *Straits Times* (Singapore, 11 June 1981)
'Seminar on Religious Aspects of Death Penalty' (*Death Penalty Thailand*, 1 September 2008) <http://deathpenaltythailand.blogspot.com/2008/09/seminar-on-religious-aspects-of-death.html> accessed 15 June 2010
'Show Mercy Mr Ong' *South China Morning Post* (Hong Kong, 22 June 1994)
'Singapore Defends Death Penalty in First Rights Report to UN' *Deutsche Presse-Agentur* (Hamburg, 26 February 2011)

'Singapore Premier Says West Coddles Citizens' *Reuters News* (London, 17 October 1994)

'Singapore, World Execution Capital' *The Economist* (London, 3 April 1999)

'Some Pardons Boards Have Not Met for Years' *New Straits Times* (Kuala Lumpur, 29 June 2006)

'Statistics of Prisoners Condemned to Death, 31st October 2014' (*Death Penalty Thailand*, 29 November 2014) <http://deathpenaltythailand.blogspot.hk/2014/11/statistics-of-prisoners-condemned-to.html> accessed 14 December 2017

'Statistics of Those Condemned to Death in Thailand: September 2016' *Death Penalty Thailand* (22 November 2016) <http://deathpenaltythailand.blogspot.hk/2016/11/statistics-of-those-condemned-to-death.html> accessed 14 December 2017

'Sultan Gives Death Row Convicts One More Chance' *New Straits Times* (Kuala Lumpur, 23 March 2015)

'Survivors, Families Mourn Bali Lost Ones' *AAP* (Sydney, 9 November 2008) <https://web.archive.org/web/20081113121122/http://news.ninemsn.com.au:80/article.aspx?id=662676> accessed 11 December 2017

'Thai Executions Condemned' *BBC News* (London, 20 April 2001) <http://news.bbc.co.uk/2/hi/asia-pacific/1287406.stm> accessed 3 September 2017

'Thailand Does Not Execute Women' (*Death Penalty Thailand*, 18 December 2013) <http://deathpenaltythailand.blogspot.hk/2013/12/thailand-does-not-execute-women.html> accessed 14 December 2017

'Thailand's King and Its Crisis' *The Economist* (London, 4 December 2008)

'The Attorney General—The Most Powerful Person in Malaysia?' INSAF: Journal of the Malaysian Bar (August 1983) <http://www.malaysianbar.org.my/index2.php?option=com_content&do_pdf=1&id=16136> accessed 29 March 2013

'The Executioners' *The Gold Coast Bulletin* (Australia, 3 December 2005)

'Thursday Special Report; Spared Death on Appeal' *The Straits Times* (Singapore, 1 March 2012)

'Time Running Out for 109 Death Row Inmates' *Jakarta Post* (26 March 2009)

'To Our Readers' (1982) 6(2) Human Rights in Thailand Report

'Update, Thailand Death Penalty Statistics' (*Death Penalty Thailand*, 27 June 2012) <http://deathpenaltythailand.blogspot.hk/2012/06/update-thailand-death-penalty.html> accessed 13 December 2017

'Vietnam Commutes Aussie's Death Sentence' *The Age* (Melbourne, 24 February 2006) <http://www.theage.com.au/news/world/vietnam-commutes-aussies-death-sentence/2006/02/24/1140670215957.html> accessed 2 September 2017

'Vui Kong's Journey' (*Save Vui Kong*, 28 August 2010) <http://savevuikong.blogspot.hk/p/yong-vui-kongs-journey.html> accessed 11 December 2017

'Western Prisoners Face Thai Firing Squad' *The Australian* (Sydney, 29 June 2001)

'When Couriers Fail to Deliver' *The Weekend Australian* (Sydney, 4 May 1996)

'When the Killing Hour Arrives' *Bangkok Post* (30 August 2009)

'Who Deserves Clemency' *Jakarta Post* (19 November 2012)

'Will King Go against UMNO? Agong Has Last Word in Anwar's Pardon—Lawyers' *Malaysia Chronicle* (26 February 2015)

'Woman Executed in Indonesia, 1st in Country's Judicial History' *Kyodo News* (Tokyo, 20 March 2005)

'Yong Vui Kong Gets to See His Next Birthday' (*Save Vui Kong*, 1 September 2010) <http://savevuikong.blogspot.com.au/2010/09/vui-kong-gets-to-see-his-next-birthday.html> accessed 25 March 2013

Aaron A, 'The Grandson of Former Minister Pay RM550,000 Damages in Defamation Suit' *utusan.com.my* (Kuala Lumpur, 22 March 2007)

Abou El Fadl K, 'The Death Penalty, Mercy, and Islam: A Call for Retrospection' in Owens EC, Carlson JD, and Elshtain EP (eds), *Religion and the Death Penalty* (Eerdmans Publishing 2004)

Abramowitz E and Paget D, 'Executive Clemency in Capital Cases' (1964) 39 New York University Law Review 136

Abu-Nimer M, 'A Framework for Nonviolence and Peacebuilding in Islam' (2001) 15 Journal of Law and Religion 217

Acker JR and Lanier CS, 'Ready for the Defense? Legislative Provisions Governing the Appointment of Counsel in Capital Cases' (1999) 35 Criminal Law Bulletin 429

Acker JR and Lanier CS, 'May God—Or the Governor—Have Mercy: Executive Clemency and Executions in Modern Death Penalty Systems' (2000) 36(3) Criminal Law Bulletin 200

Acker JR et al, 'Merciful Justice: Lessons from 50 Years of New York Death Penalty Commutations' (2010) 35 Criminal Justice Review 183

Addruse A, 'The Respective Roles of the Pardons Board and of the *Yang Di-Pertuan Agung*' (Human Rights Seminar, Kuala Lumpur, 19 July 1986)

Adzkia A, 'Ketua MA Tuding PK Berulang Jadi Dalih Tunda Eksekusi Mati' (*CNN Indonesia*, 7 January 2015) <https://www.cnnindonesia.com/nasional/20150107142245-12-22961/ketua-ma-tuding-pk-berulang-jadi-dalih-tunda-eksekusi-mati/> accessed 25 September 2017 [in Indonesian]

Agerholm H, 'Thailand Uses Lethal Injection to Execute First Prisoner in Nearly a Decade' *The Independent* (London, 19 June 2018) <https://www.independent.co.uk/news/world/asia/thailand-execution-death-penalty-lethal-injection-amnesty-international-a8405711.html> accessed 17 September 2018

Aglionby J, 'Tommy Suharto Gets 15 Years for Judge's Murder' *The Guardian* (London, 27 July 2002) <https://www.theguardian.com/world/2002/jul/27/indonesia.johnaglionby> accessed 25 September 2017

Agustin R, 'Reformasi: A Tale of Indonesia's Success' (*Free Malaysia Today*, 1 August 2017) <http://www.freemalaysiatoday.com/category/nation/2017/08/01/reformasi-a-tale-of-indonesias-success/> accessed 17 November 2017

Aisbett N, 'Echoes of Barlow and Chambers' *The West Australian* (Perth, 14 July 2001)

Akbar P and Lai G, 'Thailand Amends Drug Law to Reduce Penalties and Ensure More Proportionate Sentencing' (*International Drug Policy Consortium*, 15 February 2017) <http://idpc.net/blog/2017/02/thailand-amends-drug-law-to-reduce-penalties-and-ensure-more-proportionate-sentencing> accessed 11 December 2017

Al Saqqaf T, 'The Position of Islam' (4th World Congress Against the Death Penalty, Geneva, 24–26 February 2010)

Alarid LF and Wang H-M, 'Mercy and Punishment: Buddhism and the Death Penalty' (2001) 28 Social Justice 231

Alford P, 'Tunes Differ on Revival of Executioner's Song' *The Weekend Australian* (Melbourne, 8 January 2000)

Alfred H, 'Reprieve for Death Row Woman' *Straits Times* (Singapore, 18 February 1983)

Alston P, 'Report of the Special Rapporteur on Extrajudicial Summary or Arbitrary Executions' (UN Doc A/HRC/4/20, 27 March 2007)

Ammons LL, 'Discretionary Justice: A Legal and Policy Analysis of a Governor's Use of the Clemency Power in the Cases of Incarcerated Battered Women' (1994) 3 Journal of Law and Policy 1

Amnesty International, *Annual Reports 1978 to 2010* (Amnesty International 1978–2010)

Amnesty International, 'Against the Tide: The Death Penalty in Southeast Asia' (AI Index ASA 03/01/97, 1 January 1997)

Amnesty International, 'Amnesty International Report 1998—Thailand' (*refworld*, 1998) <http://www.refworld.org/docid/3ae6a9fb28.html> accessed 13 December 2017

Amnesty International, 'Asie-Pacifique: Les condamnations à mort pour les infractions liées à la législation sur les stupéfiants sont en augmentation' (AI Index ASA 01/003/2007, 20 June 2007) [in French]

Amnesty International, 'Cooperate or Die: Singapore's Flawed Reforms to the Mandatory Death Penalty' (AI Index ACT 50/7158/2017, October 2017) <https://www.amnesty.be/IMG/pdf/singapore_report_web.pdf> accessed 17 November 2017

Amnesty International, 'Death by Firing Squad' (1988a) 14 Inside Indonesia 2

Amnesty International, *The Death Penalty* (Amnesty International 1979)

Amnesty International, *The Death Penalty and Executions in Malaysia* (Amnesty International 1983)

Amnesty International, 'The Death Penalty in India: A Lethal Lottery' (AI Index ASA 20/006/2008, May 2008)

Amnesty International, 'The Death Penalty Worldwide: Developments in 2001' (AI Index ACT 50/001/2002, 1 April 2002)

Amnesty International, 'The Death Penalty: No Solution to Illicit Drugs' (AI Index ACT 51/02/95, 2 October 1995)

Amnesty International, 'Death Sentences and Executions 2012' (AI Index ACT 50/001/2013, April 2013)

Amnesty International, 'Death Sentences and Executions 2013' (AI Index ACT 50/001/2014, March 2014)

Amnesty International, 'Death Sentences and Executions 2014' (AI Index ACT 50/001/2015, April 2015)

Amnesty International, 'Death Sentences and Executions 2015' (AI Index ACT 50/3487/2016, April 2016)

Amnesty International, 'Death Sentences and Executions 2016' (AI Index ACT 50/5740/2017, 11 April 2017)

Amnesty International, 'Death Sentences and Executions in 2007' (AI Index ACT 50/001/2008, 15 April 2008)

Amnesty International, 'Death Sentences and Executions in 2008' (AI Index ACT 50/003/2009, March 2009)

Amnesty International, 'Death Sentences and Executions in 2010' (AI Index ACT 50/001/2011, 28 March 2011)

Amnesty International, 'Death Sentences and Executions in 2011' (AI Index ACT 50/001/2012, March 2012)

Amnesty International, 'Execution/Fear of Further Executions: Thailand' (AI Index ASA 39/01/98, 2 November 1998)

Amnesty International, 'Fear of Imminent Execution' (AI Index ASA 39/04/95, 29 September 1995)

Amnesty International, 'Fear of Imminent Execution' (AI Index ASA 28/12/97, 4 November 1997)

Amnesty International, 'Flawed Justice: Unfair Trials and the Death Penalty in Indonesia' (AI Index ASA 21/2434/2015, 15 October 2015) <https://www.amnestyusa.org/files/flawed-justice-indonesia-2015.pdf> accessed 2 September 2017

Amnesty International, 'Further Information on EXTRA 144/99' (AI Index ASA 39/07/99, 16 December 1999)

Amnesty International, 'Further Information on EXTRA 36/98' (AI Index ASA 36/03/98, 29 May 1998)

Amnesty International, 'Further Information on Fear of Imminent Execution' (AI Index ASA 39/05/99, 24 November 1999)

Amnesty International, 'Further Information on UA 27/08 (ASA 21/002/2008, 25 January 2008)—Fear of Imminent Execution' (AI Index ASA 21/010/2008, 4 July 2008)

Amnesty International, 'Indonesia—First Execution in Five Years: A Step Back' (AI Index ASA 21/016/2001, 22 May 2001)

Amnesty International, 'Indonesia—The 1965 Prisoners: How Many More Will Die in Jail?' (AI Index ASA 21/43/96, 1 August 1996)

Amnesty International, 'Indonesia/East Timor—A New Order?' (AI Index ASA 21/03/93, February 1993)

Amnesty International, 'Indonesia: A Briefing on the Death Penalty' (AI Index ASA 21/040/2004, 1 October 2004)

Amnesty International, 'Indonesia: Briefing to the UN Committee Against Torture' (AI Index ASA 21/003/2008, April 2008)

Amnesty International, 'Indonesia: Fifth Execution Confirms Shocking New Trend of Secrecy' (*Amnesty International*, 18 November 2013) <https://www.amnesty.org/en/latest/news/2013/11/indonesia-fifth-execution-confirms-shocking-new-trend-secrecy/> accessed 17 November 2017

Amnesty International, 'Indonesia: The Application of the Death Penalty' (AI Index ASA 21/27/87, November 1987)

Amnesty International, 'Indonesia: President Refuses to Grant Clemency to Brazilian while Two Australian Nationals Are Sentenced to Death' (AI Index UA-064-2006, 15 February 2006)

Amnesty International, 'Israel and the Occupied Territories: State Assassinations and Other Unlawful Kilings' (AI Index MDE 15/005/2001, 21 February 2001)

Amnesty International, 'Kingdom of Thailand: At Least 10 People (Names Unknown)' (AI Index ASA 39/001/2001) <https://www.amnesty.org/download/Documents/128000/asa390012001en.pdf> accessed 13 December 2017

Amnesty International, 'Kingdom of Thailand: Human Rights in Transition' (AI Index ASA 39/002/1997, 20 May 1997)

Amnesty International, 'Malaysia: Imminent Execution, Chu Tak Fai [M], Aged 30, Hong Kong National/N/N' (AI Index ASA 28/014/01, 13 June 2001)

Amnesty International, 'Massive Leap Backwards as Singapore Resumes Executions' (*Amnesty International*, 18 July 2014) <https://www.amnesty.org/en/latest/news/2014/07/massive-leap-backwards-singapore-resumes-executions/> accessed 14 December 2017

Amnesty International, 'Medical Concern—Asep Suryaman—Indonesia' (AI Index ASA 21/01/98, 19 January 1998)

Amnesty International, 'Power and Impunity: Human Rights under the New Order' (AI Index ASA 21/017/1994, 1 September 1994)

Amnesty International, 'Recent Executions in Indonesia and the Application of the Death Penalty', in Indonesia Publications (ed), *Law and Political Liberty in Indonesia* (Indonesia Publications 1988b)

Amnesty International, *Religions and the Death Penalty: The Case for Abolition* (Amnesty International 1990)

Amnesty International, 'Singapore—The Death Penalty: A Hidden Toll of Executions' (AI Index ASA 36/001/2004, 15 January 2004)
Amnesty International, 'Singapore: Failing to Respect Civil Rights' (AI Index ASA 36/002/2010, 1 November 2010)
Amnesty International, 'Singapore: Imminent Hanging of Malaysian National Undermines Death Penalty Reforms' (*Amnesty International*, 5 November 2015) <https://www.amnesty.org/download/Documents/ASA3628182015ENGLISH.pdf> accessed 17 January 2019
Amnesty International, 'Southeast Asia: Human Rights Violations in Brunei, Indonesia, Malaysia, Philippines, Singapore and Thailand' (AI Index ASA 03/01/87, December 1987)
Amnesty International, 'Statement of Amnesty International's Concerns in Indonesia' (AI Index ASA 21/33/85, 30 August 1985)
Amnesty International, 'Summary of Amnesty International's Concerns in Indonesia' (AI Index ASA 21/01/83, March 1983)
Amnesty International, 'Thailand: 10 Years Later—Still No Justice for the May 1992 Victims' (AI Index ASA 39/004/2002, 16 May 2002)
Amnesty International, 'Thailand: A Human Rights Review based on the International Covenant on Civil and Political Rights' (AI Index ASA 39/01/99, January 1999)
Amnesty International, 'Thailand: Executions Will Not Curb Drug Trade' (AI Index ASA 39/005/2001, 19 April 2001)
Amnesty International, 'Thailand: Fear of Imminent Execution' (AI Index ASA 39/002/2002, 25 April 2002)
Amnesty International, 'Thailand: Substantial Human Rights Progress Made' (AI Index ASA 39/02/99, 5 January 1999)
Amnesty International, 'Thailand: Time to Abolish the Death Penalty' (AI Index ACT 50/7611/2017, December 2017)
Amnesty International, 'The Trial of Opposition Parliamentarian Lim Guan Eng: An Update' (AI Index ASA 28/03/97, 1 March 1997)
Amnesty International, 'Two Executed without Trial in Thailand' (Newsletter Article, June 1977)
Amnesty International, 'Urgent Action: Malaysian Man Facing Execution in Singapore' (AI Index ASA 36/004/2009, 3 November 2009)
Amnesty International, *When the State Kills—The Death Penalty: A Human Rights Issue* (Amnesty International 1989)
Amnesty International and Human Rights Watch, 'Indonesia and East Timor: The Prisoner Releases So Far' (AI Index ASA 21/84/98, 26 August 1998)
Anand P, 'His Majesty's Role in the Making of Thai History' (14th Conference of the International Association of Historians of Asia, Bangkok, May 1996)
Anandan S, *The Best I Could* (Marshall Cavendish 2009)
Anckar C, *Determinants of the Death Penalty* (Routledge 2004)

Anckar C, 'Selecting Cases in Cross-National Political Research' (2007) 10(1) International Journal of Social Research Methodology 49

Anckar C, 'Why Countries Choose the Death Penalty' (2014) 21 Brown Journal of World Affairs 7

Andrew AM and Rapp JA, *Autocracy and China's Rebel Founding Emperors: Comparing Chairman Mao and Ming Taizu* (Rowman & Littlefield Publishers 2000)

Anti-Death Penalty Asia Network, 'ADPAN Welcomes Thailand's Commitment to the Abolition of the Death Penalty at the UN Human Rights Council's Universal Periodic Review (UPR) of Thailand in Geneva on 11/5/2016' (*Anti-Death Penalty Asia Network*, 20 May 2016) <https://adpan.org/2016/05/21/adpan-welcomes-thailands-commitment-to-the-abolition-of-the-death-penalty-at-the-un-human-rights-councils-universal-periodic-review-upr-of-thailand-in-geneva-on-1152016/> accessed 1 March 2017

Anti-Death Penalty Asia Network, 'Mongolia Abolishes the Death Penalty for All Crimes' (*Anti-Death Penalty Asia Network*, 4 July 2017) <https://adpan.org/2017/07/04/mongolia-abolishes-the-death-penalty-for-all-crimes/> accessed 3 September 2017

Anti-Death Penalty Asia Network, 'NEWSFLASH—Malaysia—A Positive First Step towards Abolition' (*Anti-Death Penalty Asia Network*, 25 October 2012) <https://adpan.org/2012/10/25/newsflash-malaysia-malaysias-proposal-to-review-the-mandatory-death-penalty-for-drug-offences-a-positive-first-step-towards-abolition/> accessed 29 November 2017

Anti-Death Penalty Asia Network, 'When Justice Fails: Thousands Executed in Asia after Unfair Trials' (*Anti-Death Penalty Asia Network*, AI Index ASA/01/023/2011, 2011) <https://adpandotnet.files.wordpress.com/2011/11/adpan-unfair-trials-asa-010232100-final-pdf.pdf> accessed 17 November 2017

Anti-Death Penalty NGO Memo (copy on file with author, 17 December 2012)

Argys LM and Naci Mocan H, 'Who Shall Live and Who Shall Die? An Analysis of Prisoners on Death Row in the United States' (2004) 33 Journal of Legal Studies 255

Aritonang M and Susanto S, 'Jokowi to Ban Clemency for Drug Convicts' *Jakarta Post* (10 December 2014) <http://www.thejakartapost.com/news/2014/12/10/jokowi-ban-clemency-drug-convicts.html> accessed 25 September 2017

ASEAN Law Association, 'Legal Systems in ASEAN: Indonesia' (*ASEAN Law Association*, 2005) <http://www.aseanlawassociation.org/legal-indonesia.html> accessed 25 March 2013

Asian Human Rights Commission, 'The State of Human Rights in Indonesia in 2012' (*Asian Human Rights Commission*, 10 December 2012) <http://www.humanrights.asia/resources/hrreport/2012/ahrc-spr-006-2012.pdf> accessed 25 March 2013

Au WA, 'Hanging Up the Hanging Rope' (*Yawning Bread*, 15 November 2011) <http://yawningbread.wordpress.com/2011/11/15/hanging-up-the-hanging-rope/> accessed 25 March 2013

Au WA, 'Singapore Reeling from Murder Spree, Drug Scourge' (*Yawning Bread*, 21 May 2011) <http://yawningbread.wordpress.com/2011/05/21/singapore-reeling-from-murder-spree-drug-scourge/> accessed 25 March 2013

Au WA, 'Singapore Retreats from Mandatory Death Penalty by an Inch' (*Yawning Bread,* 16 July 2012) <https://yawningbread.wordpress.com/2012/07/16/singapore-retreats-from-mandatory-death-penalty-by-an-inch/> accessed 11 September 2017

Au WA, 'Sleeping with Strangers, Part 1' (*Yawning Bread*, 21 August 2010) <http://yawningbread.wordpress.com/2010/08/21/sleeping-with-strangers-part-1/> accessed 25 March 2013

Aziz A, 'Rais to Meet Rulers in Move to "Activate" State Pardons Boards' *New Straits Times* (Kuala Lumpur, 25 March 2001)

Azlan Shah YAM, 'The Role of Constitutional Rulers in Malaysia' in Trindade FA and Lee HP (eds), *The Constitution of Malaysia: Further Perspectives and Developments* (Oxford University Press 1986)

Babbie E, *The Practice of Social Research* (10th edn, Thomson Wadsworth 2004)

Babulal V and Mokhtar IL, 'Nothing Can Bring Back Good Yew' *New Straits Times* (Kuala Lumpur, 28 January 2008)

Bachelard M, 'Drug Charge Britons Fear Horrors of Bali's Jails and a Firing Squad' *The Guardian* (London, 2 June 2012)

Baderin MA, *International Human Rights and Islamic Law* (Oxford University Press 2003)

Bae S, 'Is the Death Penalty an Asian Value?' (2008) 39(1) Asian Affairs 47

Bae S, 'When the State No Longer Kills: International Human Rights Norms and Abolition of Capital Punishment' (SUNY Press 2007)

Bailer S, 'Interviews and Surveys in Legislative Research' in Martin S et al (eds), *The Oxford Handbook of Legislative Studies* (Oxford University Press 2014)

Baker M, 'The Price of a Human Life in Regional Relations' *The Age* (Melbourne, 9 June 1992)

Bampton D, 'Indonesia, Australia and the Death Penalty: Options for Australians Facing Execution in Indonesia' (Law Honours Thesis, University of Sydney 2006)

Banchoff T, 'Human Rights, the Catholic Church, and the Death Penalty in the United States' in Banchoff T and Wuthnow R (eds), *Religion and the Global Politics of Human Rights* (Oxford University Press 2011)

Bangkok Corrections Museum, 'Execution by Sword' (Description of Execution Procedures under King Rama V (r.1868–1910), Bangkok Corrections Museum, Maha Chai Road, Bangkok 2012) [in Thai]

Bari AA, *Malaysian Constitution: A Critical Introduction* (The Other Press 2003)

Barkow RE, 'The Ascent of the Administrative State and the Demise of Mercy' (2007–8) 121 Harvard Law Review 1332

Barkow RE, 'The Politics of Forgiveness: Reconceptualizing Clemency' (2009) 21(3) Federal Sentencing Reporter 153

Barrow R, 'Royal Pardon' (*Thai Prison Life*, 7 June 2017) <https://web.archive.org/web/20170607142357/http://www.thaiprisonlife.com/royal-pardon/> accessed 13 December 2017

Bass J, 'Malaysia in 1983: A Time of Troubles' (1983) 24 Asian Survey 167

Baumgartner J and Morris M, 'Presidential Power Unbound: A Comparative Look as Presidential Pardon Power' (2001) 29(2) Politics and Policy 209

Baxstrom R, *Transforming Brickfields: Development and Governance in a Malaysian City* (National University of Singapore Press 2010)

Beattie J, *Crime and the Courts in England 1660–1800* (Oxford University Press 1986)

Bedau HA, 'The Decline of Executive Clemency in Capital Cases' (1990–1) 28 NYU Review of Law and Social Change 255

Bedau HA, 'The US: Institutional Obstacles and Future Prospects' in Hodgkinson P and Schabas WA (eds), *Capital Punishment: Strategies for Abolition* (Cambridge University Press 2004)

Bedi RS, '165 on Death Row Escaped the Gallows from 2007 to 2017' (*The Star Online*, 28 June 2018) <https://www.thestar.com.my/news/nation/2018/06/28/165-on-death-row-escaped-the-gallows-from-2007-to-2017/> accessed 16 January 2019

Bellamy R, 'The Political Form of the Constitution: The Separation of Powers, Rights and Representative Democracy' in Bellamy R and Castiglione D (eds), *Constitutionalism in Transformation: European and Theoretical Perspectives* (Blackwell 1996)

Bellett G, 'Court Orders New Plan for Extradition' *Vancouver Sun* (21 June 2008)

Bellivier F and Lahidji K, 'Letter on Abolition to Miinister [sic] of Justice from World Coalition and FIDH' (*Death Penalty Thailand*, 8 October 2013) <http://deathpenaltythailand.blogspot.com/2013/10/letter-on-abolition-to-miinister-of.html> accessed 26 August 2017

Bennett RR, 'Presidential Address—Comparative Criminology and Criminal Justice Research: The State of Our Knowledge' (2004) 21(1) Justice Quarterly 1

Berlow A, 'The Texas Clemency Memos' *Atlantic Monthly* (Washington DC, July/August 2003)

Black D, *The Behavior of Law* (Emerald Group Publishing 2010)

Blaikie N, *Designing Social Research* (2nd edn, Polity Press 2010)

Blumenthal EJ, 'Executive Power to Grant Reprieves and Pardons: How Can Your Client Receive the Scooter Libby Treatment?' (Section of Litigation Criminal Litigation Committee Newsletter, American Bar Association 2007)

Bonner R, 'Capital Punishment Change' *The New York Times* (10 September 2003)

Boon TO, 'Youth on Murder Rap Escapes Gallows' *Straits Times* (Singapore, 5 May 1998)

Boriboonthana Y, 'Effective Treatment Measures for Prisoners to Facilitate their Re-Integration into Society' (UNAFEI 108th International Seminar, Tokyo, September 1999) <https://web.archive.org/web/20161205011254/http://www.unafei.or.jp/english/pdf/RS_No54/No54_27PA_Boriboonthana.pdf > accessed 5 December 2016

Botsman D, *Punishment and Power in the Making of Modern Japan* (Princeton University Press 2007)

Boulanger C and Sarat A, 'Putting Culture into the Picture: Toward a Comparative Analysis of State Killing' in Boulanger C and Sarat A (eds), *The Cultural Lives of Capital Punishment* (Stanford University Press 2005)

Bourchier D, 'Behind Indonesia's Courts' (1988) 14 Inside Indonesia 10

Boxer JT, 'China's Death Penalty: Undermining Legal Reform and Threatening National Economic Interest' (1998–9) 22 Suffolk Transnational Law Review 593

Breen D, 'Buddhism' (4th World Congress Against the Death Penalty, Geneva, 24–26 February 2010)

Breen D, 'Chalerm and the Way of Death' (*Death Penalty Thailand*, 1 September 2012) <http://deathpenaltythailand.blogspot.hk/2012/09/chalerm-and-way-of-eath.html> accessed 14 December 2017

Breen D, 'Thailand and the Death Penalty' (*Taiwan Alliance to End the Death Penalty*, 16 May 2013) <http://www.taedp.org.tw/en/story/2541> accessed 3 September 2017

Bremboo A, 'Inilah Bandar Narkoba Yang Pertama Kali Dieksekusi Di Indonesia' (*Riau Online*, 16 August 2016) <http://www.riauonline.co.id/riau/kota-pekanbaru/read/2016/08/16/inilah-bandar-narkoba-yang-pertama-kali-dieksekusi-di-indonesia> accessed 25 September 2017 [in Indonesian]

Bremmer I, 'Here's What You Need to Know about Thailand's New Constitution' *Time* (New York, 11 August 2016) <http://time.com/4448655/thailand-constitutional-referendum/> accessed 27 November 2017

Breslin B and Howley JJP, 'Defending the Politics of Clemency' (2002) 81 Oregon Law Review 231

Brooke M, 'Murderer of UK Tourist "Grateful to His Majesty"' *Bangkok Post* (9 June 1996)

Brummitt C, 'Indonesia Bucks Global Downward Trend in Executions, Killing 6 since June' *Associated Press Newswires* (New York, 20 July 2008)

Buang S, 'An End to Mandatory Death Penalty?' *New Straits Times* (Kuala Lumpur, 17 August 2017) <https://www.nst.com.my/opinion/columnists/2017/08/268727/end-mandatory-death-penalty> accessed 17 September 2017

Buhmann K, *Implementing Human Rights through Administrative Law Reforms: The Potential of China and Vietnam* (Djoef Publishing 2001)

Burnett C, 'The Failed Failsafe: The Politics of Executive Clemency' (2003) 8 Texas Journal of Civil Rights and Civil Liberties 192

Burnett C, *Justice Denied: Clemency Appeals in Death Penalty Cases* (Northeastern University Press 2002)

Burns AI and Markham SJ, 'Understanding the Separation of Powers' (1987) 7(3) Pace Law Review 575

Burrell I, 'Family Claim Trafficker "Failed by Government"' *The Independent* (London, 20 December 1999)

Butler D and Low DA, *Sovereigns and Surrogates: Constitutional Heads of State in the Commonwealth* (Palgrave Macmillan 1991)

Butt S, 'Asia-Pacific: Judicial Responses to the Death Penalty in Indonesia' (2014) 39(2) Alternative Law Journal 134

Butt S, *Corruption and Law in Indonesia* (Routledge 2012)

Butt S and Lindsey T, 'Judicial Mafia' in Aspinall E and van Klinken G (eds), *The State and Illegality in Indonesia* (KITLV Press 2011)

Butt S and Lindsey T, *The Constitution of Indonesia: A Contextual Analysis* (Bloomsbury 2012)

Byrnes A, 'The Bali 9 Case—Where Has International Law Gone?' (*University of New South Wales Australian Human Rights Centre*, 2 February 2015) <http://www.ahrcentre.org/news/2015/02/02/660> accessed 27 November 2017

Cameron MA, 'Democracy and the Separation of Powers: Threats, Dilemmas, and Opportunities in Latin America' (2002) 27(53) Canadian Journal of Latin American and Caribbean Studies 133

Cassrels D, 'The Journey from Death Row' (*SBS*, 15 August 2017) <http://www.sbs.com.au/topics/life/feature/journey-death-row> accessed 17 November 2017

Chambers P and Waitoolkiat N, 'The Resilience of Monarchised Military in Thailand' (2016) 46(3) Journal of Contemporary Asia 425

Chan SK, 'The Courts and the "Rule of Law" in Singapore' [2012] Singapore Journal of Legal Studies 209

Chan WC, 'The Death Penalty in Singapore: In Decline but Still Too Soon for Optimism' (2016) 11(3) Asian Journal of Criminology 179

Chanprasert S, 'Rehabilitation for Prisoners under Sentence of Death in a Human Rights Perspective: A Case Study of Bang Khwang Central Prison' (Master of Arts Thesis, Chulalongkorn University 2012)

Choudhury F, 'Due Process and the Death Penalty in the Asia-Pacific Region' (2015–6) 22 Australian International Law Journal 15

Charoonbara S, 'The Organization of Military Courts in Thailand' (1981) 93 Military Law Review 25

Cheah R, 'Family Members Affected by Clemency Granted to Death Row Prisoner' (*The Star Online*, 27 January 2008) <https://www.thestar.com.my/news/nation/2008/01/27/family-members-affected-by-clemency-granted-to-death-row-prisoner/> accessed 11 December 2017

Chew M, 'Australia Approached Singapore Hanging with Eye on Ties' *Dow Jones International News* (New York, 2 December 2005)

Chitsawang N, 'Capital Punishment—Execution in Thailand' (*Thailand Criminology and Corrections,* 2015) <http://thaicriminology.com/execution-in-thailand.html> accessed 3 September 2017

Cho B-S, 'The Death Penalty in Korea and Japan: "Asian Values" and the Debate about Capital Punishment?' in Hodgkinson P and Schabas W (eds), *Capital Punishment: Strategies for Abolition* (Cambridge University Press 2004)

Cho B-S, 'South Korea's Changing Capital Punishment Policy' (2008) 10(2) Punishment and Society 171

Chong S, 'Publication of Prosecutorial Guidelines: Publication for Whom, and Publication to What End' (Association of Criminal Lawyers of Singapore Annual Lecture 2013, Singapore, 12 November 2013) <https://www.agc.gov.sg/docs/default-source/speeches/2013/acls-lecture-2013.pdf?sfvrsn=2> accessed 27 November 2017

Choosup D, 'Innovations in the Administration of Criminal Justice in Thailand' in Clifford W (ed), *Innovations in Criminal Justice in Asia and the Pacific* (Australian Institute of Criminology 1979)

Chotibal P, 'The Royal Prerogative of Pardon in Thailand' (Master of Laws Thesis, Chulalongkorn University 1990) [in Thai]

Clammer J, 'Framing the Other: Criminality, Social Exclusion and Social Engineering in Developing Singapore' (1997) 31 Social Policy and Administration 136

Clapano JR, 'GMA Urged to Seek Pardon for Pinoy in KL Death Row' (*Philstar*, 14 March 2003) <http://www.philstar.com/headlines/198897/gma-urged-seek-pardon-pinoy-kl-death-row> accessed 17 September 2017

Close J, 'Amnesty Provisions in the Constitutions of the World: A Comparative Analysis' (*International Law Blog*, 5 January 2015) <https://aninternationallawblog.wordpress.com/2015/01/05/amnesty-provisions-in-the-constitutions-of-the-world-a-comparative-analysis/> accessed 21 September 2016

Colgate Love M, 'The Pardon Paradox: Lessons of Clinton's Last Pardons' (2002) 32 Capital University Law Review 185

Colgate Love M, 'The Twilight of the Pardon Power' (2010) 100(3) Journal of Criminal Law and Criminology <http://papers.ssrn.com/sol3/papers.cfm?abstract_id=1569874> accessed 19 April 2012

Constant M, 'Massive Royal Pardon by New Thai King' *Anadolu Agency* (Ankara, 12 December 2016) <http://aa.com.tr/en/asia-pacific/massive-royal-pardon-by-new-thai-king/704774> accessed 3 September 2017

Conway D, 'Dealing with Death in Indonesia's Courts' *Joyo Indonesia News Service* (6 September 2006)

Cooper P, 'Competency of Death Row Inmates to Waive the Right to Appeal' (2009) 28 Developments in Mental Health Law 105

Corben R, 'Drug Stance Cruels Foreigners Chances of Royal Pardon' *Australian Associated Press* (Sydney, 28 June 2001)

Cornell Center on the Death Penalty Worldwide, 'Indonesia' (*Death Penalty Worldwide*, 6 December 2017) <https://www.deathpenaltyworldwide.org/country-search-post.cfm?country=Indonesia> accessed 11 December 2017

Cornell Center on the Death Penalty Worldwide, 'Malaysia' (*Death Penalty Worldwide*, 6 December 2017) <http://www.deathpenaltyworldwide.org/country-search-post.cfm?country=malaysia> accessed 11 December 2017

Cornell Center on the Death Penalty Worldwide, 'Papua New Guinea' (*Death Penalty Worldwide*, 6 December 2017) <http://www.deathpenaltyworldwide.org/country-search-post.cfm?country=Papua+New+Guinea> accessed 11 December 2017

Cornell Center on the Death Penalty Worldwide, 'Singapore' (*Death Penalty Worldwide*, 6 December 2017) <http://www.deathpenaltyworldwide.org/country-search-post.cfm?country=Singapore&region=&method=> accessed 11 December 2017

Cornell Center on the Death Penalty Worldwide, 'Thailand' (*Death Penalty Worldwide*, 6 December 2017) <https://www.deathpenaltyworldwide.org/country-search-post.cfm?country=thailand> accessed 11 December 2017

Cornell Law School, 'Pathways to Abolition of the Death Penalty' (*Death Penalty Worldwide*, 2016) <https://www.deathpenaltyworldwide.org/pdf/Pathways%20to%20Abolition%20Death%20Penalty%20Worldwide%202016-07%20FINAL.pdf> accessed 27 November 2017

Coyne R and Entzeroth L, *Capital Punishment and the Judicial Process* (2nd edn, Carolina Academic Press 2001)

Crawford A, 'Briton in Thai Jail Refuses to Beg for Pardon' *Sunday Herald* (Glasgow, 29 December 2002)

Cribb R, 'Unresolved Problems in the Indonesian Killings of 1965–1966' (2002) 42 Asian Survey 550

Crook P, 'Sim Kie Chon V. Superintendent of Pudu Prison & Ors: The Royal Prerogative of Mercy?' [1986] Jurnal Undang-Undang 195

Crouch J, *The Presidential Pardon Power* (University Press of Kansas 2009)

Damis A, 'Bar Council to Lobby for Review of Taiping's Natural Life Prisoner' *New Straits Times* (Kuala Lumpur, 17 November 2004)

Damis A, 'The Measure of Their Lives Is a Prison Cell' *New Straits Times* (Kuala Lumpur, 25 December 2004)

Dascalu CI, 'Elements of Comparative Law on the Individual Pardon, Between Constitutional Constraint and Discretionary Prerogative of the Head of State' (2012) 2(2) Union of Jurists of Romania Law Review 1

Davies PHJ, 'Spies as Informants: Triangulation and the Interpretation of Elite Interview Data in the Study of the Intelligence and Security Services' (2001) 21(1) Politics 73

Davis SB, 'The Death Penalty and Legal Reform in the People's Republic of China' (1987) 1(2) Journal of Chinese Law 303

Dean M and Aleksander T, *Lethal Justice: The Death Penalty* (Channel Four Television 1995)

Deans B, 'In Malaysia, Drugs Mean Death' *Atlanta Journal and Constitution* (18 March 1990)

Death Penalty Information Center, 'Clemency' (*Death Penalty Information Center*, 2017a) <https://deathpenaltyinfo.org/clemency> accessed 25 September 2017

Death Penalty Information Center, 'Executions by Year' (*Death Penalty Information Center*, 2017b) <https://deathpenaltyinfo.org/executions-year> accessed 25 September 2017

Death Penalty Information Center, 'Illinois Death Row Inmates Granted Commutation by Governor George Ryan on January 12, 2003' (*Death Penalty Information Center*, 2003) <http://www.deathpenaltyinfo.org/node/677> accessed 25 March 2013

Death Penalty Information Center, 'Jurisdictions with No Recent Executions' (*Death Penalty Information Center*, 2017c) <https://deathpenaltyinfo.org/jurisdictions-no-recent-executions> accessed 11 December 2017

Death Penalty Worldwide, *Representing Individuals Facing the Death Penalty: A Best Practices Manual* (2nd edn, Death Penalty Worldwide 2013)

DeCoste FC, 'Conditions of Clemency: Justice *from* the Offender' (2003) 66 Saskatchewan Law Review 1

Deen T, '51 States Challenge U.N. Body over Death Penalty' *Inter Press Service* (Rome, 7 August 1998)

Delaney B, 'Comment: Changing Attitudes to the Death Penalty in Southeast Asia' (*SBS News*, 25 July 2013) <http://www.sbs.com.au/news/article/2013/07/25/comment-changing-attitudes-death-penalty-southeast-asia> accessed 15 September 2013

Deliani D, 'Pelaksanaan Kekuasan Presiden Dalam Pemberian Grasi' (Postgraduate Thesis, Faculty of Law, University of Indonesia 2011) [in Indonesian]

Department of Foreign Affairs and Trade (Australia), *Human Rights Sub-Committee Report—Death Penalty* <http://dfat.gov.au/about-us/publications/corporate/australian-consular-operations-handbook/Documents/appendix-22-Death%20Penalty%20Guidelines.DOCX> accessed 29 November 2017

Donoghue T, *Karpal Singh: Tiger of Jelutong* (Marshall Cavendish 2013)

Donoghue T, *The Tiger Who Smiled: Lorraine and Aaron Cohen's Story* (William Collins Publishers 1990)

Drummond A, 'Accused Britons Face Call for Death Penalty' *The Herald* (Glasgow, 31 January 1996)

Dui Hua Foundation, 'China: Juveniles Biggest Winners in 2015 Special Pardon' (*Dui Hua Human Rights Journal*, 29 January 2016) <http://www.duihuahrjournal.org/2016/01/china-juveniles-biggest-winners-in-2015.html> accessed 7 April 2016

Eddyono SW et al, 'Update Hukuman Mati di Indonesia 2016' (*Institute for Criminal Justice Reform*, August 2016) <http://icjr.or.id/data/wp-content/uploads/2016/09/Update_Kondisi_Hukuman_Mati_di_Indonesia_2016.pdf> accessed 2 September 2017

Edwards P, *Australia and the Vietnam War* (New South Publishing 2014)

Eksa G, 'Kejaksaan Siapkan Eksekusi Mati Tahap IV' (*Metro TV News*, 27 September 2016) <http://news.metrotvnews.com/hukum/0kprpz0N-kejaksaan-siapkan-eksekusi-mati-tahap-iv> accessed 25 September 2017 [in Indonesian]

El-Awa MS, *Punishment in Islamic Law* (American Trust Publications 1982)

Elda E, 'Pengaturan pidana mati sebagai pidana pokok yang bersifat khusus dan alternatif dalam rancangan kitab undang-undang hukum pidana' (Thesis, Faculty of Law, University of Indonesia 2009) [in Indonesian]

Elson RE, *Suharto: A Political Biography* (Cambridge University Press 2001)

England V, '"Coup Men" Freed after 33 Years in Jail' *South China Morning Post* (Hong Kong, 27 March 1999)

Erdianto K, 'Panglima TNI Akui Pernah Ada Oknum Tentara dalam Jaringan Peredaran Narkoba' (*Kompas*, 4 August 2016) <http://nasional.kompas.com/read/2016/08/04/19483581/panglima.tni.akui.pernah.ada.oknum.tentara.dalam.jaringan.peredaran.narkoba> accessed 29 November 2017 [in Indonesian]

Erlanger S, 'Intensive War on Drugs by Malaysia and Singapore Shows Mixed Results' *The New York Times* (15 December 1989)

Fairchild ES and Dammer HR, *Comparative Criminal Justice Systems* (Cengage Learning 2006)

Farrar SA, 'Crime and Criminal Justice in Malaysia' in Liu J et al (eds), *Handbook of Asian Criminology* (Springer 2013)

Faruqi S, *Document of Destiny: The Constitution of the Federation of Malaysia* (Star Publications 2008)

Fauziyah M, 'Indonesian Diplomatic Policy towards Malaysia on Indonesian Migrant Workers Faced Death Penalty 2010–2013' (Bachelor of Arts Thesis, Syarif Hidayatullah State Islamic University 2015)

Fealy G, *Release of Indonesia's Political Prisoners: Domestic versus Foreign Policy, 1975–1979* (Monash Asia Institute 1995)

Federal Court of Malaysia, 'Malaysian Judicial Structure' (*Malaysian Judiciary*, 2004) <https://web.archive.org/web/20171031033103/http://www.kehakiman.gov.my/sites/default/files/document3/POJ-LAPORAN%20TAHUNAN/ENGLISH/IA-PT2.pdf> accessed 17 September 2018

Fernandez W, 'Real Villains in Nguyen Case' *The Straits Times* (Singapore, 3 December 2005)

Fidrus M, '21 Drug Traffickers Sentenced to Death, None Executed' *Jakarta Post* (14 January 2003)

Fidrus M, 'Tough Sentencing Not Stopping Drug Crime, Judge Says' *Jakarta Post* (31 May 2006)

Finch J and Tangprasit N, 'The Death Penalty Part I: Capital Punishment in Thailand' *Bangkok Post* (25 March 2012)

Firdaws N, 'Be Bold and Abolish Death Penalty, Government Told' (*Free Malaysia Today*, 26 March 2017) <http://www.freemalaysiatoday.com/category/nation/2017/03/26/be-bold-and-abolish-the-death-penalty-government-told/> accessed 17 September 2017

Fitzgerald E, 'The Privy Council and the Death Penalty—A Buried Treasure of Jurisprudence' (University of Sussex, Brighton, 4 May 2011) <http://www.sussex.ac.uk/video/sussexlectures/audio/edwardfitzgerald.mp3> accessed 11 December 2017

Fitzpatrick J, 'Nothing but the Truth? Transitional Regimes Confront the Past' (1995) 16 Michigan Journal of International Law 713

Freedom House, 'Freedom in the World: Malaysia' (*Freedom House*, 2002b) <http://www.freedomhouse.org/report/freedom-world/2002/Malaysia> accessed 8 April 2013

Freedom House, 'Freedom in the World: Singapore' (*Freedom House*, 2002a) <http://www.freedomhouse.org/report/freedom-world/2002/Singapore> accessed 8 April 2013

Freedom House, 'Freedom in the World: Thailand' (*Freedom House*, 2002c) <https://freedomhouse.org/report/freedom-world/2002/thailand> accessed 11 December 2017

Freedom House, 'Freedom in the World 2016' (*Freedom House*, 2016) <https://freedomhouse.org/report/freedom-world/freedom-world-2016> accessed 3 September 2017

Friedman H, 'Free at Last: Longest-Serving Farang at "Bangkok Hilton" Is Checking Out' (*Mail and Guardian Online*, 2 March 2012) <http://

mg.co.za/article/2012-03-02-free-at-last-longestserving-farang-bangkok-hilton-is-checking-out> accessed 25 March 2013
Friedman LM, *Crime and Punishment in American History* (Basic Books 1993)
Funston J, 'Malaysia: Developmental State Challenged' in Funston J (ed), *Government and Politics in Southeast Asia* (Zed Books 2001a)
Funston J, 'Thailand: Reform Politics' in Funston J (ed), *Government and Politics in Southeast Asia* (Zed Books 2001b)
Gallahue P and Lines R, *The Death Penalty for Drug Offences: Global Overview 2010* (International Harm Reduction Association 2010)
Gallahue P and Lines R, *The Death Penalty for Drug Offences: Global Overview 2015* (Harm Reduction International 2015)
Ganapathy N, 'Critical Realist Reflections on Crime and Social Control in Singapore' in Sheptycki J and Wardak A (eds), *Transnational & Comparative Criminology* (Routledge-Cavendish 2006)
Garland D, *Peculiar Institution: America's Death Penalty in an Age of Abolition* (Oxford University Press 2010)
Garland D, *Punishment and Modern Society: A Study in Social Theory* (Clarendon Press 1990)
Gay P, *Freud for Historians* (Oxford University Press 1985)
Ghui, 'The President's Power to Grant Stays of Execution Revisited' (*The Online Citizen,* 8 December 2011) <https://web.archive.org/web/20120110080436/http://theonlinecitizen.com/2011/12/the-president%E2%80%99s-power-to-grant-stays-of-execution-revisited/> accessed 11 December 2017
Giao VC, 'Capital Punishment in Vietnam: Status and Perspective' in Hodgkinson P (ed), *Capital Punishment: New Perspectives* (Ashgate Publishing 2013)
Gill M, 'Clemency for Lifers: The Only Road Out Is the Road Not Taken' (2010) 23(1) Federal Sentencing Reporter 21
Glasius M, *Foreign Policy on Human Rights: Its Influence on Indonesia under Soeharto* (Hart 1999)
Goodman J, *Cultures of the World: Thailand* (Marshall Cavendish 2004)
Greenberg DF and West V, 'Siting the Death Penalty Internationally' (2008) 33 Law and Social Inquiry 295
Gunawan R, 'Elegy Rodrigo Gularte: When Reason Is Executed Dead' in Koalisi untuk Hapus Hukuman Mati (HATI) (eds), *Unfair Trial: Analysis of Death Penalty Cases in Indonesia* (Imparsial 2016)
Haberkorn T, *In Plain Sight: Impunity and Human Rights in Thailand* (University of Wisconsin Press 2018)
Haberkorn T, 'The Hidden Transcript of Amnesty: The 6 October 1976 Massacre and Coup in Thailand' (2015) 47(1) Critical Asian Studies 44
Habib S, 'Pardons Board Not Sitting Regularly' (*The Star Online*, 27 September 2009) <http://thestar.com.my/news/story.asp?file=/2009/9/27/nation/4787425&sec=nation> accessed 15 June 2010

Hahm C, 'Law, Culture and the Politics of Confucianism' (2003) 16(2) Columbia Journal of Asian Law 253

Han WC, 'No Convincing Reason to Believe that the MDP Works' (*The Online Citizen*, 3 March 2010) <http://www.theonlinecitizen.com/2010/03/no-reason-that-mdp-works/> accessed 20 September 2011

Handley PM, *The King Never Smiles* (Yale University Press 2006)

Hands Off Cain, 'East Timor' (*Hands Off Cain*, 2017) <http://www.handsoffcain.info/bancadati/asia-middle-east-australia-and-oceania/east-timor-30000076> accessed 29 November 2017

Hands Off Cain, 'Indonesia' (*Hands Off Cain*, 1999–2017) <http://www.handsoffcain.info/bancadati.php?id_cont=23&id_state=30000285> accessed 13 December 2017

Hands Off Cain, 'Malaysia' (*Hands Off Cain*, 1999–2017) <http://www.handsoffcain.info/bancadati/asia-middle-east-australia-and-oceania/malaysia-30000257> accessed 11 December 2017

Hands Off Cain, 'Singapore' (*Hands Off Cain*, 1999–2017) <http://www.handsoffcain.info/bancadati.php?id_cont=23&id_state=30000254> accessed 13 December 2017

Hands Off Cain, 'Thailand' (*Hands Off Cain*, 1999–2017) <http://www.handsoffcain.info/bancadati.php?id_cont=23&id_state=30000011> accessed 13 December 2017

Hands Off Cain, 'Viet Nam' (*Hands Off Cain*, 2000) <http://www.handsoffcain.info/bancadati/schedastato.php?idstato=1136&idcontinente=23> accessed 13 December 2017

Hands Off Cain, 'Vietnam' (*Hands Off Cain*, 2009) <http://www.handsoffcain.info/bancadati/schedastato.php?idstato=12000023&idcontinente=23> accessed 13 December 2017

Hardie-Bick J et al, 'Introduction: Transnational and Comparative Criminology in a Global Perspective' in Sheptycki J and Wardak A (eds), *Transnational & Comparative Criminology* (Routledge-Cavendish 2006)

Harding A, 'Comparative Law and Legal Transplantation in South East Asia' in Nelken D and Feest J (eds), *Adapting Legal Cultures* (Hart 2001)

Harding A, 'Global Doctrine and Local Knowledge: Law in South East Asia' (2002) 51(1) The International and Comparative Law Quarterly 35

Harding A and Leyland P, *The Constitutional System of Thailand: A Contextual Analysis* (Hart Publishing 2011)

Harding A and Leyland P, *Law, Government and the Constitution in Malaysia* (Kluwer Law International 1996)

Harding A and Leyland P, 'Monarchy and the Prerogative in Malaysia' (1986) 28 Malayan Law Review 345

Hargreaves J, 'On Death Penalty' *Jakarta Post* (30 October 2004)

Harring SL, 'Death, Drugs and Development: Malaysia's Mandatory Death Penalty for Traffickers and the International War on Drugs' (1991) 29 Columbia Journal of Transnational Law 365

Harris J and Redmond L, 'Executive Clemency: The Lethal Absence of Hope' (2007) 3 Criminal Law Brief 2

Haryoso, 'Capital Punishment still Needed, Says Muladi' *Jakarta Post* (22 July 1997)

Hashim MS, *An Introduction to the Constitution of Malaysia* (2nd edn, Malaysian Government Printer 1976)

Hawkins K, 'The Use of Legal Discretion: Perspectives from Law and Social Science' in Hawkins K (ed), *The Uses of Discretion* (Clarendon Press 1992)

Hay D, 'Writing About the Death Penalty' (2006) 10 Legal History 35

Hay D et al, *Albion's Fatal Tree: Crime and Society in Eighteenth-Century England* (Allen Lane 1975)

Hector C, 'Death Penalty in Malaysia: Time for Abolition Is Now' (*Slideshare*, 12 May 2012) <http://www.slideshare.net/easytocall/death-penalty-in-malaysia-time-for-abolition-bc> accessed 25 March 2013

Hector C, 'Motion on Royal Pardon and the Death Penalty' (Resolution Adopted at the 69th Annual General Meeting of the Malaysian Bar, Kuala Lumpur, 14 March 2015) <http://madpet06.blogspot.hk/2015/03/malaysian-bar-resolution-on-royal.html> accessed 12 December 2017

Hector C, 'Putting an End to Mandatory Death Penalty for Drug Offences' (*Aliran*, 9 August 2017) <https://aliran.com/civil-society-voices/2017-civil-society-voices/end-mandatory-death-penalty-drug-offences/> accessed 29 November 2017

Heise M, 'The Death of Death Row Clemency and the Evolving Politics of Unequal Grace' (2015) 66 Alabama Law Review 949

Heise M, 'The Geography of Mercy: An Empirical Analysis of Clemency for Death Row Inmates' (2013) 39 Thurgood Marshall Law Review 3

Heise M, 'Mercy by the Numbers: An Empirical Analysis of Clemency and its Structure' (2003) 89 Virginia Law Review 239

Heng TTW, 'Life after Abdul Nasir' (1998) 9 Singapore Law Review 104

Hickling RH, 'Recent Constitutional and Legal Developments in Thailand' (1973) 3 Hong Kong Law Journal 215

Hoffman J, 'Seeking Clemency in a Labyrinth that Varies by State' *The New York Times* (4 February 1998)

Hood R, 'Enhancing EU Action on the Death Penalty in Asia' (*European Parliament,* 17 October 2012) <http://www.europarl.europa.eu/RegData/etudes/note/join/2012/457068/EXPO-DROI_NT(2012)457068_EN.pdf> accessed 18 November 2017

Hood R, *The Death Penalty: A Worldwide Perspective* (3rd edn, Oxford University Press 2002)
Hood R, *The Death Penalty: A World-Wide Perspective: A Report to the United Nations Committee on Crime Prevention and Control* (Clarendon Press 1989)
Hood R, 'The Death Penalty in Malaysia: Public Opinion on the Mandatory Death Penalty for Drug Trafficking, Murder and Firearms Offences' (*The Death Penalty Project*, 2013) <https://web.archive.org/web/20171031015226/http://www.deathpenaltyproject.org:80/wp-content/uploads/2013/07/Malaysia-report.pdf> accessed 29 November 2017
Hood R and Hoyle C, 'Abolishing the Death Penalty Worldwide: The Impact of a "New Dynamic"' (2009) 38(1) Crime and Justice 1
Hood R and Hoyle C, *The Death Penalty: A Worldwide Perspective* (4th edn, Oxford University Press 2008)
Hood R and Hoyle C, *The Death Penalty: A Worldwide Perspective* (5th edn, Oxford University Press 2015)
Hooker MB, 'Introduction: Islamic Law in South-East Asia' (2002) 4(3) Australian Journal of Asian Law 213
Hor M, 'Death, Drugs, Murder and the Constitution' in Teo KS (ed), *Singapore Academy of Law Conference 2006: Developments in Singapore Law Between 2001 and 2005* (Academy Publishing 2006)
Hor M, 'The Death Penalty in Singapore and International Law' [2004] Singapore Year Book of International Law 105
Hor M, 'The Independence of the Criminal Justice System in Singapore' [2002] Singapore Journal of Legal Studies 497
Hor M, 'Singapore's Death Penalty: The Beginning of the End?' in Hood R and Surya D (eds), *Confronting Capital Punishment in Asia: Human Rights, Politics and Public Opinion* (Oxford University Press 2013)
Horigan DP, 'Of Compassion and Capital Punishment: A Buddhist Perspective on the Death Penalty' (1996) 41(1) American Journal of Jurisprudence 271
Hubert T, 'Study Explores Variety of National Paths to Abolition' (*World Coalition against the Death Penalty*, 3 May 2013) <http://www.worldcoalition.org/international-commission-against-death-penalty-icdp-mayor-paths-abolition-countries-culture-religion-repeal.html> accessed 29 November 2017
Hubert T, 'Thai Seminars Explore Religious Perspectives on the Death Penalty' (*World Coalition against the Death Penalty*, 4 August 2008) <http://www.worldcoalition.org/Thai-seminars-explore-religious-perspectives-on-the-death-penalty.html> accessed 15 June 2010
Human Rights Commission of Malaysia, 'Report on Standing Issues' (8th Annual Meeting of the Asia Pacific Forum of National Human Rights

Institutions, Kathmandu, 16–18 February 2004) <http://web.archive.org/web/20150702132237/http://www.asiapacificforum.net/about/annual-meetings/8th-nepal-2004/downloads/report-from-apf-members-on-acj-standing-issues/malaysia_acj.pdf> accessed 12 December 2017

Human Rights Watch, 'Convicted before Trial: Indefinite Detention under Malaysia's Emergency Ordinance' (*Human Rights Watch*, 23 August 2006) <https://www.hrw.org/report/2006/08/23/convicted-trial/indefinite-detention-under-malaysias-emergency-ordinance> accessed 12 December 2017

Human Rights Watch, 'End the Death Penalty for Drug-Related Offenses' (*Human Rights Watch*, 22 June 2009) <http://www.hrw.org/en/news/2009/06/22/end-death-penalty-drug-related-offenses> accessed 15 June 2010

Human Rights Watch and Amnesty International, 'Indonesia: Release Prisoners of Conscience Now!' (*Human Rights Watch*, AI Index ASA 21/58/98, 4 June 1998) <https://www.hrw.org/legacy/reports98/indonesia/indo1-0.htm> accessed 12 December 2017

Hunt B, *Australia's Northern Shield: Papua New Guinea and the Defence of Australia since 1880* (Monash University Publishing 2017)

Ibrahim A, 'The Malaysian Constitutional System' in Beer LW (ed), *Constitutional Systems in Late Twentieth Century Asia* (University of Washington Press 1992)

Imparsial, 'A Long Way to the Abolition of the Death Penalty in Indonesia' (*Gufron Mabruri*, June 2004) <https://gufronmabruri.files.wordpress.com/2008/09/a-long-way-to-the-abolition-of-the-death-penalty-in-indonesia-december2004.pdf> accessed 12 December 2017

Imparsial, *Evaluasi Praktik Hukuman Mati Pada Era Pemerintahan Jokowi* (Imparsial 2017) [in Indonesian]

Imparsial, *Inveighing against Death Penalty in Indonesia* (Imparsial 2010)

Indonesian Ministry of Law and Human Rights, 'Amnesti Indonesia Dataset' (Unpublished list of amnesty grants 2016, copy on file with the author) [in Indonesian]

Institute for Criminal Justice Reform, *Politik Kebijakan Hukuman Mati di Indonesia Masa ke Masa* (Institute for Criminal Justice Reform 2017) [in Indonesian]

International Commission of Jurists, *Ruler's Law: The Report of the International Commission of Jurists Mission to Indonesia* (International Commission of Jurists 1999)

International Federation for Human Rights, 'The Death Penalty for Drug Crimes in Asia Report' (*International Federation for Human Rights*, October 2015) <https://www.fidh.org/IMG/pdf/asia_death_penalty_drug_crimes_fidh_wcadp_report_oct_2015_pdf.pdf> accessed 17 November 2017

International Federation for Human Rights, 'The Death Penalty in Thailand' (*International Federation for Human Rights*, March 2005)

<http://www.fidh.org/IMG/pdf/Thailand411-2.pdf> accessed 15 June 2010

International Federation for Human Rights, 'Going Backwards: The Death Penalty in Southeast Asia' (*International Federation for Human Rights*, October 2016) <https://www.fidh.org/IMG/pdf/asie682apdmweb.pdf> accessed 14 December 2017

International Harm Reduction Association and Human Rights Watch, 'Thailand's "War on Drugs"' (*Human Rights Watch*, 12 March 2008) <https://www.hrw.org/news/2008/03/12/thailands-war-drugs> accessed 3 September 2017

Ivarsson S and Isager L, 'Introduction: Challenging the Standard Total View of the Thai Monarchy' in Ivarsson S and Isager L (eds), *Saying the Unsayable: Monarchy and Democracy in Thailand* (Nordic Institute of Asian Studies Press 2010)

Jackson PA, *Buddhism, Legitimation and Conflict: The Political Functions of Urban Thai Buddhism* (Institution of Southeast Asian Studies 1989)

Jaruboon C, *The Last Executioner: Memoirs of Thailand's Last Prison Executioner* (Maverick House 2006)

Jayakumar S, *Diplomacy: A Singaporean Experience* (Straits Times Press 2011)

Jayakumar S, 'Misuse of Drugs (Amendment) Bill (Singapore)' (Second Reading Speech, 30 November 1989)

Jayaphorn C, 'The Pardoning Power of the Kings of Thailand before the Reform of Legal and Judicial Systems' (*Thailand Law Journal*, 2011) <http://www.thailawforum.com/articles/pardoning-power-king-of-thailand-history.html> accessed 3 September 2017

Johnson DT, 'Asia's Declining Death Penalty' (2010) 69(2) The Journal of Asian Studies 337

Johnson DT, 'Capital Punishment—The Death Penalty Is Unnecessary' *Bangkok Post* (29 January 2009)

Johnson DT, 'The Jolly Hangman, the Jailed Journalist, and the Decline of Singapore's Death Penalty' (2013) 8 Asian Criminology 41

Johnson DT and Zimring FE, 'Taking Capital Punishment Seriously' (2006) 1 Asian Criminology 89

Johnson DT and Zimring FE, *The Next Frontier: National Development, Political Change, and the Death Penalty in Asia* (Oxford University Press 2009)

Judicial System Monitoring Programme, 'Presidential Pardons and Commutation of Sentences: The Need for Regulation and Clarity' (*Judicial System Monitoring Programme*, October 2010) <https://web.archive.org/web/20121202111129/http://www.jsmp.minihub.org/English/webpage/pwp/JSMPSubmisaunindultubaMoJoct_e.pdf> accessed 12 December 2017

Junlakan LD et al, 'Contemporary Crime and Punishment in Thailand' in Liu J et al (eds), *Handbook of Asian Criminology* (Springer 2013)

Kamariah M, 'Amendments to the Dangerous Drugs Act, 1952' [1988] Jurnal Undang-Undang 131

Kaminer W, *It's All the Rage: Crime and Culture* (Addison-Wesley 1995)

Kaye L, 'The Killing Time' *Far Eastern Economic Review* (Hong Kong, 27 June 1985)

Kelly N, 'Australian Drug Trafficker Faces Death by Machinegun' *The Sydney Morning Herald* (22 October 1985)

Kelly N, 'Briton Accused of Drugs Dealing' *The Times* (London, 4 April 1991)

Kelly N, 'Sydney Woman Faces Death by Machinegun' *Sydney Morning Herald* (16 June 1988)

Kencana MA, 'Yudhoyono Defends Clemency Gaffe' *Jakarta Globe* (9 November 2012)

Kent SL, 'Predicting Abolition: A Cross-National Survival Analysis of the Social and Political Determinants of Death Penalty Statutes' (2010) 20(1) International Criminal Justice Review 56

Kershaw R, *Monarchy in South-East Asia: The Faces of Tradition in Transition* (Routledge 2001)

Keyes C, 'Buddhism, Human Rights, and Non-Buddhist Minorities' in Banchoff T and Wuthnow R (eds), *Religion and the Global Politics of Human Rights* (Oxford University Press 2011)

Khairulrijal R, 'Reprieve for Prisoners on Death Row' *New Straits Times* (Kuala Lumpur, 5 May 2015) <https://www.nst.com.my/news/2015/09/reprieve-prisoners-death-row> accessed 17 September 2017

Khalik A, 'Police Seek Go-Ahead to Execute Drug Convicts' *Jakarta Post* (21 June 2004)

Kim D, 'International Non-Governmental Organizations and the Abolition of the Death Penalty' (2015) 22(3) European Journal of International Relations 1

King P, 'Decision-Makers and Decision-Making in the English Criminal Law, 1750–1800' (1984) 27 Historical Journal 42

King P and Ward R, 'Rethinking the Bloody Code in Eighteenth-Century Britain: Capital Punishment at the Centre and on the Periphery' (2015) 228(1) Past and Present 159

Kobil DT, 'Chance and the Constitution in Capital Clemency Cases' (2000) 28 Capital University Law Review 567

Kobil DT, 'Due Process in Death Penalty Commutations: Life, Liberty, and the Pursuit of Clemency' (1992–3) 27 University of Richmond Law Review 201

Kobil DT, 'The Evolving Role of Clemency in Capital Cases' in Acker J et al (eds), *America's Experiment with Capital Punishment: Reflections on the Past, Present and Future of the Ultimate Penal Sanction* (Carolina Academic Press 1998)

Kobil DT, 'How to Grant Clemency in Unforgiving Times' (2003) 31 Capital University Law Review 219

Kobil DT, 'Should Mercy Have a Place in Clemency Decisions?' in Sarat A and Hussain N (eds), *Forgiveness, Mercy and Clemency* (Stanford University Press 2007)

Kobil DT, 'The Quality of Mercy Strained: Wresting the Pardoning Power from the King' (1991) 69 Texas Law Review 569

Kohli A et al, 'The Role of Theory in Comparative Politics: A Symposium' (1995) 48(1) World Politics 1

KontraS, 'Capital Punishment in Indonesia: Update 2012–2013' (*KontraS*, June 2013) <https://www.kontras.org/data/Capital%20Punishment%20in%20Indonesia%20Update%202012-2013.pdf> accessed 25 September 2017

KontraS, 'Death Penalty Log' (*KontraS*, 2010) <https://www.kontras.org/data/Update%20Death%20Penalty%20Log%202010%20-%20KontraS.pdf> accessed 25 September 2017

KontraS, 'Death Penalty Log in Indonesia: Updated 30 April 2016' (*KontraS*, 30 April 2016) <https://www.kontras.org/data/20160519_Data_Hukuman_Mati_di_Indonesia_2016_8uh1235r8uyb.pdf> accessed 25 September 2017

Kow KS, *Sentencing Principles in Singapore* (Academy Publishing 2009)

Kowitwanij W, 'Bangkok, Drug Traffickers Executed by Lethal Injection' (*Asianews.it*, 26 August 2009) <http://www.asianews.it/news-en/Bangkok,-drug-traffickers-executed-by-lethal-injection-16147.html> accessed 13 December 2017

Kraemer J, 'An Empirical Examination of the Factors Associated with the Commutation of State Death Row Prisoners' Sentences between 1986 and 2005' (2008) 45 American Criminal Law Review 1389

Kulasegaran M, 'Let's Say No to the Death Penalty' (*Malaysiakini*, 22 August 2016) <https://www.malaysiakini.com/news/353200> accessed 14 December 2017

Kuppusamy B, 'Death Penalty: Beijing Sentences Shakes Malaysia's Own Policy' *Inter Press Service News* (Rome, 23 January 2008)

Kuppusamy B, 'Death Penalty—Singapore: Stand at UN Leaves Many Angered' *Inter Press Service* (Rome, 3 December 2007)

Kurniawati D, 'Executed Indonesian Drug Dealer's Tale of High-Level Help' *Asia Sentinel* (Hong Kong, 10 August 2016) <https://www.asiasentinel.com/politics/executed-indonesia-drug-dealer-story/> accessed 29 November 2017

Kwhankhom A, 'Cold Comfort for 100 on Death Row' *The Nation* (Bangkok, 1 February 2001)

Lamb K, 'Indonesia: Families Told that 14 Death Row Prisoners will Be Executed Tonight' *The Guardian* (London, 28 July 2016) <https://www.theguardian.com/world/2016/jul/28/indonesia-death-row-prisoners-executed-tonight> accessed 25 September 2017

Landes WM and Posner RA, 'The Economics of Presidential Pardons and Commutations' (2009) 38 Journal of Legal Studies 61

Langit R, 'Indonesia: End Death Penalty, Rights Groups Urge' *Inter Press Service* (Rome, 6 October 2004)
Lardner G and Colgate Love M, 'Mandatory Sentences and Presidential Mercy: The Role of Judges in Pardon Cases, 1790–1850' (2004) 16(3) Federal Sentencing Reporter 212
Laurin JE, 'Gideon By the Numbers: The Emergence of Evidence-Based Practice in Indigent Defense' (2015) 12 Ohio State Journal of Criminal Law 325
Lavinsky M, 'Executive Clemency: Study of a Decisional Problem Arising in the Terminal Stages of the Criminal Process' (1965) 42(1) Chicago-Kent Law Review 13
Ledewitz B and Staples S, 'The Role of Executive Clemency in Modern Death Penalty Cases' (1993) 27 University of Richmond Law Review 227
Lee HP, *Constitutional Conflicts in Contemporary Malaysia* (2nd edn, Oxford University Press 2017)
Lee JTT, 'The Court of Appeal's Lack of Jurisdiction to Reopen Appeals' [1994] Singapore Journal of Legal Studies 431
Lee JTT, 'The Past, Present and Future of the Internal Security Act' (*bepress*, 4 June 2012) <https://works.bepress.com/jacklee/16/> accessed 12 December 2017
Lee SG, *From Lee Kuan Yew to Goh Chok Tong* (Shing Lee Publishers 1991)
Lee SK, 'Prosecutorial Discretion and Clemency in the Singapore Criminal Justice System' in Teo KS (ed), *Singapore Academy of Law Conference 2006: Developments in Singapore Law between 2001 and 2005* (Academy Publishing 2006)
Leech BL, 'Interview Methods in Political Science' (2002) 35(4) Political Science and Politics 663
Leechaianan Y and Longmire DR, 'The Use of the Death Penalty for Drug Trafficking in the United States, Singapore, Malaysia, Indonesia and Thailand: A Comparative Legal Analysis' (2013) 2(2) Laws 115
Lefevre A, 'Soaring Prison Population Prompts Thailand to Re-Think "Lost" Drug War' *Reuters* (London, 17 July 2016) <http://www.reuters.com/article/us-drugs-thailand-prisons-idUSKCN0ZX01J> accessed 3 September 2017
Lent JA, 'Human Rights in Malaysia' (1984) 14(4) Journal of Contemporary Asia 442
Lev D, 'The Criminal Regime: Criminal Process in Indonesia' in Rafael VL (ed), *Figures of Criminality in Indonesia, the Philippines and Colonial Vietnam* (Cornell University Press 1999)
Lev D, *No Concessions: The Life of Yap Thiam Hien, Indonesian Human Rights Lawyer* (University of Washington Press 2011)
Levett C, 'Fighting against the Tide of Opinion' *The Age* (Melbourne 5 November 2005)

Liang HL et al, 'Sources of Variation in Pro-Death Penalty Attitudes in China' (2006) 46 British Journal of Criminology 119

Liddle RW, 'Indonesia's Unexpected Failure of Leadership' in Schwarz A and Paris J (eds), *The Politics of Post-Suharto Indonesia* (Council on Foreign Relations Press 1999)

Lijphart A, 'Comparative Politics and the Comparative Method' (1971) 65(3) The American Political Science Review 682

Lilleker DG, 'Interviewing the Political Elite: Navigating a Potential Minefield' (2003) 23 Politics 207

Lim KS, 'Call on Malaysians of All Races to Respond to the Save Sim Kie Chon Signature Campaign in the Way the People Responded to the DAP's Save 13-Condemned Signature Campaign in 1968' (*Pursuit of a Malaysian Dream*, 28 July 1985) <https://bibliotheca.limkitsiang.com/1985/07/28/call-on-malaysians-of-all-races-to-respond-to-the-save-sim-kie-chon-signature-campaign-in-the-way-the-people-responded-to-the-dap%E2%80%99s-save-13-condemned-signature-campaign-in-1968/> accessed 12 December 2017

Lim L and Yong JA, '96% of S'poreans Back the Death Penalty' *The Straits Times* (Singapore, 12 February 2006)

Lindsey T, 'Drugs, the Death Penalty and the Bali Nine' (ALC/CILIS Evening Seminar, University of Melbourne, 21 April 2015) <https://storify.com/indoforummelb/tim-lindsey-drugs-the-death-penalty-and-the-bali-n> accessed 25 September 2017

Lindsey T, 'Muddling Through' (2006) 87 Inside Indonesia <http://www.insideindonesia.org/muddling-through> accessed 17 November 2017

Lindsey T, 'PM Kevin Rudd Government Dilemma over Executions' *Herald Sun* (Melbourne, 19 July 2008)

Lindsey T and Butt S, 'Unfinished Business: Law Reform, Governance, and the Courts in Post-Suharto Indonesia' in Kunkler M and Stepan A (eds), *Democracy and Islam in Indonesia* (Columbia University Press 2013)

Lindsey T and Kingsley J, 'Other Ways of Doing Justice' *Herald Sun* (Melbourne, 11 September 2006)

Lindsey T and Nicholson P, *Drugs Law and Legal Practice in Southeast Asia: Indonesia, Singapore and Vietnam* (Bloomsbury 2016)

Lindsey T and Santosa MA, 'The Trajectory of Law Reform in Indonesia: A Short Overview of Legal Systems and Change in Indonesia' in Lindsey T (ed), *Indonesia: Law and Society* (2nd edn, Federation Press 1999)

Lindsey T et al, 'Early Plea for Clemency May Be a Mistake' *The Australian* (Melbourne, 30 May 2005)

Lines R, *The Death Penalty for Drug Offences: A Violation of International Human Rights Law* (International Harm Reduction Association 2007)

Lingga H, 'Presiden Kabulkan Grasi Terpidana Mati Asal Sintang' (*Lintas Kapuas*, 22 January 2015) <http://www.lintaskapuas.com/presiden-kabulkan-grasi-terpidana-mati-asal-sintang/> accessed 25 September 2017 [in Indonesian]

Linggasari Y, 'Pemerintah Diminta Pelajari Efektivitas Hukuman Mati' (*CNN Indonesia*, 6 January 2016) <https://www.cnnindonesia.com/nasional/20160105195259-20-102392/pemerintah-diminta-pelajari-efektivitas-hukuman-mati/> accessed 14 December 2017 [in Indonesian]

Liu RTK, 'The King Can Pardon Anwar Only with Advice from PM' (*Democratic Action Party Malaysia*, 22 October 2003) <https://dapmalaysia.org/all-archive/English/2003/oct03/bul/bul2292.htm> accessed 14 December 2017

Lum S, 'Apex Court Clears Air on A-G's Power' *Straits Times* (Singapore, 11 January 2012)

Luong HT, 'The Application of the Death Penalty for Drug-Related Crimes in Vietnam: Law, Policy, and Practice' (*Thailand Law Journal*, 2014) <http://www.thailawforum.com/articles/Vietnam-death-penalty.html> accessed 12 December 2017

Lynch C, 'Indonesia's Use of Capital Punishment for Drug-Trafficking Crimes: Legal Obligations, Extralegal Factors, and the Bali Nine Case' (2009) 40 Columbia Human Rights Law Review 523

Majid MM, *Criminal Procedure in Malaysia* (University of Malaya Press 1995)

Mala D, 'Parting Words to the Condemned' (*Bangkok Post*, 13 February 2018) <https://www.bangkokpost.com/news/general/1411567/parting-words-to-the-condemned> accessed 26 September 2018

Malakunas, 'Executions on the Rise in Asia, the Death Penalty Capital of the World' *Agence France Presse* (Paris, 18 January 2004)

Mallinder L, *Amnesty, Human Rights and Political Transitions: Bridging the Peace and Justice Divide* (Bloomsbury Publishing 2008)

Mandery EJ, *Capital Punishment: A Balanced Examination* (Jones and Bartlett 2005)

Markham S and Phillips M, 'Clemency Plea Last Hope for Death Row Man' *Australian Associated Press General News* (Sydney, 20 October 2004)

Marshall G, *Constitutional Theory* (Clarendon Press 1971)

Marszalek J, 'Bali Nine Member Andrew Chan's Death Sentence Reportedly Upheld after Drug Smuggler's Clemency Bid Suffers Setback' (*news.com.au*, 27 March 2013) <http://www.news.com.au/national-news/bali-nine-member-andrew-chans-death-sentence-reportedly-upheld-after-drug-smugglers-clemency-bid-suffers-setback/story-fncynjr2-1226607459613> accessed 9 September 2013

MARUAH, 'Universal Periodic Review—Singapore' (*Office of the United Nations High Commissioner for Human Rights*, 2011) <http://lib.ohchr.org/HRBodies/UPR/Documents/session11/SG/MARUAH_WorkingGroupforanAseanHumanRightsMechanism-eng.pdf> accessed 25 March 2013

Mayberry K, 'Executing Drug Dealers in Southeast Asia' *Al Jazeera* (Doha, 22 June 2015) <http://www.aljazeera.com/indepth/features/2015/06/executing-drug-dealers-southeast-asia-150622060018374.html> accessed 14 December 2017

McDermott Y, '*Yong Vui Kong v. Public Prosecutor* and the Mandatory Death Penalty for Drug Offences in Singapore: A Dead End for Constitutional Challenge' (2010) 1 International Journal on Human Rights and Drug Policy 35

McDonald A, 'No Saving Bali Kingpins: New Envoy' *The Australian* (Melbourne, 7 March 2006)

McEvoy K, 'Beyond Legalism: Towards a Thicker Understanding of Transitional Justice' (2007) 34(4) Journal of Law and Society 411

McGann A and Sandholtz W, 'Patterns of Death Penalty Abolition, 1960–2005: Domestic and International Factors' (2012) 56 International Studies Quarterly 275

McMahon J, 'The Death Penalty in Singapore: Issues and Developments' (International Conference on the Death Penalty in Comparative Perspective: Regional Laws and Practice, Ho Chi Minh University of Law, March 2017)

McRae D, 'A Key Domino? Indonesia's Death Penalty Politics' (*Lowy Institute*, 2012) <https://archive.lowyinstitute.org/sites/default/files/mcrae_a_key_domino_web-1_0.pdf> accessed 23 September 2018

McRae D, 'Indonesian Capital Punishment in Comparative Perspective' (2017) 173 Bijdragen tot de Taal-, Land- en Volkenkunde/Journal of the Humanities and Social Sciences of Southeast Asia 1

McRae D, '"Jokowi" and His Firing Squads' *Strategic Review* (Jakarta, July-September 2015) <http://www.sr-indonesia.com/in-the-journal/view/jokowi-and-his-firing-squads> accessed 23 September 2018

McRae D, 'Shot until Dead' (2008) 94 Inside Indonesia <http://www.insideindonesia.org/shot-until-dead-2> accessed 23 September 2018

McRae D, 'Staying the Executioners' Guns?' (2013) 111 Inside Indonesia <http://www.insideindonesia.org/staying-the-executioners-guns> accessed 25 September 2017

Mehat H, *Malaysian Law and Islamic Law on Sentencing* (International Law Book Services 1991)

Merriam SB, 'What Can You Tell from an N of 1? Issues of Validity and Reliability in Qualitative Research' (1995) 4 PAACE Journal of Lifelong Learning 51

Metcalf K, *Near Neighbours: Records on Australia's Relations with Indonesia* (National Archives of Australia 2001)

Meyer LR, 'The Merciful State' in Sarat A and Hussain N (eds), *Forgiveness, Mercy and Clemency* (Stanford University Press 2007)

Michelmore K, 'Bali Bombers Deaths "Soon as Possible"' *The Australian* (Melbourne, 21 July 2008)

Miethe TD et al, 'Cross-National Variability in Capital Punishment: Exploring the Sociopolitical Sources of Its Differential Legal Status' (2005) 15 International Criminal Justice Review 115

Millar P, 'Whatever Happened to … Thailand's Abolition of the Death Penalty?' (*Southeast Asia Globe*, 30 August 2018) <http://sea-globe.com/whatever-happened-to-thailands-abolition-of-the-death-penalty/> accessed 26 September 2018

Miller RL, 'Triangulation' in Miller RL and Brewer JD (eds), *The A to Z of Social Research* (Sage Publications 2003)

Ministry of Justice (UK), *The Governance of Britain: Review of the Executive Royal Prerogative Powers: Final Report* (Ministry of Justice (UK) 2009)

Mojapelo PM, 'The Doctrine of Separation of Powers: A South African Perspective' (2013) 26(1) Advocate 37

Moore KD, *Pardons: Justice, Mercy and the Public Interest* (Oxford University Press 1989)

Morison ST, 'The Politics of Grace: On the Moral Justification of Executive Clemency' (2006) 9(1) Buffalo Criminal Law Review 101

Moucarry C, *The Search for Forgiveness: Pardon and Punishment in Islam and Christianity* (Inter-Varsity Press 2004)

Mulia SM, 'Islam' (Conference Paper, 4th World Congress Against the Death Penalty, Geneva, 24–26 February 2010)

Mulya Lubis T, 'Death Penalty and the Road Ahead: The Case of Indonesia' (2015) Centre for Indonesian Law, Islam and Society Policy Papers 9 <https://law.unimelb.edu.au/__data/assets/pdf_file/0009/1685943/ALC-CILIS-Policy-Paper-9-Lubis_final.pdf> accessed 25 September 2017

Mulya Lubis T and Lay A, *Kontroversi Hukuman Mati* (Kompas 2009) [in Indonesian]

Mulyana A, 'KIP Sidangkan Setneg Soal Transparansi Pemberian Grasi' (*RMOL*, 15 February 2016) <http://www.rmol.co/read/2016/02/15/235813/KIP-Sidangkan-Setneg-Soal-Transparansi-Pemberian-Grasi-> accessed 25 September 2017 [in Indonesian]

Muntarbhorn V, 'Deconstructing Thailand's (New) Eighteenth Constitution' (*Thailand Law Journal*, 2009) <http://www.thailawforum.com/articles/Thailand-Eighteeth-Consititution.html> accessed 16 June 2010

Murdoch L, 'McAullife's Eight Years of Torment End in Death' *The Age* (Melbourne, 19 June 1993)

Murray A, 'Decades on Death Row' *Green Left Weekly* (Ultimo, 10 April 1991)

National Human Rights Commission of Indonesia, 'Annual Report 2006' (*KOMNAS HAM*, 2007) <https://web.archive.org/web/20101202200005/http://www.komnasham.go.id/portal/files/Annual.pdf> accessed 30 November 2018

Ndiaye BW, 'Report by the Special Rapporteur, Mr. Bacre Waly Ndiaye, submitted pursuant to Commission on Human Rights resolution 1995/73' (UN Doc E/CN.4/1996/4, 25 January 1996)

Nelken D, 'Comparative Criminal Justice' in Maguire M et al (eds), *The Oxford Handbook of Criminology* (3rd edn, Oxford University Press 2002)

Nelken D, *Comparative Criminal Justice: Making Sense of Difference* (Sage 2010)

Nelken D, 'Why Compare Criminal Justice' in Bosworth M and Hoyle C (eds), *What Is Criminology?* (Oxford University Press 2011)

Neuman WL, *Social Research Methods: Qualitative and Quantitative Approaches* (6th edn, Allyn & Bacon 2005)

Neumayer E, 'Death Penalty Abolition and the Ratification of the Second Optional Protocol' (2008b) 12 (1) The International Journal of Human Rights 3

Neumayer E, 'Death Penalty: The Political Foundations of the Global Trend Towards Abolition' (2008a) 9 Human Rights Review 241

New JL, 'Anwar's Last Hope Is a Pardon from the Agong, But Do These Things Come Easy? We Check' (*CILISOS*, 15 December 2016) <https://cilisos.my/is-a-royal-pardon-the-last-resort-for-anwar-but-how-easy-is-it-to-get-pardoned/> accessed 17 September 2017

Newman G and Howard GJ, 'Introduction' in Newman G and Howard GJ (eds), *Varieties of Contemporary Criminology* (Brill 2001)

Ngoo I, 'Jaya: Untenable to Make Exception' *The Straits Times* (Singapore, 24 September 1994)

Ngui CYK, 'Lawful Battles' *New Straits Times* (Kuala Lumpur, 16 August 2005)

Nguyen TPH, 'Drug-Related Crimes under Vietnamese Criminal Law: Sentencing and Clemency in Law and Practice' (2014) 8 Centre for Indonesian Law Islam and Society Policy Papers <http://law.unimelb.edu.au/__data/assets/pdf_file/0011/1547093/ALC-CILISPolicyPaper_Hoa_finalwobleed3.pdf> accessed 23 January 2016

Nicholson P, 'Legal Culture "Repacked": Drug Trials in Vietnam' in Nicholson P and Biddulph S (eds), *Examining Practice, Interrogating Theory: Comparative Legal Studies in Asia* (Martinus Nijhoff 2008)

Nicholson P, 'The Death Penalty and Its Reduction in Asia: An Overview' (2017) 10 Asian Law Centre Briefing Papers <https://law.unimelb.edu.au/__data/assets/pdf_file/0010/2675386/Nicholson-EN_final.pdf> accessed 17 January 2019

Nicholson P and Truong K, 'Drugs Prosecutions in Vietnam: The Modern Propaganda Trial' (2008) 34(2) Monash University Law Review 430

Novak A, *Comparative Executive Clemency: The Constitutional Pardon Power and the Prerogative of Mercy in Global Perspective* (Routledge 2015)

Novak A, *The Global Decline of the Mandatory Death Penalty: Constitutional Jurisprudence and Legislative Reform in Africa, Asia, and the Caribbean* (Routledge 2014)

Novak A, 'Transparency and Comparative Executive Clemency: Global Lessons for Pardon Reform in the United States' (2016) 49(4) University of Michigan Journal of Law Reform 817 (2016)

Nygh PE and Butt P (eds), *Butterworths Concise Australian Legal Dictionary* (2nd edn, Butterworths 1998)

Oehlers A and Tarulevicz N, 'Capital Punishment and the Culture of Developmentalism in Singapore' in Sarat A and Boulanger C (eds), *Cultural Lives of Capital Punishment* (Stanford University Press 2005)

Osman N, 'Malaysia Asked to Spare 3 Traffickers Facing Death' *Jakarta Globe* (19 September 2010)

Othman Z, 'From Death Sentence to Life in Prison to Freedom' *The New Paper* (Singapore, 23 January 2012)

Oxford Pro Bono Publico, 'Zedekia Gainob and Two Others v the State: A Report on Life Imprisonment' (*Oxford Human Rights Hub*, March 2016) <http://ohrh.law.ox.ac.uk/wordpress/wp-content/uploads/2016/09/Namibia-Report-FINAL-VERSION.pdf> accessed 12 December 2017

Øyen E, 'The Imperfection of Comparisons' in Øyen E (ed), *Comparative Methodology: Theory and Practice in International Social Research* (Sage 1990)

Pakes F, *Comparative Criminal Justice* (3rd edn, Routledge 2015)

Palansamy Y, 'End of Malaysia's Mandatory Death Sentence on the Horizon' (*Malaymail Online*, 17 November 2015) <http://www.themalaymailonline.com/malaysia/article/end-of-malaysias-mandatory-death-sentence-on-horizon#EK8chhgojulCeGHt.97> accessed 17 September 2017

Parliamentary Monitoring Group, 'The Power to Pardon' (*Amazon AWS*, 2004) <http://pmg-assets.s3-website-eu-west-1.amazonaws.com/docs/2004/appendices/040218pardon.htm> accessed 2 September 2017

Parlina I et al, 'Jokowi Refuses to Budge on Clemency Issue' *Jakarta Post* (21 January 2015) <http://www.thejakartapost.com/news/2015/01/21/jokowi-refuses-budge-clemency-issue.html> accessed 26 August 2017

Parsons T, 'The Role of Theory in Social Research' (1938) 3(1) American Sociological Review 13

Pasandaran C and Sihombing EC, 'Indonesia Executes First Convict in Four Years' *Jakarta Globe* (15 March 2013)

Pascoe D, 'Clemency in Southeast Asian Death Penalty Cases' (2014) Centre for Indonesian Law, Islam and Society Policy Papers 1 <http://law.unimelb.edu.au/__data/assets/pdf_file/0003/1547094/ALC-CILISPolicyPaper_Pascoe_web2.pdf> accessed 26 August 2017

Pascoe D, 'Comparing Death Penalty Clemency in Singapore and Thailand' in Lu J et al (eds), *Comparative Criminology in Asia* (Springer 2017b)

Pascoe D, 'Explaining Death Penalty Clemency in the Socialist Republic of Vietnam' (2016a) 10(2) Vienna Journal on International Constitutional Law 165

Pascoe D, 'The Functions of Death Penalty Clemency in Southeast Asia: Comparative Lessons for Vietnam' (2017c) 7 Asian Law Centre Briefing Papers <https://law.unimelb.edu.au/centres/alc/research/publications/alc-briefing-paper-series/the-functions-of-death-penalty-clemency-in-southeast-asia-comparative-lessons-for-vietnam> accessed 21 August 2018

Pascoe D, 'Is *Diya* a Form of Clemency?' (2016c) 34(1) Boston University International Law Journal 149

Pascoe D, 'Legal Dilemmas in Releasing Indonesia's Political Prisoners' (2017a) 7(3) Indonesia Law Review 313

Pascoe D, 'Researching the Death Penalty in Closed or Partially-Closed Criminal Justice Systems' in Bosworth M et al (eds), *Changing Contours of Criminal Justice* (Oxford University Press 2016b)

Pascoe D, 'Su'ud Rusli's Constitutional Court Challenge: Overhauling Clemency in Indonesian Death Penalty Cases?' (2019a) 19(2) Australian Journal of Asian Law (forthcoming)

Pascoe D, 'Towards a Global Theory of Capital Clemency Incidence' in Steiker C and Steiker J (eds), *Comparative Capital Punishment Law* (Edward Elgar 2019b, forthcoming)

Pascoe D and Miao M, 'Victim-Perpetrator Reconciliation Agreements in Murder Cases: What Can Muslim-Majority Jurisdictions and the PRC Learn from Each Other?' (2017) 66(4) International & Comparative Law Quarterly 963

Penna LR, 'Pardoning Power and the "Saga" of Sim Kie Chon' (1987) 8 Singapore Law Review 106

Perry A, 'Mercy and Caprice under the Indian Constitution' (2017) 1(1) Indian Law Review 56

Perry N, 'Winning a Battle, Losing the War' (2009) 96 Inside Indonesia <http://www.insideindonesia.org/winning-a-battle-losing-the-war> accessed 23 September 2018

Peters R, *Crime and Punishment in Islamic Law: Theory and Practice from the Sixteenth to the Twenty-First Century* (Cambridge University Press 2006)

Peters R, 'Please Pick Mummy Up from Prison' *New Paper* (Singapore, 17 February 1995)

Phang ABL, *Development of Singapore Law: Historical and Socio-Legal Perspectives* (Butterworths 1990)

Pillai J, 'Winning Edge in War against Dadah' *New Straits Times* (Kuala Lumpur, 28 June 1990)

Pompe S, *The Indonesian Supreme Court: A Study of Institutional Collapse* (Cornell University Press 2005)

Postawko R, 'Towards an Islamic Critique of Capital Punishment' (2002) 1 UCLA Journal of Islamic and Near Eastern Law 269

Pouaree S, 'Letting Drug Pushers Off the Hook' *Bangkok Post* (3 October 1999a)

Pouaree S, 'Setting a Late Example' *Bangkok Post* (3 October 1999b)

Pridemore WA, 'An Empirical Examination of Commutations and Executions in Post-*Furman* Capital Cases' (2000) 17(1) Justice Quarterly 159

Quah JST, 'Singapore: Meritocratic City-State' in Funston J (ed), *Government and Politics in Southeast Asia* (Zed 2001)

Rachman A, 'Clemency Law Amended as Requests Spill Over' *Jakarta Globe* (27 July 2010)

Rajah J, *Authoritarian Rule of Law: Legislation, Discourse and Legitimacy in Singapore* (Cambridge University Press 2012)

Rapaport E, 'Retribution and Redemption in the Operation of Executive Clemency' (1998-2000) 74 Chicago-Kent Law Review 1501

Rapaport E, 'Staying Alive: Executive Clemency, Equal Protection and the Politics of Gender in Women's Capital Cases' (2001) 4 Buffalo Criminal Law Review 967

Ravi M, *Hung at Dawn* (Orion Books 2005)

Reprieve, 'Annual Report 2012' (*Reprieve*, 2012a) <https://www.reprieve.org.uk/wp-content/uploads/2015/06/2013_07_31_PUB-5.-Reprieve-2012-Annual-Report.pdf> accessed 26 August 2017

Reprieve, 'Chi Fai Leung, Shun Wa Ng and Kam Chuen Leung' (Unpublished NGO Case Summary, copy on file with the author, 2012b)

Reprieve, 'Chu Tak Fai' (*Reprieve*, 2013) <https://web.archive.org/web/20141201083226/http://www.reprieve.org.uk/cases/chutakfai/> accessed 12 December 2017

Reprieve, 'EC Project Manual' (*Reprieve*, 2014) <https://www.reprieve.org.uk/wp-content/uploads/2015/01/2014_08_07_INT-EC-Project-Manual-FINAL-KEY-DOC.pdf> accessed 29 November 2017

Reza BI, 'Emergencies and Executions under Jokowi' (*New Mandala*, 15 August 2016) <http://www.newmandala.org/emergencies-executions-jokowi/> accessed 25 September 2017

Richards D, 'Elite Interviewing: Approaches and Pitfalls' (1996) 16 Politics 199

Richards D, 'Inveighing against Death Penalty in Indonesia' (*Anti-death Penalty Asia Network*, 30 June 2016) <https://adpan.org/2016/06/30/indonesia-inveighing-against-death-penalty-in-indonesia/> accessed 25 September 2017

Robertson G, *Crimes against Humanity: The Struggle for Global Justice* (3rd edn, Penguin 2006)
Rojanaphruk P, 'Dump the Death Penalty, Ex-Senator Urges' *The Nation* (Bangkok, 11 March 2012)
Roy A, 'Drug Case Briton to Be Hanged' *The Sunday Times* (London, 22 June 1986)
Ruckman P, 'The Study of Mercy: What Political Scientists Know (And Don't Know) about the Pardon Power' (2011) 9 University of St Thomas Law Journal 783
Sabdo AB, *Paradoks Pidana Mati* (Forthcoming) [in Indonesian]
Safi M, '"Am I being executed?" Brazilian Killed by Indonesia Unaware until End, Says Priest' *The Guardian* (London, 29 April 2015) <https://www.theguardian.com/world/2015/apr/30/brazilian-executed-by-indonesia-was-hearing-voices-all-the-time> accessed 12 December 2017
Sagita D, 'Indonesia Not Alone in Death Penalty Reticence: Ministers' *Jakarta Globe* (17 October 2012)
Sahetapy JE, *Ancaman pidana mati terhadap pembunuhan berencana* (Alumni 1979) [in Indonesian]
Sahid K, 'Pemberian Grasi Menurut Perundang-Undangan di Indonesia' (Dissertation, Sunan Ampel State Islamic University 2014) [in Indonesian]
Sajarwo G, 'Jokowi Tolak Permohonan Grasi 64 Terpidana Mati Kasus Narkoba' *Kompas* (Jakarta, 9 December 2014) <http://regional.kompas.com/read/2014/12/09/16545091/Jokowi.Tolak.Permohonan.Grasi.64.Terpidana.Mati.Kasus.Narkoba> accessed 25 September 2017 [in Indonesian]
Sakti M, 'Tiang Gantungan buat Ramli' *Tempo* (Jakarta, 30 August 1986) [in Indonesian]
Salinger LM, *Encyclopaedia of White-Collar & Corporate Crime* (Sage Publications 2005)
Salna K, 'Huge Blow to Chan's Bali Nine Clemency Bid' *Australian Associated Press* (Sydney, 26 March 2013)
Sander G, 'The Death Penalty for Drug Offences: Global Overview 2017' (*Harm Reduction International*, 9 March 2018) <https://www.hri.global/files/2018/03/06/HRI-Death-Penalty-Report-2018.pdf> accessed 22 September 2018
Saragih BBT, 'SBY Approves Clemency for 19 Drug Convicts' *Jakarta Post* (17 October 2012)
Sarat A, 'Between (the Presence of) Violence and (the Possibility of) Justice: Lawyering against Capital Punishment' in Sarat A and Scheingold S (eds), *Cause Lawyering: Political Commitments and Professional Responsibilities* (Oxford University Press 1998)

Sarat A, *Mercy on Trial: What It Means to Stop an Execution* (Princeton University Press 2005)

Sarat A, 'Memorializing Miscarriages of Justice: Clemency Petitions in the Killing State' (2008) 42(1) Law and Society Review 183

Sarat A and Hussain N, 'On Lawful Lawlessness: George Ryan, Executive Clemency, and the Rhetoric of Sparing Life' (2004) 56 Stanford Law Review 1307

Schabas W, 'Islam and the Death Penalty' (2000) 9 William and Mary Bill of Rights Journal 223

Schabas W, 'Hard-Core Executioners' in Zapatero A et al (eds), *Death Penalty: A Cruel and Inhuman Punishment* (Ediciones de la Universidad de Castilla-La Mancha 2013)

Schabas W, *The Abolition of the Death Penalty in International Law* (3rd edn, Cambridge University Press 2002)

Scholastica Gerintya, 'Jokowi Beri Grasi Kepada Napi Politik, Narkoba Tidak' (*Tirto.ID*, 14 August 2018) <https://tirto.id/jokowi-beri-grasi-kepada-napi-politik-narkoba-tidak-cSi1> accessed 26 September 2018 [in Indonesian]

Schwarz M, 'Deadly Traffic' *The New York Times* (22 March 1987)

Scott AW, 'The Pardoning Power' (1952) 284 Annals of the American Academy of Political and Social Science 95

Sebba L, 'Clemency in Perspective' in Landau S and Sebba L (eds), *Criminology in Perspective: Essays in Honour of Israel Drapkin* (Lexington Books 1977a)

Sebba L, 'The Pardoning Power: A World Survey' (1977b) 68(1) The Journal of Criminal Law and Criminology 83

Seldon A, 'Elite Interviews' in Brivati B et al (eds), *The Contemporary History Handbook* (Manchester University Press 1996)

Shadrake A, *Once a Jolly Hangman* (Strategic Information and Research Development Centre 2011a)

Shadrake A, *Once a Jolly Hangman* (Pier 9 2011b)

Shafee Abdullah M, 'A Deeper Impact beyond the Gallows' *New Straits Times* (Kuala Lumpur, 2 November 2012)

Shafee Abdullah M, 'It's Time to End the Death Penalty' *New Straits Times* (Kuala Lumpur, 1 November 2012)

Shane PM, 'Presidents, Pardons and Prosecutors: Legal Accountability and the Separation of Powers' (1993) 11(2) Yale Law and Policy Review 361

Shankar A, 'Time to Abolish Death Sentence' (*Free Malaysia Today*, 3 April 2011) <https://web.archive.org/web/20170830140538/http://www.freemalaysiatoday.com/category/nation/2011/04/03/time-to-abolish-death-sentence/> accessed 23 September 2018

Shanmugam K, 'Parliamentary Debate on the Motion on Drugs "Strengthening Singapore's Fight against Drugs"—Speech by Mr K Shanmugam, Minister for Home Affairs and Minister for Law'

(*Singapore Ministry of Home Affairs*, 5 April 2017) <https://www.mha.gov.sg/Newsroom/speeches/Pages/Parliamentary-Debate-on-the-Motion-on-Drugs-Strengthening-Singapores-Fight-Against-Drugs.aspx> accessed 12 December 2017

Shanmugam K, 'Response by Minister for Law, Mr K Shanmugam, during the Second Reading of the Misuse of Drugs (Amendment) Bill' (*Singapore Ministry of Law*, 14 November 2012) <http://www.mlaw.gov.sg/news/parliamentary-speeches-and-responses/response-by-minister-for-law--mr-k-shanmugam--during-the-second-.html> accessed 1 April 2013

Sharif S and Veera RV, '44 "Forgotten" Convicts' *New Straits Times* (Kuala Lumpur, 14 September 1997a)

Sharif S and Veera RV, 'Plight of the Forgotten Prisoners' *New Straits Times* (Kuala Lumpur, 14 September 1997b)

Shelley FM and Metz R, *Geography of Trafficking: From Drug Smuggling to Modern-Day Slavery* (ABC-CLIO 2017)

Sheridan M and Taher A, 'Execution of Bali Bombers Divides Victims' Families' *The Sunday Times* (London, 9 November 2008)

Sherwell P, 'Thailand Honors Half Century of Monarch's Rule' *Daily Telegraph* (London, 10 June 1996)

Sidel M, 'Law, the Press and Police Murder in Vietnam: The Vietnamese Press and the Trial of Nguyen Tung Duong' in Marr DG (ed), *Mass Media in Vietnam* (The Australian National University 1998)

Sihombing EC, 'Peradilan Tidak Fair, Hukuman Mati Jangan Dipaksakan' (*Berita Satu*, 9 September 2016) <http://www.beritasatu.com/nasional/384584-peradilan-tidak-fair-hukuman-mati-jangan-dipaksakan.html> accessed 14 December 2017 [in Indonesian]

Sijabat RM, 'Lawmakers Call Poso Executions Illegal' *Jakarta Post* (30 September 2006)

Silverstein G, 'Singapore: The Exception that Proves Rules Matter' in Ginsburg T and Moustafa T (eds), *Rule by Law: The Politics of Courts in Authoritarian Regimes* (Cambridge University Press 2008)

Singapore Anti Death Penalty Campaign, 'Universal Periodic Review on Singapore: For the 11th Session of UPR' (*Office of the United Nations High Commissioner for Human Rights*, May 2011) <http://lib.ohchr.org/HRBodies/UPR/Documents/session11/SG/SADPC_SingaporeAntiDeathPenaltyCampaign-eng.pdf> accessed 2 September 2017

Singapore Government, 'The Singapore Government's Response to Amnesty International's Report: "*Singapore—The Death Penalty: A Hidden Toll of Executions*"' (*National Archives of Singapore*, 30 January 2004) <http://www.nas.gov.sg/archivesonline/speeches/view-html?filename=2004013005.htm> accessed 11 September 2017

Singapore Ministry of Communications and Information, 'New Cabinet Announced' (*Singapore Government*, 28 September 2015) <https://www.gov.sg/news/content/new-cabinet-announced> accessed 11 September 2017

Singapore Prison Service, 'Enhancing Inmates' Employability to Prevent Re-Offending' (*Singapore Prison Service*, 14 February 2017) <https://web.archive.org/web/20170517060333/http://www.sps.gov.sg/Data/Editor/Documents/SPS%20Annual%20Stats%20Release%20for%202016%20(14%20Feb%202017)_For%20Upload.pdf> accessed 23 September 2018

Singh B, *Succession Politics in Indonesia* (Palgrave Macmillan 2000)

Singh J, 'Non-Custodial Sentencing Options in Malaysia' (*United Nations Asia and Far East Institute for the Prevention of Crime and the Treatment of Offenders*, 2004) <https://web.archive.org/web/20070421210756/http://www.unafei.or.jp:80/english/pdf/PDF_rms/no67/06_Mr.Rungit__p88-p92.pdf> accessed 23 September 2018

Sithambaram V, 'The Current Form of Sentencing Is Outdated—Time for Reform' (*The Malaysian Bar*, 17 November 2005) <http://www.malaysianbar.org.my/criminal_law/the_current_form_of_sentencing_is_outdated_time_for_reform_by_v._sithambaram.html> accessed 29 November 2017

Sitze A, 'Keeping the Peace' in Sarat A and Hussain N (eds), *Forgiveness, Mercy and Clemency* (Stanford University Press 2007)

Siyuan C, 'The Meaning of "Life Imprisonment" in the Context of a Presidential Commutation Order' (2012) 1 Singapore Law Watch <https://mercury.smu.edu.sg/rsrchpubupload/20581/slwmar2012lifeimprison.pdf> accessed 1 April 2013

Skapinker M, 'Singapore's Law Sets It Apart and Makes It Hard to Imitate' *Financial Times* (London, 1 April 2015) <https://www.ft.com/content/227b5b0a-d3e3-11e4-b041-00144feab7de> accessed 11 September 2017

Skehan C, 'No Sanctuary' *Sydney Morning Herald* (1 January 2000)

Smith AL, 'Indonesia: Transforming the Leviathan' in Funston J (ed), *Government and Politics in Southeast Asia* (Zed 2001)

Smith ATH, 'The Prerogative of Mercy, the Power of Pardon and Criminal Justice' (1983) Public Law 398

Smith KE, 'Problematising Power Relations in "Elite" Interviews' (2006) 37 Geoforum 643

Sodhy P, 'Malaysia and the United States in the 1980s' (1987) 27 Asian Survey 1074

Soedarjo AD, 'Attorney General Defends Capital Punishment' *Jakarta Post* (24 March 2007)

Soeharto RKH, *My Thoughts, Words, and Deeds: An Autobiography* (Citra Lamtoro Gung Persada 1991)

Soong KK, 'The Equality of Mercy' (Paper presented at the Human Rights Seminar, Kuala Lumpur, 19 July 1986)

Soong KK, *Malaysian Political Myths* (Selangor Chinese Assembly Hall 1990)

Southwood J and Flanagan P, *Indonesia: Law, Propaganda and Terror* (Zed Press 1983)

Steiker CS and Steiker JM, *Courting Death: The Supreme Court and Capital Punishment* (Harvard University Press 2016)

Steinmo S, 'Historical Institutionalism' in Della Porta D and Keating M (eds), *Approaches and Methodologies in the Social Sciences* (Cambridge University Press 2008)

Stevenson W, *The Revolutionary King: The True-Life Sequel to The King and I* (Robinson 2001)

Strange C, 'Introduction' in Strange C (ed), *Qualities of Mercy: Justice, Punishment and Discretion* (University of British Columbia Press 1996)

Streckfuss D, 'The Intricacies of Lese-Majesty: A Comparative Study of Imperial Germany and Modern Thailand' in Ivarsson S and Isager L (eds), *Saying the Unsayable: Monarchy and Democracy in Thailand* (Nordic Institute of Asian Studies Press 2010)

Streckfuss D, *Truth on Trial in Thailand: Defamation, Treason and Lèse-Majesté* (Routledge 2011)

Streib VL, *Death Penalty in a Nutshell* (West Academic 2005)

Suh CS, 'Democracy and the Making of Contentious Policy: The Role of Democracy in the Abolition of the Death Penalty, 1950–2010' (2015) 56(5) International Journal of Comparative Sociology 314

Suh S and Oorjitham S, 'Under the King's Watch' *Asia Week* (Hong Kong, 7 May 1999)

Suhadji IP, 'No Flexibility Offered to Drug Traffickers' *Jakarta Post* (17 February 2006)

Sullivan C, 'Death Penalty Cases Test Fairness of Clemency: Critics Contend that the Arbitrariness Excluded from Sentencing Permeates the Process; Supporters Say the System Protects against Executing the Innocent' *LA Times* (Los Angeles, 29 August 1993)

Sulong W, 'Malaysia Holds to Tough Line on Drugs Trade' *Financial Times* (London, 25 June 1986)

Sumarno JT, 'Grasi dan Vonis Narkoba Kontroversial di Negeri Ini' *Suara Surabaya* (10 February 2014) <http://www.suarasurabaya.net/print_news/Kelana%20Kota/2014/130271-Grasi-dan-Vonis-Narkoba-Kontroversial-di-Negeri-Ini> accessed 25 September 2017 [in Indonesian]

Supreme Court of Singapore, 'Structure of the Courts' (*Supreme Court of Singapore,* 1 August 2017) <http://www.supremecourt.gov.sg/about-us/the-supreme-court/structure-of-the-courts> accessed 11 September 2017

Surach G, '1,122 Still on Death Row' (*The Sun Daily*, 11 April 2017) <http://www.thesundaily.my/news/2017/04/12/1122-still-death-row> accessed 29 November 2017

Swain J, 'No Mercy for Losers in the Deadly Trafficking Game' *The Sunday Times* (London, 24 April 1988)

Sya'ban N, 'Hak Presiden Dalam Memberi Grasi, Amnesti, Abolisi dan Rehabilitasi' (Thesis, Faculty of Law, University of Indonesia 1985) [in Indonesian]

Tait D, 'Pardons in Perspective: The Role of Forgiveness in Criminal Justice' (2000–1) 13(3–4) Federal Sentencing Reporter 134

Talib NH, 'The Powers and Functions of the Pardons Board in Malaysia—A Review' (Master of Laws Dissertation, University of Malaya 1989)

Tan GP, 'Time Limit to Dispose Off [sic] Petitions for Clemency' (*Attorney-General's Chambers of Malaysia*, 3 March 2010) <http://agc-blog.agc.gov.my/agc-blog/?p=117> accessed 25 March 2013

Tan KYL and Thio L-A, *Singapore: 50 Constitutional Moments that Defined a Nation* (Marshall Cavendish 2015)

Tan P and Harn LY, 'Evaluating the Mandatory Death Penalty under Section 39B of the Dangerous Drug Act 1952' (University of Malaya-Griffith University International Law Conference, Kuala Lumpur, 25–26 January 2007)

Tan WP, 'The Attorney General—What's His Job?' (*The Online Citizen*, 9 April 2016) <https://www.theonlinecitizen.com/2016/04/09/attorney-general-whats-job/> accessed 23 September 2018

Tang A, 'Thai Police Seize Half a Ton of Heroin in Bust of a Decade' *The China Post* (Taipei, 22 March 2005)

TAPOL, '1965 Tapols Released at Last' (1999) 152 TAPOL Bulletin 17

TAPOL, 'Prisoner Releases: A Slow Business' (1998) 148 TAPOL Bulletin 16

TAPOL, 'Waiting for the Executioner' (1980) 40 TAPOL Bulletin 1

Tavallaei M and Abu Talib M, 'A General Perspective on Role of Theory in Qualitative Research' (2010) 3(11) The Journal of International Social Research 570

Tey TH, 'Death Penalty Singapore-Style: Clinical and Carefree' (2010) 39 Common Law World Review 315

Tey TH, 'Limitations on Public Interest Litigation in Singapore: Internalizing Political Ideology and Institutionalizing Judicial Self-Restraint' in Yap PJ and Lau H (eds), *Public Interest Litigation in Asia* (Routledge 2011)

Tey TH, 'Singapore's Electoral System: Government by the People?' (2008) 28(4) Legal Studies 610

Thailand Department of Corrections, 'Death Penalty' (*Thailand Department of Corrections*, 12 February 2008) <http://web.archive.org/web/20080212033715/http://www.correct.go.th/eng/deathpenalty.htm> accessed 12 December 2017

Thailand Department of Corrections, 'Number of Execution and Type of Offense' (*Thailand Department of Corrections*, 27 January 2006) <http://web.archive.org/web/20060127013318/http://www.correct.go.th/death.htm> accessed 12 December 2017

Thailand Department of Corrections, *Procedures for Royal Pardon Petitions* (Thailand Department of Corrections 2008) [in Thai]

Thailand Department of Corrections, 'Royal Pardon' (*Thailand Department of Corrections*, 24 March 2009) <https://web.archive.org/web/20090324073052/http://www.correct.go.th:80/eng/RoyalPardon/Royal%20Pardon.htm> accessed 12 December 2017

Thailand Rights and Liberties Protection Department, 'A Summary of Death-Eligible Offences' (*Thailand Rights and Liberties Protection Department*, 2014) <http://www.rlpd.go.th/rlpdnew/images/rlpd_1/HRC/2557/e1.pdf> accessed 29 November 2017

Thamnukasetchai P, 'Lethal Injection for Two Ya Ba Dealers' *The Nation* (Bangkok, 25 August 2009)

Thamnukasetchai P, 'Prisoners to Be Freed in Honour of King' *The Nation* (Bangkok, 12 December 2007)

Than TH, 'It Is Govt's Duty to Protect All' *New Straits Times* (Kuala Lumpur, 26 July 2010)

Thayer C, 'Vietnam: Time to Abolish Capital Punishment?' (*Chennai Centre for China Studies*, 17 January 2015) <http://www.c3sindia.org/vietnam/4764> accessed 23 January 2016

The K, 'Vietnam to Build Five More Lethal Injection Venues' (*dti news*, 9 February 2017) <http://english.vietnamnet.vn/fms/society/172369/vietnam-to-build-five-more-lethal-injection-venues.html> accessed 1 March 2017

Thio LA, 'Pragmatism and Realism Do Not Mean Abdication' (2004b) 8 Singapore Year Book of International Law 41

Thio LA, 'The Death Penalty as Cruel and Inhuman Punishment before the Singapore High Court?' (2004a) 4 Oxford University Commonwealth Law Journal 213

Thongpao T, 'Live and Let Live' *Bangkok Post* (18 November 2007)

Thurschwell A, 'Ethical Exception: Capital Punishment in the Figure of Sovereignty' in Sarat A and Culbert JL (eds), *States of Violence: War, Capital Punishment and Letting Die* (Cambridge University Press 2009)

Tilemann H, 'Indonesia's Long Wait for Its Own Criminal Code' *(Indonesia at Melbourne*, 10 November 2016) <http://indonesiaatmelbourne.unimelb.edu.au/indonesias-long-wait-for-its-own-criminal-code/> accessed 14 March 2017

Ting R, 'Different Justice for Different People' (*Malaysiakini*, 30 January 2008) <https://www.malaysiakini.com/letters/77621> accessed 12 December 2017

Tips WE, *Crime and Punishment in King Chulalongkorn's Kingdom* (White Lotus 1998)

Toh YC, 'Death Penalty Figures Are Available Online' *Straits Times* (Singapore, 22 October 2011)

Topsfield J, 'Mentally Ill Brazilian Rodrigo Gularte Fit to Execute: Indonesia' *Sydney Morning Herald* (20 April 2015)

Torode G, 'Speedy Executions for Drug Offenders Planned' *South China Morning Post* (Hong Kong, 16 October 1998)

Traisophon T, 'Human Rights—Vatana Shrugs off Amnesty Criticism of Execution' *Bangkok Post* (4 November 1998)

Trembat B, 'Nguyen Supporters Lobby for His Life' *ABC News* (Australia, 4 November 2005)

Tremewan C, *The Political Economy of Social Control in Singapore* (Palgrave Macmillan 1996)

Tuckness A and Parrish JM, *The Decline of Mercy in Public Life* (Cambridge University Press 2014)

Turpin C and Tomkins A, *British Government and the Constitution: Text and Materials* (6th edn, Cambridge University Press 2007)

Turrell R, '"It's a Mystery": The Royal Prerogative of Mercy in England, Canada, and South Africa' (2000) 4 Crime, History and Societies 83

UN Economic and Social Council, 'Capital Punishment and Implementation of the Safeguards Guaranteeing Protection of the Rights of Those Facing the Death Penalty' (UN Doc E/2010/10, 18 December 2009)

UN Economic and Social Council, 'Crime Prevention and Criminal Justice: Capital Punishment and Implementation of the Safeguards Guaranteeing Protection of the Rights of those Facing the Death Penalty' (UN Doc E/2000/3, 31 March 2000)

UN Human Rights Committee, 'Consideration of Reports Submitted by States Parties under Article 40 of the Covenant—Initial Reports of States Parties: Indonesia' (UN Doc CCPR/C/IDN/1, 19 March 2012)

UN Office of the High Commissioner for Human Rights, 'Moving Away from the Death Penalty: Lessons in South-East Asia' (*Office of the United Nations High Commissioner for Human Rights*, 2014) <http://bangkok.ohchr.org/files/Moving%20away%20from%20the%20Death%20Penalty-English%20for%20Website.pdf> accessed 17 September 2017

Unidjaja F, 'President Commutes Oki's Sentence to Life' *Jakarta Post* (31 October 2003)

Union for Civil Liberty, *Prisons in Thailand 2011* (Union for Civil Liberty 2011)

Unmacht E, 'Indonesia Sending a Message with Death Penalty' *Arab News* (Jeddah, 28 March 2005) <http://archive.arabnews.com/?page=7&section=0&article=61194&d=28&m=3&y=2005> accessed 15 June 2010

US Department of State, '2009 International Narcotics Control Strategy Report' (*US Department of State*, 2009) <http://www.state.gov/j/inl/rls/nrcrpt/2009/> accessed 25 March 2013

US Department of State, 'Country Reports on Human Rights Practices for 2011: Singapore' (*US Department of State*, 2011) <http://www.state.gov/j/drl/rls/hrrpt/humanrightsreport/index.htm?dlid=186306> accessed 11 September 2017

US Department of State, 'Thailand: Country Reports on Human Rights Practices 1999' (*US Department of State*, 23 February 2000) <http://www.state.gov/j/drl/rls/hrrpt/1999/307.htm> accessed 25 March 2013

US Embassy Thailand Bangkok, 'Executions Resume in Thailand after Six Year Break: Two Methamphetamine Dealers Die by Lethal Injection' (*WikiLeaks Public Library of US Diplomacy*, 9 September 2009) <https://wikileaks.org/plusd/cables/09BANGKOK2286_a.html> accessed 29 November 2017

VanBrocklin P, 'Comparison of the Clemency Procedures in the Four Census Bureau Regions' (2003) 28(7) Corrections Compendium 1

van den Berg EM, *Influence of Domestic NGOs on Dutch Human Rights Policy* (Intersentia Publishers 2001)

van Oosten K, 'Kamma and Forgiveness with Some Thoughts on Cambodia' (2008) 37(3) Exchange 237

Vietnam Ministry of Public Security, 'Tổng kết 05 năm thi hành Luật Thi hành án hình sự trong Công an nhân dân (2011–2016)' 10 (Hanoi, 4 January 2017) [in Vietnamese]

Vijayan KC, 'A Pardon to Mark National Day?' *The Straits Times* (Singapore, 26 August 2007)

Vijayan KC, 'AGC: Robust Reviews before Discretion is Exercised' *The Straits Times* (Singapore, 21 January 2012)

Walker S, *Taming the System: The Control of Discretion in Criminal Justice, 1950–1990* (Oxford University Press 1993)

Warren M, 'Foreigners under Sentence of Death Worldwide' (*Foreign Nationals, Consular Rights & The Death Penalty*, 30 September 2017) <http://users.xplornet.com/~mwarren/world.html> accessed 12 December 2017

Watts J, 'Family of Brazilian Executed in Indonesia Campaign for Pardon' *The Guardian* (London, 3 May 2015) <https://www.theguardian.com/world/2015/may/03/bali-nine-family-of-executed-brazilian-rodrigo-gularte-campaign-for-posthumous-pardon> accessed 29 November 2017

We Believe in Second Chances, 'Singapore's Problematic Death Penalty System' (*We Believe in Second Chances*, 8 December 2011) <http://webelieveinsecondchances.wordpress.com/2011/12/08/singapores-problematic-death-penalty-system/> accessed 25 March 2013

Weber M, 'Politics as a Vocation' in Owen D and Strong TB (eds), *The Vocation Lectures* (Hackett 2004)

Weightman BA, *Dragons and Tigers: A Geography of South, East and Southeast Asia* (3rd edn, John Wiley and Sons 2011)

Whiteman H et al, 'Australia Recalls Ambassador after Indonesia Executes Prisoners' (*CNN*, 29 April 2015) <http://edition.cnn.com/2015/04/28/asia/indonesia-firing-squad-executions/index.html> accessed 25 September 2017

Whiting A, 'Emerging from Emergency Rule? Malaysian Law "Reform" 2011–2013' (2013) 14(2) Australian Journal of Asian Law 1

Willcox S, 'The King's Pardon Explained' (*Steve's Life in the Bangkok Hilton*, 5 August 2008) <http://web.archive.org/web/20080805000909/http://www.steveatbangkwang.bravehost.com:80/mp.html> accessed 12 December 2017

Winchester S, 'The Politics of Death Row: In Malaysia, Two Westerners Ponder Their Fate for Smuggling Drugs' *The Sunday Times* (London, 29 June 1986)

Windle J, 'Drugs and Drug Policy in Thailand' (*Brookings Institution*, 2016) <https://www.brookings.edu/wp-content/uploads/2016/07/WindleThailand-final.pdf> accessed 3 September 2017

World Coalition against the Death Penalty, 'Brunei Darussalam, Asia (South-Eastern Asia)' (*World Coalition against the Death Penalty*, 31 March 2011) <http://www.worldcoalition.org/Brunei-Darussalam> accessed 12 December 2017

World Coalition against the Death Penalty, 'Ratification Kit: Cambodia' (*World Coalition Against the Death Penalty*, 2014) <http://www.worldcoalition.org/media/resourcecenter/Cambodia-EN.pdf> accessed 29 November 2017

World Coalition against the Death Penalty et al, 'Meeting with General Director of the Department of Rights and Liberty Protection under the Thai Ministry of Justice' (Meeting Agenda, 4 July 2013, copy on file with the author)

Yesuiah S, 'Give Judges Discretion in Death Penalty' *The Star Malaysia* (Petaling Jaya, 25 April 2017) <https://www.pressreader.com/malaysia/the-star-malaysia/20170425/281831463619606> accessed 17 September 2017

Yimprasert J, 'The "Voter's Uprising" that Is Changing Perceptions in Thailand' (Consultation on Gender, Development and Decent Work: Building a Common Agenda, OECD Headquarters, Paris, 27 April 2009)

Yudhoyono SB, 'Transkripsi: Sambutan Pengantar Presiden Republik Indonesia' (*Presiden RI*, 2 August 2011) <https://web.archive.org/web/20111010084215/http://www.presidenri.go.id:80/index.php/pidato/2011/08/02/1682.html> accessed 12 December 2017 [in Indonesian]

Zakaria F, 'The Rise of Illiberal Democracy' (*fareedzakaria.com*, November/December 1997) <https://web.archive.org/web/20170705032924/https://fareedzakaria.com/1997/11/01/the-rise-of-illiberal-democracy/> accessed 23 September 2018

Zee J, 'Defending Singapore's Internal Security Act: Balancing the Need for National Security with the Rule of Law' (2011) 18(1) Murdoch University Electronic Journal of Law 28

Zeng R, 'Kho Jabing Executed at 3.30pm, First Execution in Singapore Not Carried Out at Dawn of Friday' (*The Online Citizen*, 20 May 2016) <https://www.theonlinecitizen.com/2016/05/20/kho-jabing-executed-at-3-30pm-first-execution-in-singapore-not-carried-out-at-dawn-of-friday/> accessed 29 November 2017

Zhang D, 'By the Numbers: Indonesia's Executions of Foreigners' *ABC News* (Australia, 27 February 2015) <http://www.abc.net.au/news/2015-02-26/zhang-indonesia-likely-to-execute-more-foreigners/6263122> accessed 17 November 2017

Zwartz B, 'Spare the Bali Bombers, Church Urges' *Brisbane Times* (3 January 2008)

List of Interviews and Statements Cited

Interview with American academic expert on the death penalty (Hong Kong, 7 November 2011)
Interview with Australian academic expert on Asian Studies (Canberra, 15 September 2009)
Interview with Australian academic expert on Indonesia (Melbourne, 14 December 2011)
Interview with Australian academic expert on Indonesia #2 (Telephone Interview, 30 January 2013)
Interview with Australian academic expert on Indonesia #3 (Canberra, 15 September 2009)
Interview with Australian academic expert on Indonesia #4 (Canberra, 16 September 2009)
Interview with Australian academic expert on Malaysia (Melbourne, 15 December 2011)
Interview with Australian academic expert on Thailand (Canberra, 16 September 2009)
Interview with British academic expert on the death penalty (Oxford, 25 January 2010)
Interview with Canadian academic expert on the death penalty (London, 26 August 2011)
Interview with former employee of the Thailand Department of Corrections (Bangkok, 17 September 2012)
Interview with former Malaysian Federal Court judge (Kuala Lumpur, 1 December 2011)
Interview with Indonesian deputy minister (Jakarta, 15 April 2013)
Interview with Indonesian human rights activist (Jakarta, 10 April 2013)
Interview with Indonesian human rights lawyer (Jakarta, 11 April 2013)
Interview with Indonesian human rights lawyer #2 (Jakarta, 12 April 2013)
Interview with Indonesian NGO staff (Jakarta, 16 April 2013)
Interview with Indonesian Supreme Court judge (Jakarta, 26 April 2013)
Interview with international human rights NGO staff (Hong Kong, 3 November 2011)
Interview with international human rights NGO staff #2 (Kuala Lumpur, 25 October 2011)
Interview with international human rights NGO staff #3 (telephone interview, 4 February 2010)

Interview with international human rights NGO staff #4 (Geneva, 26 February 2010)
Interview with international human rights NGO staff #5 (Bangkok, 5 September 2012)
Interview with international human rights NGO staff (Bangkok, 18 September 2012)
Interview with London-based death penalty lawyer (London, 8 September 2011)
Interview with London-based death penalty lawyer #2 (London, 12 December 2009)
Interview with London-based Indonesian human rights activist (London, 22 August 2011)
Interview with London-based NGO staff (London, 30 January 2012)
Interview with Malaysian Human Rights Commissioner (Kuala Lumpur, 7 December 2011)
Interview with Malaysian criminal defence lawyer (Kuala Lumpur, 3 December 2011)
Interview with Malaysian human rights lawyer (Kuala Lumpur, 26 October 2011)
Interview with Malaysian Member of Parliament (Kuala Lumpur, 3 December 2011)
Interview with Malaysian prosecutor (Kuala Lumpur, 30 October 2011)
Interview with Singaporean criminal defence lawyer (Singapore, 20 October 2011)
Interview with Singaporean criminal defence lawyer #2 (Singapore, 10 October 2011)
Interview with Singaporean human rights activist (Singapore, 12 October 2011)
Interview with Singaporean human rights lawyer (Singapore, 18 October 2011)
Interview with Singaporean NGO staff (Singapore, 21 October 2011)
Interview with Singaporean NGO staff #2 (Singapore, 20 October 2011)
Interview with Singaporean NGO staff #3 (Singapore, 17 October 2011)
Interview with Singaporean NGO staff #4 (Singapore, 16 November 2011)
Interview with Singaporean law professor and Singaporean NGO staff #5 (Singapore, 21 October 2011)
Interview with Singaporean prosecutor (Oxford, 10 November 2009)
Interview with Thai Human Rights Commissioner (Bangkok, 21 September 2012)
Interview with Thai criminal defence lawyer (Bangkok, 20 September 2012)
Interview with Thai criminal defence lawyer #2 (Bangkok, 8 September 2012)
Interview with Thai criminal defence lawyer and Thai NGO staff (Bangkok, 20 September 2012)

Interview with Thai human rights activist (Geneva, 25 February 2010)
Interview with Thai human rights activist (Bangkok, 7 September 2012)
Interview with Thai human rights activist #2 (Geneva, 26 February 2010)
Interview with Thai human rights activist #2 (Bangkok, 16 September 2012)
Interview with Thai human rights lawyer (Bangkok, 23 September 2012)
Interview with Thai law professor (Bangkok, 14 September 2012)
Interview with Thai prison caseworker (Bangkok, 11 September 2012)
Interview with Thailand Department of Corrections staff (Bangkok, 24 September 2012)
Statement by Australian academic expert on Indonesia #5 (personal email correspondence, 15 November 2011)
Statement by former Singaporean politician (personal email correspondence, 8 December 2011)
Statement by Indonesian human rights lawyer (personal email correspondence, 3 October 2017)
Statement by Malaysian human rights lawyer (personal email correspondence, 4 February 2010)
Statement by Malaysian human rights lawyer #2 (personal email correspondence, 15 September 2017)
Statement by Singaporean law professor (personal email correspondence, 4 February 2010)
Statement by Thai human rights activist (personal email correspondence, 22 February 2010)

Index

The manufacturer's authorised representative in the EU for product safety is Oxford University Press España S.A. of el Parque Empresarial San Fernando de Henares, Avenida de Castilla, 2 – 28830 Madrid (www.oup.es/en or product.safety@oup.com). OUP España S.A. also acts as importer into Spain of products made by the manufacturer.

www.ingramcontent.com/pod-product-compliance
Ingram Content Group UK Ltd.
Pitfield, Milton Keynes, MK11 3LW, UK
UKHW020846150926
475595UK00003B/25
9780198809715